The Spectacular Modern Woman

The Spectacular

Feminine Visibility in the 1920s

Modern Woman

LIZ CONOR

INDIANA UNIVERSITY PRESS

Bloomington and Indianapolis

This book is a publication of

Indiana University Press

601 North Morton Street

Bloomington, Indiana 47404-3797 USA

http://iupress.indiana.edu

Telephone orders 800-842-6796

Fax orders 812-855-7931

Orders by e-mail iuporder@indiana.edu

*The paper used in this publication meets the
minimum requirements of American National
Standard for Information Sciences—Permanence of
Paper for Printed Library Materials, ANSI Z39.48-1984.*

MANUFACTURED IN THE UNITED STATES OF AMERICA

Library of Congress Cataloging-in-Publication Data

Conor, Liz, date

The spectacular modern woman: feminine visibility in the
1920s / Liz Conor.

p. cm.

Includes bibliographical references (p.) and index.

ISBN 0-253-34391-7 (cloth : alk. paper)—
ISBN 0-253-21670-2 (pbk. : alk. paper)

1. Mass media and women—History—20th century.
2. Women in popular culture—History—20th century.
3. Visual sociology—History—20th century.   4. Self-
perception in women—History—20th century.   I. Title.

P94.5.W65.C677 2004

302.23'082—dc22

2003022618

1   2   3   4   5   09   08   07   06   05   04

In memory of my New Women Grandmothers,

Agnes O'Connor (1907–1998) for her
kitchen Charlestons

and Edith Ellen Hoy (1905–1996) for the
quiet regard of her Kelly Country gaze.

What is more subtle than this which ties me
    to the woman or man that looks in my face?
Which fuses me into you now, and pours my
    meaning into you?
                    —Walt Whitman,
                    "Crossing Brooklyn Ferry,"
                    Leaves of Grass

Contents

Illustrations

Preface

This book begins with a confession from its author—
I was a teenage kitten. During the 1980s, I occupied the image of new-
wave retro glamour and was given notice, everywhere I went, that
this look was provocative, even "asking for it." Most significantly for
this book, it was evidently inconsistent with my feminism. For these
were the turbulent days of anti-porn feminism, in which heated debate raged about the significance of popular and pornographic representations of women and their impact on women's safety, mobility,
self-perception, cultural authorship, and political inclusion. I was
among legions of women who found many feminine visual ideals appealing, and who even adopted those ideals into their own visual style.
It was, however, ill-advised to attend collective meetings in fire-truck-
red lipstick and stiletto heels. Appearing to actively solicit the "male
gaze" while debating its patriarchal impetus didn't fit within the polarized positions that began to characterize the discussion: masculinist,
sadistic voyeur or pro-censorship, sexually repressed prude. And if one
dressed girlie, then one was girlie. Visual style was not mediated by
representation, it was a literal reflection of immutable identity.

More recently a series of slogans appeared as graffiti on walls in
my neighborhood. "More Hairy Women on TV," one bannered. "More
Older Women on TV," another read. Of course they were promptly
prefixed with "NO," and the squabble continued with much haphaz-
ard crossing out and revising. It struck me as a good illustration of the
atrophied state of the discussion inherited from decades before. This
discussion starts with an unexamined assumption that feminine visibility, as I will call it, has political significance, with erratic protesta-
tions from various quarters, none of which pose the primary questions: When did the visibility of women become important? Why have
visual representations been said to have a greater effect than text on
gender relations and the status of women: what of bumper stickers
which exhort drivers to "harpoon fat chicks"?

Anti-porn feminism unduly focused the critical gaze on the visually explicit. Nuances, not to mention blinding distinctions, were lost
in the genuine shock many women felt when exposed to violent, mi-
sogynist, and racist pornography. Why did the explicit, more than
other material, bear a causal relation to sexual violence? How did
explicit imagery manage to "reflect" the real danger of male sexuality
and simultaneously "construct" the false masochism of women's sexuality? Such questions went unanswered because underlying questions about the relation between visual representation and gendered
identity went unasked.

As someone who saved her orange peels to hurl at men who ges-
ticulated with their tongues, offered money, and threatened violence
on the streets of all the cities she had visited, I was not about to relinquish feminist analyses of the prohibitory and damaging effects of
being relegated to spectacle. If some feminists' disapproval of my
"look" was censorial, it had nothing on the palpable hostility coming
from some men, who stalked, groped, hurled abuse, and worse—all
in response, they made it known, to my "looks." "You don't deserve
to be a blonde," one man screeched when I responded to his "sit on
my face" with a raised middle finger. It seemed I was wielding a very
ambivalent kind of power.

After many years of speculation, I began this book to answer the
paradox of my own experience: my status as spectacle both singled
me out for censure and hostility and granted me a range of privileges
and cultural access. What I had invested in my looks was quite the
opposite of desiring to be objectified, with its association of being
barred from available subject positions. I sought a subjective identity
based on my visibility, rather than precluded by it. I encountered images with a simultaneous desire to occupy them, and to subject them
to my own critical scrutiny. The significance and sense of agency I
attached to this public visibility was the outcome of discourses concerned with cultural participation, political representation, self-
mastery, self-articulation, and sexual agency that I shared with Western feminists and modern women across the twentieth century. And,
it has to be owned, a measure of narcissism was thrown in; I took
pleasure in my looks, just as a century of women's commodity culture
simultaneously promised I would and reviled me for doing.

My research for this book confirmed my hunch that the modern
industrialized production of images had forged a new relation between
feminine visibility and public visibility, and that this relation continues

to inform the production not just of images of women, but of our very identities as women today.

Visual representations of women may construct a range of meanings, imaging them as anything from willing victims of male violence to assertive feminist heroines. However, across this spectrum of meanings there remains one constant: images of women are always producing meanings of women's visibility. Visual representations are important because modernity has intensified the visual scene and spectacularized women within it. Consequently, feminine subjectivity has come to be increasingly performed within the visual register. The conditions of modernity constituted certain visually typed subject positions—Business Girl, Flapper, Screen-Struck Girl, Beauty Contestant, and others—which I call types of the "modern appearing woman." These subject positions were marked by a dramatic historical shift: women were invited to articulate themselves as modern subjects by constituting themselves as spectacles.

These developments had global effects as imagery circulated, along with capital, between nation-states: the United States, Britain, Australia, Europe, Japan, and China. Australia was part of the web of globalizing capital that mobilized the image of the Modern Woman to manage expanding markets. It adopted her image into its own idiosyncratic, late colonial visual lexicon. Australia's interpretation of this increasingly globalizing modern visual economy reveals a great deal about how distinct nation-states attempted to define their relations with one another through, of all things, popular imagery of women. Australia's liminal status as both a British colonial outpost and a massive consumer of American cinema and other visual media submerged it within global commodity and cultural currents which conveyed the Modern Woman on a tide of raced, gendered, and national tropes. As Australia struggled to assert a national identity, it found itself awash with representations of the Modern Woman that were arriving from many national locales. It wrestled with the modernist narratives that traveled with these representations, such as nation-building, cosmopolitan urbanity, and the racialized formations of African American jazz and Asian nouveau aesthetics. In denial of the brutal land theft by which it was founded, it used images of whiteness to signify colonial dominance, and by persistently depicting Aboriginal women as failing to achieve modernity it disqualified them from the modern scene.

This book explores the impact of popular imagery of women, as

it developed through the modern period, on feminine subject formation through the concept of "appearing." In the end it articulates the
paradox of my own experience: that to be a spectacular woman is to
occupy imagery invested with myriad forms of gendered and racialized
power, capable of allowing and forbidding cultural participation. It will
always be important to assess the varied effects of that power. In order
to do so, we need to invent less polarized and more supple ways of
thinking about the relation between feminine visibility and identity.

Acknowledgments

Earlier versions of parts of this book were first published as "The Flapper's Ontological Ambivalence: Prosthetic Visualities, the Feminine and Modernity," in *Dealing with Difference: Essays in Gender Culture and History*, ed. Patricia Grimshaw and Diane Kirkby (History Department, University of Melbourne, 1997), pp. 178–96; "The Beauty Contestant in the Photographic Scene," in *The Show Girl and the Straw Man: Journal of Australian Studies*, no. 71 (2001), pp. 33–44 by the API network; "The Flapper in the Heterosexual Scene," *Jumping the Queue: Journal of Australian Studies*, no. 72 (2002), pp. 43–58 by the API network; "The City Girl: Appearing in the Modern Scene," in *Lilith: a Feminist History Journal*, no. 11 (2002), pp. 53–72.

Every effort has been made to contact the holders of copyright material reproduced in this book, but the creators of some images were impossible to identify and/or locate. The publishers would be happy to hear from any descendants and copyright holders we were unable to contact. For permission or assistance in reprinting images I am grateful to the documentation collection at ScreenSound: The National Screen and Sound Archive; The State Library of New South Wales; The State Library of Victoria; The Museum of Victoria; The National Library of Australia; Viscopy; Curtis Brown; H. A. and C. Glad; Jane Sullivan; Sue Cross and Craig Thompson of Visual Merchandising at David Jones.

I have been assisted in the realization of this work with grants from the Australian Research Council and La Trobe University Research and Graduate Studies. I am grateful to the Australian Academy of the Humanities for granting the book a publication subsidy. The research that forms the basis of chapter five was conducted in the employ of Professor Marilyn Lake as part of an Australian Research Council large grant on the subject "Women and Nation."

I wish to advise readers that, in some Aboriginal and Torres Strait Islander Communities, seeing photographic images of deceased persons may cause sadness or distress, particularly to the relatives of these people. In addition, terms and images which reflect the attitude of the period considered in the book may be considered inappropriate today.

I have been extremely privileged with the support and assistance I have been given in the process of writing and producing this work—though I am solely responsible for its shortcomings. I would like to express my heartfelt thanks to Marilyn Lake, Alison Ravenscroft, Jodi Brooks, Katie Holmes, and Phillipa Rothfield, all of whom brought their considerable and diverse talents to the process and sustained me, with their experience and wisdom, through the formidable task of writing. Thanks also to Patrice Petro, Barbara Creed, Scott McQuire, and particularly to Rita Felski who has given me encouragement. Joan Kerr was an accomplished guide through the convoluted problems of copyright permissions, and Tess Flynn, Rita Fraser, and David Cresswell, at La Trobe University's Centre for Online and Multimedia Educational Technologies, did painstaking work on the images. My appreciation also to Marilyn Grobschmidt, Shoshanna Green, Richard Higgins, and Miki Bird at Indiana University Press. The meticulous editing of Jordie Albiston and Jeremy Ludowyke has been as indispensable as their affection. Jeremy in particular should be awarded a medal for his fortitude, teeth-gritted endurance, hot dinners, and inadvertent funding. Hattie and Faith, who were born into the process, are probably scarred for life, along with their brother Jake Ludowyke, but I thank them for putting up with being continually put off. Claire Sawyer, Bridget Tehan, Madeline Toner, Deborah Kelly, Kathryn Bird, Zelda Grimshaw, and Allan Thomas listened generously to all manner of fretting. Ruth Ford offered reams of advice as we went through the process together. I also want to thank my award-winning mother, Biddy (at least, if there were awards for mothers, she would win one), for Wye River and all the grossly exploitative childcare, and my father, Jocky, whose own thesis coexisted with most of my childhood—his complete rapture and lifelong immersion in his discipline have also made him my most inspiring teacher. Finally, I chewed through enough paper in writing, drafting, photocopying, and editing this book and associated materials to make a rain forest and its collective inhabitants cower. I pay homage to the natural world I've inevitably plundered.

The Spectacular
Modern Woman

Introduction

The Spectacular Modern Woman

As cinema was changing in the 1920s, Lev Kuleshov, a Russian film experimenter and theorist of montage, made an observation germane to this book. He spoke of the possibility of using these new visual technologies, particularly the technique of montage, to edit into being "a new geography, a new place of action," adding,

> What I think was more interesting was the creation of a woman who had never existed—I shot a scene of a woman at her toilette: she did her hair, made up, put on her stockings and shoes and dress—I filmed the face, the head, the hair, the legs, the feet of different women, but I edited them as if it was all one woman, and thanks to my montage, I succeeded in creating a woman who did not exist in reality but only in cinema.[1]

In February 1924, the Australian screen star Lotus Thompson went to Hollywood to pursue a film career, like many such young, "screen struck" hopefuls. Using precisely the technique of montage that Kuleshov had eulogized for its creative potential, her legs were filmed and attributed to other actresses. In a poignant and desperate protest against her treatment within these new conditions of women's public visibility, Thompson poured acid over her legs.[2]

Thompson's response to her legs being made spectacle, or to her spectacularization within these new visual technologies and techniques, suggested that *being* the image gave her a different take on Kuleshov's illusory new woman. In withdrawing her disembodied limbs from future such editing techniques she drew attention to the relation between visibility, feminine subjectivity, and the identification of self as image. Her reaction suggested that one's image could not be cast off like a shed skin, that it was not separate from and incidental to one's subjectivity. Rather, becoming a spectacle was deeply implicated in the parameters of modern subjectivity, which included cultural presence, public visibility, and participation in the circulation and exchange of looks in the urbanized and commodified modern scene.

Through cinema, Kuleshov could indeed edit into being a "new geography," specifically of the feminine body, as a new "place of action" in the modern visual field. His spatial metaphors aptly describe a relocation of feminine identity within an altered social field—the modern visual scene—for it was as visual images, spectacles, that women could appear modern to themselves and others. Through what I will term *techniques of appearing*—the manner and means of execution of one's visual effects and status—women's bodies became a place of action in modern visual culture.

Kuleshov's cinematic techniques placed the spectacle of a "new woman" before the public. She was contrived from a tradition of signifying the feminine taken from high art—woman eroticized at toilette—yet her image was also constructed in unprecedented ways through the use of new visual technologies. Kuleshov deployed the changed conditions of visual technologies to effect a particular representation of the feminine, as constituted through the process of her spectacularization. His montage is allegorical of the New Woman of modernity because her spectacularization within modern conditions of visibility was constitutive of her representation as a modern feminine type. Moreover, in the part(s) these representations of women played in constructing this characteristically modern spectacle, the feminine not only was spectacularized within the modern visual field, but contributed to the constitution of this field as spectacular. Kuleshov assembled a representation of his new woman from images, just as types of the New Woman emerged through the visual conditions of modernity, and these conditions produced a new formation of subjectivity, which I call the *Modern Appearing Woman*.[3]

By contrast, Thompson's protest seemed to occupy the underside of Kuleshov's filmic and phantasmatic projection. It was a remarkable and disturbing intervention by a young Australian starlet who attempted to assert ownership of her own spectacle within similar techniques of image production. She brought into view the often hidden or unconsidered relation of her visibility to her subjectivity. She seemed to reply to Kuleshov that she might indeed have become a representation, typical of the Screen Star, but the implications of this status for her subjectivity went beyond surface, beyond visual effects. Specifically, Thompson seemed to assert that her visibility was a central aspect of her subjectivity, and she sought to reclaim herself from the new techniques that brought her to mass public visibility as an array of corporeal dismemberments. She was less than content, she was profoundly disturbed, not to appear recognizably and altogether as herself. Tellingly, her desire was not to become *invisible,* but rather to achieve mass visibility within contemporary terms of fame. While Thompson may have seemed to refuse her construction as image, she nevertheless sought and later achieved the status of Screen Star, the notoriety resulting from her acid protest catapulting her into new roles. Thompson, like the modern appearing woman I believe emerged at this time, professed a desire to appear within the modern visual scene.

Kuleshov's new woman was contemporaneous with a number of feminine types that emerged as specifications of feminine identity as it was being visually constituted. They produced new locations of feminine identity that were particularly modern—the City or Business Girl, Screen Star, Beauty Contestant, and Flapper—and each was implicated in (and potentially implicated other women in) the conditions of the modern perceptual field.

However, there is more to the spectacularization of women than their objectification, with its longstanding association with the loss of self-determination. I want to propose *appearing* as an alternative term, and to investigate the impact of visual representations of women on the production of a new modern feminine subjectivity, *the appearing woman.* I want to use it to explain how the modern, as an altered visual scene replete with spectacles, modified the category "woman" in ways that altered the relation between feminine visibility and the production of feminine subject positions. My intention is to rethink the relation between women and cultural forms, feminine identity, and visibility.

The term "appearing" is used in the work of feminist philosopher Judith Butler. "Masquerade" and "appearing" are instrumental designations in Butler's influential theory of gendered performativity.[4] Butler is committed to a theory of subject formation that posits sex as "a cultural norm which governs the materialization of bodies," that is, the subject becomes culturally intelligible through the assumption of a sexed body.[5] Butler's subject is thus embedded in significatory systems, or produced and made intelligible within discourse, since gender is itself an organizing principle of discourse. Many poststructuralist theories have made this claim, but Butler argues that gender identity continues to be positioned as natural or prediscursive within some poststructuralist writing. She also uses poststructuralist theories to critically explore and make subversive use of the idiosyncratic placement of the feminine in linguistic and significatory systems. Butler's use of "appearing" resonates with this book for the ways in which it specifies the operation of sexual difference in the discursively produced subject.

In her first book, *Gender Trouble: Feminism and the Subversion of Identity,* Butler investigates the potential of psychoanalytic theory to support one of her central claims: that the subject does not precede discourse, but is constituted within it. Butler's concept of gendered performativity is a theoretical riposte to the radical exclusion of the feminine from the phallic signifying economy. Through masquerade the feminine enacts the repetitive performance of "appearing to be" the phallus. "Appearing," in this usage, is an aspect of the idiosyncratic placement of the feminine subject within language. In the Lacanian symbolic order—the order in which language, meaning, and subject positions are culturally intelligible through the paternal metaphor of the phallus—men are said to "have" the phallus, but not to "be" it, since the penis is not equivalent to the phallus as the transcendental signifier.[6] Paradoxically, women are said to "be" the phallus to the extent that they signify its loss, or lack.[7] For Lacan, this differentiation of positions in language describes the sexual difference between "being" and "having" the phallus. And yet both positions are "comedic" failures, since neither male nor female can fully signify these positions because both are grounded in lack. As Butler comments, "both masculine and feminine positions are signified, the signifier belonging to the Symbolic that can never be assumed in more than token form by either position."[8]

This proposition is important because it positions sexual difference and gendered identity as operating at the level of representation within culturally contingent signifying systems. It also specifies the particular place of the feminine within the dominant signifying economy. Her lack must be masked, since the male depends on her apparent fulfillment of the position of "being" the phallus in order to posture as a self-grounding subject. In order to signify lack, the feminine must paradoxically appear to "be" the fulfillment of that lack, appear to "be" the phallus. Effectively, "being" the phallus is an appearance, which itself must be masked.

This feminine appearing-as-being is taken from Joan Riviere's 1929 essay "Womanliness as a Masquerade," where appearing to be the phallus is described, precisely, as a masquerade.[9] However, Butler finds the term troublesome for the contradictory ways in which it reflects on gender identity. She writes,

> On the one hand, if the "being," the ontological specification of the Phallus, is masquerade, then it would appear to reduce all being to a form of appearing, the appearance of being, with the consequence that all gender ontology is reducible to the play of appearances. On the other hand, masquerade suggests there is a "being" or ontological specification of femininity *prior to* the masquerade, a feminine desire or demand that is masked and capable of disclosure, that, indeed, might promise an eventual disruption and displacement of the phallogocentric signifying economy.[10]

This prior "ontological specification of femininity" is at odds with Butler's central argument that no "I" precedes signification, but rather that "the enabling conditions for an assertion of 'I' are provided by the structure of signification."[11] Is the feminine subject constituted through this play of appearances, or through masking an essential lack that also designates her sexual difference? Does one appear to be a woman in accordance with a preordained designation as woman, or come into being as woman through appearing to be feminine?

Importantly, this problematic of the subject, as a substantializing effect, needs to be located within practices of signification so that "rule-governed discourses that govern the intelligible invocation of identity" become apparent as the scene wherein these identities are signified. Butler provides for the subjects' agency through their everyday and ongoing insertion into "the rules" of the "pervasive and mundane signifying acts of linguistic life." She lodges the agency of the subject within ritualized repetitions, a "politically enforced performativity," in order to display, through parody and even participation, "the performative status of the natural itself." The context of any signifying field is thus crucial in the enactment of the subject. The appearance of the feminine subject can show that she comes into being within and through discourse. Butler's "scene" of signification encompasses all formations of language and meaning.[12]

I have been pondering the nature of the significatory scene which, through the repetitive acts carried out within it, becomes the site of the subject's generation, regulation, and intervention. In Butler's own words, signification is a "scene" in which the play of gender as an "act" is open to "hyperbolic exhibitions"[13] of the mirage of the prediscursive subject. I want to cast an eye over Butler's significatory scene in order to ask: If the visual is a privileged part of the modern significatory scene in which the feminine subject is both generated and intervening, could "appearing" become a particularly visual performance? Having accepted that appearing potentially demarcates the linguistic operation of feminine performativity, I want to extend the concept of appearing, to locate it within the modern signifying scene, and to propose that in a cultural field that privileges the visual, the visual itself might become privileged in repetitive signifying acts that constitute gendered identity.

In the context of the modern scene, the term "appearing" could refer to performance while taking on new reference to the visual. Appearing facilitates rethinking how the visual extent of the modern significatory scene spectacularized the feminine and produced a new subjectivity in which the performance of the feminine became more concentrated on the visual. It works from two claims: firstly, that the modern is a spectacular age, or that the significatory scene of the twentieth-century West privileges the visual; and secondly, that through a discursive web that includes the mechanical reproduction of images, commodity fetishism, illusion, and visual scandal, the modern feminine has been spectacularized. Having specified these visual conditions, we can ask: What are the consequences of this visual privileging in the production of feminine subject positions? Did women come into being as modern subjects through their practices of appearing? I want to conceptualize appearing as a mode of gendered performativity, as a particularly visual practice within the significatory scene of modernity. This is not to argue that the visual can exhaust the multi-sensory scope of any context in which gender is performed, but simply to single it out for analysis.

"Appearing" is the central term of this work, as it considers the visual as a critical element in the production of feminine subjects through historically contingent significatory systems.

In the early twentieth century, women's visibility extended from their earlier incursions into public space, particularly that of the metropolis, to their iconization within the mechanized production of popular images and the conventions of display in commodity culture. In effect, this visually intensified scene provided new conditions for the feminine subject. To appear within it was to literally make a spectacle of oneself, to configure oneself as spectacle, to apprehend oneself and be apprehended as image. Some types of the Modern Woman which emerged at this time—the Screen Star, Beauty Contestant, and Flapper—were manifestly, though not solely, constructed around their visibility. "Appearing" describes how the changed conditions of feminine visibility in modernity invited a practice of the self which was centered on one's visual status and effects. "Feminine visibility" refers to the entire range of women's capacity to be seen: from self-apprehension in a mirror, to being seen in public space, to becoming an image through industrialized visual technologies such as the camera.[14] The Modern Woman was spectacularized. For women to identify themselves as modern, the performance of their gendered identity had to take place within the modern spectacularization of everyday life.

There are three aspects to this argument. Firstly, the historical conditions of women's visibility, the perceptual fields in which modern women appeared. These include visual technologies such as popular cinema, professional and domestic photography and print media, and commodity culture with its proliferating strategies of display. The modern appearing woman was prevalent within six visual scenes of the Australian 1920s: the metropolis, the cinematic scene, commodity culture, beauty culture, the late colonial scene, and the heterosexual leisure scene. Australia shared the experience of these scenes with industrialized Western nation-states, particularly Britain and the United States, which were major cultural producers. Indeed, it has been argued that the Modern Girl was a global phenomenon before the invention of the term "globalization": the first cultural figure to travel along the multi-directional, intersecting flows of transnational capital.[15] In the local reception of these cultural forms this increasingly global visual economy brought changing relations between Western nation-states which were acted out in attitudes to the modern feminine spectacle.

Secondly, an expanding range of representations of women during the 1920s were produced within these visual conditions. Women were cast as Screen Stars within the flood of block-booked American silent productions. They were represented as local favorites within productions of the nascent but already struggling Australian film industry. They began to appear as "pin-up girls" on postcards, posters, and calendars. Indeed, the Australian swimmer and health advocate Annette Kellerman is credited with being America's first pin-up girl.[16] They were represented as vaudeville and stage stars, and the feminine was used as a decorative motif on the covers of popular sheet music. Women were represented as advocates for products and appeared as *mannequins vivants*—living mannequins, or models. The feminine appeared as replica mannequins and in visual designs on billboards and in print. Women were photographed in studio portraits and household "snaps," and they appeared in the increasingly "illustrated" print media in countless guises, from motoring pioneers to Rexona-Girls, the celebrity advocates in advertising for Rexona products. Types of the New Woman were also the targets of humor in thousands of black-and-white drawings and cartoons.

Thirdly, and most significantly, these representations could have a significant impact on feminine subjectivities—or appearing, which prompts a series of hitherto unasked questions: What meanings of visibility do representations of women construct? What does it mean for women to appear as spectacles? Does appearing as such discount a woman's status as subject, through positioning her as object?

Appearing disrupts the foundational dichotomy of subject and object by disrupting the traditional articulation of sexual difference along this divide, as I'll discuss in the next chapter. However, the complex interplay of power and cultural forms makes it crucial to attend to the investments of power and its potential to assign cultural inclusion or exclusion through visibility and invisibility. Rather than visibility being consigned to a secondary status in the arrangement of subjectivity around psyche, sexuality, corporeality, and ideology, or to an enactment of a construction already in place, the mutability of that construction of subjectivity—its being in process—is effected in part through self-representation. In the modern teleology of the feminine subject, the "field of vision"[17] becomes foundational.

Modernity's visions of women became part of women's self-perception as modern: gendered representations became embodied. However, the modern is to some degree dependent for its own meaning on its images of women, as well as being their condition of possibility. The modern appearing woman did not step into modernity's symbolic systems, but was textually inscribed within its panorama. The picture formed part of her and she formed part of the picture as she became emblematic of the pictorial life of the modern scene. This is

FIG. INTRO.1. "The Misses Madge and Edith Fennell, who were awarded first prize at the Louise Lovely Ball, Melbourne, for their representation of the Simplex Twins," reprinted from *Everyones— Incorporating Australian Variety and Show World*, 26 November 1924. Courtesy of the Mitchell Library, State Library of New South Wales.

beautifully illustrated in figure Intro.1 by the first-prize winners at the Louise Lovely Ball, held in Melbourne in November 1924. The sisters Madge and Edith Fennell did indeed become part of the picture, by costuming their bodies as film projectors. Their pantomime commented on changed technological conditions, the fact of modern feminine spectacularization, and the fact that occupying an image is a performative act. Of the many and diverse meanings that did accrue to feminine visibility—including artificiality, heterosexual appeal, celebrity, commodity display, metropolitan presence, fashion, whiteness, youth, and scandal—the one of overriding significance was the modern.

In Australia in the 1920s, the transnational processes of industrial capital, mass media, and consumption through Western modernization are apparent in six scenes that form the basis for the chapters making up this book. As a late colonial nation-state, imbricated in twentieth-century imperial relations, Australia was entangled within industrial trends through local formations of national, gendered, and raced identities. Its local iteration of types of the Modern Woman traces her emergence into the interstices of global formations of communication, production, and consumption. As the authors of the collaborative research project "The Modern Girl around the World" argue, the Moga, as they call her (adopting the Japanese term as a heuristic through which to investigate her global recurrence), "emerged through international commodity flows, colonial relations, the new media, popular culture, political and social scientific discourses, and far-reaching economic policies."[18] The chapters of this book each describe a unique Australian visual scene and draw on different formations of modern feminine types as motifs for these respective scenes. The first chapter deals with the origins of the articulation of sexual difference through the divide of subject and object, and the implications of this articulation for the modern positions of spectator and spectacle. The following six chapters are divided into two parts. The first part, entitled "The Modern Scene," explores three visual scenes arising from the basic conditions of twentieth-century modernization. These chapters historically contextualize the modern perceptual field. The second part, entitled "Modern Appearing Women," investigates the relations of power in three more scenes. These chapters are case studies of appearing.

In the first part urbanization, visual technologies, and commodity culture are foundational to the modern perceptual horizon. The second chapter investigates the entrance of women into the industrialized workforce and their movement into the growing metropolitan centers. Such urban migration played a significant role in the construction of the Modern Woman as a metropolitan presence through the emergence of urban types such as the City Girl, Office Girl, Business Girl, and Factory Girl. The City Girl was used to illustrate the cultural intersections forged between ideas of the metropolis, the entrance of women into public space, and altered perceptual relations on the street. The meanings that accrued to feminine visibility on the pavements and in the offices of the Australian urban scene were often filtered through notions of the urban spectacle, such as the commodity object, and then displaced onto constructions of cosmopolitan feminine types. The type of the City Girl was discursively negotiated alongside older feminine street presences, such as the prostitute, and this association was played out in changing perceptions of commodity exchange, traffic, movement, contemplation, and visual distraction. Representations which constructed meanings of feminine visibility in the Australian metropolis, such as the marketing of disposable napkins, complicated the traditional status of the woman-object.

In the third chapter, the Screen Star illustrates how women appeared and cast themselves as modern within the popularization of photographic and cinematic technologies. Their status as feminine visual icons threw into doubt foundational distinctions between representation and reality, illusion and substance, artifice and essence. The Screen Star and her emulator, the Screen-Struck Girl, acted as cultural relays between the feminine and visual technology. In Australia these types also brought to the fore Hollywood's dominance of the Australian film industry. An enthusiastic, and perhaps coercive, process of Americanization took place in Australia as U.S. film corporations mobilized the figure of the Screen Star to secure and manage the local market. Commentators related the incursion of these exhibitions to an invasion of moral lassitude from the United States. The illusory qualities of the reproduced image were employed to identify the spectacularized modern feminine as American: not being British, she was not to be trusted and was seen to bear a deceptive relation to truth. The Screen-Struck Girl characterized young women spectators as impressionable, which explained their desire to become spectacles or, more particularly, Screen Stars. These related types hold at once two contradictory meanings: by appearing as images women made themselves modern, yet as spectacles women offered an ambiguous picture of globally recurring visual culture.

In the fourth chapter, the Mannequin, as both a live fashion model and an inorganic replica, is shown to have acted as a motif for the iconization of the feminine created by globalizing commodity culture. She embodied the ways that changes in modern consumer practices affected notions of display and the refiguring of commodity aesthetics in the department store and the ready-to-wear industry. Unlike the City Girl, the Screen Star, and some other types of the Modern Woman, the Mannequin did not emerge in the 1920s as a descriptive type. The Mannequin had existed prior to this period but was now transformed from wax moldings of body parts and dressmakers' dummies, which had acted as clothing supports, into assembled, detailed, mass-produced reproductions of the idealized feminine body. The replica Mannequin embodied the primacy of the visual in characterizing women as modern in contemporary discourses. It also stood in for street presence, inviting women to strike a pose within the play of looks in the metropolis. As a literal reproduction of idealized women, it was like the Screen Star and the unstable real-but-not-quite-real status of her image, both of them drawn under the logic of looks within capitalist exchange. As a commodity fetish, it acted as a host and guide, illustrating women's modes of access to the modern scene through practices of appearing, and it emphasized that the terms of this access rested within the increasingly global visual register.

The fifth chapter investigates a rash of beauty competitions which spread over the popular print media in the 1920s. International newspaper syndicates used such competitions to increase reader participation. A broader and sometimes troubled discussion of feminine visibility was incited by the Beauty Contestant. As an ideal image of modern womanhood, she was placed in a relation to the public gaze that was always predetermined by her relation to her own image. The young women who sought their own publicity by submitting photographs of themselves to newspapers were ambiguously received by the public. The fact that the entrants were judged from reproduced images altered ideas of feminine beauty. Meanwhile, the visual scene created by beauty culture made techniques of appearing essential to the correct performance of the modern feminine subject.

Yet if practices of appearing—the performance of techniques of appearing—became a means to produce oneself as the ideal modern feminine subject, they were also deployed to disqualify women from the modern scene. The sixth chapter shows how Aboriginal and Islander women were systematically constructed as premodern or "primitive" precisely through their perceived failure to *appear* modern. Feminine visual ideals were delineated by size, age, and race as practices of appearing were circumscribed by colonial visions. Whereas whitening creams emerged at this time in the United States and later in India and Africa, Australian Indigenous women were perceived as beyond the reach of commodity markets that mobilized a racially coded aesthetics. That is to say, they had little or no spending power, and unlike Indigenous consumers in other colonial and semi-colonial locales, they were cast as inassimilable to the cosmopolitan consumerism which was integral to the modernist ideology of nation-building.

Representations of Aboriginal women in the 1920s repeatedly cast them as visual anomalies across the modern perceptual horizon. In a converse (but related) move the Modern Woman herself was essentialized as primitive because of her childlike enthrallment to spectacle and her excessive fascination with her own visual effects. Meanwhile, a disavowed but nevertheless voyeuristic colonial gaze was imposed on Aboriginal women. A kind of visual tenure was evident in popular imagery, which used Aboriginal women's naked breasts, in particular, to signify their primitiveness—they "showed" Aboriginal women to be outside the conventions of modesty that marked civilized women. As visibility within the modern scene became increasingly important to women's claims to cultural presence and participation, the casting of Aboriginal women as anomalies in this scene underscored the political implications of invisibility and of pictorial vilification in the construction of visual minorities.

The Flapper's attention-seeking and desire to be seen is the motif of the final chapter. Like the Screen Star, the Flapper was an international practice of modernist bodily aesthetics, and she is still a figure of nostalgia for the 1920s. Everywhere she appeared she was marked by scandal because, by constituting herself as spectacle, she was asserting her sexual agency. Her love of spectacle—particularly as it manifested in mass culture—made her symbolic of modern youth and the transnational flows of communication. She was an allegory for spectacular modernity and its libidinized fascinations, and she represented modern youth as full of energetic movement and in perpetual flux. The Flapper was perceived as both naive and calculating about her public exposure as spectacle. While she was closely associated with and constructed through spectacle, her own desire to appear— particularly to men—complicated the woman-object's traditional inability to attain subject status. The Flapper's practices of appearing were seen to be symptomatic of an excessive desire to be objectified by a heterosexual, anonymous, and often transitory gaze, which was itself encouraged by her appearance in the cinema and popular culture. She became a cultural thought-balloon, in which the questions of globalizing visual technologies and their effects on local heteronormative rites and feminine sexuality were thrashed out. This desire to attract sexualized, anonymous attention left her standing in the shadow of the street prostitute, at times standing alongside Australian renditions of the "street Fairy," "privateer," and "amateur."[19] By constituting herself as a spectacle, the Flapper seemed to assert that she was not merely a modern subject, but a sexual subject.

This book relies on a definition of modernity that emphasizes the alteration of human perception, initially through the invention of optical devices in the eighteenth century, and then through visual technologies such as photography and cinema in the nineteenth century.[20] The significance of twentieth-century industrialized image production to modern structures of identity reverberated across national boundaries as types of the modern appearing woman were reiterated within local significatory regimes of race and gender. If modernization has been defined by changing modes and relations of production—new commodity markets and the expansion of cultural consumption, urbanization, migration, democratization, and technology and its popularization in leisure forms[21]—the visual realm was constituted through these changes and became a primary site for contesting the significance of these innovations for identity. The emergence of types of the modern appearing woman within a complex web of visual scenes suggests that women in the 1920s were implicated in the overall extension of social meaning, gender, race, and power relations into the realm of the visual and conversely, in the intensification of the visual in the production of identity.

Chapter 1

The Status of the Woman-Object

In her quest for a female flâneur, "overlooked" and rendered "invisible" in the literature of modernity, the feminist historian Anke Gleber writes that "[t]o be able to speak of a female flâneur would offer the new figure of a resistant gaze, an alternative approach, and a subject position that stands in opposition to women's traditional and prevailing subsistence as an image on the screen and in the streets."[1] The traditional "subsistence" of woman as image that Gleber refers to found new impetus through the spectacularization of modern women, both as they entered public space and as they were produced as images in cinema, print, and commodity cultures. The subject position of the flâneur was effected from the position of the modern spectator, adjacent to the spectacle. Without access to a position of looking, Gleber's argument continues, modern women were relegated to image.

Gleber's analysis reveals a pervasive ambivalence about feminine visibility. She seeks to reclaim modern women from "their status as an overdetermined image" and their subjection to "massive scrutiny and daily objectification" when they ventured out into public space. "The image status of female existence"[2] prevented modern women from exercising an autonomous gaze that would allow them access to the visual stimulus and, more broadly, to a subjective experience of the modern. This correlation between spectatorship and modern subjectivity is crucial. It not only underpins the claim that modernity centers on the visual, but it implies that only spectators can be included in the category of the modern subject. The traditional divide between subject and object is reproduced between spectator and spectacle. In this instance the "subject" comes to associate with a position of identity and the "object" takes on the qualities of the spectacle. If this division is also gendered, an alternative view of the feminine spectacle is obscured: one that is not exclusionary, one that challenges rather than confirms the traditional division between spectator and spectacle, subject and object. The newly emerged subject position of the modern appearing woman subverted those divisions, inviting a reappraisal of their appropriateness in the analysis of visual culture.

The spectacularization of modern women created a deep ambivalence about the cultural, political, and subjective status of their newfound visibility. Did women's magnified visibility render them merely objects, "subsisting" as images, or could it have been integral to their cultural presence and political representation, even to realizing the emancipated ideal of the Modern Woman? What is the origin of this ambivalence about feminine visibility, which is shared by writers, commentators, and theorists across the decades of the twentieth century? How does it continue to inform, and even restrict, our ways of seeing women, retrospectively and presently?

The dichotomous and mutually exclusive relation of subject to object underpins the argument that, as overdetermined objects, women have been barred from the subject position of the spectator essential to modern identity. For instance, George Sand reveled in her *in*visibility the first time she cross-dressed: "No one paid attention to me, and no one guessed at my disguise. No one knew me, no one looked at me, no one found fault with me; I was an atom lost in an immense crowd."[3] Sand appropriated the invisibility and anonymity that were the privilege of the male flâneur. Through her invisibility she was literally able to lose herself as she chose in the proliferating spectacles of the modern streetscape. Walter Benjamin has written of the mobile and distracted gaze induced by the spectacularized modern city in terms of flânerie. Movement through the city, such as by public transportation, meant that people were put in the position of "having to look at one another for long minutes or even hours without having to speak to each other." This deflected contemplation, which threatened the conventions of anonymity, was not "pleasant," according to Benjamin. It was the reason that "interpersonal relationships in big cities are distinguished by a marked preponderance of the activity of the eye over the activity of the ear."[4] The need to grasp the crowd's significance, sometimes in a passing glance, sometimes in prolonged proximity, led to the emergence of a new observer, "the Flâneur." This type belonged to the emerging literary genre of physiologies of urban types published in France before 1841.[5] These bourgeois transformations of earlier political caricature into an innocuous parade, in which "everything passed in review," were "bonhomie," "leisurely descriptions" that fitted the style of the Flâneur.

Benjamin's trope of the Flâneur described the nineteenth-century Parisian, contemplatively strolling through the panorama of the city. Flânerie was the distracted gaze of the metropolitan dweller who ambled through a cluttered and indistinct landscape of proliferating signs and meanings. Benjamin's modern subject is largely defined through the distractions of mass spectacle and the city. The Flâneur perambulated the arcades of Parisian modernity, where he was "at home," "botanizing on the asphalt."[6] He sought out the opaque crowd, in which, like the hero of the new detective stories, he could move without leaving a trace. Finally, the Flâneur's "last hangout" is figured (in Edgar Allan Poe's work) in the department store, where he could surrender to "the intoxication of the commodity around which surges the stream of customers."[7]

But like many theories of modernity, Benjamin's critique of the modern exchange of looks is gendered. His Flâneur figured a metropolitan masculinity, who made commodity culture and the spectacular pleasures of the street a new masculine territory of discovery—if not in the old sense of blazing a trail through an inscrutable wilderness, then in a new sense of exploring the tantalizing and multiplying sights in the urban landscape. Benjamin's metropolitan men, who seemed to realize their distinctly modern identity through positioning themselves as observers, looked at women as spectacles within this panorama. An indistinct stream of unidentified women must have floated before men's unblinking eyes, for a taxonomy brought women into focus as types almost as soon as they appeared, constructing the significance of their presence, movement, and visual style. Feminine visibility became subject to the logic of typing, itself a response to the anonymous metropolitan crowd and the fleeting, transient gaze that

oversaw its every movement.[8] Through the self-fulfilling logic of scrutiny and appraisal, women were also often cast as sexually deviant, as
were the prostitute and the lesbian.

The stifling and inhibiting effects of women's spectacularization
have led Gleber to claim that only by finding refuge from the male
gaze in the darkened, anonymous spaces of cinemas did modern
women fully realize the subject position of spectator.[9] Since the production of the spectator in modernity's perceptual field so intrinsically
defined the modern subject, Gleber's claim implies that only as un-
impeded spectators were women able to identify as subjects.

Gleber rightly identifies the restrictions arising from women's
status as spectacle. Many feminist theorists of modernity have drawn
attention to the gendered regulation of movement through metropolitan space. Women, including myself, have been subjected to an
intensive, intrusive, and disciplinary surveillance.[10] The subject position of the spectator was ostensibly forbidden them by the cumulative
effect of threats to their safety, unrelenting and sexualized scrutiny,
harassment and intimidation, the ghettoization of their "limited excursions"[11] of consumption, and the commodification of their stylized
images. Women were excluded from the privileged standing of spectator, with its attendant visual pleasures and uncurtailed mobility,
along the gendered divide of scopic relations, namely that men look
and women appear. Altered conditions of feminine visibility com-
pounded the traditional status of Western women as objects, particularly through industrialized and commodified image production. But
these altered conditions also had surprising consequences. At the very
time when modernity found new ways to articulate sexual difference
through the gendered divide between spectator and spectacle, new
ways were also inadvertently opened to women to articulate themselves as gendered, modern subjects, by constituting themselves as
spectacles. The objectification of women was and is real. It has never,
however, been absolute. In modernity women began to negotiate the
increasingly strict terms of self-presentation, prising open their object
status to subvert its inhibiting effects and exhibit themselves, by enacting the subject position of the Modern Woman. I call the habitual,
mutually binding relation between the feminine and objectification
the "woman-object," to uncover its origins and implications for modern women. The woman-object deserves a closer look, one that complicates her status.

The binary polarization of subject/object, so foundational to Western epistemology, has been paradigmatically aligned with sexual dif-

ference, and this has kept us from seeing women as, in fact, the image of the modern subject—that is, as modern because they are spectacular.

Subject/Object under the Modern Gaze

If the modern conditions of feminine visibility produce new formations of feminine subjectivity, then ways of seeing are significant in the apprehension and articulation of gendered identity. Yet that vision is historically variable seems counter-intuitive, since the human eye is a biological constant. The subject/object divide, itself a historical construction of vision, was deployed in modernity's articulation and assignation of sexual difference. Ways of seeing that have gendered the positions of looking and appearing make it difficult to appreciate that the modern appearing woman is "acting."

Vision is historicized more easily by distinguishing between the natural properties of vision and a culture's "entanglement" with these properties in the discursive and historical effects of "visuality":[12] the ordering of reality, knowledge, identity, and sexual and racial difference, and of the disciplinary procedures of government, through visual experience and observation. In the modern scene, not only was vision privileged above other senses, but the traditional subject/object divide was further consolidated through modernity's rational, instrumental gaze.

"Ocularcentrism" is the privileging of vision in the hierarchy of the senses and in metaphors of knowledge. It is said to be the outcome of centuries of thinking in terms of seeing, a manner of thinking which gained dominance in antiquity.[13] The material visibility of Greek gods, the provision for the spectacle of human action and drama, the idealization of the visual form in Greek art, the centrality of the eye in Greek mythological literature (such as the stories of Medusa, Narcissus, and Oedipus), and Greek mathematics' emphasis on geometry all testify to "an Hellenic affinity for the visible."[14] This affinity had marked effects on Greek culture's episteme. Detached, disinterested objectivism, a feature of the Enlightenment's ocular bias, is said to have its origins in the Greek belief that theory (*theoria*) is superior to practice because "consciousness can hover over its object and simply illuminate its essence or form, without affecting the object in any other respect."[15] This split between the object observed and the observing subject recurs under the modern instrumental gaze. But the subject/object divide is itself contingent on ideas about human visual perception and on another bifurcation, this one between the sight of the human eye and the vision of human intelligence. This bifurcation has its origins in the writings of Plato. His distinction between corporeal sight and the visionary mind influenced the sexual differentiation of the looking subject (masculine) and the looked-at object (feminine).

For Plato, sight has an immaterial quality which it shares with the source of light, the sun. He positioned sight as distinct from the other senses, which were clustered with the material human body. Sight belonged with the intellect and soul. Because of this distinction, he was able to call the intellect "the eye of the mind."[16] Visual historian Martin Jay discerns in this a distinction between vision, as "the inner mind of the eye," and the two imperfect eyes of perception, the latter susceptible to illusion and the mimesis of representation.[17] It is the material body that sees, often imperfectly, but the mind that is capable of accurate vision of "the good." A platonic visionary, as such, could be blind.

In Plato's simile of the cave, the prisoners perceive only imperfect shadows, that is, representations of real objects, cast upon its wall. Believing these shadows to represent truth, they are held in a state of illusion until they are "let loose" and emerge into the light of the sun. Though initially dazzled, they are eventually able to directly face it and have "vision of the form of the good." This ascent into daylight represents "the upward progress of the mind into intelligible reason."[18]

For feminist theorist and psychoanalyst Luce Irigaray, the primacy of the visual mind in Plato's simile of the cave itself produces a "blind spot" which forgets the materiality of the eye. The cave is the womb, and the "role of the mother in engendering culture is elided in favour of the father, the solar origin of Ideas, the specular fount of sameness." The maternal cave inscribes the feminine into a particular relation to representation and to subjectivity for Irigaray. It shows that the feminine has a deeply ambiguous relation to representation itself, for feminine reproduction takes the form of images. She writes,

> The cave gives birth only to phantoms, fakes or, at best, images. One must leave its circle in order to realize the factitious character of such a birth. Engendering the real is the father's task, engendering the fictive is the task of the mother—that 'receptacle' for turning out more or less good copies of reality. . . . Semblance exists, it seems, only because of the scene of reproduction that remains *material, matrical.* Here the cave is the 'lowest' representative of that place. Thus the mother-matter gives birth only to images, Father-Good only to the real."[19]

This discrediting of the material or corporeal basis of sight, because of its susceptibility to the illusions of representation, re-emerges in the modern articulation of sexual difference. Young women spectators in the 1920s were said to be susceptible to cinema's chicanery and amorality because they were unable to distance themselves from its images. Their proximity was born out of their being, or materially embodying, spectacles themselves. However, this bodily occupation of the modern spectacle only served to introduce the prospect of the subject into the scene of the object.

Historically contingent conceptions of human sight were crucially implicated in the construction and gendering of the subject/object binary. The question of what the mind could know through the eye, that is, how reliably the eye could relay information from the exterior world to the mind—the interior anchorage of reason—spawned the study of optics. The construction of the vision of the observer as immaterial, through situating it in the interior mind rather than the corporeal eye, furthered the spectator's separation from the exterior, material object he surveyed. The observing subject was configured as a distant witness through the "quattrocento system" or the geometric perspectivalism of the Renaissance.[20] But the eye of the observer remained open to question. The Dutch astronomer Kepler had turned his attention away from what lay before the human eye to the eye itself, to study the impression of light on the retina. His distinction between the image of the world outside the eye and the picture cast on the retina defined visual perception itself as an act of representation. It "split apart the hitherto unified field"[21] of human vision, dividing it into the physical formation of images and their psychological perception. And yet it kept intact the Platonic association between the imperfect eye and its susceptibility to the illusion of representation. Nor did it disturb his distinction between this imperfect eye and the "eye of the mind." This split is also symptomatic of the Cartesian mind, purifying itself of the body, "taking leave of its senses,"[22] so that through his work on optics Descartes could assert that it is "the mind that sees, not the eye."[23]

The earliest prototypes of modern visual technologies, such as the camera obscura of the 1500s, are said to have further disembodied the gaze of the observer. Their look was interiorized, as objects were perceived as arrayed across a field exterior to the machine. Nevertheless the act of seeing was sundered from the corporeality of the observer, as it was no longer a perceivable part of the representation: the look of the observer was supplanted by the look of the machine. The new visual domains opened up through visual technologies confirmed the suspicion that the material eye often erred, and these technologies were important in correcting its deficiencies. As Jonathon Crary argues, the relation between the two was ambiguous:

> On the one hand the observer is disembodied from the pure operation of the device and there is a disembodied witness to a mechanical and transcendental re-presentation of the objectivity of the world. On the other hand, however, his or her presence in the camera implies a spatial and temporal simultaneity of human subjectivity and objective apparatus.[24]

If the spectator-subject lost proximity to the object observed, perhaps this loss was compensated for by the coupling of the spectator-subject's look with that of the machine. This "conquest of the world as perspective,"[25] together with the regulation of both the observer and the objects before "him" through a deepening dualism between subject and object, has been described as the defining lineament of modernity. It laid the ground for the radical schism between object and subject in positivism. The ocularcentrism that marked Western thought came to assume a "distinctively modern historical form." David Levin considers modernity to have begun with "the 'discovery' of perspective and the rationalization of sight in the Italian Renascimento of the fifteenth century."[26]

Social theorists and cultural historians of modernity have claimed that the modern is "spectacularized" or "ocularcentric."[27] It has been called "the society of the spectacle."[28] Levin sees modernity as a culture increasingly dominated by "the hegemony of vision." The contention that the eye is the elemental organ of modernity arises from the invention of the spectator, or the repositioning of the eye of the subject within a field of reproduced and proliferating images.[29] The scene was set as early as the fifteenth century by the invention of the woodblock. Images could now be more easily disseminated, but even in the printing of words vision became the "single mode" of perception.[30] Print produced a "typographic man" who "began to link visual perception to verbalization," which, in Walter Ong's estimation, led to the Cartesian "campaign for a visually conceived cognitive enterprise."[31] It argued that only through visual observation could knowledge be acquired and characterized as truth. This reduction of knowledge to visual contact exemplifies the modern instrumental, rational gaze. Modernity is regarded as having a spectacular logic not purely because of the proliferation and reproduction of images, its "promiscuous range of effects,"[32] or the rationalization or Fordism of its gaze,[33] but because its visual field inaugurated a new ontology of observing and, I believe, of appearing.

People's world-view and everyday encounters were dramatically altered through the advent of mass-communication technologies and modernity's spectacularization of daily life. Developments in architecture and transport created new vantage points from which to behold the globe.[34] The reproduced image was industrialized when mass-produced Kodak cameras became commercially available in 1888; prepackaged film, the picture postcard, and the half-tone block (which allowed photographs to be reproduced in print) soon followed.[35] And although the preclassical cinema of the 1910s often offered a diverse "variety show" format, modernity was about to witness a hegemonization of textual response through mass culture's aesthetic commodification. In the 1910s the feature narrative format began to gain ascendancy, laying the ground for the classical Hollywood studio system and the textual colonizing of distinct significatory locales, such as Australia. Miriam Hansen notes that "the term 'spectator' implied a shift from a collective plural notion of the film viewer to a singular, unified but potentially universal category, the commodity form of reception."[36] Commodity culture itself was prolific in modernity's "frenzy of the visible."[37] In the modern perceptual field the eye of the observer was positioned to allow for "optimum conditions of circulation and exchangeability, whether it be of commodities, energy, capital, images, or information."[38] Modernity had a capacity "to generate forms of 'outward show,' brilliant designs, glamorous spectacles."[39]

The scopic technologies of modernity repositioned the eye through the hegemonic ideals of positivism. As Scott McQuire writes in his cultural history of the camera, it not only removed the observer from the scene of the image but bypassed the documented vagaries and irregularities of human vision, "seizing" reality through its incontestable replication and through the regular, universal laws of chemistry and optics. The "carnal density of vision"[40] was deposed by a "photographic retina"[41] which seemed able to meet positivism's requirement for a fully rationalized, disembodied objectivism in which image was equivalent to object, replication to reality, and image to truth.

The certainty of vision provided by the camera was no doubt central to the "apparent dominance in the modern age of the conviction that vision provides us with the most appropriate paradigm for knowledge."[42] As an overarching epistemic tendency from Greek antiquity through to Enlightenment objectivism and modern instrumentality, ocularcentrism is the mark of Western perception. Theodor Adorno, cultural theorist of the Frankfurt school, has said that "all Western metaphysics has been a peephole metaphysics."[43] And in his damning critique of the operations of the spectacle in late capitalism, the situationist Guy Debord writes, "the spectacle is heir to all the weakness of the project of Western philosophy, which was an attempt to understand activity by means of the categories of vision."[44]

However, vision's susceptibility to the processes of representation arguably laid the ground for the sense of false perception and illusion that filtered through the modern image. Modern visual technologies and their popularization had a profound effect on notions of representation: on the one hand, the reproduced image was perceived as illusory; on the other hand, it was believed to be more accurate than human perception. The belief that modern images could be more truthful—particularly by utilizing the rational gaze of modernity, which brought into view elements that had been invisible because of their distance, movement, interiority, or minuteness—was constantly contended, as representation, mimesis, and reproduction retained their Platonic association with illusion. As semblance, the reproduced image was always in disrepute despite its verisimilitude. This contradiction between the accuracy and realism of photographic technologies and the illusory, almost magic quality of mechanically reproduced imagery underpins the ambiguity and complexity through which the spectacularized woman-object was perceived. Was the spectacle of the Modern Woman true to modern women? Or was it indeed the truth *of* modern women: Did spectacularization come to produce their identities as modern and as women?

In the modern scenario, the radical schism between the object and the observing subject, and the visualization of the object through industrialized techniques of image production, rendered it passive to scrutiny. Agency resided within the replicating machinery and its operation. If the object was looked into being, it was almost discarded in favor of its replicated image. To some extent the object was disembodied and rematerialized within a replication—initially often thought of as a shadow or even a death of sorts[45]—through which its truth could then be deciphered. But the object takes on curiously illusory effects through its reproduction, in spite of the realism of visual technologies, and in spite of attempts to know its truth through its image. Modern visual technologies intensified the distinction between object and subject, but rendered ambivalent the status of the object when reproduced as image.

The changed treatment of the object through its visual reproduction affected the status of the woman-object and seemed to confirm the distinctness of women as objects and their removal from the position of the subject-spectator. However, the very articulation of sexual difference that was facilitated by the gendering of spectator and spectacle also unlocked ways for women to articulate their modern femininity, through appearing. Most of the accounts of ocularcentric modernity focus on its viewing positions[46] and consider techniques of observation[47] as being decisive in modern formations of subjectivity. Inadvertently they also intimate that women's "becoming" image, along with looking at themselves as image, could be central to formations of modern femininity. Modernity had thrown into doubt so many aspects of feminine identity that it is hardly surprising that when women constituted themselves as "glamorous spectacles" they were viewed with both fascination and distrust.[48] When women began to realize their modernity through practices of appearing, they complicated the significance of their visibility. In doing so they confounded the reiterated alignment of sexual difference with the binary subject/object. If men are assigned subject status and women object status through their respective relation to vision and image in Western epistemology, in modernity this distinction extended to mass culture. The picture of women presented in modernity became profoundly contradictory as their objectification through illusory, reproduced imagery seemed to diminish their originary "essence" as feminine on the one hand, while assigning them the status of the modern feminine subject on the other.

The Object of Sexual Difference

The object status of the feminine has been instrumental in the construction of women as unknowable, mutable, and non-originary. Women cannot be self-grounding subjects as objects and, under modern visual techniques, they were increasingly associated with second-order reproductions and mimics.[49] Yet the articulation of sexual difference through subject or object status had profoundly contradictory effects which point to the growing complexity presented by the picture of women in modernity.[50] For instance, the accuracy of photographic technologies opened new realms to view, including the "mysteries" of the feminine body. In the 1928 advertisement aimed at film exhibitors and distributors shown in figure 1.1, the spectacularization of previously unseen parts of the feminine body signified a particularly modern self-consciousness of access to truth through new visual technologies. The visibility of women's legs was an allegory of modern visual access, as distinguished from the visual

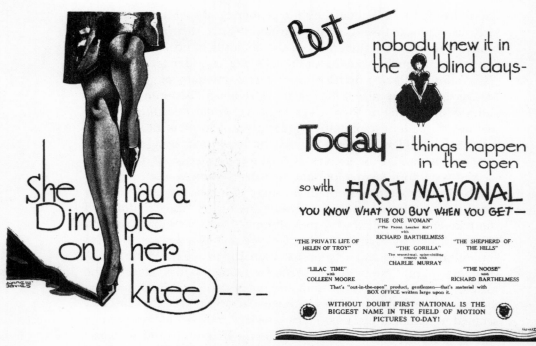

FIG. 1.1. Advertisement for First National, reprinted from *Everyones*, 22 February 1928. Courtesy of the Mitchell Library, State Library of New South Wales.

obstructions in the "blind days" of the past. It signified the genuineness of promoters and the accuracy of cinema—and the attendant pleasures of voyeurism. The objectification of women revealed more than new parts of their bodies. It showed that the articulation of the feminine was seen as a natural extension of visual technologies that, by their nature, revealed the truth of things. This relation, or the expectation of a relation, between feminine spectacle and truth in the modern perceptual field was concisely expressed by the rather risqué cartoonist Brodie Mack in the humor gazette *Beckett's Weekly* in 1928.[51] A young woman suggestively holds open the flap and lapel of her loudly printed coat, revealing her thigh up to the hint of underwear. She looks knowingly at us under the rim of her cloche hat. Mack's caption reads, "Since seeing is believing is it any wonder that people believe in the Modern Girl?" We are able to identify the girl as modern because she exposes so much of herself to view that her femininity is unmistakable.[52] But it is not just the lineaments of her body that make her identifiable as feminine; it is her status as object that assigns her femininity, and the cultural tendency to see her as an object articulates not just her femininity but her modernity. Unlike so many of the feminine nudes in Western art traditions, she is conscious of the gaze she appears before and actively seeks to captivate it by revealing herself. She is tangible through a longstanding epistemological equation between vision and truth: "since seeing is believing." She is the Modern Girl through the shift of this axiom from the epistemic to the cultural realm, a shift facilitated through mass visual technologies that makes her gender known through her object status.[53]

And yet Mack's cartoon discloses that this relation between feminine spectacle and truth is not automatic, otherwise why would he need his caption to guarantee the meaning of his picture? Vision may have already been equated with verification, object status with the feminine; however, modern feminine identity was still not made self-evident by the objectification of women. Indeed, the Modern Girl posed a particular problem to this ancient epistemic relation. As many popular representations in the 1920s of the Modern Woman demonstrate, the feminine-as-spectacle could upset ordinary faith in the correspondence between image and reality on two counts. Firstly, modern feminine visibility harbored meanings of artifice, superficiality, standardization, and mechanization: Mack's Modern Girl is "made up," with dress and cosmetics, to represent the image of modern femininity. Secondly, the very process of her imaging, as mass-produced, recalled another epistemic relation, that between representation, illusion, and the feminine.

The feminine seemed commensurable with the representational intangibilities of modern technologies. In posters and advertisements the feminine was specifically figured as illusion, in that woman could embody that which is resistant to vision, such as speed and electricity.[54] The 1923 Hoskins & Hoskins advertisement in figure 1.2 is reminiscent of earlier uses of feminine spectacle in many emerging nation-states to visualize intangible imperial ideals such as victory and nationalism. Almost as a warning, the woman-object was used to figure illusion. Any claim to veracity through vision could not also accommodate the meanings that accrued to modern feminine visibility: mutability of identity, distractibility, a continuous search for the new and fashionable, and therefore instability, unreliability, compulsiveness, and superficiality.

The contradiction between visual truth and illusory spectacle re-

FIG. 1.2. Advertisement for Hoskins & Hoskins, reprinted from *Bulletin*, 5 April 1923. Courtesy of the State Library of Victoria.

curred in perceptions of and commentary on the Modern Girl. "The artful flapper"[55] may have been considered "frank" and "open"— perhaps because her spectacularization was associated with this very positioning of vision as the "trustworthy sense" of reason.[56] But she was also said to be downright deceitful in her appearance, a figure of trickery and illusion whose real hair color, complexion, age, and moral nature could not be visually ascertained. The figure of feminine Pandora has recurrently invoked the unknowable feminine, taking the form of Lulu in Franz Wedekind's 1925 play *The Loves of Lulu*, adapted to the screen by G. W. Pabst in 1929 under the title *Pandora's Box*.[57] Within these works, well known and much discussed in their period, Lulu was also positioned as spectacle.[58] She unleashed libidinal excess and irrational, regressive appetites through her susceptibility to the visual pleasures of commodity display, as if to prove her inability to master the subject position of spectator. Modernist historian Rita Felski notes that Lulu is thought of, in the writings of Gail Finney, as an instance of the modern feminine exhibiting "the passive, hedonistic and decentered nature of modern subjectivity."[59] The modern spectacle of women may have appeared seamless, but it was also profoundly destabilizing, volatile, and complex.

Yet it is not only the content of what Lulu exhibits but the perverse activity of exhibiting herself that, in my estimation, places her as a feminine symbol of the modern. Felski notes that Lulu is "actress, sex object, prostitute, performer, spectacle," and she argues that "all these identities render her the paradigmatic symbol of a culture increasingly structured around the erotics and aesthetics of the commodity." The feminine was characterized in modernity's cultural imagination by Lulu's "combination of eros and artifice" and was made an object of visual fascination.[60] But Lulu-as-spectacle symbolized not only the expanding effects of commodity aesthetics but also the spectacularization of the Modern Woman. This spectacularization did not, in itself, mean that women could not produce or occupy modern subject positions. Indeed, by turning themselves into spectacles women could enter new feminine categories even as they were being imaged and typed by modernity's representational systems. These spectacles undertook their cultural work from two key sites: the aestheticized feminine caught under the spectacular logic of commodity fetishism, and the presentation of self within representational systems: the consumption and production of the self as image.

For perhaps the first time in the West, modern women understood self-display to be part of the quest for mobility, self-determination, and sexual identity. The importance of this association of feminine visibility with agency cannot be overestimated: the modern perceptual field reconfigured the meanings of feminine visibility. This dramatic shift from inciting modesty to inciting display, from self-effacement to self-articulation, is the point where feminine visibility began to be productive of women's modern subjectivities. The Modern Woman was more likely than earlier women to be positively identified by "her love of looking nice and having beautiful clothes."[61] In *Helen's Weekly*, a women's magazine published in the late 1920s,[62] the columnist "Evangeline" wrote, "The modern girl, neat of head, daintily incarnadined of cheek, and trim of dress fits right into the modern picture and carries her charm with her."[63] Her practices of appearing were inextricably bound up with her presence and participation in all that modernity offered. For example, she was said to have "studied hygiene in studying dress"[64]—her techniques of appearing thus endorsed the modern rationalization of the feminine body.

Commentators were cognizant of the historical discontinuities in modern women's visibility. They praised the Modern Woman as "bored" by the decorum, "ridiculous suppressions and false modesties of our grandmothers."[65] Of course, women in earlier periods had their own techniques of visibility, but rarely did they see these techniques as ways of achieving freedom, emancipation, and social action. The premodern woman reacted to the condemnation of vanity and display by cloaking her techniques of visibility, in effect disavowing them through modesty, dignity, and self-restraint.

Within modernity, tension emerged over the altered significance of feminine visibility. While the woman-object now enabled the articulation of sexual difference to be visually articulated, new opportunities also arose for women to "make spectacles of themselves" in the modern scene. At the same time that women were asked to associate emancipation and self-definition with their visibility, that is, to assert and even flaunt their subject status through positioning themselves as spectacles, they came face to face with the limits of this newfound visibility. Images of women were increasingly homogeneous—young, slender, attractive, and white—and women of other ages, weights, looks, and races found it increasingly more difficult to "make spectacles of themselves." And the reading of women-objects as pleasing heterosexual spectacles seemed to confirm that the woman-object was the opposite of the modern subject, who looked and who was male. At first glance, it would appear that the traditional and exclusive status of the woman-object was modernized by employing the gendered divide between spectacle and spectator to articulate and assign sexual difference. However, I believe that this newfound ability to articulate sexual difference through significatory modes, particularly image production, enabled women themselves to articulate their gendered, modern, and sexual identities using techniques of appearing. Although the images were narrow, homogenized, and racist, the new significance they gave to feminine visibility facilitated women's occupation and subversion of such images in turn.

The conditions of feminine visibility are produced by the ongoing interaction of the changing nature of social space within the modern perceptual field and what Denise Riley, following the subtitle of her book *Feminism and the Category of "Women in History,"* would undoubtedly call the changing density of the category "modern woman."[66] This density was altered through women's own practices of appearing. The tension between the feminine as cultural form and as subjective practice has been exacerbated by our inability to theorize the interface between representation and subjectivity.[67] We need to ask, following Teresa de Lauretis, how visual technologies not only produced images of women but reproduced them as images, or, for my purposes, made the identity of women intelligible as modern through their spectacularization.[68] What did the woman-object mean to women subjects? To answer this question we must read the woman-object not only as one of the impediments holding women back from subject status, but also as a practice of identity in itself.

The subject/object binary became another means to articulate sexual difference through the significatory modes of the modern perceptual field. But it also significantly limited our understanding of modern women's visibility to seeing them as passive objects evacuated of subjectivity at the point of becoming spectacles. Within an exclusive or, more accurately, excluding view of women as spectacles, this dichotomy then consolidated the status of the woman-object. However, that status had contradictory implications for how women might negotiate the subject/object divide. Women were able to challenge that object status rather than participate in confirming it, by occupying the space of those images and appearing within the visual and cultural domain they created. Throughout the twentieth century thinkers have grappled with the implications of the subject/object divide when it was deployed to articulate and assign sexual difference. Those who have broached the question of feminine visibility and its relation to feminine subjectivity offer alternative visions of the woman-object. Feminine spectacle presents a more complex, contradictory picture than first meets the eye.

Bridging the Subject/Object Divide

For Simone de Beauvoir "woman is an object" and it is a lie, an act played to men, that "she accepts her status as the inessential other." Beauvoir believes that this play-act is woman's "vocation"; because she is not "able to fulfil herself through projects and objectives" she becomes a narcissist, "forced to find her reality in the immanence of her person."[69] This social requirement is central to Carole Pateman's explication of the social contract,[70] in which woman is given to man as his property, in response to his demand that "she represent the flesh purely for its own sake."[71] Woman is nothing to man when he "is not making use of the object that she is to him."[72] Her body then becomes "a thing sunk deeply in its own immanence."[73] Woman as object is passive, and in Beauvoir's language, also immanent, alienated, and "Other." But Beauvoir is not absolute about the status of the object. She also writes of woman's objectified body as "her glorious double" and a site of redemption from the bad faith of immanence and passivity: "she is dazzled in beholding it in the mirror; it is promised happiness, work of art, living statue; she shapes it, adorns it, puts it on show. When she smiles at herself in the glass, she forgets her carnal contingence."[74]

It is the young girl's ability to double, to "exist outside"[75] herself, that enables her to see herself as an object and thus to find erotic transcendence. This redemption of object status through its relation to sexual agency configures the sexual emancipation of woman as crucial to their release from object status.[76] Beauvoir was not prepared to dismiss women's object status as unredeemable in her wider scheme of the transcending subject. To be an object—if this is not an oxymoron—"is not to renounce all claim to subjectivity," for "woman hopes in this way to find self-realization under the aspect of herself as a thing." Insofar as "all existents remain subject," despite the demand of men for her to be Other, passive object, "she makes herself object; at the very moment when she does that, she is exercising a free activity." This activity confounded the struggle between men and the modern women who sought emancipation: "woman is opaque in her very being; she stands before man not as a subject but as an object paradoxically endued with subjectivity; she takes herself simultaneously as self and as other, a contradiction that entails baffling consequences."[77] Crucially, Beauvoir sees subject and object cohabiting in the female body.

The feminist philosopher Iris Marion Young draws on the existential contradiction that Beauvoir locates in femininity, through a woman's "doubled experience of being an objectified subject," in her book *Throwing Like a Girl*.[78] In her examination of the "basic modalities of feminine bodily comportment, manner of moving and relation to space,"[79] Young argues that visual space is like phenomenal or lived space in that it has its own modalities of feminine motility and spatiality. At the root of these modalities, which handicap and enclose, "is the fact that woman lives her body as an object as well as a subject," and this "objectified bodily existence" is largely due to visual objectification. "An essential part of the situation of being a woman is that of living the ever-present possibility that one will be gazed upon as a mere body, as shape and flesh that presents itself as the potential object of another subject's intentions and manipulations, rather than as a living manifestation of action and intention."[80] This splitting, or dual occupancy, of subject and object in the visual modalities of femininity resurfaces in John Berger's famous axiom that I have been making use of: "men act and women appear." Berger also leaves open the possibility that woman's object status does not preclude her subject status. However, unlike Beauvoir and Young, he identifies the subject in woman as male. He writes, "men act and women appear. Men look at women. Women watch themselves being looked at. This determines not only most relations between men and women, but also the relation of women to themselves. The surveyor of woman is herself male: the surveyed female. Thus she turns herself into an object—and most particularly an object of vision: a sight."[81]

While Berger is at least willing to consider the relation of the woman-object to herself, he retains the gendered dichotomy in which the cultural roles of subject and object can be taken up only by men and women respectively. Once again, the status of woman as object assigns her sexual difference. In order to see herself as spectacle, she must identify with the male spectator and disavow her own sexual identity. In the discussion leading to the passage quoted above, Berger writes of a woman's self as "being split in two"; these two parts coexist within her as "the surveyor and the surveyed," "the two constituent yet always distinct elements of her identity as a woman."[82] In a similar attempt to consider women's subjective experience of themselves as objects, which also inadvertently keeps intact the alignment of sexual difference with the subject/object binary, feminist theorist Sandra Bartky explores how women's subjectivity is in part determined by the male gaze. She writes, "a panoptical male connoisseur resides within the consciousness of most women; they stand perpetually before his gaze and under his judgement. Woman lives her body as seen by another, by an anonymous patriarchal other."[83]

Berger's and Bartky's split gaze has a commonality with Laura Mulvey's generative and much contested essay "Visual Pleasure and Narrative Cinema."[84] Mulvey originally argued that women's spectatorship was precluded by the inscription of a male gaze into the dominant codes of cinematic representation. For Mulvey the objectification of women within the cinema, on the screen, eliminated any possibility of a woman spectator. Using Freudian psychoanalysis, Mulvey argued "the male gaze" fetishized the woman star as an overvalued object in an attempt to disavow the threat of her castration. The star was controlled by a scopophilic, sadistic voyeurism. She relegated the feminine to what she called "to-be-looked-at-ness," an inherently passive, even masochistic position and the one with which the woman spectator could identify. Her configuration of the feminine spectacle "as the bearer of meaning, not the maker of meaning" poses a dichotomy more radical than Berger's in its disqualification of feminine subjectivity. It served to confirm feminist theory's suspicion of feminine spectacle until its reappraisal during and after the anti-pornography "sex wars" of 1983–87.[85] Most critiques of Mulvey's position, including Mulvey herself in later works, have concentrated on the implied "lack" of possibilities in women's spectatorship.[86] Other feminist film theorists resisted Mulvey's gendered split between to-be-looked-at-ness and the spectator's subjectivity by means of the male gaze. In theories of masochism and fantasy, they proposed a more mobile gaze and same-sex identification. They postulated that transgendered and multiple points of identification were available to the spectator, and these allowed them to theorize an active female spectatorship, which transcended the strictures of Mulvey's initial polarization.

The status of the woman-object has an almost self-defeating logic. When it manifests in feminine spectacle and is understood to preclude women's subject status, we feel that there must be some way out of its paradox. The difficulty feminists face in analyzing and critiquing the status of the woman-object is that, having identified it, their very reading compounds the split between subject and object and gives women no scope to appear other than as objects. But the critique of the status of the woman-object cannot stop at identifying it. A way out of the subject/object binary as it applies to sexual difference must be found. Needless to say, this binary thinking has shaped Western feminism, from Mary Wollstonecraft to Catherine Mackinnon.[87] Whilst some feminists have emphasized the need for women to become cultural producers, the anti-porn movement pursued less convincing campaigns to stop the objectification of women, particularly and inexplicably in sexually explicit imagery. Interestingly, these campaigns repeatedly foundered on the counter-claim by some porn stars that they were not reduced to "sex-objects," but became high-earning sex-subjects through their performances.

Feminist critique remains strongly influenced by the assignation of sexual difference through the subject/object divide. Even when women are acknowledged as subjects, the subject is often characterized as a male tenant in the female body. Beauvoir and Young are notable in that they go beyond this bifurcation of sexual identity, by arguing that women *themselves* might be subjects in becoming objects, although Young is concerned with the prohibitive effects of this "doubling." "All existents are subjects," Beauvoir reminds us, and interestingly, like other modern women, Beauvoir identified sexual agency in women's object status.

The articulation of sexual difference through the assignment of woman to object status as spectacles and men to subject status as spectators has a long history. In modernity, the subject/object divide was constituted differently through the changing historical constructions of human vision. Within the modern perceptual field the status of the woman-object was consolidated through the spectacularization of the Modern Woman. Ancient associations of representation with illusion were played out over the feminine spectacle, in ways which furthered the construction of an unknowable, unstable, and illusory modern feminine identity. A new relation between scopic technologies and truth was also established with regard to the feminine spectacle, in the application of modern ocularcentrism to the mysteries of the feminine body. Different types of the Modern Woman, such as the Flapper, emerged within this complex visual field and negotiated the disabling and enabling impacts of women's spectacularization.

As a visual field, modernity marked an era in which industrialized and commodified image production provided a new way to articulate sexual difference. Although this articulation reinforced the status of the woman-object, it also opened up new cultural spaces for women to occupy. Women were enjoined to make themselves in the image of feminine spectacles they encountered, which produced new meanings of their visibility, such as social, political, and sexual agency. The very spectacularization of women which reiterated their object status also encouraged and sometimes explicitly instructed women in the techniques of appearing, which enabled them to enact different types of the subject position of the modern appearing woman. Through these historical negotiations new ways of seeing and being seen were created for women in the modern scene.

Part I

The Modern Scene

Chapter 2

The City Girl in the Metropolitan Scene

At the conclusion of the First World War, the American company Kimberly-Clark found itself with a surplus of absorbent bandaging made from wood fibers and cellulose padding. Having already learnt that army nurses had used bandages as sanitary napkins, the company turned its surplus into such napkins for the retail market, naming them "Kotex." Although they were discreetly introduced, because of the nature of the product, and despite their expense at ten cents apiece, the disposable napkins caught on quickly.

But their marketing was caught in a cultural paradox. The image of the commodity was crucial in advertising, and yet the napkins had to remain hidden. Sophisticated techniques of display and visual promotion had already become customary. But menstruation was certainly not in the public eye; it had no ready visual referents and was verbally cloaked by terms such as "the curse," "the rags," or, in one sex education pamphlet for parents and daughters, "the monthly sickness."[1] Kimberly-Clark depended upon the new significance of visual images for its product's exposure. But it had to make visible to women a product that would not attract undue attention and that would guarantee modesty, discretion, and the ability to make menstruation invisible.[2] The marketing of the disposable napkins encapsulates the contradictory reception of women in the cosmopolitan urban scene. While women's visibility was construed as part of their modern adventure, commentary in print culture warned women of the dangers of visual exposure and indecency. The advertisements are replete with the contradictory meanings of feminine visibility in reaction to women's, especially middle-class women's, increased street presence.

Against the scopic logic of modern commodity culture, the disposable napkins had to promise invisibility and be brought to women's attention from behind a cultural veil.[3] Advertising was at this time adapting to changing conditions of visibility, which included photojournalism and its new techniques of layout and image production, in a proliferation of women's magazines. Displays of merchandise in department stores, through mirrors and light, "were designed to produce, illuminate, reflect and direct images of femininity to women who shopped there."[4] If the value of the commodity was shifting to the realm of signification, and this process of commodity fetishism was being consolidated by new techniques of display and imaging, then the disposable napkin had to somehow negotiate the complex meanings of feminine visibility in the public sphere and promise invisibility *through* its widespread visibility.

It was a paradox which, like the pads being marketed, incorporated many layers. The product itself had to be visible without being too obvious about its purpose, and in addition the discretion it promised was designed precisely for women entering public space and subject to multiple forms of scrutiny—namely, for the out-and-about Modern Girl. Unlike many products directed at women at this time, which promised that women could become modern through their spectacularization, disposable napkins guaranteed the concealment of a defining aspect of the feminine. Yet they also guaranteed that women could enter into the new freedoms outside the home and enjoy their newfound visibility with confidence, without fear of "exposure" or "embarrassment."

Like so many of the vagaries of the feminine body that required intervention and correction—such as facial and underarm hair— menstruation was deemed "unsightly," the designation of the culturally inadmissible. Many of the advertisements implied that if it were not for disposable napkins, women would have to remain closeted at home when they menstruated. In one Kleinert's advertisement two young women are seated indoors, one in hat and open coat, the other in a frock, cushioned on a chaise longue with an open magazine on her lap. "My Dear! . . . of course you can go!" the advertisement pronounces; the product "makes you feel perfectly safe and comfortable anywhere any time!"[5] Without these products, women would continue to languish, fragile and sickly, on chaise longues in premodernity. If women could not be visible in public space, they could not truly think of themselves as modern. Public space posed real dangers to women, such as violence and sexual harassment; nevertheless it was from the exposure of unsightly aspects of their own bodies that women needed "protection."

Kimberly-Clark's Kotex napkins were not the first product marketed for menstruation. Since 1854, twenty different patents had been taken out for "sanitary napkins," "catamenial supports," "monthly supports and protectors," and "menstrual receivers and receptacles." In 1890, Johnson and Johnson had produced a disposable gauze pad which it named "Lister's Towels,"[6] avoiding any direct textual reference to menstruation. By the 1920s, the product deployed the Victorian feminine ideals of modesty and discretion, but now within the context of the public exposure that was endemic to modern life. Johnson and Johnson renamed its product "Modess" for its association with "modesty."[7] The items offered became instead "sanitary napkins" or "towels," "ladies' protective necessities," "santalettes," or "sanitary lingerie."

In the 1920s, a variety of disposable napkins swept through transnational markets, including the British "Menex," the American "Modess" and "Kotex," and the Australian "Lister's Towels" and Kleinert's "Kez." The "years-old problem of personal hygiene"[8] was exacerbated for the Modern Woman, the advertisements reasoned. An ad for Menex showed a drawing of a young woman seated on a train with a man in the distance glancing at her through the window; the caption read "May be [sic] you have wondered at them—these women who fling themselves light-heartedly into the whirl of life—dance, motor, play tennis in the sheerest of frocks with no fear of embarrassment. Gone is that awful old-time feeling of conspicuous bulkiness."[9] In a 1928 advertisement in the *Australian Woman's Mirror*, Kleinert pointed out the ways the Modern Woman might be caught out and embarrassed without its Kez pad. It trumpeted, "Modern Womanhood Must Know No Embarrassment" [sic]. "Woman with her increased outdoor activities, her wider circle of social engagements, has learned in the past few years to look to science for hygienic aids." Modern science was able to give "PROTECTION ABSOLUTE!" as "deodorised, sterilized, aridized," and with "solubility."[10] The modern imperative of hygiene—which set out to make germs and disease visible, in order to destroy them—was applied to the vagaries of the feminine body.

The visible feminine body threatened women's modernity. Women had to keep watch over their own bodies by identifying with the multiple points of view of a scrutinizing gaze—that is, by thinking of themselves as spectacles, and by regulating and managing their visibility through techniques of self-mastery. To appear correctly modern women had to invite science into the secrets of their bodies so that it could teach and supply, through the commodity, techniques of control and discretion.

To fear exposure was to be relegated to the premodern. The advertisements claimed that menstruation was woman's "age-old hygienic problem,"[11] that "every women [sic]" had sought "sure protection" from "the old-time fear and dread of embarrassment."[12] Although the feminine body was subject to change, in woman's "increased outdoor activities"[13] her body's timelessness could not be forgotten, normalized as it was by sexology, eugenics, and social Darwinism.[14] But even when these discourses were used in contradictory ways, the imperative of modern womanhood was to exhibit self-mastery through techniques of appearing. Modern women had to know their visual effects in order to become active participants in their spectacularization.

Women had to be taught how to watch themselves. Mothers were called upon to "Show Her the Way" and use Kleinert's Ladies' Protective Necessities because their daughters "should be taught to appreciate that undue embarrassment is unnecessary."[15] Advertisers of sanitary napkins offered the Modern Girl as a figure with whom potential customers could identify. She was in need of maternal guidance, being "acutely sensitive"[16] and subject to the contradictory desires for visual appeal and modesty—the necessity of "keeping oneself immaculate and sweet" and yet doing away with "the slightest fear of embarrassment."[17] "Immaculate" means "free from spot or stain"; "embarrassment" became a gendered condition.[18] The new conditions of feminine visibility are inscribed in a Menex advertisement (fig. 2.1) in the frank gaze of the "modern girl" whose hand discreetly covers the opening of her tunic. Her poignant look seems to demonstrate her awareness of being before a public, indeed a mass, gaze. Equipped with these understandings and with the new products that can protect her against exposure, she has "safely solved the age-old hygienic problem" and can partake in the pleasures of modern feminine visibility.[19]

FIG. 2.1. Advertisement for Menex, reprinted from *Home*, 1 May 1930. Courtesy of the Mitchell Library, State Library of New South Wales.

These pleasures included "freedom the whole day through," according to the caption on an advertisement's sketch of a young woman stepping out of a car wearing a skirt of lightweight fabric—a particular "danger" for the menstruating woman. Menex promised that its wearers would have "No doubts or fears—even though you wear the sheerest of frocks—those dangerous light things that once were a source of never-ending anxiety."[20] Wrinkles made in the backs of skirts by the rubber panels of sanitary "lingerie" were as much to be guarded against as menstrual staining itself, as was "silhouetting," or, napkin bulk showing through clothes.[21] In another peculiar image, a young woman in golfing apparel is discernible behind a floating pair of sanitary knickers.[22] As the danger that public visibility offered to women was met with assurances that aspects of the feminine body would remain veiled and private, menstruation became an outdoor activity, an aspect of life for the "Outdoor Girl." But menstruation remained as "secret" as ever, and companies used this contradiction to market their products. "It's an Open Secret," a Menex advertisement announced, under a drawing of a young woman smoking in a light party frock, with dancers behind her.[23]

By the 1920s women were a notable presence on city streets. While working-class women had been visible much earlier, the everyday presence of middle-class women intensified anxiety about the meaning and intentions of their visibility. Commentators received them with the same ambivalence that can be seen in the marketing of the disposable napkin. Their visibility was seen as integral to their identification as modern, but it was also viewed with distrust for the ways that it might sabotage the gendered rituals of looking and being seen as they traditionally articulated sexual difference. The representations of women in the metropolitan scene that follow come primarily from print culture, with some from actuality (non-dramatized) footage. Photography would soon dominate newspaper illustration, but in the 1920s animated and even roguish social commentary was still often conveyed in cartoons and line drawings. They mined the City Girl and Business Girl types, unearthing that peculiarly Australian aptitude for colloquialism, implicating visibility in their production as types. If the visibility of the Modern Woman helped to produce this subject position, the sanitary napkin advertisements, comics, and cartoons reproduced here show that women had to negotiate often contradictory meanings of feminine visibility: there was a great deal at stake in achieving fitting visual effects.

The Flâneuse and Separate Carriages

On 30 November 1894, only five weeks after the Edison Kinetoscopes had premiered in London, James McMahon set up five of these peep-hole film-viewers in Sydney. Cinematograph footage, often of novelty sequences, such as trains traveling at high speed toward the camera, was first projected before an Australian audience by the magician Carl Hertz.[24] In September 1896 the chemist Maurice Sestier, the Lumière brothers' agent for India and Australia, screened footage he had shot in India and elsewhere. By the end of the month, he and photographer Walter Barnett had completed the first film sequences ever shot in Australia. They screened their footage in Melbourne at a J. C. Williamson theatre production, *Gin Gin,* and went on to film the Flemington race season, beginning on 31 October

1896, including the Melbourne Cup. This footage is the earliest Australian film known to survive and includes sequences of women walking along footpaths, crossing streets, and traveling by public transport.[25]

One scene in this film shows a crowd disembarking from a train at Flemington railway station, and the difference in the ways men and women occupy and move through public space is striking. The women stand out because of their top-heavy hats and light-colored dresses. They leave the train after most of the men, and usually descend from it without help. Judging from a quick headcount through slowed frames there are approximately fifteen women among the crowd of male travelers.[26] None appear to be alone in public; each is part of a larger group or accompanied by a man. In footage of a Melbourne street filmed by the Salvation Army's Joseph Perry, only two women appear to be walking along the relatively well-populated street alone.[27] The same pattern of women embarking and disembarking after the men recurs in footage of a Sydney paddle ferry shot circa 1910.[28] As the ferry fills, only eleven of the women appear to be traveling alone. However, it is possible that men and women used separate entrances and joined their opposite-sexed companions later (just as men often congregated in smoking carriages on trains).

The much pursued flâneuse makes few appearances in this early footage. In a sequence that follows a tram car in Sydney, only twelve women appear alone in a street crowded with men.[29] In other scenes as well, the gender ratio is markedly unbalanced. Women are well represented in the crowd outside Sydney's Horden Brothers store, but even there, they group together under a cloud of white parasols and attentively balanced hats.[30] In 1910 footage of Melbourne crowds, isolated women make lonely expeditions outside a number of landmarks and thoroughfares: five women at a railway station, three on a bridge, one outside the town hall.[31] Another sequence shows workers leaving a Swallows and Ariel factory in 1905.[32] Men swarm out of the small door, larking and hamming it up for the camera, filling the pavement and street. As they trail off, the women begin to appear, leaving in tight clusters, sometimes giggling, rarely leaving the pavement when alone. Three men wait by the door to accompany their womenfolk, who join them unceremoniously, while other women pass them in pairs. Women who are alone round the doorframe closely and march off down the pavement under low hat-brims, sometimes leaving so fast they blur in the frame.

The actuality footage gives the impression of a slow but evident change in the manner in which women occupied the street. By the 1920s, women no longer scuttle through the streets shielding themselves with their hats, as if dreading the possibility of being seen. Rather, they walk erect, their comportment suggesting an outward-directed gaze, encountering and negotiating the gaze of others. In this footage, women appear to be purposively projecting an image. The ratio of women to men has increased, with women seen negotiating traffic jams,[33] approaching traffic police,[34] and filling their separate train compartments.[35] By the late 1930s, the ratio of women to men on the street is as you might see it today. In one whimsical sequence, women walking into the wind across Sydney's main square seem to salute the camera as they reach up to hold their hats.[36]

During the 1920s the number of women in public space increased noticeably. Ways of occupying this space still differed by sex: most obviously women's movement through space was regulated and, at times, segregated. While early actuality footage shows a steady increase of women from the mid-1890s to the 1930s, the 1920s were a cusp decade in which women's public presence increased dramatically and, while still regulated by the habits of the past decades, began to be a normal part of daily life. By then, traversing public space implicated women in scopic relations in which they looked, and were no doubt conscious of being looked at. Managing the popular meanings that came to surround their public visibility must have been an indispensable aspect of orientating themselves in the cosmopolitan scene. Modern appearing women had to strategically place themselves on the spectrum of these meanings, as part of their performative enactments. Perhaps because of this perceptible change in women's public visibility, their modes of appearing and their street presence were the subject of intense commentary, and also cause for alarm.

His Last Stand

The modern metropolis was one of the formative conditions of feminine visibility. Urbanization, it has been argued, is one of the "normative systems" of modernity, instituting similar modes of identity, movement through space, temporal alignment, and spectatorship conventions in industrialized countries. Just as modernity was a spatial formation, the metropolis was a human geography that configured urban feminine types through their spectacularization, both on the street and within its proliferating and mass-reproduced imagery.

In print culture, new formations of public visibility provoked comment and concern. Commentators in the 1920s held the social repercussions of the war responsible for the "swarms" of women to be seen on the pavements. However, as the actuality footage demonstrates, working- and middle-class women had entered the commercial sector throughout the previous decades, as Business Girls and Shop Girls, in response to industrial and economic changes.[37] By 1891, they made up 10.6 percent of the burgeoning tertiary occupations workforce. Later, women would fill the gap in the workforce created by 417,000 men enlisting for the war, and by 1921 they constituted 22.4 percent of the tertiary occupations workforce.[38] From the early years of the twentieth century white-collar jobs were opened to white women in public service, banking and insurance, nursing, teaching, and retail, and it was in these jobs that women faced the public across counters and desks. Their new visibility was often considered scandalous.

The entrance of women into metropolitan space was a challenge to the Victorian doctrine of "separate realms"[39] and was read as "new" and indicative of the modern from the 1850s to the 1920s. It was embodied in the figures of the "New Woman" and the "Modern Woman."[40] The New Woman came onto the Australian cultural stage in the 1880s from Britain, with a reputation gained in the British press through a series of articles by Mona Caird questioning the morality of marriage and "compulsory motherhood."[41] The articles were reprinted in Australia at the same time as the New Woman "Nora" appeared on the stage in Ibsen's play A Doll's House. The New Woman had much in common with the single woman: both were new categories that provided alternative identities for women. The number of unmarried Australian women peaked in 1921, and the modern types who became prominent in Australian visual scenes were young women who, because of their economic independence, now had the option of not marrying. Such a woman was often depicted as seeing herself as "an object of desire and as capable of evoking strong sexual responses: she saw herself as sexual. The danger of this was that her sexuality was uncontained: it was not controlled within the marital framework."[42] Young women were increasingly discussed in commentary and cartoons in part because of interest in the now indeterminate meaning of their visual appeal. Women might make themselves visually appealing for their own satisfaction, and beautification was just one of the growing number of activities women engaged in with no intention of pleasing men.

In the United States, Britain, and Australia, modern womanhood was defined by women's entrance into public space. American historian Glenna Matthews calls this new category of women "public womanhood." She argues that their presence was fostered by "the development of a corporatized industrial economy" in which typewriter girls visited department stores and other public places, "marching into the terrain" along with temperance activists, women from the settlement house movement, members of women's clubs, and radical speakers such as Emma Goldman and the suffrage leader Elizabeth Cady Stanton. Public womanhood gained "cultural influence" by earning academic degrees, lecturing and speaking in public, traveling alone, attending theaters and dance halls, shopping in department stores, and riding bicycles. These women had to negotiate the still commonplace association of unchaperoned women in public with the "common" street prostitute. But modern women "were less likely than their predecessors of any class to be driven from public space or public roles by aspersions on their chastity."[43] Such "aspersions" were still commonly cast in Australian visual representations in the 1920s. They contributed to the belief that women's new freedoms were dogged by the threat of dangerous exposure. Marilyn Lake writes of Australian feminists' perception that "the sexualisation of women increasingly evident in the wider culture seemed inimical to the advancement of women as citizens."[44] Because feminine visibility was maligned, efforts were made to consign these new, visible modern women to unqualified object status.

Women's presence in city streets has been figured as an effect of the agitation of first-wave feminists who claimed their right to public inclusion. However, it is more likely that the need to earn a living impelled young women to pursue the "freedom of the factory."[45] Young women increasingly sought to avoid the "demeaning" relations of domestic service. The associations of women on the street with spectacle, commodity, and visual traffic meant that these women were often left to deflect their identification with the prostitute as best they could. The distinction between the independent "woman about town" and the prostitute seemed unclear to commentators and cartoonists, or perhaps they enjoyed blurring it. The meanings that accrued to women's visibility in public space situated them in cultural proximity to the commodity spectacle. They were caught up in the exchange of

FIG. 2.2. "How She Got the Notion to Shorten Her Skirts." Illustration by Geoffrey Keith Townshend, reprinted from *Aussie*, 15 May 1929. Courtesy of the Mitchell Library, State Library of New South Wales.

looks that became as much a part of metropolitan traffic as the Model T Ford.

The entry of women into metropolitan space was shaped by representations of feminine types who were not at home in the home, who relished participating in the urban traffic and, possibly, the ambiguities this participation created in their sexuality. These types were marked by a desire to enter into the cosmopolitan perceptual field as more than spectators—they wanted to be part of the scene as spectacles, reputedly shortening their skirts to excite more attention (and not to avoid dragging hems in the mud—see Townshend's illustration in figure 2.2). Part of the pleasure offered by the city lay in attracting attention within an anonymous and fleeting gaze. Pavements and offices became theaters to these types of City Girl, places where she distracted, displaced, and visually overpowered men. This was her way of partaking in the adventure of the city, the excitement of (hetero)sexual attraction, anonymous display, and urban style. The siren call of the city was even heard in rural centers. Young countrywomen who called themselves Flappers insisted that the local Friday night promenade had to take place on the main street. "That's the only street that people were interested in": the open shops meant that "the whole place was lit up"—not unlike a theater.[46]

City types upset the traditional heterosexual visual economy by partaking in the confusion of street traffic. The territory of the street was undergoing an upheaval, wherein public and private experience were being resituated, remapping the experience of physical proximity, captivation, romance, and intimacy.[47] The City Girl challenged the split between masculinized and desexualized productivity and the sexualized and feminized pursuits of mass entertainment, which were associated with the constant flux of images and commodities. Merely by their presence on the pavements, City Girls befuddled and disoriented men who did not know how to assess them visually, and therefore morally, as is shown in the cover illustration for the humor magazine *Aussie* in figure 2.3. Writing of the unprecedented attention given to young women in the city street, one American commentator said, "people still are amazed by seeing women anywhere except in the time-honored places."[48] In another *Aussie* cartoon a lone, bewildered man stands in a tram car surrounded by rows of stylish young women smoking cigarettes in elongated holders and talking animatedly. The cartoon is captioned "His Last Stand."[49]

The City Creates Wants in Queer Forms

Women's street presence was one outcome of a general shift in production and manufacturing which reconfigured the landscape and therefore people's sense of place and national identity. As rural populations in industrializing nation-states drifted to the cities, those metropolises, which were centers for production, resonated with anxieties about national identity that were informed by gendered characterizations.[50] The visibility of young women, their susceptibility to city spectacles, and their visual (and therefore sexual) transformation were commonly invoked to describe the moral fall of country girls who came to the city—and in Australia that fall was itself seen as a symptom of the loss of country virtue in the national character. A quarter of a million people moved to urban centers; by 1921 Sydney's population had reached one million, as did Melbourne's population by 1928.[51] As cities industrialized, they were felt to be drawing the people and primary produce off the land, consuming them "like a giant octopus, stretching forth its suckers throughout the state,

FIG. 2.3. Cover illustration, reprinted from *Aussie*, 15 June 1923. Courtesy of the Mitchell Library, State Library of New South Wales.

draining its life blood in a vain effort to satisfy its insatiable stomach," as one farmer lamented.[52]

The metaphors of consumption and engulfment here were congruent with a pervasive fear that the national identity of the outback and its associations of mateship and men's self-determination were being undermined by the rise of manufacturing industries and consequent urbanization.[53] This opposition of country and city was overlaid with and overdetermined by sexual difference in the Norman Lindsay cartoon of 1919 that is shown in figure 2.4. The country was represented as the locale of an idealized version of coherent masculine identity, the self-made man; the metropolis was the fragmented site of confused and feminized consumption, embodied by the Flapper—who, with her audacious ways, baffled and disoriented men.

The City Girl represented a challenge to national identity, as embodied in the figure of the Australian bush, the Outback Man. But she also challenged the traditional gender divide. Young women coming to the city from the country were transformed into spectacles of decadence and familial rebellion. In a 1925 Melbourne *Bulletin* cartoon,

FIG. 2.4. Cartoon by Norman Lindsay, reprinted from *Bulletin*, 6 November 1919. © H. A. and C. Glad. Courtesy of the State Library of Victoria.

the returned daughter sports bobbed hair and a sleeveless cocktail frock; perched provocatively on the dining table blowing smoke rings, she is indifferent to the aghast gaze of her family.[54] Parental supervision failed in the city, and the libidinous Modern Girl was all too keen to take advantage of that.[55] Newspapers such as the Melbourne *Truth* published alarmist broadsides with titles such as "Tarts about Town: Girls Who Take the Wrong Turn," in which young women living unsupervised in the city "work in offices and shops during the day, and seek the bright lights at night." *Truth* sorted such young women into the types "Flappers," "Love Birds," and "Privateers": "[t]hey pay for their pleasures with smiles and kisses and if they have in the end to pay more dearly—well 'it's all in the game'. Such is the reckless philosophy of the typical tart about town."[56] *Truth* cited letters from the *Brisbane Patriot* which hotly debated the issue of young single women moving into bachelor flats and "giddy girls using them for parties and orgies."[57] Opportunities for such revels were represented as a major aspect of the city's "lure" and its seductive power over young women in particular. Importantly, such women were transformed visually. In 1922, *Truth* wrote of the city as "the Vortex" which "draws" country girls in: "Rural in appearance as she is, unformed, without poise, she glimpses the promise of herself transformed and citified."[58]

The Country Girl, in coming to the city, "unconsciously" and "wistfully" absorbs the "elusive" style and "artificial laughter" of smart city ladies, until she too discards the "serious, self-respecting" values of her former arcadian identity and acquires "hardness and a cynical veneer" by way of adopting "the fashionable scepticism and unbelief which women cultivate in the name of smartness."[59] The Country Girl, that is, enters the city in a state of pastoral simplicity and natural grace, but the city enchants her, leaving her wandering its thoroughfares in an almost phantasmic state of scopic marvel and libidinal disorientation. She succumbs as though dazed to the distraction of commodity display and the pleasure of appearing "citified," losing her moral bearings principally because of her desire to appear as spectacle. Her gaze and the gaze she seeks to attract are key to her vulnerability to the city's transfixing, transforming power.[60]

The trope of ruined country girls appears again in the *Green Room Pictorial* in 1926. The magazine admonished the sons and daughters of the "strong, hardy Saxons" of old days for returning to the city, which their fathers had left to extract "golden harvests" from harsh remote places. "The city creates wants in queer forms," the article lamented above a sketch of a calculating, smartly dressed woman wedged between two police officers.[61] The desire to be visually integrated as smart, modern, and "citified" could distract "bonnie" girls from country virtue, sometimes with fatal results. "Mary" went to Sydney specifically to escape her parents' control. She turned to thieving in order to obtain smart clothes and, on being discovered, had to leave the department store where she worked. "Within six months . . . at least three men went 'broke' over her." "It was clothes made me do it," she confessed to the *Green Room Pictorial*. Accepting a fur coat from a married man was the beginning of her demise, but the acceptance of such gifts became a habitual impulse in her dealings with men.[62] If the country girl had sexual relations with men it was to fulfill her desire to become spectacle in the metropolitan scene: her transformation into spectacle precipitated her moral fall. The City Girl's "love of finery" and desire to appear were cast as libidinal, irresistible attractions.

Industrial cities invited young women to appear publicly as modern, and this appearance was seen as transforming them, contaminating and mutating the feminine body until it was unsuited for domesticity. Traditional constructs of sexual difference were defended by associating them with the premodern, virtuous country girl. Publicity for Beaumont Smith's film *Satan in Sydney* (1918) mobilized the theme of scandalous metropolitan sexuality. A poster shows a country heroine drawing back a curtain to reveal Satan looming over the city horizon and "that side of Sydney you do not know about."[63] The Country Girl was unaccustomed to the city gaze, and her shyness and discretion exemplified the respectable premodern woman's rejection of object status. In verse in the *Bulletin*, the country wife's virtue, typified by her domestic endurance and maternity, is also defined by her not having been seduced by the mirage of city light and spectacle:

> She does not know the fascinating lights:
> The splendid city streets; the crowded ways;
> The wondrous palaces where hours are shod
> With magic shoes that cheat the aching nights.
> She toils, she bears, she weeps. She hears no praise—
> Unless perhaps, it be the praise of God.[64]

In a 1924 *Bulletin* cartoon, the economy of heterosexuality is undone by the urban girl who is too tainted by city odors to touch pure country milk and be the "helpmate" wife.[65] The young "City Visitor" stands matter-of-factly returning the "Cow Cocky's" gaze and asks, "so you wouldn't allow your son to marry a girl who smoked cigarettes?

Surely that is very narrow-minded." The other replies, "No it ain't that. But every milkin-time that nicotine on 'er fingers wouldn't do the milk no good." If the polluted metropolis threatens to contaminate the agrarian ideal, it is young women who are the agents of this pollution as a result of pursuing their own pleasures. Many of the traits of the modern metropolis—artifice, sophistication, and the standardization of appearance—are attributed to urban feminine types, whose visual style completes the transformation of the City Girl to symbolic representative of the metropolis. So H. H. B. writes in *Aussie* in 1923 that City Girls "live in a totally artificial atmosphere. The very pavement on which they walk is man-made. The air they breathe is stale with the lies of the million. The food they eat has been prepared, preserved and cooked until it has lost all the freshness with which Nature endowed it. Their faces are modelled until God's original creation is merely the canvas upon which the artist lays her colors."[66] Similarly, in a letter signed "Old Fashioned" in *New Idea*, a women's magazine, the "semi-woman"—smoking, drinking, and disregarding the "true man's ideal of womanhood"—is described in terms of "standardisation and the dearth of individuality," as an "imitation" and a "revolting spectacle."[67] The ancient equation of spectacle with imitation and fallacy is recast in the modern scene in the figure of the City Girl whose behavior makes a spectacle of her—and her being a spectacle is necessarily "revolting." Beneath these pervasive censures of young City Girls as standardized and artificial was the sense that feminine essence was being lost. Young women symbolized the power of the city to transform, and their moral and visual mutability were disturbing indicators of social instability.

Defrauding Nature

The inability to visually determine the moral nature of City Girls informed the contemporary discourse on eugenics and population decline. Femininity was said to wither in the precincts and overcrowded slums of the city. The concentration of the population in towns was blamed for the declining birthrate,[68] as slum living conditions and equally difficult working conditions were believed to cause sterility in women.[69] Anxiety about urbanization and women's new opportunities to discard domesticity was evident in the 1914 New South Wales Royal Commission to investigate the decline of the birth rate, as well as in the ongoing discussions about the shortage of white working-class female domestic workers. They too were effectively leaving the home, though someone else's home rather than their own. If the domestic servant became the Factory Girl, she would sit eternally within "smoke-darkened walls" and confined under a "smeary ceiling." The Factory Girl, in a verse by Myra Morris published in the *Lone Hand,* is daily drowned under the clamor of "brazen tongued machinery" and mocked by "the groan of lathes and wheels / and cylinders that swoop and spin." She asks God why she cannot watch the flowers, trees, and grass: "I would be a part of these."[70] When the Country Girl was lost to the city, so were her "better nature" and her potential motherhood. Concerns that underpopulation would render the nation vulnerable to an influx of inferior racial types, particularly the "yellow peril" from Asia, intersected with discourses on eugenics and racial hygiene in the popular press to decry the City Girl as unable, even selfishly unwilling, to "continue the functions of motherhood." The city worked against women's having children, through both "cramped and sordid surroundings" and "the shameful prevention and the slaughter of the unborn." In the cities, Australia faced "a future of permanent sterility" because of the "constant stream" of women "defrauding nature," who were already "bleeding the country white."[71] Middle-class women, especially, would fail to carry the reproductive burden of the nation because of their urbanization and particularly their attraction to spectacle.[72] One commentator warned that "machinery products, canned goods, and city crowding, cut away from the life of the average woman, not giving her time to a young child . . . leaving time that would hang heavily on her hands, if not filled by a 'movie,' the casual shopping the object of which is not to buy but to see, the tea-party and the gossip fest."[73] "The Moloch of Industries" produced "mutilated spectres of womanhood," as unhealthy industrial conditions combined with "a callous disregard for nature's requirements." Cities removed women from homemaking and child-rearing, thrusting them into the "notorious haunts of vice."[74] The liberatory potential of the city, the escape it offered women from the confinement of the home and surveillance of proprietorial sexual relations, led some men to declare they would not marry the "modern girl." They said, "I will make a house—will the women make a home," when she was "always asking, 'Where shall we go now?' "[75] Women who wanted to go out and be seen could hardly be attentive to the demands of the home.

In a British treatise on the "future woman," commentator A. M. Ludovici similarly lamented the impact of industrialization on Britain's four million spinsters and "unmated women-workers." The city de-sexualized women through "dehumanising labours," denying them "the ardent embrace of a lover, the ecstasy of consummated love, and the clinging devotion of adoring offspring." Here sexuality is attached to an idealized femininity, which should stand against the soiling and corrupting realms of masculine industry and commerce. In Western cities, the feminine body became either pathologized or, like the Mannish Woman, deviant. The "unmated spinster workers" who filled trains, trams, and omnibuses in Britain became "withered and broken by long years of typing." Removing women from the home rendered them "conspicuously inferior in passion and equipment." The industrialized urban woman became a "neuter."[76] In these scenarios of lost feminine essence, the urban woman became a "revolting" spectacle, recognizably "unfeminine" because of her withered charms. She failed the modern ideal of self-mastery, vigor, and health because she traded her premodern, agrarian femininity for that of the modern, city-soiled laborer. She contributed to a view of the metropolis as grimy and despoiled, and symbolized nature as corrupted and failed by modernity.

The Concretive Impulse

In her *City of Dreadful Delights*, Judith Walkowitz notes the "dense cultural grid" which discursively mapped the city as dangerous terrain for women. She discusses the charity worker and platform speaker of the 1870s not only as representational types, but as women who were "social actors" and "political actors," who both inserted themselves into prevailing discourses of sexuality and social space and charted the city as space in which they could feel at home. By situating their home in public space, such women breached the dichotomy of private and public as consigned to sexual difference and effected a powerful "new urban style." Walkowitz attends closely to the meanings which accrued to the visibility of such women, who, like the lady shopper, "seemed to exhibit a penchant for 'egotistical' self-display, that disquieted many observers."[77] She also outlines the conditions of this visibility, noting that new or "advanced" women, though few in number, nevertheless, through the wide distribution of print media, became an influential discursive presence within the landscape of contested meanings of femininity, social space, and sexual danger. These women's practices of appearing produced meanings of feminine visibility in the metropolis.

For Walkowitz, self-creation and self-expression are central to the "systems of meaning articulated by social actors of the past."[78] She sees them as the actions of the socially self-including subject. Appearing was arguably an important way in which Walkowitz's "social actors" created themselves as independent and autonomous, that is, as modern, in the face of sexual harassment and the construction of women's sexual vulnerability. As Walkowitz notes, their visual style was part of modern women's assertion of themselves as social actors in metropolitan space. Similarly, Kathy Peiss notes that for the working-class immigrant girl, the "public presentation of self was one way to comment upon and mediate the dynamics of urban life and labor."[79] Representations of types of the City Girl may have encouraged young women to appear as these types, as "social actors," mediating the dynamics of this dense cultural grid.

In 1913, Jessie Ackermann published a book called *Australia from a Woman's Point of View*. Interestingly, her title stakes her claim to subject status by positioning her as an observer. Ackermann addressed women's lack of public access, writing that it was a "disgrace to a free and equal country where women and girls are supposed to be equal with men and boys" to demand that girls be kept off the street.[80] For Ackermann, women's presence on the street was an indisputable expression of their Australian citizenship. Rather than defining young women's desire to be part of the street scene as morally dubious and a response to the seductive "call of the street," she sees the street as the setting for learning a "new love through street experience." Ackermann redeems the Victorian prostitute's beat, making it into a romanticized realm of civic inclusion, where young women can learn to "repair the injuries a defective social order has inflicted." "The fullness of life may be seen on the pavement and footpaths. There all classes, occupations, nations, cults, creeds, and conditions wend their way. Happiness and misery, poverty and wealth, health and disease in the streets teach girls in a very special way they are part of life."[81] Yet, like many writers of this period, she vacillates between celebrating women's street presence as indicative of their emancipation and dreading the effect of city disorder on the sexuality of young women. Feminist organizations sought to reduce this effect by appointing women police to patrol streets.[82] A meeting convened by the Women's League of New South Wales in 1928 agreed that such patrols should firstly aim "to try and prevent the young girls, from 17 upwards, from being on the streets at night, by the appointment of more women police, or women patrols, who would act in the interests of girls' welfare and not with a view to getting her [sic] into gaol or to extract fines."[83] Ackermann was also influenced by more conventional representations of the street as a site of social and sexual contamination. The human diversity she lauded was precisely the city's danger in other commentaries. The difference between men and women is at the root of her "alarm" at the "wholesale sweeping of thousands of girls into factories" from the chaperoned shelter of the home. Her call for the improvement of young women's working conditions in the newly industrialized and urbanized labor market, for example, is motivated by the desire to install young women in a workplace which could provide moral supervision. Following from this, Ackermann commended a recent commission which had called for the separation of the sexes in the workforce. She was particularly concerned about how encounters between men and women in the factory might carry into the street after work, and advocated that men and women be dismissed from work at different times.[84] The Business, Shop, and Factory Girls needed to be spatially segregated from the indiscriminate mingling with men on the street that characterized their counterparts, the Flapper and the Amateur, who exchanged sexual favors for leisure treats such as car rides and cinema and dance hall tickets.[85] But this spatial and sexual regulation was only possible if the different types of urban women could be visually distinguished.

The modern city created a perceptual field in which images proliferated. As the metropolis became a trope of modern industrialization, urban women were attached variously to its gendered meanings, and were looked upon to describe, recognize, and contain the meanings of modernity. Urban types such as the City Girl, Office Girl, Business Girl, Factory Girl, and the more morally dubious Flapper and Amateur emerged because popular print culture relied on taxonomies developed by the nineteenth-century social sciences in order to assess the dramatically changing street presence of women.

These taxonomies both effected and relied on the spectacularization of urban women. And it was women's street visibility in particular that came in for close scrutiny and classification. Some accounts posit an alternative typing of women in the urban scene, as respectable, anonymous, and visually discreet. These older modalities of appearing were fused with aspects of the modern, including independence, easy movement through city space, and visual self-possession. This version

FIG. 2.5. Linocut by Ysobel Irving, reprinted from *Undergrowth: A Magazine of Youth and Ideals*, July–August 1928. Courtesy of the Mitchell Library, State Library of New South Wales.

of the modern urban woman was seen to harbor the meanings of the modern subject: efficient, self-advancing, independent, forthright in her manner, and "sporting" with men in sexual matters, as distinct from entrapping and mercenary. In the linocut by Ysobel Irving shown in figure 2.5, the City Girl was purposive in her movements, sensible, and not distracted by the scopic attractions of the city. Such a young woman moved through shared spaces with men without seeking to distract them. Respectable women brought "privacy" back into play through the conventions of anonymity, of never revealing personal information, of not drawing undue attention to themselves, of moving purposively through city space. Older notions of visual discretion recurred as a defensive response to object status. The figure of the upstanding urban woman, who barely looked up and certainly did not exchange glances, underscores that the meanings of feminine visibility that were being constructed were not coherent.

On the pavement, young urban women appeared to contradictory effect. The City Girl could be represented as dangerously close to men; she seemed to thrive on attention which associated her with the pavement distraction of commodity aesthetics, and she seemed willfully artificial in her appearance—all of which identified her with previous

FIG. 2.6. Cartoon by David Henry Souter, reprinted from *Bulletin*, 30 July 1925. Courtesy of the State Library of Victoria.

RIVAL SCENERY.

YANK: *"I guess there's nothing on earth to equal what we can show on our Murrikan observation railway-cars."*

AUSSIE: *"Oh, well, what we can see on our Sydney observation-trams is good enough for me."*

constructions of the street prostitute. Insofar as the street offered opportunities for a prurient peep, the women exposed were likened to the city's scenery, as in the 1925 D. H. Souter cartoon shown in figure 2.6. The City Girl was a visual offering to outsiders taking in the sights. The city itself was likened to women on show in verse such as this, which appeared in *The Mustard Pot,* a short-lived "naughty" magazine for men.

> A city and a chorus girl
>   Are much alike,'tis true.
> A city's built with outskirts
>   And a chorus girl is, too.[86]

This association with city spectacle left modern women exposed to the dangers of misapprehension. Percy Puller was fined two pounds when, in 1922, he mistook a shop girl for a street prostitute as she was walking toward the Cooee Café to have her tea break. When he whistled at her, she turned and invoked the protection of crowd anonymity, responding, "How dare you whistle at me. I don't know you." Puller must have thought his appraisal of the girl was more accurate than her own, because he persisted in offering her money, which she refused. *Truth* described Puller as a "Street Pest." In its view "a respectable young girl [had been] molested and insulted in a main street in broad daylight." Perhaps the fact that the misconstrued shop girl was "a young girl with hair down her back" rather than a bob-haired Flapper allowed *Truth* to give a sympathetic account.[87]

Truth was generally more likely to be unsympathetic to young women harassed on the street. It made a regular feature of "skirted footpath philanderers," "Precocious Pavement Perts," "Giddy Girleens Who Take to the Town" and "Flighty Flappers on Parade." Indeed, the newspaper argued that "these semi-nude hot natured little sirens who roam the city thoroughfare at all hours of the day and night," these "street strolling strumpets," were "mantraps" and should be "severely smacked with a good sized leather strap and sent off home."[88] *Truth* was stretching colloquialism to its limits in an effort to place and type the urban woman. It wrote that "the skirted footpath philanderer is more difficult to classify" than male loiterers or "greasy gutter-guns and fag-sucking 'sports.'"[89] Whereas the "vacuous-minded, if worthy matron" was classed as "a necessary nuisance," obstructing pedestrians because she was captivated by the commodity spectacle, a certain "type of flapper" was directly connected with sexual transgression. For her, "contact with the opposite sex—even chance contact—affords a pleasure. It is flappers of this type who form obstructive groups on the footpaths of crowded thoroughfares, and who persistently defy the 'keep to the right' injunction. Sex hunger, sub-conscious perhaps, but a yearning, nevertheless, for the vicarious satisfaction afforded by the bumping and squeezing of passing males."[90]

As *Truth* drew on a salient cultural repertoire of promiscuity, danger, and contagion in the city, it conjured an association between the city and the feminine. The public learned more about women's potential for sexual pleasure through the work of British sexologist Havelock Ellis,[91] and women were encouraged to claim a right to sexual pleasure by Marie Stopes's *Married Love* (1918).[92] The British sexologist Bernhard A. Bauer, M.D., wrote of young women becoming overwhelmed by what he called "the concretive impulse," wherein parts of the body that had been sexually neutral acquire sexual sensibility, and erotogenic zones "awaken" a woman's "voluptuous feeling." Again, the accidental proximity of men and women in public space is the mise en scène for women's new sexual potential:

THE DANGER ZONE

FIG. 2.7. Reprinted from *Truth*, 23 August 1923. Courtesy the State Library of Victoria.

A Visitor's Impression of Melbourne

Whereas, previously, a girl or woman noticed nothing remarkable when shaking a man's hand, or in any other intentional or unintentional contact between her body and a man's, now such contact causes quite a disturbance in the woman, send the blood to her head, flush her cheeks, and for the first time produce something like a tumult of the senses [*sic*].[93]

In figure 2.7 the street presence of the City Girl is in dangerous proximity to men, and sex invaded public space like a contagion. Like the disorderly menstruating body, the irrational feminine body, with its involuntary responses, could set in motion a chain of likewise involuntary responses on the street. They destabilized the reliance on crowd disengagement which would otherwise counter this libidinized, gendered proximity. Representations of the City Girl's petting antics with "roving young men in automobiles," in darkened picture palaces, on campuses, and in bosses' offices sexualized public space.[94]

As the crowd came to symbolize disorder in Western cities throughout the nineteenth century, it was increasingly perceived as feminine. Poor hygiene and contamination, squalid and sprawling slums, impersonal encounters, criminality, and migrant minorities left their mark on the rationalized twentieth-century city, despite attempts to bolster social order by regulating and channeling space through urban planning. As in the sanitary napkin advertisements, this sense of disorder and insalubriousness was marked by notions of feminine visibility and exposure. The feminine, whether endangered[95] or heroically bringing virtue into the city, still evoked disorder.

The popular taxonomy of feminine city types also "invited women readers to 'measure' themselves against a given typology, or rather, to place themselves in it. It encouraged them to construct an image of themselves and their identity, and to consider their own contributions to the promotion or impairment of modernity and progress."[96] In the street shots increasingly common to 1920s photojournalism, featuring anonymous women in the street, the depiction of visual style allowed the woman reader to identify with cosmopolitan spectacle.[97] In this sense, representations of city visual style and urban typologies in print culture were available discourses: they were representations that women could occupy. The type offered them visual codes they could adopt and use to regulate themselves within certain subject positions. Appearing women were engaging with and making themselves subject to regulatory and sometimes disciplinary procedures.

Holding up the Traffic

In a cartoon in the *Green Room Pictorial* a Shop Girl dangles a garter before a young woman customer, saying, "Now here's a stout garter which will really hold up your stockings." The shopper replies, "I want something a bit more ornate. Something that will really hold up the traffic."[98] Women's mobility within the city was likened to the visual diversion of its traffic, and women were subjected to a gaze increasingly constructed around the fleeting commodity distraction. The City Girl, though paradoxically anonymous as generic, subverted the conventions of street anonymity, using familiar terms such as "dearie" on the street, lingering and loitering at shop windows captivated by spectacle, and captivating as spectacle. Her love of finery exemplified the narcissistic void of commodity and mass culture, which obstructed the productive flow of the city. In figure 2.8 the attractiveness of the City Girl distracts the drivers, causing the accident of desire.

If the street spatially ordered a kind of disengaged flow for men, a purposive and impersonal conduit, the City Girl derailed this movement and reinstated the intimate proximity of contemplation. She

"THE OPEN ROAD."

FIG. 2.8. Illustration by J. L. Jukes, reprinted from *Bulletin*, 6 February 1929. Courtesy of the State Library of Victoria.

lured men from their preordained destination, not unlike the prostitute or commodity spectacle. The City Girl bodily forced innocent passing men into fleshy frottage and unintended tactile encounter. *Beckett's Budget* reported on the trial of three young women in 1928, whose raising of skirts and giggling to passing men forced several men "to step off the pavement in order to pass by." The sergeant (who admitted that he had had to take up a strategic position to watch the girls) reported to the court that "it was impossible for a man to pass without being accosted."[99] The "Pavement Nymphs" flooded the streets in frightening masses of anonymous feminine flesh:

> Each morning, like a mighty iridescent river, there flows into the city a huge volume of gaily dressed, sparkling young womanhood, on the way to office and shop, careless of everything else but what the day will bring forth in the way of amusement. A big percentage of the women have no need to work and devote the money earned to dress and pleasure. Many are totally ignorant of the rudiments of housekeeping and could not be trusted to boil an egg.[100]

Truth feigned moral outrage in order to ogle a "smart young Yankee tourist" who appeared on a main street in 1922. A "bare-legged belle," it reported, "paraded the streets in an extra short skirt, and with her stockings rolled down below the knees." When questioned by a constable, she "exclaimed indignantly: 'Why, in New York City everyone is wearing bare knees. It is fashionable to have them rouged and tattooed.'" The report has the young woman then produce a powder puff to demonstrate to the gathering crowd, and is accompanied by comic sketches detailing the vagaries of powdered knees. While the constable moves the onlookers "hastily" along, depriving the young woman of the audience she seems to wantonly solicit, *Truth* readers are invited through the comic sketches into a more prurient encounter.[101] In face-to-face encounters on the street, such scopic interactions were regulated by systems of spatial control, in this instance the policeman moving the crowd along, keeping the gaze mobile and fleeting, rather than proximate and disruptive. In *Truth*'s account, the feminine-as-crowd demands visual attention; women discarded their productivity in the home to pursue nothing but pleasure, itself an adjunct to dress. Urban men are perilously positioned. Their lost power to locate and contain the feminine within confining space correlates with a prostrated gaze as they remain riveted by the City Girl as spectacle, and yet are unable to control her implications for the feminine subject.

The appropriate spaces for feminine display and a prolonged reciprocating male gaze are carefully set out in the R. W. Coulter cartoon appearing in *Aussie* in 1928 that is shown in figure 2.9. Feminine display is accepted in certain bounded contexts, but on the street, it outrages other women and leaves the surrounding men limp-shouldered and helplessly agog. Again, it takes a policeman, keeping his wits about him and his cap pulled firmly over his eyes, to break up the scene and keep people, and their relations of looking, moving on.

The City Girl's power to distract could even be put to good use in traffic control. In 1926 the humor magazine *Adam and Eve* published an article on the efforts of Sydney authorities to enforce new regulations requiring motorists to indicate their intentions with hand signals. Above the article, the magazine placed an image of a seated young woman with "Detour" and "Stop" inscribed down her stockings. The caption read, "When Miss Mae Downey appeared on the streets of Boston, USA, with her novel traffic stockings everyone obeyed the injunction to 'stop' and there were many who detoured to get a closer look."[102]

In 1928, the Melbourne broadsheet *Argus* reported that traffic "light signals" had been ordered from the United States for the city's most congested intersection. In 1929 *Royalauto* printed an illustration

FIG. 2.9. Cartoon by Reginald Walter Coulter, reprinted from *Aussie*, 15 February 1928. Courtesy of the Mitchell Library, State Library of New South Wales.

FIG. 2.10. Cartoon by
Geoff Litchfield, reprinted
from *Bulletin*, 26 July
1923. Courtesy of the State
Library of Victoria.

HERS WAS THE HIGHER MIND.
MAY: "We're safe for a motor-ride, anyway, darling."
VIVIENNE: "Don't waste time on them, dearie—can't you see me throwing the glad eye
to the chap in the aeroplane?"

of a traffic aid: a life-sized rubber model of a young urban woman
reportedly used in Detroit, Michigan, to slow traffic. Her hand was
raised, and down the front of her dress were amber and red lights
which formed the buttons of her garment.[103] Such imagery associated
technology with modern women, highlighting the "mesh of signifi-
cations" between the feminine and technology that cultural theorist
Andreas Huyssen has described.[104]

Modern technologies altered existing vantages and spatiopercep-
tual relations. Technologies of mobility, such as the car and, in the
1923 Geoff Litchfield cartoon shown in figure 2.10, even the airplane,
facilitated a gaze that, like city traffic, was mobile, bereft of the virtues
of contemplation, and therefore promiscuous. Technology, feminine
sexuality, and the mobile gaze were discursively linked to types of the
City Girl to construct her as morally dubious, specifically "fast." Her
"fastness" was in part construed through the play of looks made possible from the new vantages created by modern technologies. To a
certain extent, the mobility allowed by those technologies rendered
the City Girl's gaze and apprehension fleeting, and she represented
the anonymous interchange of voyeurized glances so wonderfully en-

capsulated in the 1920s Australian slang phrase the "glad eye." Tellingly, the glad eye did not just appreciate passing women; it could also be "cast" by women to indicate a desire to be looked at.

The car, a private mobile space, also set in motion at least three perceptions of the City Girl: the unchaperoned City Girl could, within it, slip from being a joy-rider to an "Amateur"; women motorists attracted attention by mastering this potent symbol of the modern;[105] and, by becoming spectators within the panorama through which they traveled, women became part of the social landscape.[106] The association of unabated movement with the Flapper made it easy to link her to the aviatrix. Amy "Johnnie" Johnson was described as a "Flapper-Ace" who took on her 1930 flight from London to Darwin the peculiarly modern mix of self-determination and preoccupation with visual appeal: "a vanity case and mirror there / And grit in a Feminine Breast."[107] By encroaching on men's conquest of distance, the aviatrix came to represent the Modern Woman as technologically proficient and as a pioneer herself. But as mobile spectacles the aviatrix and the woman motorist also engendered new points of view for women. Their coverage in the press inaugurated the ability of visual technologies to follow their movements and render the mobility of women as spectacle. This potent combination of mobile gaze and unfixed feminine spectacle encapsulated and reinforced anxieties about the instability, mutability, and indeterminacy of the modern feminine. The common description of her as "fast" is indicative of the influence of changing scopic relations on conceptions of the Modern Woman.

Pocket Money Industrialists

In the office scenario, the Business Girl was construed as usurping men's position, as sexually entrepreneurial, and as calculating. In the 1928 R. W. Coulter cartoon shown in figure 2.11, the audacity of the Business Girl is rendered visually. She was described as a "Fair Interloper," having usurped men's places during the war. When returning soldiers sought to regain their productive seats within the industrializing economy, there she was, coyly occupying, in evocative words of capture and dissent, "unsurrendered office stools," undermining one of the limited expressions of masculine identity: work. She was represented as deliberately disrupting the productivity of the office, flaunting her attractiveness and inviting sexualized appraisal. In one 1925 *Bulletin* cartoon, entitled "The Age of Indiscre-

FIG. 2.11. Cartoon by Reginald Walter Coulter, reprinted from *Bulletin,* 14 November 1928. Courtesy of the State Library of Victoria.

WHEN INTEREST IS CAPITAL.
"I wonder if I could interest your boss in a new card system?"
"No, I don't think so. The only thing he's interested in at present is me."

tion," the Business Girl leans provocatively over her prospective employer's desk, with her hand over his. Asked, "What age are you?" she replies, "well some take me for eighteen, others take me for a little motor trip."[108] This was the real business of the Business or Office Girl. Hers was a sexual economy of entrapment, luring Bosses from their seats of productivity, her "capital" the "interest" she could excite in wealthy employers through appearing.

Not surprisingly, any "show" of inefficiency was almost vengefully seized upon in popular representations. Again and again narcissism and love of finery were symptomatic of women's innate lack of industry. Modern types such as the Office or Business Girl and the Factory Girl were sexually ambiguous. Through their practices of appearing they flirted with the category of the Flapper, a leisure figure and the period's most exaggerated expression of feminine exhibitionism. In their dual presence in the city as workers and pleasure-seekers, they illustrated the self-referential redundancy and unproductivity of the feminine. Representations of the Business Girl enforced women's status as objects in the exchange economy, sexualizing them as spectacles in order to contain their incursion into this most masculine of domains.

The economy of feminine spectacle in office spaces reverberated through popular culture. A verse in the *Bulletin* in 1919 lampooned "The Self-Respecting Typiste" who spurned the gifts and advances of her boss. "Since she resisted his attack / The legal penalty was 'sack.' " However, as she confided, she had intended to inflame her boss's "base intent" by making him "yearn a while." In fact, what offended her most was that he had treated her like a "stupid novice," for "[w]hen men have wicked ends to gain / They ought to plead and plead in vain / and buy one oysters and champagne."[109]

Yet, as another 1919 cartoon showed, the ensnaring pageant of the Business Girl might be designed to gain her marriage and a bread-winner husband, releasing her from minimum-wage labor. The cartoon's caption quotes a New South Wales judge: "Thirty shillings a week is the minimum wage for single women." The "First Business Girl," preening before the mirror, responds, "Thirty bob a week and find a husband!" "Second Ditto" replies, "Impossible! Why it only provides tucker and a room and no powder and hats or pretties."[110]

One commentator, writing in a special "Business Woman" issue of the Sydney feminist magazine *Helen's Weekly* in 1927, denounced the Business Girl as a " 'Pocket Money' Industrialist," a young woman with "gold digging propensities" who spends her working day powdering, rouging, and arranging her hair. "They have no flair for work, no desire to make themselves valuable, no ambition to be anything, but elegantly turned out."[111] Many readers responded. One reply lampooned the business man: "Now we know that every hour he is doing his utmost to foster beauty, that his aesthetic taste is developed to such a degree that he will employ these preening dolls by the half-dozen—and pay them wages—can you wonder that these pouting and preening misses spend their time and money in exterior beautification?"[112]

In a piece in *Adam and Eve* in 1927, a Business Girl described her boss as a "cunning old Lothario," relating the tale of a previous employer who "worked to formula" on his typists, testing their ideas on fidelity, buying them silk stockings, and flirting: "he kissed me twice—none of your pecks, either, but the real movie thing." Nevertheless, the writer had no patience for the "silly flapper" who fell for such "designing devils." This type of girl was not a typist, she stated emphatically; she was "an adventuress," as exploitative of her boss as he was of her.[113] The Business Girl's usefulness as office decoration was ridiculed in 1931 by the socialist feminist magazine *Working Woman*. It satirized "Wanted" advertisements: "Wanted a high speed, slap-up tart

/ A genteel slave quite prim and smart / This maid will dress to suit the time / And look select, serene, sublime."[114]

In the same issue of *Helen's Weekly* that spoke of "pocket money industrialists," Business Girls were offered advice on " 'Grooming' as an Asset": "thoroughly groomed looking women" have an "appearance which augurs well for the care and precision they will bring to their work." This precision should extend to being "particular about those little depressions at the side of the nose, where blackheads are likely to flourish."[115] "Smartness" was required of the Business Girl and Shop Girl as a condition of their employment. Yet uncertainty prevailed about what exactly was conveyed by good looks and attention to appearance. Two 1927 articles in *Beckett's Budget* debated the meanings of visual appeal in the city office. A self-described "plain girl" wrote that she knew, through having to depend solely on hard work, what an asset beauty was. Describing the office as akin to the exhibition space of the theater, she wrote, "To put it plainly, we are the scene shifters and extras of life's stage, not decorative ourselves, but sacrificed so that those who are more presentable may strut in front of the footlights." She was smirked at in job interviews and tormented with insults by office boys.[116] A good-looking Sydney girl, on the other hand, had her own complaints. As a shop assistant, a mannequin, and an office girl she was pawed at and felt "the eyes of all men—nice or otherwise—focused on her." In the end she could not find a job where she wouldn't be forced "to submit to the attentions and horrible caresses of some flabby middle-aged man with a perfectly good wife at home."[117] Culpability in attracting the gaze remained important in drawing the fine line between appropriate and inappropriate attention to dress and style. Retailers, commentators, and even government inquiries were preoccupied with the appearance of urban working women.

Although the "smartness" of shop girls functioned as part of the employer's capital, it was conflated with the "love of finery" narrative that culminated in moral demise. Great trepidation surrounded an apparent "orgy of adornment" in young working women.[118] This "orgy" was carefully monitored by commentators such as Ackermann, and by government inquiries such as those conducted between 1918 and 1921 by the Board of Trade on the cost of living. Their minute descriptions of amounts of clothing included discussion of how many bloomers the average female employee would wear through annually.[119] In first 1907 and then 1912, Justice H. B. Higgins considered the question of working women's "needs" and how to determine an appropriate wage. Whereas the "normal needs of the average employee" (still assumed to be male) included "the need for a domestic life," the female employee did not work to meet domestic needs; rather, she "merely wants some money for dress."[120] In this gendered reversal, it is men who are at home, dutifully providing, while women are entering public space as workers merely to furnish themselves for the pleasure they take in their visibility. A similarly reversed logic spawned the later claim that, for women, the "glamour of wage earning is tinsel."[121] The cloth and cut of feminine visibility patterned the reserve labor market status of women.

Contemporary feminists such as Jessie Street came to the defense of "scarlet lipped" and "overdressed" working women, recognizing that women had shifted from being "ornamental adjuncts" to the home to playing an integrated role within capitalist models of exchange. If women were overdressing for work it was because, she wrote to the press, "the employers prefer them so," and because "girls have to compete in the open market for jobs."[122] This implicit sexual economy was rendered sadly in the journal of the Socialist Labor Party of Australia in 1927. In an article entitled "Story of a Woman," Alice, "the little daughter of a wage worker," is forced to relinquish her girlhood dreams of freedom and integrity and "capitalise the only valuable asset she possesse[d]—her sex-personality." She survives on "scrappy" meals in order to buy beautiful clothes and, through them, eventually comes to be thought of as a "sound investment" by her employers rather than "cheap labor." Alice realizes that her clothes have "merely drawn attention to her sex, and that her sex is being exploited for commercial purposes."[123] Her story follows the established trajectory of moral demise through the excesses of finery, although this socialist account is marked by exploitation and the intrusive boss's gaze.[124] For feminists and members of the labor movement, the construction of women's worth in terms of their sexual appeal was reductive and invasive. Feminists participated in discursive traditions in which women who made themselves spectacles were objects, a categorization that anticipated the later, much protested process of "sexual objectification."[125] Yet accounts of both finery and femininity placed women in a relation of exchange and saw their visual appeal as both their own and their employer's capital, and both accounts were therefore pervaded with the historical residue of the prostitute.

The Business Girl's discursive approximation to the feminist ideals of economic and sexual independence and her uncomfortable affinity

THE EVOLUTION OF THE OFFICE GIRL.

FIG. 2.12. Illustration by Grace Burns, reprinted from *Bulletin,*
23 February 1922. Courtesy of the State Library of Victoria.

with sexual commerce incited anxiety and confusion over the meanings of modern feminine identity that women enacted by appearing.
As Ackermann wrote in 1913, the "vanity of dress is the besetting sin
of girls."[126] The excessiveness of the Business Girl's exhibitionism, consumerism, and appetite for male approval confused the smart, professional, economically independent unmarried woman with the lurid,
sexually bargaining Amateur. In figure 2.12, these confused categories
become an expression of cosmopolitan woman's modernization.
Smartly dressed working women defiantly paraded their wage-earning
as a practice of self-reliance, self-definition, and independence, af-
fronting middle- and upper-class expectations of service which remained visually associated with the uniform of domestic workers.

In popular representations of young women in the metropolis,
types such as the Business Girl were collapsed within two distinct
modes of vision. They were seen as both workers and spectacles. As
workers they encountered the Taylorist visual imperatives of industrialism, which organized sight into rationalized segments of engagement between worker and produce or workplace. As spectacles they
were among the constant distractions and seductions of the commod-

ity and entertainment scene paradigmatically aligned with the irrational, the libidinal, and the feminine.

Working women were represented as occupying both office stools and picture-palace seats, creating a new duality in public space. By making themselves at home in department stores, in automobiles, along the beachfronts, and in the picture palaces, these modern feminine types were instrumental in feminizing public space. Yet when they dressed similarly to occupy office stools, they were represented as failing to respect the conventions of masculine industrial space, threatening to feminize this as well. Newspapers such as the *Bulletin* fought hard to keep the categories of Business Girl and Flapper distinct, but the Flapper tantalized on the street and in the office, rendering the categories shifting terrains of indeterminate meaning. The Business Girl was a liminal figure whose "smart grooming" could identify her as exemplary of the self-made modern subject, but when her visual style seemed to indicate that she was calculating about her appeal, any incursions she may have been making into men's business could be sharply rebuffed by relegating her to object status. In order to walk this fine line, women must have had to pay careful attention to their visual effects and adopted highly refined techniques of appearing.

The entrance of women into metropolitan space had profoundly unsettling effects on the meaning, regulation, and rituals of sexual difference as they were enacted through scopic relations. An inventory of "types" created a representational reference system which attempted to contain and order the increasingly "unfixed" and mutable meanings of modern femininity. Feminine spectacle carried the burden of meaning for many of the changed conditions people experienced in the modern city: from mechanization to the traffic in looks, to the distraction of the commodity image, exposure, and anonymity. The Modern Woman was historically distinct from her predecessor in that she did not retreat into modesty as a defense against object status, but rather asserted her modernity through her visibility. Even when women in urban space were depicted as "respectable types," they were shown to be deploying the street conventions of anonymity rather than being modest. They may not have flaunted their public visibility, but neither did they shrink from it. This shift was of profound significance since, instead of retreating from object status and its modern manifestation as spectacle, the appearing woman demonstrated mastery over that status as she put it to use in her self-articulation as modern. Her practices of appearing required her to be highly aware of the meanings accruing to feminine visibility, to avoid the regulatory and disciplinary effects of a censuring gaze that relegated her to object status as sexualized spectacle. Attracting such a gaze could prove genuinely dismissive (from her job) for the Business Girl but, as the victims of "street pests" like Percy Puller also knew, women in public space could not rely on their own practices of appearing to deflect a soliciting, censuring, or menacing gaze.

In the entanglement of cultural meanings linking the metropolis, the spectacle, and the feminine, urban feminine types emerged which carried their symbolic function into the realm of subjective realization. I agree with feminist historians who see the metropolis as problematic for women because of their being positioned as the touchstone for moral judgment and control. However, women may have been able to partake in the modern city's commitment to spectacle by identifying with and performing the new subject positions opened up by and within the representation of types, through their own practices of appearing. As Elizabeth Wilson states, "There is no identity without visibility, and the city spectacle encourages self-definition in its most theatrical forms."[127] For young, urban, white women, this meant appearing as modern subjects, within a metropolitan scene, by imaging themselves or self-consciously becoming spectacles. Women encountered a tide of combative representations which sought to contain the feminine within the traditional symbolism of the home, along with the exclusionary forces of harassment, surveillance, spatial and traffic regulation, and the scandal of exposure. These forces attempted to curtail the new relation between women's symbolic utility as cultural objects and their performative enactments of this symbolism as cultural subjects through practices of appearing.

Chapter 3

The Screen-Struck Girl in the Cinematic Scene

In 1924, the Australian stage actress Louise Carbasse returned from the United States "having become Louise Lovely, a film star."[1] Famous, charismatic, and a firm advocate of the Australian film industry, Lovely devised a vaudeville act in the form of a talent drive called "A Day at the Studio," in which young women from the audience, armed with newspaper coupons and admission fees, were screen-tested.[2] Lovely tested more than twenty-three thousand applicants, drawing capacity audiences and breaking previous theater attendance records around Australia.[3] "A Day at the Studio" was characteristic of the Hollywood experience, including auditions, screen tests, and inciting mass interest in the screen star. She hoped to import Hollywood-style production values into an industry that she also knew would fail without protection from American dominance. She advocated government funding for Australian productions and restrictions on the importing and block-booking of American films before the 1927 royal commission inquiring into the Australian film industry. Lovely was among a number of women who made films in the 1920s; others included the McDonagh sisters, Lottie Lyell, Mary Mallon, Kate Howarde, and Juliette De La Ruze.[4] As many as fifty-five of the young women screen-tested in Lovely's "A Day at the Studio," such as the "smartly flapperish" Billie Sim, won parts in her productions.[5]

Louise Lovely's "screen test" was jealously derided by *Truth* as a "newspaper circulation stunt," since the coupons required for admission were from a competing paper. *Truth* claimed Lovely's initiative would result in thousands of girls queuing in Hollywood for screen tests. The young woman who showed ambition for a screen career was typed in popular representations as the Screen-Struck Girl. Such women were characterized as "human derelicts," "fighting a woman's battle with men whose appetite for girl flesh has no limitation."[6] The naive Screen-Struck Girl overidentified with the cinematic image, which itself was viewed with suspicion as being untrue to life. Because Australian audiences—among the most eager cinematic audiences in the world—were viewing a glut of American films, the reproduced image was condemned as untrue to Australian character and sentiment.

The construction of the Screen-Struck Girl as courting mass recognition through her transformation into reproduced spectacle was used to condemn young women with screen ambitions as morally lax; their ambitions would lead them into a type of moral fall. The icon of the Screen Star was viewed as part of what captivated the Screen-Struck Girl. Louise Lovely's vaudeville act was perceived as "luring" young women with the "Movie Virus" into moral danger by preying on their susceptibility to the image of the Screen Star, which was illusory and deceitful. "Glittering Glamour of Stardom Hypnotises the Adolescent," *Truth* headlines warned, because "the glamour of a star dazzles the eyes of the foolish." *Truth* compared Lovely to a madam, "pushful, capable, and with a solicitous eye to her own welfare," "capitalising" and "cashing in" by luring "feather-headed" "screen emotionalists" with "mushy dope" into the quest for stardom.[7] Alongside the condemnation, however, existed a competing version of young modern women's relation to cinema, portraying them as savvy and discriminating. Their desire to emulate the Screen Star was, in these accounts, simply a natural expression of their modernity.

The visual culture that sprang up because of the mechanically reproduced image, particularly the cinema, both relied on and incited feminine spectacle. The types of the Screen Star and her fan, the Screen-Struck Girl, emerged as part of the cultural inventory of spectacularized modern women. They were used in popular commentary to represent the pervasive and all-consuming desire of modern women to become spectacles. This desire was construed either as a loss of feminine essence in the Modern Girl, or conversely (and particularly by those with a vested interest in the cinema) as an expression of the Modern Girl's modernity.

The construction of the Screen-Struck Girl as a type who emulated the Screen Star underscores the relationship young women were believed to have with the reproduced image as spectators, and how this relationship was seen to influence their desire to be spectacularized. Newly popularized visual technologies profoundly affected the meanings of feminine visibility, many commentators believing that, once exposed to the chicanery and visual deceit of the reproduced image, young women became captivated by its spell and imagined themselves appearing within its emotionally and sexually intensified scenes long after they had left the picture palaces. Cultural imaginings about the intense and loving bond between the Screen-Struck Girl and her same-sex idol, the newly emergent Screen Star, were fraught with deeper anxieties about how feminine spectacle confused important cultural distinctions. Screen Stars were scrutinized in order to distinguish, within the mechanically reproduced image, between representation and reality, illusion and substance, artificiality and essence. Was Mary Pickford really a great beauty, it was asked, or was her image due to make-up and tricks of the camera? Did her image in fact represent her, or the illusion of the modern spectacle? Underpinning all of these concerns was a pervasive sense of the loss of feminine essence in the Modern Girl, who was characterized by the desire to become spectacle. This loss became an emblem for the instability and mutability of modern identity. The sense of loss of feminine essence was conflated with suspicion of the reproduced image as illusory, hypnotic, artificial, and deceptive.

An Inexplicable Emptiness

In his famous essay "The Work of Art in the Age of Mechanical Reproduction," cultural theorist Walter Benjamin writes of photography and film as capitalism's attendant technologies of image reproduction, capable of removing the presence of the object from itself and from the viewer. This constitutes the loss of the object's "aura" for Benjamin. He posits that human beings, when considered as objects, could be equivalent to artworks, in their potential to be commodified. The loss of the aura, Benjamin writes, "reveals entirely new structural formations of the subject." When the subject matter of the camera is human, the subject he is principally concerned with, however, is male. As well as thinking about the effects on the observer of looking at the mechanically reproduced object, Benjamin also considers the effects on the subject imaged through this process. He writes of the screen actor, who, unlike the stage actor, must forego the aura of his whole living being through the camera, since "aura is tied to his presence; there can be no replica of it."[8] This loss of an individual's aura is compelling, for Benjamin is thinking through the subjective effects of being interpellated into cultural form (in the Althusserian sense of how a discursive regime calls the subject into being). He quotes the playwright Pirandello:

> The film actor feels as if in exile—exiled not only from the stage but also from himself. With a vague sense of discomfort he feels an inexplicable emptiness; his body loses its corporeality, it evaporates, it is deprived of reality, life, voice, and the noise caused by him moving about, in order to be changed into a mute image, flickering an instant on the screen, then vanishing into silence. . . . The projector will play with his shadow before the public, and he himself must be content to play before the camera.[9]

This screen actor is appearing within the specific conditions of silent cinema, where his muteness assists in his transformation into image and the associated loss of aura and the other things tied to presence, such as voice. Here objectification through visual technologies refers back to a "seeming" death, the emptying of subjectivity that was a common perception of early cinema audiences, who sometimes believed they were witnessing ghosts or shadows.[10] Benjamin believes this "shrivelling of the aura" in the screen actor is publicly offset by the star cult, as "an artificial build-up of the 'personality' outside the studio." Although Benjamin is clearly bothered by film's reconstituting the "unique aura of the person" into "the phony spell of the commodity,"[11] he never explicitly claims that such imaging effected a loss of subjectivity. Yet cultural theorists Paul Kelly and Susan Lord argue that Benjamin's "auratic object" corresponds to the humanist subject in that it is woven through with "the strands of 'authenticity,' 'uniqueness,' 'singularity' and 'authority.'"[12] In the instance of the male screen actor, Benjamin is able to argue that the process of spectacularization effects a "shriveling of the aura"—the loss of which arguably corresponds to a threat to masculine subjectivity. But what might he have made of actresses? Could women have an authentic, authoritative cultural presence to start with, which they then risked losing in modernity?

Since Benjamin perceives the modern observer's subjectivity as altered, he is ambivalent toward mass culture. He believes that its reproduction of imagery extends both perception and the "optical unconscious," yet also fragments perception and drains memory of its content. But Benjamin's ideas about the modern reproduced image are expressed in terms of gender. As feminist cultural theorist Patrice Petro argues, Benjamin's ambivalence toward mass culture is "expressed through reference to the metaphorical figure of a woman (a figure that stands for modernity as much as it does for the continually renewed search for a lost plenitude)."[13] However, Rita Felski points out that the modern feminine undermines this very imagined plenitude. She writes, "through its very artificiality, femininity was to become the privileged marker of the instability and mobility of modern gender identity."[14] Benjamin links this modern, artificial feminine to mass culture and commodity production through the figures of the prostitute, the lesbian, and the masculinized woman. In doing so, he is again concerned with a radically fragmented subject. Petro believes that although Benjamin expressed his disquiet about mass culture in terms of the commodification of women, he was in fact afraid that the erotic aggression of "masculinized women" threatened masculine subjectivity. It is striking that such women were, in the modern scheme of things, sexually deviant, and that this deviancy was read principally through the visual taxonomy of women in public space.

The division of gender is brokered by a play of looks in Benjamin's work: his "collector" and "flâneur" are principally lookers, whereas the prostitute and lesbian are looked at. It seems that when women were spectacles, they were more likely to shock, be sexually deviant, or become aggressive. Although Benjamin's women are not spectacularized as mechanically reproduced images (as his stage actor is) but are visible as street presences, his writing highlights the contradiction lying at the heart of popular discussion about the Screen Star and the Screen-Struck Girl. On the one hand, the modern feminine seems to have no essence to lose; on the other hand, her reproduction as image is posed as the truth of her modern identity. If Benjamin's screen actor were a woman, what "aura" would she lose, given that the process of her spectacularization was constitutive of her modern feminine identity? And if this "aura" in any way correlates with an essence or selfhood, how can the artificial, unstable, mutable modern feminine have an aura to lose? Benjamin had the same habit of situating women as objects or spectacles and men as subjects or spectators. As a result, he was ambivalent about the feminization of the reproduced image. In popular commentary, the figures of the Screen Star and Screen-Struck Girl were used to speak about women's desire to become spectacularized through the reproduced image of modern visual technologies, and this desire was presented as a loss of feminine essence. While Benjamin's lost aura does not necessarily correlate with popular constructions of this lost feminine essence, it is interesting that both discourses encounter the same stumbling block. Both implicitly posit a feminine essence prior to the spectacularization of the feminine, failing to see that, rather than being undone by her spectacularization, the modern woman was produced by it.

While Benjamin's modern masculine subjects are enunciated through a position of looking, but threatened with "shriveling" if reproduced as spectacle, his feminine types occupy a "presence" in his writing because they are looked at; they exist only because they are seen. They materialize on being apprehended, or come into being as spectacles. The commodified Screen Star did not need to rely on her status within the personality cult to offset her lost aura. Part of her fascination was due to the questions of whether there was any essence behind her image, and whether her mechanically reproduced image was accurate. Doubt would remain because the modern feminine was already associated with artifice, visual deceit, and illusion. The more the modern feminine was spectacularized, the less she seemed either to have an essence to begin with or to be able to represent that essence truthfully. In Benjamin's writings, the object loses its aura when its image is separated from the object itself, the image's referent. This was the tension between representation and subjectivity that the Screen Star embodied. It was the perilous terrain of a subject position that seemed to be born out of a trick of mirrors, specifically American mirrors, that the Screen-Struck Girl was seen to court.

The Hollywood Offensive

As a Screen Star who used her image to seduce impressionable young women into becoming spectacles, Louise Lovely had some commentators bristling. The fact that her real fame had been achieved in America made her motives even more suspicious. Many felt that American culture was swamping the Australian national character through the ephemeral and evasive devices of flickering, shimmering, enchanting images.

The Screen Star and Screen-Struck Girl existed within the wider cultural anxiety about perceived "Americanisation" resulting from changing economic alignments between Australia, Britain, and the United States from the 1890s. From 1913 to 1920 the proportion of Australian import trade from the United States doubled, from 12 percent to 24 percent. As historian Jill Julius Matthews notes, "the interests of America were identified with the unencumbered working of the market place"—unencumbered by "older hierarchical values" seen to be representative of "civilisation," which was undermined by the American appeal to the popular.[15] The American film industry and its stars were seen as symptomatic of a "Hollywood offensive."[16] The Hollywood film was perceived as "an agent of American economic and cultural imperialism"[17] which undermined the prestige of the British empire and British/Australian trade relations. The pervasive perception of American films as sexually immoral was thus informed by colonial and class relations.

American cinema not only exposed a diverse American population to "unprecedented forces of cultural uniformity in the 1920s," but also "operated to carry the American image abroad."[18] Americanization through celluloid, an omen of modernity's globalizing effects, is said to have resulted from "a fascination with movies, soaring towers, powerful machines, and speeding automobiles. But behind this was a growing recognition that the USA was providing the world with a new model of industrialism."[19] Both Australia's growing economic ties with the United States and the general influx of American cultural imports irked the fiercely nationalist *Bulletin*, which named them "sickening piffle and pornography" and "American slop."[20]

Nothing provoked this nationalist fervor more than the American film distribution system, called the "combine." Australia offered the American motion picture industry the highest per capita attendance rates in the world during the interwar years, with admissions to Australian cinemas totaling 68,364,016 in 1920 alone out of a population of 5,303,000.[21] World War I had left Australian film producers vulnerable: film stock was scarce because its chemical ingredients were needed to make explosives and European sources were cut off. "The pre-war diversity of film culture available in Australia disappeared,"[22] in part for lack of film stock and in part because American entertainment features became more popular than European war films. From this foothold, Hollywood studios established powerful distribution networks in Australia and exploited the absence of restrictions on foreign films. The Melbourne *Bulletin* particularly resented the fact that Roscoe "Fatty" Arbuckle and other "dumb clowns and buffoons who pull faces in front of foreign cameras" did not pay a penny in tax on income drawn from Australian screenings of their films. When Arbuckle was accused, in 1921, of raping and causing the death of an actress named Virginia Rappe, the paper's anger increased.[23]

In 1912–13, a group of American distribution companies formed a combine to book their films in Australian theaters at the price of expected box office income, which meant Australian offices consistently showed a loss and gross income went back to the United States untaxed. Australian exhibitors were allegedly obliged to accept the combine's entire program "or get none at all." This system was called the "blind" or "block" contract system. The *Bulletin* wrote of its effect on Australian production companies (which it saw as laudable compared to American studios, because they were "engaged in filming Australian subjects in an atmosphere of Australian sentiment"): "their collapse was as immediate and complete as if the omissaries [sic] of the combines has [sic] put poison in their breakfast food."[24] By the middle of the decade American films constituted 94 percent of foreign feature film imports.[25] American society classics such as *Flapper Wives* (1924), *Sinners in Silk* (1924), and *Our Dancing Daughters* (1928) overshadowed Australian renditions of femininity such as *Girl of the Bush* (1921) and director Charles Chauvel's *Moth of Moombi* (1925).

The moral reform lobby, which included women's organizations, returned soldiers, empire loyalists, clergy, and sections of the press, objected to the "American" character of these films, associating the Screen Star with licentious and disingenuous behavior, and demanded government intervention. Even the *Bulletin* joined the clamor, despite its anti-"wowser" standpoint.[26] Many of these complaints focused on the visual trickery and illusion of the reproduced image. In 1925 Hugh D. McIntosh told the New South Wales Legislative Council how moviegoing was being used for "American Propaganda":

> You go into a darkened theatre, you listen to music, and the mind is lulled to rest, and is in a condition to receive impressions which are unconsciously formed. The purpose of these pictures is to make us think America is a far greater nation than the British Empire. . . . they hold up to public ridicule the British people, British traditions, and all British sense of honesty and justice; while they idealise the prostitute, and hold up the crook of every sort for public approbation.[27]

FIG. 3.1. "The Higher Education," by C. H. Percival, reprinted from *Bulletin*, 14 August 1924. Courtesy of the State Library of Victoria.

Modern visual technologies and popular understandings of spectatorship led other commentators to think that cinematic images were absorbed "directly through the eye and not . . . the mind. . . . it skips a process that has to be gone through in reading, the very process that is the safeguard of the immature mind." Women's groups believed children's "visual sense" was so strong that "what is seen seems so much more real than what is read or heard." The cinema was "the strongest influence in modern life."[28] Too much realism manipulated the viewer into a false view of life. In the 1924 drawing shown in figure 3.1 American films wallpaper the vista available to an indiscriminate public, including women and children, who cluster around the promotions, gaining "higher education" in the once private pursuit of seduction.

Cinema was commonly expected to accurately reflect national life, and American feature films' failure to do so reinforced people's suspicion of them. "The slushy sentiment of the average American picture" was "untrue to life, and art is bound up with truth," argued the *Bulletin*, suggesting that cinema was not of the stature of art and literature, but belonged to "the truthless" entertainment forms of mass culture.[29] British efforts to restrict the importation of American films were reported to be due to "alarm at the prevalence of pictures from the USA disseminating ideas of American importance, industry, wealth and prosperity and distorted Hollywood morals."[30] Empire loyalty and the sense that distinct national character was being lost through transnational flows of visual culture (as when an American star, Eva Novak, was cast as the lead in the 1927 Australian film *For the Term of His Natural Life*) led for calls to support Australian film productions to counter "the inanities . . . of that fantastic village," Hollywood.[31] The Returned Sailors and Soldiers Imperial League requested that the Tariff Board restrict foreign films to 50 percent of local screenings,[32] while the Good Film League of New South Wales sought to encourage the release of "good British and Australian films."[33] The importation of American film was decried by the Prince of Wales himself, who said, "The film is to America what the flag once was to Great Britain. By its means, America may hope some day to Americanise the world."[34]

Under the pressure of such complaints, in 1927 the conservative federal government appointed a select committee, which became the Royal Commission into the Moving Picture Industry. The government responded to the desire for accurate national representation in film, with pictures drawn from Australian life and character, as advocated in the press throughout the decade. Because cinematic technologies could reveal the truth, many people saw the cinema as "the greatest educator of today."[35] An Australian type of film "would depend on quiet drama and a realistic atmosphere," providing a "contrast with the tricks and sentimentality of Hollywood."[36] This Australian authenticity was depicted through a divide between the backcountry Bush and the Town, which was perhaps truer to the radical nineteenth-century ideal of agrarian utopianism than to the reality of Australia as a "highly urbanised and increasingly suburbanised society."[37] Filmmakers such as Raymond Longford with *The Sentimental Bloke* (1919) and Charles Chauvel with *Greenhide* (1926) perpetuated this divide, as can be seen in figure 3.2, a promotional poster for *Greenhide*. As in many silent films, this partition was constructed through stories of the heroines, who moved to the city to be exploited by parasitical men,

FIG. 3.2. *(opposite)* Promotional poster for *Greenhide* (1926). Documentation Collection, ScreenSound Australia, The National Film and Sound Archives. By arrangement with the copyright owner, The Estate of Charles Chauvel © Curtis Brown (Aust PTY LTD).

or moved from the city out of boredom with "eternal seaside sheiks and Hotel Lounge Lizards" to marry the "real man—a cave man" she could count on finding in the Australian bush.[38] Yet the location and content of "the Australian picture" was always contested. Some commentators argued that Australian films should be "redolent of the bush . . . and the stirring deeds of heroism and hardships" of the early pioneers.[39] However, filmmakers such as the McDonagh sisters studied the conventions of shots in American films to create emotional scenarios suited to their cosmopolitan society melodramas. While the cabaret scenes they included were regarded by the press as "not perhaps the familiar figure in Australian life,"[40] the three sisters' films could nevertheless be claimed as Australian because of their "sweeter tone, cleaner story, and unaffected acting quite foreign to many American productions."[41]

The depiction of national character as "unaffected" also influenced Longford's direction. He argued that a portrayal of such a character needed to stay close to the "average Australian," who in Longford's estimation was a "casual, carelessly natural beggar." Longford sought to achieve "realism" and "naturalness" in his pictures, and believed that "the true art of acting is not to act." But Longford took a particular view of the woman spectator—unlike many commentators, he aimed to appeal specifically to women's emotions: "You see one might say that three parts of your audience is composed of women, and women, above everything else, are impressionists."[42] Whether Longford was referring to impressionist painting and literary conventions or meant that women were impressionable, he believed them to have a relation to the reproduced image that was specific to their gender. Unlike most commentators, he believed this relation should be properly catered to, rather than disparaged.

The Screen Star embodied this difference between the "artificial" American and the "unaffected" Australian. *A Girl of the Bush* (1921) was promoted with the headline "A Real Australian Girl in a Real Australian Picture! She can ride the 'killer' to a standstill—brand a steer in ten seconds and rob a sheep of its wool while you're winking."[43] Similarly, Marie Lorraine (Isobel McDonagh) was admired for her understated acting style, and because "the lips of the actress were not smothered with paint, with an extra coat of glue for kissing."[44] Lottie Lyell, who played lead in some twenty-four films between 1911 and 1923 and was a screenwriter and production partner in Raymond Longford's company, told *Theatre Magazine*, "I have often been asked what make-up I find best for pictures. I do not put anything on my face, not even powder."[45] Lyell was revered for her naturalistic depiction of the quintessential Australian Girl, Doreen, in *The Sentimental Bloke* (1919).

But if the reproduced image was so accurate that audience members (at least Australian audience members) could see through its chicanery and detect excessive make-up and overacting, then the national feminine ideal might be hard to capture on film. What woman could stand up to the harsh exposure of the moving camera? In giving evidence to the 1927 Royal Commission, filmmaker Gayne Dexter stated that Australian young women simply failed the motion picture's standards of beauty. The very realism of the reproduced image required perfection in women. He and a leading Melbourne dentist could find only one set of perfect teeth in this nation "barren of beauty," from Western Australia. He admonished, "The screen requires perfection of minor points, in addition to a beautiful face, perfection of hands, wrists and ankles. In our girls there is a tendency toward premature development and even where the physique is correct, they lack the art of making the most of themselves. They have not been trained to walk in beauty."[46]

When an individual named Mason asserted that "the female species" of Australia "were lacking in the many essentials that go to make the perfect woman," Australasian Films chivalrously rose to the challenge (not without scoring "heavily by the amount of publicity"). They held screen tests for more than one hundred applicants at A. F. Studios in Rushcutters Bay in Sydney. *Everyones* magazine endorsed the screen test experiment, but, like Dexter, commented on the failure of the applicants to appear perfect. They reported an "intensely amusing" process, "not unmixed with an amount of pathos, as one or another of the girls, whose beauty was a thing of the past, if it ever existed, made her the butt of many derisory remarks from a majority of 'cats' who were waiting their respective turns." A contradiction marks press reports of Screen Star aspirants, between the derision of deluded young women "whose audacity far exceeded their beauty," and the investment the newspapers shared with the Australian film industry, and the public, in producing Australia's own Screen Star. It was a contradiction ensuing from two incompatible sets of desire: on the one hand for new visual technologies to reveal the truth of modern feminine identity and on the other for young women to be true to their image.[47]

In Australia, the search for national authenticity, indeed cultural distinctiveness, was carried on by opposing the fraudulent American cinema to a naturalistic Australian cinema and investigating illusion and visual ambiguity in the cinematic image. The American Screen Star and even the Americanized Australian Screen Star, such as Louise Lovely, colluded in the cinematic illusion, their spectacularization helping to seduce Screen-Struck Girls into improper desires. As one contributor to *Woman* complained of American films, "The tender minds of girls . . . are sullied by bedroom and bathroom scenes . . . and the gorgeous undress of . . . Movie actresses!" Another commentator added, "What local girl could escape a mood of sulking discontent when viewing the extravagant cabaret scenes and lavish dress in a Hollywood production?"[48] American films were unreal, featuring "butterfly women with marvellous clothes." "The wonderful dresses of these spoilt darlings make the average girl dissatisfied with her lot," her lot being the reality which she was increasingly unable to grasp once seduced by the cinematic illusion.[49] If American films were false, it was the spectacle of its stars and their practices of appearing which were so often cited to illustrate the counterfeit tricks of cinema. Within the scopic conditions of Australian modernity, feminine identity became an illusion, which could not be known through the meanings constructed around the Screen Star's spectacularization and the Screen-Struck Girl's desire to appear as reproduced image.

A Disillusionment that Is Positively Painful

As a representational trope the Screen Star came to visual prominence in Australia at a time when cinematic reception was evolving from what film historian Tom Gunning has named "the cinema of attractions."[50] Early cinema used film as an apparatus of magical illusions, thrilling and shocking the audience beyond previously held perceptual thresholds. Throughout the 1920s, film transformed into narrative format which drew the spectator into a voyeuristic relation to the image, eliding the cinematic apparatus from the text to achieve the classic realism of the Hollywood studio system. However, narrative films in Australia were still presented together with "flesh and blood" acts in the 1920s, including beauty competitions, to increase audience appeal and offset the huge costs of the picture palaces.[51] Arguably, screening films between vaudeville acts drew attention back to the cinema as spectacle, since such screening foregrounded its illusory effects instead of hiding its optical techniques from view. This was very much the case with Louise Lovely's vaudeville act. She brought together the spectacle of cinema with the fascination of the Screen Star. As a live act, Lovely played on the same enthrallment with the Screen Star that the paparazzi capitalize on to this day: the desire to verify—or disprove—the Screen Star's beauty in a "live," ostensibly unmediated encounter between star and audience.[52]

The Screen Star, more than any other type of the Modern Woman, embodied the tension between generic type and individualized woman, between cultural form and its occupation. Her star status relied on the narrative of her rise to fame, her pre-stardom history, and particular knowledge about her own way of adapting to stardom and managing to live as a celebrity.[53] And yet the Screen Star was also much discussed as a type who reflected aspects of other types of modern women through her peculiar illusory qualities and because of the media of cinema and photojournalism through which she appeared. Her illusory qualities were used as evidence that the spectacularized modern feminine was not to be trusted. She posed two contradictory meanings: by appearing as image women made themselves modern, yet as spectacles, women offered a deceptive picture of femininity.

Screen Stars, of all modern types, were the most difficult to appraise, because they relied on visual deceit: they are "artists when it comes to making up their faces."[54] Their main attraction, beauty, was exposed as a contrivance of camera and other trickery. Mary Pickford was reported to be "homely without layers of thick yellow make-up" which photographed white. Indeed, the discrepancy between her screen image and reality was said to cause a "disillusionment that is positively painful."[55] Screen make-up reportedly was the means by which "girls and women, who had little if any claim to beauty, were given screen faces of supreme loveliness." Until the "Talkies," the illusion was further secured through an auditory veil; some stars' voices were said to be no more harmonious than "a comb and a piece of paper."[56]

Visual deception was an allegory for moral chicanery. Screen Stars were thought to be of dubious morality, the contrast between their onscreen and offscreen conduct held up as proof that illusions could be constructed by publicity and camera technique. *Truth*'s depiction of Lovely is a good example. In 1922, responding to the "Fatty" Arbuckle scandal, the Motion Picture Producers and Distributors of America appointed William Hays, a former postmaster general, to draft a voluntary moral code for the industry, including "morality clauses" inserted into artists' studio contracts which policed their sexual conduct offscreen.[57] The Arbuckle scandal had figured prominently in the Australian press and contributed to the image of the Screen Star as belonging to a "sordid and unsalutary" industry.[58] Her "artistic temperament" caused her to "crave excitements" and "the latest fads," such as "native dances" in the "altogether" at beach parties, moonshine, "drug parties," and "prize fights" between "pretty well stripped ladies."[59] In a cartoon in *Humour* in 1924, the visual technologies and clothing in which Screen Stars appeared to the public afforded a pun on the nature of their morality. A young woman on the beach is surrounded by cameras, and the caption reads, "The Hollywood Girl. Under-developed and Over-exposed."[60] Women who actively sought a desiring gaze were associated with visual deceit, artifice, and the entrapment of men. They exhibited their desire to become sexual subjects by positioning themselves, rather duplicitously, as sexual objects.

In Australia, the construction of Hollywood luminaries as inhabitants of "The New Sodom" contributed to the suspicion of American visual culture.[61] Because young Australian women were allegedly susceptible to the hypnotic glamour of the Screen Star, national concern developed that their desire to be spectacularized would modernize—that is, liberalize—their sexual morality. The Screen-Struck Girl's desire to appear as a Screen Star was construed as the expression of a subjective desire to become an image to herself and others, to become an object. Because she was susceptible to the reproduced image, it was held, she was unable to create any distance between herself and the Screen Star, with whom she appeared to have a fanciful and misplaced overidentification. She was thought to be morally disoriented by the modern cinematic illusion.

Movie Stricken Girls

When Lotus Thompson poured acid on her legs, the news was reported in the raft of Australian magazines that had sprung up around the Hollywood and local film industries, such as *Green Room, Stage and Society, Everyones* (which had several incarnations and appeared under several names), and *Film Weekly,* which billed itself as the "showman's journal" (see fig. 3.3 for some of its coverage on this topic). *Everyones,* a magazine designed for Australian film distributors which favored the American film-distribution combine and also reviewed local theater and vaudeville acts, first reported the incident in a column in February 1925. It cast Thompson as the disillusioned,

HERE'S A SMASHING NEW ANGLE FOR SHOWMANSHIP!

An opportunity to "play up" one of the most sensational real-life stunts ever perpetrated by a real live girl. And she is an Australian!

You remember how Lotus Thompson, the beautiful Australian, in order to attract the attention of Movie Producers to her acting ability, and to dissociate her beautiful limbs from their minds, actually poured acid on her legs so as to disfigure them—and give her Art a chance.

The Press of the world rang with the news of the daring gesture!

"LOTUS OF THE LIMBS"

they called her! Then Universal gave her her big chance. And now, at last, Lotus is a full-fledged star—making screen history in the powerful Universal Feature.

Lotus Thompson

in

"The Yellowback"

This Block is available to the Showman who wants to put this picture, this star, this stunt OVER to a tremendous Box Office success!

Get the real sensation "dope" on Lotus in America. Her "rise" to ballet girl, her fall to obscurity because directors could not see further than her beauty—her sudden leap into the limelight—and then her great triumph—the Contract with Universal to Star!

"The Yellowback" is a knockout winner — if you go after it!

FIG. 3.3. Reprinted from *Film Weekly*, 14 April 1927. Courtesy of the Mitchell Library, State Library of New South Wales.

inexperienced, and exploited screen hopeful who wanted to attract attention both to and away from her good looks: "Miss Thompson, despairing of attracting attention to her good looks, decided upon such drastic action." By its estimation, Thompson, who had won a beauty contest in Australia and appeared in local film productions, was a "misguided beauty" whose quest for lead roles was thwarted by her good legs and "shapely form," which "attracted most attention," confining her screen work to bathing-suit comedies.[62] Thompson had in fact already played a number of lead roles in American films, but the notoriety which grew out of the scandal—a particular formation of twentieth-century fame—won her a starring role in Universal Studios' *The Yellowback* (1926), which film historians have said launched her career.[63] *Everyones*, with its capacity for publicity and promotion, was prophetic when it concluded its piece on Thompson with the surmise: "Maybe, if the publicity is well arranged, Miss Thompson's recent action will have its compensations."[64]

Many other commentators similarly suggested that Thompson was under some kind of illusion in thinking of herself as a Screen Star. The impressionability of Screen-Struck Girls seemed to prime them for a kind of moral disorientation that made them vulnerable to seduction and misuse by "movie sharks." *Everyones* had run, since 1920, columns about the influx into Hollywood of "foolish," "Movie-Mad Maids," "taxing the ingenuity and resources" of Los Angeles welfare workers; one hundred girls tried out for every film part, with many left destitute and stranded.[65] The phenomenon of young aspiring starlets finding themselves in dire straits in Hollywood caught the popular imagination and generated a number of films, such as *A Star Is Born* (1937), as well as numerous chorus-girl narratives about the process of discovery and the bittersweet rise to fame, such as *42nd Street* (1933). *Everyones* believed such girls "fall victims of the cheapest flattery of men."[66] Perhaps because of their supposed immodesty, young women with "movie fever" were said to be surprised, once in Los Angeles, "to find that no one wants them, and that it is hard work and not moral laxity that will get them a place."[67] The editors reminded readers that they had already published warnings issued by Los Angeles authorities to dissuade young women with the "movie bug," "no matter how beautiful or otherwise attractive they were," from coming to seek "elusive screen notoriety."[68]

The moral stupefaction of Screen-Struck Girls was made clear, it was argued, by their willingness to do whatever was necessary in order to appear as a Screen Star. The "villainous director" preyed on the "delusion" of young women who flocked to Los Angeles with "movie fever." Such girls were "lured" by the patronage of "movie kings," only to find that their patronage was "obtained at a price." Their moral fall was perceived as precipitated by their desire to be spectacularized. The young girl who "was drawing pictures of herself as Mary Pickford" was later found in a "house of ill-repute" addicted to "the dope habit." From youth until her demise, then, she was susceptible to altered states of reality, created initially by the cinema and then by narcotics. Her initial overidentification with the Screen Star reportedly placed her amongst an "alarming" number of "foolish maidens" in a "steady flow toward Film land," who falsely believed "that they resemble certain stars and therefore have an advantage."[69] According to *Home* magazine, they became only "Ladies of Poverty Row," movie failures too proud to return to their small towns and admit defeat, who ended up "living little romances of their own" through being part of the "grand Hollywood adventure." Their delusion was in believing the modern day "fairy-story" of "Extra-Girl today—Star tomorrow," "to be found often enough on the screen but very rarely behind it."[70] Like the Screen Star, such young women were deceptive in their appearance, since they "dress rather better than they can afford to,"[71] and their excessive desire for visual style led them to poverty and made them vulnerable to "sharks who prey on film-struck girls."[72] They walked "penniless but wonderfully clad,"[73] "lamp-blacking their eyelashes"[74] in the hope they would be discovered.

The discrepancy between reality and representation was illustrated by the Screen-Struck Girl's mistaken belief in her visual appeal, which was fostered under the direction of the cinematic image. In figure 3.4, a comic sketch in *Aussie* in 1928, the Screen-Struck Girl is completely oblivious to her own context, her own duties, and her own lack of physical appeal when she identifies herself with the image of the Screen Star. Through her overidentification with the reproduced image she lost any ability to relate to her own visual context: she saw glamour where there was the squalor of poverty and chores. Hers was a whole new kind of madness, more formally spoken of as "Film Neurosis." "Nerve specialists" associated with the League of Nations conducted a survey of girls' classes and found that going to the cinema produced a "startling effect to the girls' mental condition." Cinema's illusoriness was foremost in this discussion; terms such as "mesmerised" and phrases such as "falseness of . . . impression," "the strong impression created by over-sensational films," and "unfulfilled craving for more and more excitement," crescendoed into a description of

MOVIE MAD.

FIG. 3.4. Comic sketch by Alice Solly, reprinted from *Aussie*, 15 October 1928. Courtesy of the Mitchell Library, State Library of New South Wales.

young women "growing up into a neurotic race whose standards of courage, honesty and morality will be those of the artificial and frequently insane behaving creatures of the film story." The moral decline of such young women resulted from a kind of scopic disorientation which caused them to act "mechanically" under the direct influence of films. Their marked preference for romantic and sentimental themes "creates an erotic emotionalism among young girls that has far reaching consequences."[75] The pejorative use of "sensational" and "sentiment" recurred in the discourse surrounding mass visual technologies in their association with the feminine.

The Screen-Struck Girl's desire to appear propelled the plot in the narrative of her modern-day "fall." She became "easy pickings" for "motion picture swindlers" said to be setting up numbers of fraudulent acting classes in Sydney and Melbourne.[76] Once "bitten by the longing for movie fame," "movie stricken girls" were "dazzled" by the "highest artistry" of "masquerading" and "alluring advertisements" and their money, innocence, and virtue were finally "filched" by such "confidence men."[77] The Screen-Struck Girl's susceptibility to the fantastic and the fraudulent made her credulous, leading her to misjudge her physical appeal and star potential. The *Green Room* essentialized this susceptibility as a feminine condition, expounding that "lurking within every woman's soul is vanity." The magazine drew attention to modern types, by adding, "Flappers, too, have their full share in cold storage."[78] The famous American director Cecil B. DeMille concurred in *Everyones*, declaring, "nearly every woman in the world feels in her heart that she could be a famous actress if the opportunity would present itself." The idea was "ridiculous" and such women were "weak, unreal"; they should be able to discern the skill and art behind the glamorous idol of the great actress.[79]

Older women cinema spectators were also criticized for being too emotional, unable to be objective before the reproduced image. When the federal government was urged to appoint a woman censor by the Victorian Women Citizens' Movement and the Perth Women's Service Guild, the appointment was strongly opposed by members of the National Association of Film Exhibitors, who argued that "women did not possess sufficient knowledge of the world."[80] When Eleanor Glencross, a prominent feminist and president of the Housewives' Association, did take up the woman's seat on the censors' board, she was described as "sour and silly" for warning that American film exporters might think more carefully about the kind of films they sent to Australia, once they knew a woman was a censor.[81] Perhaps, as a feminist and representative of housewives, Glencross was perceived as too identified with the feminine, for according to *Everyones* she was swayed by "sentiment" and "political leanings" and was therefore incapable of impartiality.[82]

Women's susceptibility to the illusion of cinema appeared again in early theories of women's spectatorship in modernity. In her analysis of Weimar cinema, Petro notes, "While mass culture in general was frequently associated with modernity (and hence, as several theorists have pointed out, with woman) the cinema in particular seemed to crystallize the relationships among modern life, modes of perception, and male responses to gender differences." Petro finds the same tendency to construct women spectators as "willingly duped by the image, but also most deceived by its lies" at work on a number of levels: in popular representations of the woman spectator, in early theories of gender differences in perception, but also in contemporary explanations of spectatorship in film theory.[83] The significant aspect of Petro's linking of early theories of women's spectatorship to contemporary film theory is the way women's overidentification with the image

continues to be central. Woman is still equated with image and assumed to be unable to separate from it. The woman-object has a tenacious hold. Petro finds the same belief in overidentification in Mary
Ann Doane's argument that the woman spectator is constituted differently through structures of looking and forms of perception. She
quotes Doane:

> For the female spectator there is a certain overpresence of the image—
> she is the image. Given the closeness of this relationship, the female spec-
> tator's desire can be described only in terms of narcissism—the female
> look demands a becoming. It thus appears to negate the very distance or
> gap specified by Metz . . . as the essential precondition of voyeurism.[84]

Petro believes such constructions of female spectatorship have their
origins in early theories of mass culture and perception in modernity,
including those of Martin Heidegger, Walter Benjamin, and Siegfried
Kracauer. Contemporary film theory conceals "a fairly complex history rooted in responses to modernity and male perceptions of sexual
difference."[85] Early theories strongly echoed popular constructions of
the Screen-Struck Girl, focusing on her naive spectatorship, her deluded overidentification with the Screen Star, and her desire to appear.

In 1923, when one "Screen Struck Foolish Flapper" was "decoyed"
and abducted by an American actor, Leslie Holiday, the dangers of this
desire were once more given a public airing. Many Adelaide girls had
answered his newspaper advertisement for "students in the film pictures," from whom he selected Alice Vincent. However, Vincent became less enamored of the romance of Hollywood once she was taken
to Melbourne by Holiday, and she sought protection with the Salvation Army. *Truth* was careful to elaborate on the various levels of
deception at work: that of "picture lure" and its "feather fancied female fans"; that of Holiday himself, who was unknown and "did not
look the part" of an actor; and, most interestingly, that of Vincent,
who "did not look romantic, and there was little to distinguish her
from the multitude of flappers who frequent picture shows and other
haunts of gaiety." Still, *Truth* aptly concluded, "one can never judge
from appearance."[86] Perhaps this sense of confusion over representation and reality, symbolized by the gullibility of young women attending the cinema and by the visual deceit of the Screen Star, formed
part of the imperative in the 1920s to make precise judgments based
on the appearances of young modern women. The same mania for
beauty that erupted in print beauty competitions recurred in a prolif-

eration of competitions for the perfect "film face" or "film type." The thousands of entrants to these competitions resisted *Truth's* recommendation not to judge from appearances, for this was precisely how these young women wished to be judged. They were not deterred by the disapproving popular commentary on the deceptive Screen Star and on the gullible, sexually vulnerable Screen-Struck Girl. Instead they responded with alacrity to invitations by those with vested interests to occupy the pictures they were enthralled by and to make themselves in their image.

The Stuff Stars Are Made Of

"Girls! Which of you have not longed to be a MOVIE STAR?" This was the rhetorical question posed in 1923 by Ashby Studios, of Pitt Street, Sydney, in the promotion shown in figure 3.5, when advertising their competition for a first-class passage to the United States and introduction to a "leading movie studio."[87] "The girl who makes up her mind to-day to take advantage of this unri-

FIG. 3.5. Promotional ad for Ashby Studios, reprinted from *Everyone's— Incorporating Australian Variety and Show World*, 8 August 1923. Courtesy of the Mitchell Library, State Library of New South Wales.

valled and unprecedented offer may change the whole course of her life, and bring happiness and prosperity not only to herself, but to every one of her friends," the studio enthused.[88] The *Picture Show* wrote that Ashby's competition would prove "alluring" to "the thousands of Australian girls who sigh for 'just a chance.' "[89] It would also prove lucrative for Ashby, which accepted only photographs from its own workshop. The campaign assumed that all modern young women fervently desired mass visibility, and this assumption offered innovative avenues for Ashby and others to exploit the new spending power of the Modern Girl.

Film studios enthusiastically noted the avid spectatorship of young women in their advertising to film exhibitors. "Have You Booked Miss 1928?" Paramount Studio asked the film exhibitor. Young women constituted 70 percent of Australian film audiences and were "eager for entertainment but mighty shrewd in choosing it." Spectatorship was decreed by fashion and Miss 1928 rejected "old fashioned pictures"; she "scorns them like last year's hat." Miss 1928's up-to-the-minute visual style—with her "bobbed hair and knee high skirts"—identified her in the film exhibitor's audience as a representative of modernity. As a self-possessed and movie-savvy spectator, Paramount said the Modern Girl "dictates motion picture styles to-day just as she does clothes and cars." Aware of her consumer power, Paramount called Miss 1928 the "pacemaker of to-day. Every business must please her or perish." Paramount touted itself as having "pioneered" in the studio lots by keeping up with her "swift pace," declaring that youth "rules the lot" within its gates. Paramount advised local film distributors to give Miss 1928 "what she craves; new era pictures made in her own sprightly mould. Tuned to her own bounding hopes and desires. Bright shining stars of her own shining age."[90] Since youth was a forceful sign of modernity, young women were emblematic of modernity's altered perception as they "craved" the image of all things modern. Their particular understanding of the symbiotic relation between visual culture and a self-conscious modernity earned them seats from the film distributor's box office. Spectatorship, visibility, youth, and femininity were not just indicators of the modern; in this homage to the Modern Girl, they defined it.

Miss 1928's attraction to the Screen Star was desexualized; instead of being under the dubious spell of an overly eroticized same-sex idol, she was now represented simply as fond of her "girl pals." This fondness was part of a legitimate and very modern quest to be like her. Magazines, distributors, photographic studios, and even jewelry stores fell over themselves to assist in this aspiration, promoting themselves with competitions for film faces and perfect screen types. Many of these competitions were held in picture palaces, either before or after film features. Edith Jones, president of the Victorian Women Citizens' Movement, appeared before the 1927 Royal Commission into the Moving Picture Industry. She testified that the new, lavish picture palaces (already numbering 1,250 by 1920) were holding competitions "in which young girls are paraded clad only in scanty bathing costumes. Worse still, boys are asked to vote having 'disastrous' moral consequences."[91] Like Ashby Studios, some theaters offered round trips to the United States and introductions or trials at "leading" film studios.

Such competitions not only took for granted the desire of young women to become spectacle, particularly mass-reproduced spectacle, they also asked women to position themselves in a specific relation to their own images. They had to be able to *picture themselves as image*, that is, to see their spectacularization as facilitating the performance of their modern identity: they had to hone their techniques of appearing. When *Australian Variety and Show World* advertised in 1920 that a representative from Universal-Jewel had arrived in Australia to seek a "potential star," young women were expressly asked to "ponder over these stars at your nearest theatre . . . and analyse yourself—your looks, your ability, and then if you still have the desire, have a good photo taken."[92] A short month later, Lillian Clark had been selected on the basis of her photograph.[93] The prize: a trip to "Universal City, California," and a year of training under directors "trying to discover whether or not she is the stuff stars are made of."[94] Young women were asked, "Are you fit for the films?" and film stars offered advice and endorsements of beauty products.[95] While the self-appraisal of young women and the meaning of their desire to appear was construed as symptomatic of their vulnerability to the cinematic illusion, it was also construed as essential to the success of the Screen Star. Young women were featured in photo spreads with titles such as "Australian Screen Types."[96] They gained entry into the screen type not only through expression, features, and beauty, but by being able to picture themselves while being pictured, or in short, by striking a pose.

In collecting oral histories, Sally Alexander found that young British women acquired "images and identifications" through the Hollywood Screen Star, which promised daydreams and dramas that they could rehearse and elaborate in their imagination "with every new pair of shoes or special outfit." Alexander sees fantasy as having historical and therefore changing "content, form and context," and she therefore pursues the relation between the Screen Star and working-class girls. Although she finds that "only some drew a sharpened sense of self from the images on the screen," one young woman related that "you acted out what you saw the rest of the week." Another recognized that the performance was appropriately carried out in public, saying, "you used to walk along the road imbued with it."[97] While Alexander sees this as a "mimetic" relation, the particular visibility of the Screen Star (through the new cultural import of moving pictures and their marketing) could suggest that something more than Garbo and Crawford, and their visual style, was being enacted, namely the status of the Screen Star as spectacle.

In introducing her work Alexander writes that she is concerned with "women's first jobs, and their changing appearance." However, she names "the one a condition of femininity, the other a symbol."[98] If the practices of appearing enacted by these young women were an aspect of the symbolic performance of their gendered identity, then their appearance was also a condition of their femininity. The responses of her interviewees suggest that they viewed and performed their visibility as conditional to their sense of themselves as feminine and modern. They responded to the Screen Star by performing her visual status as they went about their daily lives, using fantasy to invest the roads they traversed, and the newly mass-marketed clothes they purchased, with the visual properties of a cinematic scene, situating themselves within it as made (modern and feminine) in the image of the Screen Star. They used their changing techniques of appearing to balance the demands on them for decency, hygiene, and respectability with their own desire for glamour and self-definition, altering their hemlines and hairstyles to become modern women.

Commentaries on the Screen Star and Screen-Struck Girl viewed young women as so influenced by the cinematic image that they effected their likeness in its image. Beneath the widespread discrediting of the reproduced image through censure of the "fake" Screen Star and her "deluded" screen hopeful, there lingered a pervasive hope that the realism of the camera would secure truths about modern identity. The feminine, with its indeterminate nature, came under particular scrutiny, and while the reproduced image was deployed to uphold concern about the increasingly illusory nature of feminine identity, hope was nevertheless held out (and perhaps still is) that the truth of the feminine would finally be revealed by the realism and accuracy of new visual technologies.

The longstanding association of the feminine with representation, reproduction, and semblance was revived in the modern scene and played out over the mechanically reproduced feminine spectacle. The perception of the Screen-Struck Girl referred back to vision remaining with the body, as material, corporeal, and imperfect. If she looked herself into being the semblance of a Screen Star, she could not fail to be mistaken in what she saw of herself, as well as being a poor copy of the Screen Star she attempted, with imperfect eyes, to reproduce. Yet the feminine spectacle is always more complex than first appears. Simultaneously, it became, and has remained, the duty of the feminine to verify that the reproduced image is in fact true to life. "Motion Picture Aspirants" were therefore charged with the task of being true to their image.[99] To become successful, the Screen Star needed to put aside all artistry and performance and build "emotional resource so that she becomes plastic in the hands of a director." She was not to indulge in anything as false or feigning as acting; rather, she should call on what she had within her to "register" when she stepped before the camera. She was advised that "Tears come as a result of natural emotion and are not forced. Remember that if you do not feel a situation, you cannot expect the audience to feel it."[100] While this advice seemed to rely on an "essence" which young women could draw on before the camera, the use of language such as "build," becoming "plastic," and "registering" suggests that the reproduction of modern young women as images *was* the truth of their modern identity: they made themselves modern by coming into view.

When Benjamin wrote about the capability of the mechanically reproduced image to open up an escape from the "prison-world" of offices and factories through which we "calmly and adventurously go traveling," he seemed to promise that when modern subjects entered into the new visually prostheticized landscape, they were assured of "an immense and unexpected field of action." Moreover, these scopic innovations figured the subject in ways that enabled an apprehension of the self that was entirely unprecedented. "With the close up, space expands; with slow motion, movement is extended. The enlargement of a snapshot does not simply render more precise what in any case was visible, though unclear: it reveals entirely new structural formations of the subject."[101] When the subject matter of the camera was young women, the new formation of subjectivity that was revealed and produced was the modern appearing woman. It was a formation constructed through the conditions of modern visibility: the metropolis, the cinema, and, as I will argue in the next chapter, commodity culture. These conditions enabled the emergence of popular types such as the Screen Star and the Screen-Struck Girl, who represented this quest for objectification precisely because of the ways in which it seemed to map women into the social landscape as modern subjects. Women who identified with these types also participated in the particular technologies of gender in the 1920s; they were intimately and meticulously aware, as they were required to be, that femininity was produced as a performative and visual effect. Their appearing was a procedural production of modern feminine identity through modern visual conditions, neither a disclosure of their truth or essence nor a loss of that essence, since the truth of their identity was effected through their reproduction as image. It is this that describes a new structural formation of the modern subject. The spectacle of these types represented a self-disclosure through appearing, which did not correspond to feminine essence, yet could still delineate the parameters of modern feminine identity. The illusion of the Screen Star did not dissuade thousands of screen aspirants from wanting to be seen as just like her, as the image of the modern appearing woman.

Chapter 4

The Mannequin in the Commodity Scene

In 1921 a short story appeared in *Aussie* magazine which told of "Smugg," a blushing young man with thick glasses and myopia. After pestering Mabel at the buttons and ribbon counter for a week, he finally asked who the woman was who always stood at the end of the counter. Mabel scornfully "dragged the timid youth to where the beautiful apparition stood. . . . Smugg peered nervously through his glasses, but in return he got only a cold and even more glassy stare than his own. A deep sob was wrung from his heart, and he rushed out into the street. The lady of his dreams was only a mannequin."[1] Poor Smugg—with his compromised sight, his misapprehension of and captivation by a Mannequin mirage, and his emotional flight headlong into the regulated flow of the city street—he hardly epitomized the self-possessed, rational, modern male spectator.

Smugg's confusion over the hyperrealism of the Mannequin indicates something new in the modern scene: he had encountered a woman who was simultaneously life-like and lifeless, a *trompe l'œil* of commodity aesthetics. This paradoxical status of the Mannequin was realized through the cultural interplay between constructions of the Modern Woman and the status of the woman-object in modern commodity displays. Women and commodities were increasingly imbricated through the scopic relations instituted in the visual economy of commodity culture, its logic of display, and the positioning of feminine spectacle within this logic. While on the one hand the Mannequin confirmed the traditional status of the woman-object, it also invited women to occupy the space of its image. It modeled the feminized commodity spectacle. The Mannequin's life-like and lifeless *trompe l'œil* was effected through its being cast specifically as a commodity sign. As I will explain later, this would have important implications for the ways that women could cast themselves as spectacles. It would mean that the processes of commodity aesthetics entered into the production of the modern appearing woman. This was to be an important aspect of the constitution of this new feminine subject position, for it would mean that by becoming spectacle women were also positioned within the capitalist exchange economy.

In the 1920s, the commodified perceptual field impacted indelibly on prevalent discourses concerned with feminine visibility. These newly influenced discourses included that feminine essence was being lost, that changing visual styles made modern feminine identity mutable, artificial, and deceitful, that mass-reproduced images of women were illusory, and that young women overidentified with and were vulnerable to modern spectacle. The feminine was associated with commodity exchange and distraction in the traffic of looks within the visually cluttered metropolis. The Mannequin stood over the vicissitudes of commodity display as escort and guide to women's consumerism and techniques of appearing. It gave women something to look at, while inviting them to make themselves modern in its image. It modeled the incursion of the commodity image into feminine subjectivity, while exhibiting new meanings of women's public presence and display.

Molded to His Heart's Desire

The Mannequin had its origins in the dressmaker's dummy used by drapery emporiums in the display of dress materials. Prior to the 1920s, Mannequins had been wax-molded figures, which tended to melt under lights and were headless and limbless. In the 1920s these figures assumed new dimensions ostensibly duplicating those of "real" women—at least as retailers imagined them. They were transformed into life-like, fully assembled, mass-produced reproduc-

FIG. 4.1. Replica of 1920s mannequin from the David Jones visual merchandising collection. Photo: Jeremy Ludowyke.

tions of the idealized feminine body. As they evolved into commodity icons they acquired limbs, and even hands and feet that were carefully postured to suggest the ownership and handling of goods.[2] In the *Australian Woman's Mirror* a Mannequin's photograph was captioned with the comment, "How far we have travelled since the days of the old stiff draper's 'dummy.' "[3] The newly realistic Mannequin was featured at the Paris Exhibition of Decorative Art in 1925, which was covered by the fashionable *Home* magazine (which had relied on the older custom of using society débutantes in its fashion spreads).[4] They were given heads with elaborately designed faces, features, and hairstyles demonstrating contemporary trends. Indeed, faces meticulously made up like the Mannequin shown in figure 4.1 proved the modern doctrine that beauty need not be natural. Rather it was produced through elaborate regimes and techniques of appearing. After Man Ray used mannequins for a *Vogue* cover in 1925, they became increasingly popular images in globally circulated fashion iconography.[5]

As they took their places in the department stores and shop windows, they stood like sentinels over the modern vicissitudes of feminine visibility. William Leach has observed,

> Female mannequins were perhaps the most radical display fixtures to appear in the store window. They helped transform the character of the female public image. Unlike the female statuary of the past, which personified such classical virtues as justice and truth, as well as the domestic virtues of purity and maternal nurture, these figures owed little allegiance to earlier traditions. They invoked individual indulgence in luxury as often as they did domestic behaviour. Indeed as devices to excite desire for goods, mannequins were used explicitly to suggest not one kind of behaviour, but a range of behaviours and roles.[6]

The Mannequin excited more than a desire to purchase goods. It became a "role model" inviting women to identify with feminine spectacle. It stood for the belief among retailers and advertisers that women would respond to the suggestion that they use goods in order to appear modern. The transformative power of commodities—encapsulated in the "make-over" and "before and after" advertising that began to appear in the 1920s—did indeed open "a range of behaviours and roles" to modern women, but these behaviors and roles were in fact made commensurate with extant types, and these types were visually inscribed. In order to conveniently identify and discriminate among consumers, as new targeted marketing methods required, types were used in advertising iconography to represent new consumer groups. Types such as the Flapper were appropriated by retailers as fashion standards.[7] The Mannequin negotiated the apparent diversity of consumer behaviors by providing a simplified, but changeable, visual icon for their identification and cultural reflexivity. While able to specify types, she also represented a normative version of the consuming woman as beautiful, white, young, and slender. Needless to say, these criteria excluded the vast majority of women from identification, but they were promised that they could be included in this category of visually idealized women by using the products and merchandise the mannequin displayed to fashion an improved self.

The lingering residue of the physiologies Walter Benjamin wrote of found new application in this quest for clusterings of consumerist subjectivity.[8] The Mannequin was clearly not a type in herself, but her alterable surface typified the primacy of the visual in characterizing women as modern. The Mannequin displayed the centrality of the commodity object in specifying the field of action for the modern woman's self-articulation in the relation between looking and being looked at.

But Smugg's confusion between live women and their replicas was in part justified by the fact that live women, called *mannequins vivants*, were employed to model "haute couture." The first such living mannequin was credited as Marie Worth, who began modeling the clothes designed by her husband Charles in the 1860s. Between 1920 and 1940, the term "mannequin" could refer to both display dummies and live models.[9] During this period, the "haute couturier" Poiret toured Europe with models and photographed them.[10] This new practice of exhibiting live women could be compromised by attempts to use them in visual scenarios that were intended for a fixed, highly proximate gaze. By the 1920s, it was no longer clear that live mannequins could enact the idealized feminine commodity spectacle. Department stores had tried using shop assistants and factory workers as models in shop windows in 1916, but the experiment was unsuccessful. "The models were apparently ungainly, wore too much face powder, and had pimply backs."[11] In addition, live women could make troublesome claims about the terms of their visual reproduction, not to mention wage entitlements.[12] For instance, a 1902 advertisement in the United States used Abigail Roberson's photograph without her consent, and led the New York state legislature to pass a law prohibiting the use of photographic portraits for commercial purposes.[13] These newer forms of feminine visibility remained subject to older traditions of disrepute and censure despite attempts to make modeling respectable through the establishment of institutions such as Lucy Clayton's modeling agency in Britain in 1928.[14]

Not only did the inorganic Mannequin overcome the lingering stigma associated with women on public display, it would not flinch before shoppers' scrutiny. As the public pored over the Mannequin, they became fascinated with how its realism related to real women—whether as doll-like idealization or the vestige of a wax mold. In the 1920s press the Mannequin was figured as a novelty and curiosity. The *Sun* captioned a photo of a mannequin produced by a recently opened factory in London with "Moulded Her to His Heart's Desire," as if to admit that it was a fantasy object of perfected womanhood.[15] The process of molding from live women was photographed and reproduced in human-interest layouts,[16] as shown in figure 4.2. But the most interesting relation between animate and inanimate Mannequins

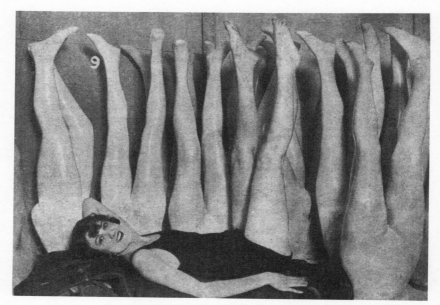

FIG. 4.2. "Mannequins and Mannequin Vivant," reprinted from *Beckett's Weekly*, 16 August 1927. Courtesy of the State Reference Library, State Library of New South Wales.

was that both embodied the feminization of commodity aesthetics as a condition of the spectacularization of the Modern Woman.

The Mannequin drew together some of the features of the City Girl and Screen Star. It presided over feminine street presence as a reproduced and commodified spectacle of the Modern Woman. It remained fixed before the fleeting, distracted gaze of the metropolis, while reinforcing the sense of anonymity in city presence as spectacle without identity. As a commodity spectacle it maintained the ambiguity of women's street presence, standing in the shadow of the prostitute before the distracted gaze of the street. The inanimate Mannequin's fixity of image countered the fragmentary and transitory images or "moving pictures" of women. Its statuesque stillness may have accommodated a yearning for visual constancy in modern women that was itself a desire for a discernible feminine essence. The Mannequin also exemplified the rationalization of the feminine body through scientific management, and exhibited the importance of advertising and merchandise in that rationalization. Standardized, assembled, ideal-

ized, and fixed before the cosmopolitan gaze, the Mannequin embodied the effects of integration into modernity's visual economy.

Strategies of Display

The 1920s witnessed a marked increase in mass
production through the growth of manufacturing.[17] Improved printing
techniques had helped to transmit modern commodity culture in the
nineteenth century, and photography and cinema now did so as well.
These advances in image production resulted in a cosmopolitan landscape replete with advertising. William Leach calls these intersections
of commodity forms and modern visualities "strategies of display."
Their histories are inextricably interdependent and globally linked,
borne along by the transnational flows of capital. The "modern display
aesthetic" and the introduction of "display" into "everyday merchandising language" date from 1899.[18] The "vertically integrated corpo-
ration" of monopoly capitalism was marked by its management of the
increase in consumer demand. The development of advertising and
packaging not only instigated the era of the consumer, but inaugurated the advertising agency and revolutionized the print media,
which dropped their prices as a result of advertising revenue, enlarged
their circulations, and invented the general mass-circulation magazine. Cultural theorist Richard Ohmann names this development the
invention of "mass culture."[19] He explains that the magazines "had hit
on a business formula new to national media: sell the magazine for
less than its cost of production, build a huge circulation and make
your profit on advertising revenues. In other words, they were no
longer dealers in their physical product and became dealers in groups
of consumers."[20]

In the formation of a mass culture of consumption, "show" became a compulsion. Among the interventions in display and advertising listed by Leach are electric light and its revolutionizing of the architecture of commodity sites, plate glass and its impact on window
and counter display, and brilliant new artificial colors made from an-
iline coal-tar dyes.[21] These more general cultural transformations
found particularly gendered expressions. The logic of display invaded
the domain of culture and sexuality. But for all their flamboyance,
these display conventions remained rather coy regarding the feminine
spectacle in the earliest years of the century.[22] Though the situation

would change, Gail Reekie documents that turn-of-the-century displays featured mostly men. She suggests this was due to a lingering sense of propriety that discouraged the public display of women and argues that prior to 1900 the displays of department stores "courted their female customers with the same ritualised set of heterosocial conventions that governed male-female relations outside the store. The sexual forms of interaction, display and enticement they initiated were couched in the language of respectability and domesticity."[23]

However, the entrance of women into public space instituted a distinct gaze that the newly self-conscious advertisers were all too keen to exploit. Commodity culture was defined by a rising managerial class who were highly aware of women as consumers and wanted to manage their consumption.[24] Shopping was one of the earliest legitimate reasons for women of means (or with spending power) to be present and unchaperoned in metropolitan space. As a condition of feminine visibility, commodity culture had first affected the spectacularization of modern women by encouraging women to enter public space, to look and to spend. "The promotion of the 'new woman' image, bound up with the world of consumption . . . emphasized freer behavior and greater social mobility for women."[25] Leach describes "how much middle-class women had come to occupy and to move comfortably within the public domain. Their new freedom was made possible by the emergence of a quintessentially feminine world constructed around the commodity form that had come to dominate the urban scene."[26] From the 1890s women constituted between 70 and 95 percent of shoppers and spent three times more than men.[27] The spatially sex-differentiated department store contained and ordered this presence.[28]

The new class of advertisers began to understand the importance of capitalizing on women's metropolitan presence and directing their gaze, not only to products but back to themselves and their potential to be visually transformed through the use of goods. They increasingly placed the feminine as a display icon within "strategies of display"— and this placement went hand-in-hand with the commodification of the feminine body or the look of the body. The scientific authority of "new experts" on health and beauty was invoked in specific commodity sites such as the department store and print advertising, as well as within the broader perceptual horizon of mass culture. Imagery circulated among the industrializing nations. Kerreen Reiger writes, by the 1930s the encouragement of virtue had been replaced by a multitude of specific instructions on modifying the person, both physically and psychologically. Local models of womanly virtue had been replaced by American packaged images of feminine beauty; the Hollywood image was brought closer to Australian women not only by a variety of articles but by photographic and advertising techniques.[29]

In the imaging of the commodity, the home and the very body of the consumer became increasingly sex-differentiated and feminized locations. From the turn of the century, retailing strategies both constructed and relied on sexual difference, bringing "sex and sexual difference out from the shadows and into popular discourse." Gendered identity began to play a particular role in modern commodity culture, since "[r]etailing and commerce were not beyond questions of sex and sexual difference, but constituted by them."[30] Sexual difference began to be elaborated through techniques of display as retailers, advertisers, and marketing experts became convinced that women were inherently attracted to the commodity spectacle. Bertha Fortescue Harrison told advertisers, "Men and women view advertisements from different points of view. . . . a clever advertisement will be called 'smart' by a man, while a woman will think it is 'nice.' "[31] This was because image and illustration were more "pleasing" to women, she said.[32]

As commodities from linoleum to soap became gendered, the logic of display was itself feminized, not only because women were seen to be more susceptible to spectacle but because they were seen to identify with it. "Modern store displays were premised on the assumption that women would be seduced by the revelation of (sexed) commodities, sexual display and exhibitionism." That seduction, according to research conducted by the sales writers of the time, was likely to be effected through women's narcissism, "typically expressed in their innate if inexplicable desire for personal adornment." Consumption was gendered principally through display: "the colour in the stores, the fashion and the theatre, the indulgence and the impulse became ever more associated in the minds of both sexes with the feminine." An emphasis on mirrors in women's retail spaces elaborated the "rules of sexual segregation in departmental display" in both window and interior settings.[33] Through this mirroring women were invited to picture themselves as part of the commodity scene. Appeals to women to look at displays and to display themselves through the visually transformative power of goods meant that commodity culture entered into the domain of subjectivity. The new goods manufactured and made available to women, such as ready-to-wear clothing and brand-name cosmetics, proposed feminine display as the correct and natural expression of modern women. A perfume advertisement featured a modish young woman at her dresser. "Do you want to be like her," it asked rhetorically, "well-groomed, modern and beautiful?"[34]

All Eyes Are on the Woman

The Mannequin had an important place in these historical shifts. As consumerism played directly upon the entrance of women into metropolitan space, the Mannequin was cast as host and guide to their street excursions. It not only gendered the department store as feminized space, but configured women as at home among commodities and even as part of the commodity and city spectacle. Despite the Mannequin's welcoming presence, however, meanings of feminine visibility continued to vacillate between emancipation and regulation. Elizabeth Wilson discusses how the gendered nature of public occupancy was shaped by the scopic relations of consumerism: "With the coming of 'modernity' the cities of veiled women have ceded to cities of spectacle and voyeurism, in which women, while seeking and sometimes finding the freedom of anonymity, are often all too visible. They are in fact a part of the spectacle, and the kaleidoscope of city life becomes intensely contradictory for women."[35] Similarly, Judith Walkowitz points to the sexualization of "Shopping Ladies." They were subjected to "the intrusive gaze of men" and could be mistaken for prostitutes.[36]

The emergence of the Mannequin into this complicated relay of looks seemed to encourage women not only to look but to accept the inevitability of their being looked at. It supports Wilson's contention "that only by becoming part of the spectacle can you truly exist in the city."[37] From behind the plate glass windows of the department stores, the Mannequin's hands seemed to reach out not only for goods, but to extend welcome.[38] Commodity displays such as the Mannequin not only gave women something to look at, they also urged women not to retreat from their spectacularization, but to respond to public scrutiny by striking a pose within it. At first glance, Mannequins "peopled" the grandly decorated "palaces of consumption" as décor but, in fact, they played host in the city street, encouraging women to identify with public presence even as they incited women to consume in order to enhance that visibility.[39] Through the congruence between commodity display and feminine display, consumption was positioned as

FIG. 4.3. Advertisement for Bond's Sylk-Arto hose, reprinted from *Canberra Times*, 3 September 1926. Courtesy of the National Library of Australia.

a site where the feminine subject could be produced and transformed within the myriad procedures of display as techniques of appearing.

In the 1926 stockings advertisement shown in figure 4.3, a woman enters a restaurant through a raised entrance like a *mannequin vivant,* commanding the look of those present as a mark of her consumer proficiency. Images such as this were common in advertising iconography during the 1920s. When looking at the Mannequin, women were incited to imagine themselves being looked at. In 1920 the *Australian Home Journal* tutored them in the elaborate techniques of "the mannequin walk," which included walking very slowly, placing weight first on the ball of the foot "and the heel an instant later," and keeping the upper body immobile, while moving with "correct poise" from the hips.[40] Modern women had to appear correctly by demonstrating a mastery of the self and their visual effects. *Helen's Weekly* cautioned, "Now that our frocks display our mode of walking and standing every fault has been made conspicuous."[41] Women did not simply wear clothes, they displayed them and themselves, and this heightened self-consciousness required correct techniques in appearing. Public visibility threatened exposure unless, as with sanitary napkins, women practiced regulatory interventions with the help of commodities.

Attracting a gaze was posited as one of women's ultimate goals and adventures enabled by their guided participation in consumerism. But women had to practice in order to "hold" the fleeting gaze of transient urban spectators. In one 1927 Lux advertisement, the Shopping Girl positions herself as a street spectacle by standing on one side of the department store window.[42] She emulates the Mannequin much as the Screen-Struck Girl does the Screen Star: icons of feminine visibility were culturally imagined as producing new types of young women. In a 1924 advertisement for face cream, a young woman saunters before a crowd of onlooking men in black tails and ties. "All eyes are on the woman with the soft, lovely and clear radiant complexion. She wins admiration wherever she goes."[43]

This admiration was often perceived to give women a covert power over men, as they stood enthralled and entrapped by visual pleasure. In the 1925 sheet music cover shown in figure 4.4 the Mannequin enters into conventions of the heterosexual gaze. Lit behind glass, with the emphasis on dress (and equally, by association, on undress), "Sarah" is asked to draw her shade and presumably release her helpless Peeping Tom from paralysis. Women positioning themselves as spectacle in public space wielded an ambiguous kind of power. However gratifying it was to her, she was also deemed responsible for the reactions of men, which could range from a welcome compliment, to an intrusive gaze, to hostility and violence. In one 1920 advertisement for Shave tailors and dressmakers in Melbourne, men were assured that should their wives become clients they would then "stand alone" (not unlike the Mannequin) in "holding" their husbands' gaze—as if the wives' patronage of Shave's would guard against their husbands' gaze straying to other women.[44] Men were encouraged to view their wives with the same fascination with which they beheld the commodity image, and women were obliged to respond by shaping themselves in its image. Sexual agency, which was associated with object status in the organization of gendered scopic relations, ostensibly rested with women: they were encouraged to enjoy its equivocal pleasures.

Identifying with advertising promised romance; but romance was about being subject to the same intense scrutiny and appraisal as the commodity image, and this required self-surveillance. A 1922 adver-

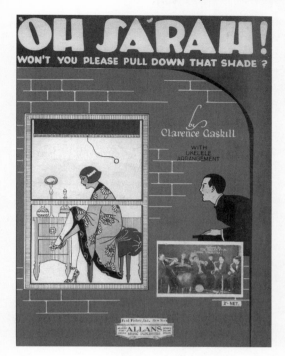

FIG. 4.4. Cover illustration for sheet music of Clarence Gaskill's "Oh Sarah! Won't You Please Pull Down That Shade?" Allans Music (1925). Courtesy of the National Library of Australia.

tisement for Palmolive soap advised, "Happy the girl who knows that her fresh, clear skin and smooth white neck and arms must command admiration." The young woman in question looks back at us, remarkably relaxed under the looming inspection of her beau.[45] If women were to achieve a sense of self-mastery in their objectification, they needed to incite men's gaze. The seeming paradox that their subject status was confirmed in their being gazed at is resolved at the point of consumption. Palmolive advised that a girl can only be "herself, natural, unaffected," and "conscious of the scrutiny of interested eyes which appraise every detail of your appearance" when she is "sure of her skin" and not self-conscious about her "complexion defects."[46] Not until she approved of herself could she be confident of the approval of others. This double-edged approval was won by the transformative intervention of the commodity. But it not only transformed her visually, it transformed her into a vision. She both used it and took on its imperative to become spectacle. "Fascination" through "purity of complexion" was the promise of Beecham Pills.[47] And it was the "Girl with the wavy hair," boasting "waviness of such potent magic charm," of whom people asked, "Who is the Popular Girl?"[48] Similarly, "Plain Jane" may have had "natural attractions," yet these had never qualified her to "achieve wider social success." But she was spotted by an old friend at "quite a select event" who marveled at her transformation. Jane, who "was now the centre of attraction," had discovered Lustre Dress Fabrics.[49] The woman who possessed, through consumer prowess, mastery over her visual effects was a cut above the rest: her power to enthrall gave her potency. In the competitive realm of heterosexual appeal and social desirability, self-transformation into riveting spectacle was the key to being a successfully modern woman.

At the time, commentators saw more menacing implications of this newfound desire to appear. The "lure of finery" emerged again in the discourse of women's impressionability to consumer display, which led them into "momentary weakness"—another version of women's perceived susceptibility to the mesmerizing effects of spectacle. In 1928 the *Bulletin* reported a "growing epidemic in shop-pilfering" among, horror of horrors, "respectable" married women. They noted that such women were put under "some entirely exceptional strain" by store displays which encouraged women to handle goods "brought under their noses" on countertops in the lavish department stores. If "pilferers" were to be punished, the *Bulletin* reasoned, so should "the provocateur."[50] English social commentator Bernhard A. Bauer, in his explanation of deviancy and criminality, relied on the longstanding sense that women's desire to appear and consume was somehow perverse. In 1927 he wrote,

> When we remember that every woman is vain, and animated with a love of adornment, that woman thinks a great deal of externals, and that a woman in love wishes to make herself appear as beautiful as possible, we shall readily understand how a loving and light minded woman to whom the necessary means of adornment are lacking, will be readily induced to steal in order to get possession of these means. It is in keeping with woman's lack of objectivity, with her credulousness, with the inferiority of her powers of judgement, that petty thefts such as the theft of a ribbon or some other minor object of adornment, are apt to be regarded as a trifling matter, not worth speaking about.[51]

Commodity display encouraged women's excessive preoccupation with superficial attraction, and the "love of finery" was again invoked to condemn a femininity to which "a certain amount of superficiality and levity must be ascribed." Young women were "cultivating habits of extravagance" by spending their disposable incomes on readily available mass-produced goods. The spreading "make-up habit" spoke of their financial imprudence and irrepressible attraction to surface effects. Narcissism was called "self-abuse," and "exceptional firmness" from mothers was required to prevent girls from being "marred" for life by poisonous "cheap paint."[52]

Consumption of beauty aids was blamed for the loss of traditional femininity. Modern femininity was brazen; it sacrificed discretion for the pleasures of spectacle, and in doing so became calculating and visually deceitful. The carefully constructed allure of the Business Girl and her schemes to entrap a wealthy husband were reiterated in countless comic sketches about the Shopping Girl. Onlookers in one 1919 *Bulletin* cartoon remark on the cleverness of a young woman "economist." "Yes, so I should think," a disgruntled older woman rejoins; "certainly she can make a maximum of display on a minimum of chiffon."[53] Consumerism signaled a self-conscious and actively constructed appeal to the male gaze through adopting the self-fulfilling logic and economy of display of commodity culture. One father complains, "you girls get clothes, clothes, clothes just to get a husband." "Yes," his daughter replies, "but dad, remember we get husbands to get us clothes, clothes, clothes!"[54] The once sacred ideal of marriage was simply a means to an end. The economic benefit of taking up the position of the commodity object was the subject of a 1928 cartoon by Betty Patterson. One precocious and overdressed girl says, "My trustee wants me to invest my money in shares. What would you do?" Her friend replies, "Oh, I think shares are silly. I'd put all my money into clothes. They'll fetch you far more interest you'll find."[55] In Patterson's cartoons intoxication with their own appearance infantilizes women; they are like little girls not quite grown out of dressing up, who refuse to adopt some of the moderation, and perhaps domestic and reproductive responsibilities, of adult womanhood. But popular images that played on the visual appeal of young women, such as the sheet music cover in figure 4.4, rarely missed the opportunity to simultaneously voyeurize their self-absorption.

This association of consumption with disreputable exhibitionism had to be overcome for the growing ready-to-wear and cosmetics industries to profit from women's attraction to, and identification with, the commodity spectacle across the socioeconomic spectrum. Ready-made mass-produced clothing brought fashion and its pleasures within the reach of working-class women.[56] Dress no longer specified class, and in modernity class markings became less clear. In one 1923 *Bul-*

letin cartoon, whose caption "The Servant Problem" plays on the short-age of domestic servants (as they too left the home and sought shorter hours and better working conditions in factories, department stores, and offices), one young woman declares, "My maid is so extravagant! She tries to copy all my clothes." Her companion replies with admirable egalitarianism, "I'm as bad darling. I try to copy my maids."[57] Self-adornment had to be divested from its earlier associations with aristocratic excess or, conversely, the "painted" character of the working-class amateur; it had to be both democratized and made respectable. Commodity display was crucial in this endeavor.

The Mannequin had implications for the production of feminine subjectivity through the consumption not just of goods but of images. Modern women did more than simply mimic the content of imagery seen in the display Mannequin; they became implicated in the processes by which the Mannequin was constituted as a commodity image of commodity aesthetics. In adopting the fashionable image of the Mannequin, modern women identified with the construction of the feminine as commodity image, internalizing its object character. The life-like qualities of the Mannequin left open the subjective effects of becoming spectacle, but because it was lifeless, it also seemed to warn against a complete reduction to object status. The Mannequin's ambiguity in being both alive and lifeless perfectly represents the contradictory and complex standing of feminine visibility. As a commodity image it also had strong allegiances to other forms of image commodification, such as the cinema.

Fluffy Dears upon the Screen

The logic of display in commodity culture ratified some of the new meanings of feminine visibility that were also emerging through the cinema, consolidating the broader association of the feminine with mass culture, visual technology, and cultural icon.[58] As a result, the locations and thereby the meanings of being seen were reorganized. Women pictured in advertising were subject to the close-up; they were aware of the scrutiny of strange eyes in public spaces. They appeared before a collective gaze and competed to be singled out from the passing crowd for their compelling visual effects. The *mannequin vivant* and Screen Star also exchanged cultural posts, appearing in each other's media and performing each other's roles. The 1928 film *Woman Triumphant* featured footage of "the most beautiful Pari-

sian mannequins arrayed in the newest of Continental creations."[59]
The Screen Star was sometimes characterized as a *mannequin vivant*.
Young women going to the cinema were said to have been "given a
pass to a fashion parade."[60] The importance of fashion to cinema's
visual pleasure was not lost on print publications, which carried pictures of prominent stars acting as *mannequins vivants* and modeling
gowns they had worn in their film roles. *Adam and Eve* reported that
Hollywood engaged the world's top designers "for the sole purpose of
making the stars the leaders of the world's fashions."[61] Articles surveyed Screen Stars on the tactile pleasures of silk.[62] In one article, the
Screen Star transformed the cinema spectator into spectacle just as the
Mannequin invited women shoppers to change from lookers to
looked-at: "the metamorphosis of plain Jane to fluffy and entirely captivating June is a miracle directly due to the appearance of fluffy dears
upon the screen to point the way."[63]

The transitory site of the cinematic screen was perfect for the cy-
clic images of fashion. They were both "crossed by a multiplicity of
transient appearances and rapid disappearances."[64] But these two feminized exhibition spaces truly converged in the ways they both commodified the image itself. Miriam Hansen notes that cinema and advertising both aimed to stimulate new needs and desires through
"visual fascination." She writes that "the abundance of images—and
images of abundance" meant that the reception of both the cinema
and commodity spectacle was structured in terms of possessions. But
this sense of possession was now affected at the level of the eye—by
"turning visual fascination itself into a commodity."[65] In "capitalist film
practice,"[66] Hansen argues, "the boundaries of 'looking' and 'having'
were blurred,"[67] and "the cinema became a powerful vehicle of reproducing spectatorship as consumers, an apparatus for binding desire
and subjectivity in consumerist forms of social identity."[68]

The congruence of the Mannequin and Screen Star through their
reproduction into mass-produced icons, and through their modes of
commodified reception, attested to the powerful cultural formations
at work in the modern appearing woman. But there were particular
ramifications not only in the content of these dominant images, but
in the processes by which they were commodified. Modern women
were invited to enact the "semiotic virtuosity" of the modern commodity image as demonstrated by the Mannequin.[69]

As reproduced, even "cast" from live women, the inanimate Mannequin replicated the cinema's ability to reproduce reality into image.[70] Ever in pursuit of the Modern Woman's truth, commentators

questioned the substance of her image, and the prominence of the Mannequin and Screen Star exacerbated the perception that she was increasingly illusory, since she was produced in relation to a chimera-like image. Film theorist Raymond Bellour has argued that "the actual process of substituting a simulacrum for a living being directly replicates the camera's power to reproduce automatically the reality it confronts. Every *mise en scene* of the simulacrum thus refers intrinsically to the fundamental properties of the cinematic apparatus."[71] Though it may not have been, strictly speaking, a simulacrum, the Mannequin emerged as people adjusted to cinematic conventions that were capable of reproducing reality into image.[72] As Hansen contends, "the reality conveyed by the cinematic apparatus is no more and no less phantasmagoric than the 'natural' phenomena of the commodity world it replicates. . . . The primary objective to capitalist film practice was to perpetuate that mythical chain of mirrors" in the "media of consumption."[73]

The Mannequin and Screen Star also illustrated "the textual mediation of identity," demonstrating what Felski has identified as "the *fin-de-siecle* preoccupation with style and appearance [which] itself reflects an expanding aestheticization of everyday life, a mediation of experience through the consumption of images and commodities."[74] This aestheticization expanded into the emergence of a new feminine subjectivity, and this modern appearing woman was inflected with the consumption and production of self as commodity image, as a means of access to and presence in the modern.

Remote as a Sleep Walker

Luce Irigaray has written:

> Participation in society requires that the body submit itself to spectacularization, a speculation, that transforms it into a bearing object, a standardized sign, an exchangeable signifier, a "likeness" with reference to an authoritative model. A commodity—a woman—is divided into two irreconcilable "bodies": her "natural" body and her socially valued, exchangeable body, which is a particularly mimetic expression of masculine values.[75]

A Berlei lingerie advertisement in 1929, "At a Mannequin Parade," toyed with the contradictory status of the Mannequin as both life-like and lifeless. Curtains parted, disclosing "a mannequin, exquisite, fro-

zen, remote. A sigh runs through the audience. It wakes the mannequin—she stirs, she comes to life. Remote as a sleep walker."[76] The
suggestion here of lifelessness draws again upon the pervasive sense
that women's overidentification with spectacle, and their imitation of
both its look and its status as object, rendered them mechanical,[77]
"remote," and "frozen," as though their life-essence were sacrificed to
their performance—specifically, as though women could not be objects and subjects at once. But the Berlei Mannequin also "came to
life" upon apprehension. She was animated by the gaze, as though
her spectacularization were one with her subjectification, or her coming into view were commensurate with her coming into being. In this
sense, the Berlei advertisement did more than equate women's spectacularization with their loss of individuality—it also suggested that
the practice of appearing animates the modern feminine subject into
cultural intelligibility.

The Mannequin's dual status as life-like and as lifeless, and its
contradictory characterization here as mechanical yet animated upon
apprehension, have much to say about the relation between subject
and object through the spectacularization of the Modern Woman. As
an icon of both consumerist subjectivity and the commodity image,
the Mannequin encapsulated the profoundly complex and newly contradictory status of the woman-object in modernity. In its lifelessness
it exhibited the object character of the spectacularized feminine, whilst
by being life-like it hinted at the spectacle's potentially subjective effects. It demonstrated that the changed conditions of women's public
visibility reconfigured the relation between representation and subjectivity, rendering them synchronous in the performative enactment
of the Modern Woman.

For some writers, the fact that women made themselves into spectacles enacted the ills of a mechanized and fragmented kind of perception, peculiar to modern capitalism. These writers also argued, co-
vertly, that this standardization and lifelessness were particular to
feminine spectacle. The commodity image did have a particular relation to the feminine, and it had contradictory effects. When women
constituted themselves as spectacles indebted to the capitalist scopic
economy they risked being commodified and reduced to object status.
However, the commodity image also had subjective effects, rendering
the modern appearing woman a consumerist subject position.

The motifs of mechanization, feminine spectacle, and lifelessness
evident in the Berlei advertisement above were linked in Siegfried
Kracauer's influential essays "The Mass Ornament" (1927) and "Girls

BEAUTY HONORS BEAUTY.—Madge Miller, of the Ziegfeld Follies, New York, was adjudged Queen of the Beaches. Sixteen of the Tiller Girls, a touring English party, visited Brighton Beach to pay homage. The queen is at the head of the swarm.
—Kadel and Herbert photo.

FIG. 4.5. Photograph of the Tiller Girls, a dancing troupe, reprinted from *Sun News-Pictorial,* 4 November 1922. Courtesy of the State Library of Victoria.

and Crisis" (1931).[78] Kracauer wrote about the Tiller Girls, an American dancing troupe that toured Europe, pictured in figure 4.5, in order to demonstrate the streamlining and rationalizing of perception under capitalism. He argued that capitalist modes of perception could distract people from "the intransigence of the capitalist rationale to reason,"[79] masking "disintegration" rather than alerting overburdened workers to "their own way of life."[80] The mass spectacle, or "mass ornament," as he called it, displayed how rationalized, exploitative labor relations had infiltrated modes of representation and perception: "the hands of the factory correspond to the legs of the Tiller Girls."[81] However, this mass ornament simultaneously disabled any critical response to such imagery and exploitation. In "Girls and Crisis," this correspondence between body parts and working tools reflected the fragmentation of the industrialized body through the atomized tasks of the Fordist conveyor belt. Kracauer wrote,

> When they formed an undulating snake, they radiantly illustrated the virtues of the conveyor belt; when they tapped their feet in fast tempo, it sounded like business, business; when they kicked their legs with mathematic precision, they joyously affirmed the progress of rationalization; and when they kept repeating the same movements without ever interrupting their routine, one envisioned an uninterrupted chain of autos

gliding from the factories into the world, and believed that the blessings
of prosperity had no end.[82]

Kracauer's assemblage of girls' bodies into components representing
the Fordist division of labor recalls Kuleshov and the techniques of
cinematography that spliced the feminine body into fetishized zones
and purely manufactured, assembled unities. It also resonates with the
assembled, mass-produced body parts of the Mannequin.

In this correlation of women, technology, and mass production,
Kracauer relied on the woman-object's mechanicalness and lifelessness to represent his disapproval of capitalist perceptual and representational modes. Kracauer characterized the fragmented legs of the Tiller Girls as "the abstract signs of their bodies" to claim that when
reason does not permeate and allow critical appraisal of the mass ornament, the capitalist design which produced such spectacles can then
"expunge life from the figures," whose "patterns are mute," as this
uncritical and weak rationale "uses abstract signs to portray life itself."[83] Women who were constituted as spectacles sacrificed something akin to language and life-essence to the capitalist design. As
other theorists have noted, the feminine is crucial to Kracauer's de-
nunciation of uncritical capitalist perception.[84] Petro discerns in Kracauer's thinking "a correspondence between the untrustworthiness of
the image and the vulnerability of the mass cultural spectator, since
both run the risks he associates with femininity—the risks of passivity,
uniformity, and uncritical consumption."[85] The use of the mute, inanimate Mannequin during the 1920s as an "abstract sign" for the
uncritical, consuming woman, enthralled by the commodity spectacle,
would tend to confirm this analysis. However, the Mannequin was
also persistently characterized as life-like, and her performative animation as a modern subject required that, like the Tiller Girls, she
become a spectacle. It is this characterization as life-like that invites
an analysis of the subjective effects of the commodity image.

The feminine *as spectacle*, and the affinity of the woman-object
with not only capitalist exchange but the commodity image, enable
Kracauer to equate mass spectacle with expunged life, life replaced by
"abstract signs."[86] But I would counter this equation by arguing that
capitalist modes of representation were effected through the operation
of commodity aesthetics and these modes of perception inaugurated
the production of a consumerist subjectivity. Commodity aesthetics
helped to recast the relationship between representation and subjectivity.

Kracauer is correct that capitalism alters perception. New manufacturing and advertising conditions obscured the labor relations under which commodities were produced, establishing the dominance of the commodity fetish.[87] Jean Baudrillard describes consumer society as fetishistic insofar as commodity objects exercise their fascination at the level of the sign.[88] The fact that it is not the material Mannequin which is sold, but rather its image, illustrates this visual abstraction of the commodity object to sign through the processes of the commodity fetish. It demonstrates the shift in the practice of looking into having, by which the value of the commodity is located at the level of its signification rather than its existence as a material product. This process has been described by Wolfgang Fritz Haug as "commodity aesthetics":

> It designates a complex which springs from the commodity form of the products and which is functionally determined by exchange value—a complex of material phenomena and of the sensual subject-object relations conditioned by these phenomena. The analysis of these relations reveals the subjective element in the political economy of capitalism insofar as subjectivity is at once a result and prerequisite of its functioning.[89]

The shift of the commodity object into the realm of language and signification charted directions for the consumption of meaning itself. Fredric Jameson argues that consumption involves not so much "the thing itself [as] its abstract idea capable of libidinal investments ingeniously arrayed for us by advertising."[90] In the 1920s advertising illustrations began to be dominated by people rather than products. The use of highly individualized imagery in advertising made consumption requisite to creating and maintaining a sense of place and legitimacy to modernity.[91] Lauren Langman describes the importance of the commodified image in naturalizing this process: "Everyday life has been transformed into an extension of consumer capitalism and the person rendered a consumer or spectator in whom the commodified meanings, the symbolic and affective values embedded in the sign system, have been interiorized as representations of reality."[92] With the extension of advertising into subjectivity, the techniques of the self in everyday life became mediated by new commodity forms, and the practice of the modern self characterized by consumer preferences.

Consumerist subjectivity grew out of a major historical shift in the social construction of vision. For Felski, modern commodity culture was the context in "which mass-produced signs, objects, and commodities constitute increasingly significant yet unstable markers of subjectivity and social status."[93] Commodity objects had extended their value into the realm of subjectivity. American sales writing did this knowingly, as it shifted "from the 'factory viewpoint' to concern with 'the mental processes of the consumer', from 'the objective to the subjective.' "[94] The "Americanisation" of the Australian advertising industry in the 1920s created a similar individualism in consumption through an emphasis on interpersonal relations. Here the " 'massified' individual beset by anxiety over his/her youth, sexual desirability, marital relations and social acceptability" overcomes feelings of inadequacy—often configured as a lack of place within modernity—through consuming.[95] Insofar as the people dominating these advertisements had to convey the meaning of a product visually—even if it was mouthwash—their success as modern consumers was communicated through the way they appeared, that is, whether they constituted appropriate spectacles to the public eye. Appropriateness came to be encoded by increasingly homogenized images which enforced normative appearances according to gendered, sexual, and colonial prescriptions.

The shift in value from commodity product to commodity sign created the optimum conditions for the pre-eminence of the scopic in this production of the consuming subject. Cultural theorist Guy Debord writes that "[t]he spectacle is *capital* accumulated to the point where it becomes image." He claims the modern spectacle is capitalism's "own peculiar décor."[96] However, Debord seems to have missed that the motifs in this décor are repetitively gendered, and that the woman-object so saturates its designs as to seem a pointed reminder of the traditional status of women as objects of exchange. Like Kracauer, Debord does not consider the implications of occupying the space of the capitalist spectacle, of women entering themselves into this visual economy and thereby asserting their modern worth. As the commodity spectacle became increasingly feminized within the new conventions of commodity display, women's object status was consolidated. However, if women consumers were being interpellated into these conventions of display, the fluid, unpredictable, and subversive potential of subject status was made available.

The replica Mannequin emerged as a hyperreal feminine commodity spectacle which demonstrated the shift in value from commodity object to commodity image. The modern feminine subject was produced not only through consuming, but also through the impact of consumer choices on her production as an appearing woman. The

Mannequin became a head-to-toe replica of woman, not only to look better to consumers, but to model how women might look as successful modern subjects. The Mannequin demonstrated that modern women became appearing women primarily through their interpellation into a consumerist subjectivity marked by the pre-eminence of women as spectacle.

The Mannequin invites us, as does cultural theorist Meaghan Morris, to see a shopping center as "a good place to begin to consider women's 'cultural production' of modernity."[97] For while women have been paradigmatically aligned with consumption, and men with production, commodity culture does nevertheless invite women to produce their modern selves through techniques of appearing. The iconization of the Mannequin invited women into new viewing positions within culture, and this self-reflexivity helped to produce their subjectivities as consumers. It was a commodity spectacle that offered to help women access the modern, and instructed them that the terms of this access were within the visual register.[98] Through encapsulating the newly forged relation between commodity aesthetics and consumerist subjectivity, the Mannequin demonstrated the intersubjective potential of new visual forms. It helped to produce a consuming subject by elevating the spectacle to a site available for occupation by women.

The exact nature of techniques of appearing, and their involvement in plays and ploys of power, are yet to be described. The visual scene created by beauty culture and the emergence of the Beauty Contestant are rich resources with which to explore the inception and dissemination of techniques of appearing. But modern notions of feminine beauty also proved to be implicated in the colonial oppressions enacted by race relations. If the Mannequin pointed to the incursions of the commodity spectacle into consumerist subjectivity, the Mannequin as ideal also pointed to the exclusions on which this rested—of women who were not white, young, and slender. When they constituted themselves as commodified spectacles that were indebted to the capitalist visual economy, modern women were restricted to delimited types. The modern appearing woman proved to be a subject position with restricted access.

Part II

Modern Appearing Women

Chapter 5

The Beauty Contestant in the Photographic Scene

In 1922 a new tabloid, the *Sun News-Pictorial*, printed the photograph and measurements of the winner of a San Francisco "most perfect figure" competition. The *Sun* asked its women readers, "Can You Beat It?" Taking up the challenge, Dorothy Woolley contested the San Francisco winner. Woolley, a physical culturist, measured up almost exactly with "the most perfect woman," and outdid her by half an inch "to the good" in the bust.[1] This unofficial competition was joined by five other young women who sent in their measurements with photographs of themselves clad in bathing suits.[2] They were among thousands of young women who believed they compared well with popular representations of idealized feminine beauty. They sent their photographs in to the plethora of beauty competitions conducted in the 1920s by Australian regional and metropolitan newspapers. The Mildura *Sunraysia Daily*, the Sydney *Evening News*, the Melbourne *Herald*, and the *Sun News-Pictorial* all conducted beauty contests in their pages in the 1920s. This craze for photographed, competitive beauty instituted a more proximate gaze, and beauty culture would both foster and profit from this gaze by instructing women in new techniques of appearing: self-scrutiny and comparison to idealized beauty.

The photographic portrait, its use in print media, and its effects on commodified beauty culture altered the meanings of feminine beauty. This proximate gaze magnified the importance of a flawless face and a body that correctly measured up. Criticism of the new importance young women attached to their visual appeal was countered by naturalizing their attachment with jingoistic rhetoric. But the way in which the celebrity beauty was said to represent the nation led to the exclusion of some women from the modern scene on the bases of age, body type, and race. Feminine visibility was increasingly constructed around restrictive ideals of beauty.

The Beauty Contestant, even if not self-nominating, was required to be complicit in her recognition and definition as beautiful. Young women were instructed through the mass marketing of beauty products to look in the mirror and closely consider how they were seen and, on the basis of that consideration, submit themselves to a gaze they knew was public. Beauty Contestants had to have faith that their self-perception was accurate and could be transmitted through mechanically reproduced images. They were required to recognize and participate in modern definitions of feminine beauty. Self-scrutiny and comparison to an ideal were the techniques of appearing that became the measure of the Modern Woman, and these techniques were formalized by the beauty competition and compelled by commodified beauty culture, which sold an expanding range of products, from blackhead removers to corsets. The imperative that they appear beautifully required young women to take the visible self as constituting the real meaning of self.

Beauty prowess afforded modern women the look of recognition. Beautiful women were welcomed into the visual scene created by beauty culture, and esteemed within the anonymous and chance scopic encounters that characterized the metropolitan scene. In a 1925 advertisement for Palmolive soap, a group of men in black ties gaze at a passing young woman, whose eyes are modestly averted. It is captioned, "Who Is She? They Want to Know."[3] The question was answered in the print beauty competitions that emerged during the 1920s, through the obliging evidence of the photographic portrait. The celebrity beauty put a name to the face of the anonymous and newly visible Modern Woman.

Appearing beautifully afforded women public recognition and

Keep your skin soft and smooth all through winter

YOU love Winter ... but no woman loves the pinching and coarsening of her skin, the harsh, drawn feeling suffered by her face when chilled by the buffeting of a cutting westerly.

To counteract the ill effects of winter winds it is necessary to keep the skin as healthy as possible; to free the minute pores and glands of clogging impurities of dust, powder, and natural oil secretions, so that they may function properly. Cold winds may sting but cannot harm a skin wisely cared for and properly cleansed and nourished.

Cold creams alone cannot be depended on to do this cleansing and nourishing—nor can ordinary soaps. A soap is needed rich in natural oils; a healing, soothing cleanser that you may massage thoroughly into your skin with utmost safety.

Use Palmolive.

Use it because it contains the bland and beneficial oils of the palm and the olive, known and highly prized as beautifying cleansers by the women of Ancient Egypt. These natural oils are so efficient and so pleasant in themselves that *Palmolive* Soap does not require to be medicated nor artificially perfumed or colored.

Palmolive penetrates. Gently but certainly it reaches the minutest pores, cleansing and freeing them from all impurities that impede the natural healthy action of the skin.

How to use it.

Work up a soft, creamy lather with Palmolive Soap and pleasantly warm water; massage it, gently but thoroughly with the finger tips into your skin, then rinse with clear warm water and finish with a dash of cold.

Your skin is now not only perfectly cleansed but soothed and well able to withstand the harshness of Winter weather. If exceptionally sensitive it will benefit by an application of Palmolive Cold Cream before exposure to the cold, and powder is harmless when dusted upon a complexion so perfectly prepared.

Palm and Olive Oils were the highly prized cosmetics of the women of Ancient Egypt who found them of inestimable value in the preservation of their beauty. To-day these valuable oils are far more potent than in their earlier crude form and easier of application for, scientifically blended, they form the principal content of a fragrant cake of *Palmolive Soap*.

Prove also the Perfection of

Palmolive Cold Cream; Palmolive Vanishing Cream; "Violet of the Nile" and "Egyptian Rose" Talcums; "Palmole" Face Powder; Palmolive Face Powder; Palmolive Rouge; Palmolive Shampoo.

PALMOLIVE SOAP

Sells everywhere at 1/3 per cake

The *quest size cake of Palmolive Soap will be sent post free, on request, by the Palmolive Company (Australasia) Limited, Broughton House, Clarence Street, Sydney.*

Fig. 5.1. Advertisement for Palmolive, reprinted from *Bulletin*, 15 June 1922. Courtesy of the State Library of Victoria.

sometimes celebrity. While the captured gaze of passing men was a common trope in the advertising of beauty aids during the 1920s, as in the Palmolive advertisement shown in figure 5.1, the conventions of celebrity already at play in modern visual technologies—particularly photojournalism—bestowed the honor of beauty on individual women. "Who Is She?" was the very question first put by the Sydney *Evening News* in April 1922, when it announced its quest for the most beautiful woman in New South Wales.[4] It was as though beauty had now to fulfill the promises of commodity goods—of notice, distinction, recognition, and public acclaim. Beauty also became the way to investigate the vexed question of the Modern Woman: "Who is she?" meant also "what is her relation to her image; what can her image say about her?"

I have argued that the gender asymmetry of "looks" became a key means of assigning and articulating sexual difference in modernity. The print beauty competitions of the early 1920s were significant partly because of the extent to which women actively participated, by appearing within them. Beauty contestants devised techniques to appear attractively within the photographic medium, aided by commodified beauty culture. More broadly, they adhered to definitions of beauty altered by the new conditions of feminine visibility. It is their participation, both in beauty competitions and in commodified beauty culture, that suggests that in the modern perceptual field women's visibility was not just an assignation of sexual difference but, through techniques of appearing, became a practice in the performative enactment of modern feminine subjectivity.

Commodified beauty culture promised self-mastery and transformation through the intervention of beauty aids. It made this promise within the expansion of discourses that constructed techniques of appearing as integral to definitions of the Modern Woman. It implicated the operation of commodity aesthetics in the production of the modern appearing woman specifically through these techniques of appearing. If commodity culture's logic of display produced a feminine consumerist subjectivity, commodified beauty culture—dealing as it did in women's visibility—instructed the consuming woman in the techniques of appearing she should employ in her quest to make herself in the image of the idealized celebrity beauty.

Duty to Beauty

In April and May 1922, the Sydney *Evening News* invited its women readers to send in their photographs to be judged by a panel appointed by the newspaper. It was the first Australian newspaper in the 1920s to adopt the beauty competition as a means to expand its readership. It selected as winner a stage actress, Eve Gray, from more than two thousand entrants. Taking the cue, the Melbourne *Herald* ran its own competition beginning in May 1922, asking, "Can a Victorian girl be found to match her?"[5] The *Herald* selected Betty Tyrrell in August, from 3,300 entrants. From July to October 1922, the *Illustrated Tasmanian Mail* also conducted a beauty competition, seeking, like its competitors, to discover the representative beauty of its state. It judged Gladys Gard to be the rightful holder of that title. These competitions were followed in 1926 by the *Daily Guardian*'s quest for Miss Australia. The following year the Miss Australia competition was run by *Smith's Weekly* and Union Theatres.

Prior to the rash of popular print beauty competitions in the 1920s, the beauty contest had generally been run as a local fundraiser for charity. The winner was the young woman in the district who was able, or whose committee was able, to win the most votes. The smaller Mildura Grand Carnival 1923 beauty contest in northwest Victoria ran along these lines. It took place after the larger state newspapers had searched for and announced their representative beauties. But it combined some of the older stipulations of popularity and district charity fundraising with the newer ideals of photographed beauty. It judged girls who had been selected by eight district committees. Voters had to make penny contributions and the £3,200 raised was divided between district hospitals. The entrants had to be nominated by "a lady or gentleman," rather than themselves, and their "bust photograph" (suggesting a sense of three dimensions in fact lost) sent to the *Sunraysia Daily*. While this competition was organized in conjunction with the local carnival, its competitors submitted their photographs to the local newspaper, which followed the lead of the bigger state papers by adopting an administrative role.

The *Sunraysia* competition drew on the tradition of crowning a Queen at local festivals, including occasional political anniversaries. Such festivals invoked the allegorical functions of feminine spectacle (for instance, in the character of Britannia) and had their precedents in medieval pageantry.[6] In her history of the Miss Australia competitions, Judith Smart sees the influence of these earlier uses of feminine spectacle. She writes, "for all the nineteenth-century prohibitions on women displaying themselves in public, this highly ritualized, idealized and decorous use of the female form precluded protest."[7]

Young women had long been competing against each other in a variety of activities, including elocution, singing, dancing, and calisthenics. An earlier national beauty contest had been organized by the *Lone Hand,* running from November 1907 until February 1909.[8] The newspaper had worked with state papers to select girls who then competed to be a national winner.[9] A Victorian, Alice Buckridge, won this competition and her photograph was submitted to the *Chicago Tribune*, which announced an American winner chosen from 200,000 submitted photographs. The Australian and American beauties were submitted to an international competition for "supremacy of beauty" run through national papers.[10] International communication through print media made possible this expansion of ideas about national beauty. It essentialized national characteristics in looking for definitions of racialized beauty, while it struck non-Western women off the global register of comparative beauty. The beauty of these women tended to be cast as fetishized and unassimilable: a curiosity.

During the 1920s, the beauty competition began to combine competition and popularity with commodified notions of beauty as a democratized achievement, available to all women. In an era in which "every" woman had a claim, indeed a "birth right" and a "duty to beauty," the competition inspired the "most cheering of modern discoveries"—that "hopeless plainness" was a thing of the past.[11] It reinforced the claims of commodified beauty culture: comparing oneself and measuring up to an ideal of feminine beauty through diligent self-scrutiny were indispensable techniques in the quest to become a truly modern beauty. The large-scale promotion of both the competitions and beauty aids persistently guided women toward the correct techniques of appearing.

The shift from district fundraisers at social events to competitions run by state and national newspapers, which offered monetary prizes and celebrity status to the winner, could not have taken place without the by-now-commonplace photographic portrait. Because initial judgments were now based upon this visual fragment, beauty had to be redefined as evident in visual and measurable qualities, such as facial proportions, bodily measurements, the shape of the head, and its placement on the shoulders. Notably, "coloring" became less important since the pictures were in black and white. This worked to downplay cultural difference but also to confirm whiteness as an invisible category, so much so that the term "coloring" had no application beyond the variety of white women's hair and complexion, a diversity that was not overtly racialized. Women "of color" were not present in the competitions and thus the notion of "coloring" worked to keep the requirement of racial sameness invisible. Expression, however, remained important to the lingering ideal of beauty as the manifestation of the inner self and feminine virtue. The face became a meaningful zone, a complex interplay of planes, angles, form, shape, and expression. But in each case, once the competitors had been initially screened, they were asked to present themselves to the judges in the flesh, to live up to their image and to demonstrate that the modern image could be accurate to an ideal as intangible as feminine beauty.

The 1920s Beauty Contestant, as she appeared within the conditions of commodified beauty culture and through the pictorial print media, was marked by many of the meanings of visibility that accrued to other types of the modern appearing woman: to the Screen Star as celebrity and reproduced image, the City Girl as public spectacle, and the Mannequin as commodity sign. The Beauty Contestant's linkage to the Screen Star was reinforced by competitions for the most beautiful Screen Type and Screen Star double, and best figure competitions were run as publicity stunts by major picture palaces.[12] Competition winners were often filmed and offered opportunities in film studios and fashion houses.[13] Beryl Mills, who in 1926 became the first Miss Australia, allegedly earned higher sums than the state premier when she toured Union picture theaters in New South Wales to capacity audiences, with record crowds turned away. She had already toured the United States as a "splendid sterling advertisement" for Australian girlhood. The Union theaters tour was a phenomenal success, with showmen and exhibitors declaring it had "smashed all the house records."[14] The following year, the Miss Australia competition was jointly run by *Smith's Weekly*, the *Daily Guardian*, Australasian Film Ltd., and Union Theatres,[15] who rushed to secure rights as though they were distributing the latest film vehicle of a leading Screen Star. By this time, newspapers had a clear idea of the lucrative potential of the celebrity beauty.

Comparing oneself with ideal feminine beauty was construed as part of modernity's adventure of romantic heterosexual love. The Beauty Contestant was, to some extent, on the (marriage) market; she put images of herself to work to localize herself in the heterosexual modern scene. A Parisian competition for the longest kiss[16] was a logical extension of the implicit heteronormality of the competitions, whose winners were reported to be inundated with marriage proposals. During its competition, the *Illustrated Tasmanian Mail* ran a short story about a young woman in love with a wealthy pastoralist who promised to marry the winner of the competition. She was transformed by a French beauty parlor and photographed to advantage, becoming a mystery entrant. She came second and won his love, as the woman placed first refused his offer. He was bewitched by her when he met her.[17] Hopeful suitors put aside the persistent doubt expressed about the accuracy of the photographic portraits and pinned their hopes on the images. Even if "the enchantment of female loveliness" was "expressed in the cold prosaic selling of a daily newspaper," and even if "the most ardent Cyrano cannot woo a photograph," the conventions of visual possession fostered by the commodity image and fascination with the beauty celebrity could override such dampenings of these "roseat visions of romance."[18] Popular advocates of health and beauty, such as Annette Kellerman, believed the imperative to modern beauty had eugenic as well as romantic dimensions: "man must have feminine beauty as a flower must have water." Women were entitled to beauty as insurance against desertion and infidelity. In the heterosexual modern scene, beauty was a "right" and the charges of vanity against "pride in beauty of body" were therefore an "immorality," a sin against the modern dictums of romance and health.[19]

Insofar as winners could become Screen Stars (Clara Bow), physical culturists (Annette Kellerman and Dorothy Woolley), or national ambassadors (Beryll Mills), the Beauty Contestant was a career woman. Indeed, "professional beauty" was said to have become "the most lucrative career opening to woman today."[20] However, as a figure seeking to reach the pinnacle of 1920s beauty culture—with its doctrine of self-surveillance, its scientific beauty treatments and techniques—the Beauty Contestant still had to appear to the public as a figure who disavowed these techniques of appearing. Her self-promotion was condemned as the greatest malfeasance; she was accused of succumbing to vanity, and worse, of being "a seeker of publicity."

Seekers of Publicity

There are probably very few entrants for beauty competitions who are not either vain, vulgar or immodest. Therefore they cannot be beautiful in the true sense of the word. At best they can lay claim to the prettiness of the wooden, soulless, brainless mannequins in the windows of drapery shops.[21]

This 1926 correspondent to Melbourne's *Argus* newspaper would no doubt have been very displeased to be advised that by writing his letter to a newspaper he aspired to participate just as Beauty Contestants did when they sent their pictures in, hoping, like him, to be published. This reader complicity in the textual production of print media was a hallmark of the modern periodical and its quest to establish a community of readers, itself a factor that made newspapers fertile ground for the mushrooming of beauty competitions in the 1920s. With the first appearance of the popular periodical form in London in 1691, with the publication of the *Athenian Mercury*, the preconditions for the eruption of beauty competitions in print media were in place. The epistolary periodical sought to figure its audience within its text through publishing its correspondence. Reader participation was a calculated appeal to a community of readers who turned to the periodical to confirm a sense of continuity "between readers' lives and the medium of print, between extra-textual experience and textual expression." Such programs of audience building were directed particularly at middle-class women, whose literacy was increasing throughout the nineteenth century and who were perceived to have leisure time that could be spent reading. Their personal correspondence created a "public intimacy" and "permitted an unprecedented opening up of the mechanisms of print to women's concerns and self-representations."[22] In responding to invitations in the 1920s to send their photographed portraits to newspapers for publication and judgment—hundreds of thousands of women across the Western world and tens of thousands in Australia did so—women broke with traditions of humility, modesty, and reserve. The contests were a new pictorial mode of reader participation, which made particular appeals to women, in which their self-representation contributed to their textual and cultural presence. The community of readers they belonged to might be as narrowly regional as *Sunraysia*'s Mildura, but through transnational print media syndication their readerly horizons encompassed the globe. Readers' participation as beauty contestants was symptomatic of the new agency that women assigned to their visibility as a means of access to modern public life. But despite these appeals to women's desire for public presence, entrants were often marginalized; the portraits submitted to the Melbourne *Herald* newspaper competition, for instance, were published on the page titled "Woman's World."

Portraits were submitted in the context of increasing use of fashion photography. In fashion photography, "the image is not simply something we 'wear'. The mass circulation of photographic images emphasizes our awareness of self-image, and establishes a relationship between the particular and the typical."[23] In seeking to get their photographs published in newspapers, young women established a relationship between themselves as particular, individual women and the typical woman, who had become the representative beauty. Women's "extra-textual" potential was wrought from an awareness that they could be considered beautiful if they complied with the directives of commodified beauty culture. They had to be able to appraise themselves, and image themselves as textual. And they had to willingly fly in the face of the views represented by the above correspondent and adopt the new meanings of beauty as surface effect rather than inner virtue. The Beauty Contestant had to be willing to appear alongside the Mannequin and the Screen Star as reproduced image, typifying a cultural ideal. Increasingly, representing the prevailing ideal became the *raison d'être* of feminine representation.

During the 1920s, print media invented new visual formats as newspapers adapted advertising's use of banner headlines and spacious layouts. The rotary press had been established in the 1890s as the basic technology for mass-circulation dailies, and the *Illustrated Australian News* first used the half-tone block for reproducing photographs in 1889.[24] The *Australian Home Journal* occasionally used color front pages from 1919.[25] Although the 1920s saw the demise of five labor metropolitan dailies, in 1924 the *Australian Advertisers' Manual and Newspaper Directory* told advertisers that "[p]ractically half of the inhabitants can be reached through the principal metropolitan newspapers."[26] Australian newspaper and magazine ownership became concentrated during this period in the hands of three major companies as newspaper empires competed for circulation.[27] *Smith's Weekly* gained two hundred thousand subscriptions from the 1926 Miss Australia competition.[28] The illustrated mass-circulation dailies relied on the Beauty Contestant and Bathing Beauty to catch readers' eyes, using syndicated images of winners of beauty competitions from around the world, including Romania, Paris, Rome, India, and New York.[29] Some of these competitions judged fragmented parts of the body and face, such as the eyebrows,[30] thus alerting women that these were beauty features that could be subject to special treatment and modification. They also alerted women to the fact that the camera instituted a highly proximate gaze, which made comparison to idealized beauty routine. It was one thing to be beautiful in the common acceptance of the term—in the modern scene it was more important to be photogenic.

The Necessity for Closer Scrutiny

To further encourage reader participation, all of the print beauty competitions invited readers to guess the winners, promising cash prizes. While none of the other beauty competitions were correctly predicted by their readers, despite hundreds of thousands of forecasts, the Tasmanian winners in 1922 were guessed in their correct order by a C. M. Deegan. Deegan wrote a lengthy explanation of the "methodology," "formulae," and "guiding principles" he had used in arriving at his result. It is a document replete with modernity's perceptual relations: the regulated, compartmentalized, classifying gaze wanting to scrutinize the reproduced feminine spectacle to gather clues about the identity of the Modern Woman and to understand the meaning of her publicized visibility. Deegan readily employed the imperatives of comparison to an ideal in his undertaking, but claimed his "task" was reduced to a minimum, "thanks to the camera." Unlike Paris, the mythical, original adjudicator of beauty, Deegan claimed the *Tasmanian Mail* "selectors" only had, "chiefly, to compare the symmetry of features as depicted by the camera; Paris had not only to select the most beautiful of countenances but to appraise the flashes of a sparkling eye, the charms of a smile, the blushes of modesty, and many other incommensurable assets."[31]

Photography reduced the perception of beauty to a purely ocular experience, making it, Deegan suggested, subject to more objective, scientific appraisal. Whereas Paris might have been swayed by the deliberately seductive wiles of his vying beauties, the modern adjudicator of feminine beauty could look with remote, detached objectivity. And yet always of concern in the print competitions was how representative of beauty the mechanically reproduced image could be. How was a man like Deegan to reconcile the fact that these modern girls quite literally posed themselves as beauties? And how to reconcile the traditional ideal of beauty as the outward effect of inner virtue, and most certainly not an affectation for the camera?

To compensate for the lack of first-hand contact with the beauty contestants, Deegan worked meticulously and formulaically. He snipped out the competitors' photos and "classified them according to type" of beauty—the Madonna cast, the intellectual, the artistic, and "other pronounced types." Thus he could make comparisons between types and within groups of types, "arranging the order of merit in each class" and bringing his "classification up to date" with each issue. He was left to guess at complexion, "wealth of hair, and the figures likely to be associated with the various types of countenance." But he subjected each face to all the minute examination of the close-in shot of a Screen Star. This scrutinizing, comparative gaze would become central to the promotion of beauty products and the directives beauty culture gave women for techniques of appearing. Deegan wrote,

> As a general principle I look, in any type of face, for the nose (whether it be of Grecian, Roman or retrousse order) to be the most commanding feature. It should be sufficiently long and strong to attract attention without claiming too much notice. I look for eyes to be large, set at right angles with the nose, and prominent without being bulged out; I look for

a forehead varying according to type, of moderate width and height; and a mouth curved slightly upwards at the corners, of medium size, with lips of the mediumly thin rather than the "mulatto" pattern. A chin with a short sharp turn at the end, and of about the same prominence as the eyes.[32]

Deegan's methodological principles demonstrate some of the themes that recurred in popular discourses as they reacted to and produced the meanings of modern feminine beauty. He expected beauty to be both nationally representative and evidence of moral character. He was ambivalent about the potential for women's beauty to command attention, and what it might mean if women used their beauty to claim "too much notice." He deliberated over facial charm by fragmenting and isolating features, then examining them in relation to one another, with predetermined specifications for the best feature both in context as well as standing, as it were, on its own merits. He measured a feature's physical dimensions to determine its worth. He deployed racially specific language—"mulatto" lips—to remind the reader that the boundaries around the category "beauty" were racially determined, and conversely that beauty was racially representative. And finally, Deegan presided over the measurement, classification, and ranking of women's beauty with a numbing kind of conceit as a spectator, with women positioned as the spectacles he judged.

"Typing" was again central to the appraisal of modern beauty. Types reflected eugenic visual taxonomies and also indicated what exactly could be known of women from their appearing as reproduced image. In the 1922 *Herald* selection process, one young woman was chosen purely because she expressed "a decided type."[33] Eve Gray, shown in figure 5.2 (*right*), was said to be the "Dolly" or "Venus" type, as distinct from Betty Tyrrell, also shown (*left*), who embodied the "Madonna type" (which one reader believed expressed "the highest womanly virtues").[34] Such a classification was thought to enable "analysis" beyond the intuitive glance of first impression (or perhaps of urban space). Features which belonged to "clashing types[,] however perfect in themselves, must spoil the ensemble." Letters to the *Herald* repeatedly fragmented women's visual "assets."[35] "Old Bloke" averred that only 10 percent of a woman's beauty—features—could be discerned from a photograph. He allotted 30 percent to skin and hair, 20 percent to eyes, 20 percent to deportment and a "well-proportioned body," and 20 percent to general expression.[36] The shift in emphasis from popularity to photography redefined beauty as objectively measurable and universally perceivable. And yet so much doubt and qualification was expressed in the discussion surrounding

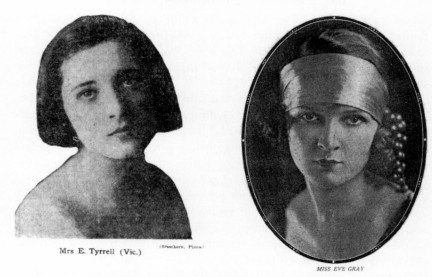

Mrs E. Tyrrell (Vic.)

MISS EVE GRAY

FIG. 5.2. Photographs of Mrs. E. (Betty) Tyrrell and Miss Eve Gray, reprinted from *The Herald*, 17 August 1922. Courtesy of the State Library of Victoria.

the print beauty competition that it would seem reproduced feminine spectacle was doubly dubious—neither the veracity of the reproduced image nor the significance accorded to feminine spectacle was certain.

When Deegan reported that his task was "reduced" by the camera, he suggested that as a purely visual, surface effect feminine beauty had become easier to judge. In fact, precisely because it was photographed, this modernized beauty enabled a closer, more scrutinizing gaze while raising questions about whether these girls merely "posed" as beauties, using artificial aids and trick photography. This uncertainty about the veracity of the reproduced image recurred throughout reports of the print competitions:

> The camera frequently flatters the lady whose complexion, eyebrows, ruby lips and sparkling "bella donna" eyes come from the nearest beauty parlours. In real life, while paint and powder, rouge and carmine, may attract and deceive in the glare of artificial light, the "made up girl" does not stand the test of daylight. The only kind of beauty which will stand all tests is that which nature bestows on those enjoying perfect health.[37]

The *Evening News* asked some entrants to attend studios at their own expense and have another portrait taken, because of "the necessity for closer scrutiny."[38] Eve Gray was herself subject to such scrutiny as winner when, during an interview, she was measured against the wall in front of the reporter. Beauty had to be objectively proven as a literal measure against the potential deception of the reproduced feminine spectacle.

The photograph was said to "truthfully indicate the eye satisfying neck contour, the firm clean modelling of nose and chin, the tender expressiveness of the mouth and brilliance of the fine eyes."[39] Yet in all the competitions, the final face-to-face encounter with the judges was counted on to reveal beauty features such as "tender winsomeness" and eyes that were "pools of passion and compassion never yet plumbed." These traits could not be reproduced mechanically, disadvantaging those young women whose expression might "have been lost in the making and printing of the block."[40] The *Herald* closely reported the judging process, conducted by artists it had appointed, and women qualified for initial selection on the strength of their portraits alone. Discussion centered on the limits of photographs. Many entrants were "spoiled" by their images, or could not be judged because of obscuring hats or poor light. One correspondent expressed disquiet about the concentration on face, and warned of "thick ankles" and "indifferent figures" lurking beneath "bewitching features."[41] In addition, the judges sought to read qualities of not only "physical beauty" but "spiritual charm" from reproduced images, drawing on types of beauty in literature—such as Conrad's "strange, tense, semi-mystical" beauty. Images were "examined" with "dissecting knives"[42] by artists who, while said to be expert in judging from images, nevertheless maintained that the competition had not rendered the women images and believed the photographs able to show the inner traits of character. Judith Smart found that in the Miss Australia contest "[t]he judges—artists, sculptors and doctors deemed to be scientific experts in the fields of aesthetics or the body's physiology—were selected because their gaze was necessarily elevated above the merely sexual."[43]

Their objective gaze, however, had to initially overcome their ambivalence toward modern visual technologies. They were ambivalent not just about print media beauty competitions, but about the photograph itself. Susan Sontag writes that "it is not reality that photographs make immediately accessible, but images." She adds that "to possess the world in the form of images is, precisely, to reexperience the unreality and remoteness of the real."[44] The "real" was staged in studios from the time of the first daguerreotype portraits. The first such studio in Australia opened on the roof of Sydney's Royal Hotel on 12 December 1842. Sitting was reported as a ritual of execution that included "decapitation." The early visual technologies, photographic and cinematic, were often perceived as stealing life essence, even beauty.[45] Women fared particularly badly in the reproduction process. Their exposure when lit by sunlight was unflattering, leading one reporter to remark, "from some specimens we have seen of photographic likenesses of ladies of our acquaintance, we were almost disposed to think the sun had a down on the whole sex." By the 1920s, however, the photographic reproduction of modern feminine beauty did not dispel the idea that "the camera cannot help but reveal faces as social masks."[46] Pose and camera angle were thus potentially procedures of masking; the *Herald* judges noted that they created anomalies and warned that "the girl who is as effective in a profile as she is in full face is a rarity."[47] Still the newspapers continued to maintain, overshadowed by mountains of photographs, that what they were judging was the beauty of young women, and not reproduced images of young women, or more simply, photographs.

As with the Screen Star and Screen-Struck Girl, the distrust of modern visual technologies centered on feminine spectacle and modern women's penchant for appearing within mechanically reproduced imagery. In the scenario of the print beauty competition, the reproduced image altered definitions of beauty, creating the need, it seemed from newspaper commentary, for community consultation. To a reader's question, "Who is eligible?" the *Sunraysia Daily* answered that "the prime qualification is beauty of the face"[48]—as far as a reproduced image could be entrusted to convey such beauty, it might have added. The paper elaborated: "the competition does not concern itself with morals, or brains or anything else, but beauty and popularity."[49] The *Herald* put it even more narrowly: "only one thing is necessary—Beauty."[50]

In Mildura in northwestern Victoria, members of the close-knit rural community were not prepared to judge from photographs alone when they were likely to know the competing girls in person, unlike the judges for the metropolitan dailies. As a gesture to local knowledge of the young women selected in their districts, the Mildura Grand Carnival Committee allowed votes for popularity and beauty to be separately registered and counted. Thus the *Sunraysia Daily* could assure readers that even a housemaid was eligible, since there are "scores of housemaids with the necessary facial charms—she merely needed to attract a committee to organise, energise, advertise."[51] This "scheme" supposedly gave the comparatively unknown woman "a chance," "if she [was] really a beauty," against girls with "thousands of friends or admirers."[52] This readmission of "popularity" into the Mildura score sheets suggests that the community balked at perceiving its contestants as images alone.

In the metropolitan dailies, popularity was expressed through the votes of readers who could judge only from the photographs. Papers may have called for reader participation in part to validate their judgments. The readers of the *Illustrated Tasmanian Mail* were invited to "test whether you have an eye for beauty" by forecasting the final order of winners as determined by a combination of the popular vote and the choices of the artist judges. The expectation that readers' choices would correlate with actual results constructed beauty as universally verifiable, its appreciation within the reach of "99.9 percent of us."[53] But as Deegan's assessments also made clear, it was often assumed that rendering beauty inanimate as reproduced image meant that it could be measured only by objective means; it was not "in the eye of the beholder." However, the fact that only Deegan, out of the hundreds of thousands of forecasters, was correct suggests that despite his assertions, ideas of beauty were not objectively provable. Rather, they intensified a subjective gaze that would, increasingly throughout the twentieth century, seek verification from face-to-face contact with celebrity beauties and ostensibly spontaneous, less "posed" imagery, such as that provided by paparazzi.

In the 1920s, print competitions found ways to validate their results. Along with the portraits, all the newspapers asked the contestants to submit their "particulars" of height, weight, measurement, and coloring. In the 1907 *Lone Hand* competition, when the field in each state had narrowed to ten, the contestants were required to present themselves to the special boards. The *Lone Hand* reported, "the camera had not borne false witness in their favour," but appearing in person added "many subjects" on which they could be judged, including "complexion, eyes and eyebrows, features in full-face and profile, hair, figure and deportment, animated expression, teeth, character of countenance, and general physique."[54]

Nonetheless, the Queensland board was reported to have lamented, "Deception, thy name is photography," as young women who had presented as "fascinating pictures" dashed the hopes of the board "on personal inspection."[55] The photographs of competitors published in the *Lone Hand* were generally not discussed in the way that photographs in the later competitions were. They were, however, laid out

The seven finalists appear before the judges on the day of the final voting. (Left to right): Miss Doris Beattie, Monica Mack, Ivy Mackay, Beryl Mills, Peggy Mount, Mascotte Ralston and Myrie Ridgway.

AUSTRALIA *in* SEARCH *of a* DAUGHTER

FIG. 5.3. Photograph of contestants' line-up, reprinted from *Home*, 2 August 1926. Courtesy of the Mitchell Library, State Library of New South Wales.

within art nouveau motifs, an aesthetic attestation of their decorativeness and status as image. Expressions stayed within the conventions of early feminine portraiture, modest, serene, and never animated.[56] Some of the women posed with veils over their heads, and only one smiled.[57] In these earlier portraits, the women made a greater effort to convey inner qualities such as virtue. Later, contestants' expressions and poses seemed calculated to appeal to the eye alone.

During the 1920s, beauty was increasingly judged with reference to the body as well as the face. The 1922 *Evening News* judging panel included the artist Thea Proctor and relied on two medical men and two medical women "to take the necessary measurements."[58] If definitions of beauty had lost "depth" because beauty was being "objectively" judged from surface effects, they nevertheless became more totalizing as they took in the entire surface of the feminine body, while the new imperative of measurement singled out particular body parts. In a competition for "Sydney's Prettiest Ankles" in 1926, entrants filled out a form requiring the circumference of the leg at the ankle, at the calf, and below the knee; the distance from kneecap to floor; and shoe size.[59] In the line-up, as shown in figure 5.3, the body was positioned to allow not only close evaluation of gradations in bodily measurement ratios, but also ready comparison between identically posed women.[60] Not coincidentally, the same imperatives for self-scrutiny and comparison against the ideal issued by the print beauty competitions emanated as well from commodified beauty culture. Beauty products lost no time in capitalizing on the close up, yet public gaze to which beauty contestants submitted.

Before the Mirror

In 1922 an article in the *Illustrated Tasmanian Mail* was entitled "What Constitutes Charm: Photographic Failures." The photographic portrait figured as a new inducement for women to avoid "detracting effects" such as shiny skin due to enlarged pores, and not to "allow such horrors as blackheads" to disfigure their photographs.[61] The gaze which could recognize beauty—whether that gaze was women's own, that of men passing in the street, or that of beauty contest judges—took its cue from the proximate, exposing camera. Scrutiny by camera, husband, friend, or passing stranger was construed as powerfully accurate about women's identities and worth. Accordingly, one was obliged to look one's best at all times. This disciplinary gaze would generate new techniques of appearing. Not surprisingly, it was a gaze encouraged and cultivated by commodified beauty culture.

The pervasiveness of advertisements, columns, and commentary on beauty products in 1920s print media indicates that women during this period were deeply implicated in the practice of beauty, and acutely responsive to the wider discourse of beauty culture.[62] Beauty instructions spoke directly to the pleasure of experiencing the self as image but were also coercive and patronizing. They construed appearing as a procedure of knowledge of the self, achieved through the surface effects of the body and a calculated regime of self-care, and by placing oneself before one's own eyes and the eyes of the public. They discursively positioned techniques of appearing as integral to the formation of the modern feminine subject—modern, precisely because self-formed through modernity's ideal of self-mastery.

Women consulted "beauty specialists," who deployed the iconography of science by dressing as nurses in clinical white and who had elaborate "methods" to perform miracles such as "build[ing] the skin tissues."[63] Women were admonished to submit to "Beauty Schedules"[64]—at 8 A.M. to immerse in parching (hot) bath water, to use special creams at 12:30 P.M. to combat the fatigue of shopping, at 4

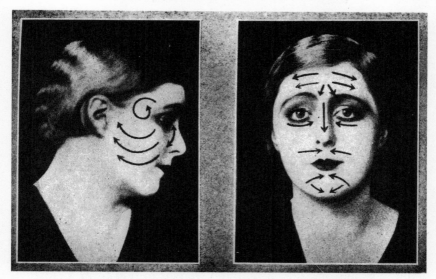

FIG. 5.4. Illustrations of massage technique from Josif Ginsburg's *Hygiene of Youth and Beauty*, Cornstalk Publishing Company, Sydney (1927). Courtesy of the National Library of Australia.

to 5 P.M. to safeguard against windburn with more creams, at 7 to 8 P.M. to finish the toilet again with creams, and to do so a last time at 10 P.M. to midnight to dissipate "that tired look."[65] They were instructed in massage procedure—effleurage (stroking), friction, and petrissage (kneading)[66]—with illustrations such as that shown in figure 5.4 in which arrows indicated movement over the face. The mouth was to be "managed" against the unsightly effects of "careless speech."[67] Blowing a feather in the air would bring "the reward of increased attractiveness."[68]

Technologies of gender, in feminist semiotician Teresa de Lauretis's thinking, can include epistemological and institutional discourses and cultural apparatuses such as cinema, which "have power to control the field of social meaning and thus produce, promote and 'implant' representations of gender."[69] De Lauretis borrows Althusser's notion of "interpellation" in order to consider this process of absorption by individuals of social representations as one of engagement at the level of the subject. What is striking about her work on technologies of gender is the resonance it has for the significatory apparatuses of modernity, and their engagement with women through a discourse that technocratized the feminine body through elaborate regimes of self-care and techniques of appearing. This has resonance with the third volume of Foucault's history of sexuality. Foucault constructs a genealogy of regimens in the care of the self from the first centuries of ancient Greek writing, saying that "[w]hat stands out in the texts of the first centuries—more than new interdictions concerning sexual acts—is the insistence on the attention that should be brought to bear on oneself; it is the modality, scope, constancy, and exactitude of the required vigilance; it is the anxiety concerning all the disturbances of the body and the mind, which must be prevented by means of an austere regimen."[70] Modern beauty culture would become such an austere regimen, preventing the anxiety of exclusion from the modern scene.

The doctrine of beauty culture—and the discourse was too systematized, too regulatory, and too directive not to be acknowledged as a doctrine—positioned techniques of appearing as techniques of modern femininity. Beyond this, it required women to transform themselves into adept and proficient technicians of gender and to emit the signs of self-mastery through their modes of appearing. Representations of women in beauty culture were "technologies of gender" in a dual sense: they engaged women at the level of their subjectivity, and they did so through appropriating the highly technocratized discourses of modernity. These images constructed gender through meanings of what it meant to be visible, to appear as a Modern Woman. Appearing was this point of "engagement" with women's subjectivities.

The Beauty Contestant symbolically evinced key markings of the modern subject—namely, attention to the self and self-modification. She also displayed the markings of modern efficiency as extended into techniques of appearing, which included being "well-groomed, soignee, alert and in all essentials young."[71] The Modern Woman knew herself through new systems of bodily accounting. In the 1920s, the entire feminine body was co-opted into new body scenes as they were imaged in beauty culture. Commodified beauty culture could greatly profit from constructing the modern feminine body as fashion-able. Modern women were told, "There is no better indicator to health than your weight; watch it carefully; regularly."[72] Woman's beauty was a sign of her health, efficiency, hygiene, line, correction, and regularity of care, all of which rested on the first principle: "study yourself."[73] Modern women were positioned "Before the Mirror,"[74] as one column was titled. From this close vantage, which simulated the close-up photographic portrait, women were advised on how to correct freckles, blackheads, double chins, and superfluous hair. Advertisements, particularly for complexion products, recurrently pictured young women before mirrors, "Face to Face—as if you were another girl."[75]

This identification with the self from the place of another precipitated the trope of transformation in advertising, in which the self could in fact become another.[76] The Modern Woman was made a "new woman" with beauty treatments, which empowered "the triumph of little Miss Ordinary" by winning "glances of wondering admiration—glances that are a homage to beauty."[77] A 1925 advertisement for Lasseter's tonic scripted "a dialogue between a young woman and her reflection," in which the reflection was not merely an image but an animated friend, "not afraid to speak her mind."[78] Awareness of being potentially subject to the critical scrutiny of another made "searching scrutiny" of oneself necessary, in order to "pass judgement on defects."[79] One advertisement for a product to remove wrinkles and blemishes pictured a woman behind a magnifying glass.[80]

Finding that one did not compare with idealized beauty amounted to being exiled from the modern scene. Sadly, "Truform" sent in his eighteen-year-old girlfriend's measurements, saying she "does not like to take part in social affairs on the plea that her figure is not what it should be for a girl of her age."[81] The *Home* would have shown little sympathy. It commended beauty competitions as part of the "frankness of the century" and a necessary "continual reproach to the imperfect sample of man and woman"—although there were no such competitions for men.[82] Women with imperfect complexions could not "hope to command real success, socially or any other way."[83] In a Kruschen Salts ad a young woman cowers in the dock before a benevolent judge. The mock-up of a newspaper report, "In The Hygiene Court of Justice," carries the headline "Girl of 19 Accused of Bad Complexion." The unbeautiful woman was deliberately careless and a malpractitioner of modern femininity, guilty of "serious neglect."[84] She was an anomaly within the contemporary visual landscape, and if she did not become "frankly intimate with the interior of salons" and have a "battalion of jars and bottles" on her dresser she "might just as well retire to the seclusion of a desert isle and let the world wag unheeding on."[85]

Kathy Peiss argues that cosmetic marketing "reshaped the relationship between appearance and feminine identity by promoting the externalization of the gendered self, a process much in tune with the tendencies of mass-culture."[86] However, because techniques of appearing were positioned as central to the enactment of the modern appearing woman, the relationship was reshaped as not so much externalized as subjectified. In this broader context, the visual signs of dereliction of duty and care crept insidiously over new body scenes as they were exposed. Bare skin meant that areas of the body, particularly legs, underarms, and backs, emerged from commodity dormancy and were rezoned as commodity-dependent.[87] Under "a merciless spotlight of attention" these new body scenes had to become "satiny-smooth in texture—youthful—exquisite."[88] They must also be white. The modern appearing woman had to carry the imperatives of domestic management over her body when she went into public space— she was a polished product from head to toe, and could not miss a spot.

Urban proximity and image production invented new body scenes that could be exposed and appraised in the modern scene. But the beauty competition and commodified beauty culture repeatedly admonished women that the modern scene was competitive, and their inclusion depended on their ability to "measure up."

The Muscular Corset

The Australian Annette Kellerman was one of the first celebrity beauties who was seen by the public both in close-up and at great distance.[89] Her primary activities and earning capacity were bound up with her self-promotion as a beauty. She self-consciously exposed her body in her career as a physical culture advocate, Screen Star, and reputedly the first pin-up girl in America.[90] She was renowned as a Bathing Beauty from as early as 1907, when she was arrested in Boston for wearing a one-piece swimming costume, designed along the lines of men's costumes, to complete a twenty-mile swim.[91] She became known as the "Australian Venus."

Her belief that beauty depended on health and her directives on techniques of appearing made her an influential advocate of bodily discipline. Kellerman considered the body "physical machinery" that must meet the doctrine of modern health and hygiene, and of "general perfection of bodily form and activity . . . all of them closely related to the problem of bodily beauty."[92] In Kellerman's thinking, the comparative ideal was important in this "working" of the body, and she was it. She gave her measurements, from neck to ankle, as taken by a "leading authority on physical culture" and a doctor, and listed them against those of the Venus de Medici and the average American college girl.[93] Her proportions were "correct," the college girl's "under-developed."[94] As a physical culture advocate she endorsed the view of "healthful beauty (you cannot separate the two words)."[95] Beauty was a manifestation of health rather than virtue, though for up-to-date modern women like Kellerman, health was to become a virtue.

Kellerman considered bodily form, carriage, grace of action, features, complexion, and dress all essential to beauty, and believed that all of these but features could be enhanced. Her feminine body was able to participate in beauty culture as malleable parts to be worked upon and transformed. She was particularly concerned to shake off the "trickery" of corsets, in which mere fat could be squeezed and laced and passed off as form, writing, "Fat is a weakening and in a society where woman's weakness was a virtue, fatness in women may have been desirable. But weakness is no longer a virtue, but a handicap to women; and the development of such natural health and strength as she possesses is a privilege and a duty." Although some accounts associated women's abandonment of the corset with liberation, Kellerman held that freedom from such constraints involved a new bodily discipline. Women themselves now had to contain the boundaries of feminine flesh which threatened to capsize in a metaphorics of spillage. Women had to depend on their own bodies as the basis for dress and style and "replace the corset of cloth and steel with one of her own making of firm muscular tone," a "muscular corset" by which the Modern Woman "laced up by the tissues of her well knit muscles."[96] As shown in the poses struck in figure 5.5, Kellerman was not only inventorying techniques of the body, but was "constructing" the modern feminine body as a technique in itself. In fat was localized the symbolics of feminine engulfment. "Hold yourself erect and do not let the fat crowd the muscle tissue," advised an article on Screen Stars.[97]

Nevertheless, manufacturers continued to market the corset as an embracing, reassuring second skin women could count on when exposed to the public eye.[98] The corset paradoxically exemplified "the charm of being natural," as the feminine body naturally required "assistance"[99] in achieving harmony of line. By "tailoring underneath,"[100] corsets could ward off and control "threats of unwanted flesh."[101] Modern corsets enabled "increased efficiency"[102] and shook off old-fashioned ideas of "compression." Instead they claimed to "permit free breathing, heart action, digestion, circulation and muscular activity."[103] Thus the corset embodied women's participation in "progress."[104] It had to negotiate newer notions of bodily transformation,

FIG. 5.5. Illustrations of posture from Annette Kellerman's *Physical Beauty— How To Keep It: Annette Kellerman Illustrated*, George H. Doras Company, New York (1918). Courtesy of the National Library of Australia.

THE CARELESS ATTITUDE.   THE PERFECT CARRIAGE.

maintenance, hygiene, mobility, and health, and to help women ward off the claims of physical culturists such as Kellerman that corsets allowed the muscles of the diaphragm and abdomen to weaken and slacken. Thus the corset was not a relic of an older, premodern scene. Gossard claimed that its "hygienically correct" corset gave "scientific support to abdominal and back muscles with no chance of undue pressure at the waistline; the organs of nutrition will be free from pressure; the erect posture which is induced will encourage deep breathing and the diaphragmatic muscles become strong with use."[105] Without such products the feminine body threatened to spill beyond the permissible boundaries of the category Modern Woman.

The freedom, mobility, and leisure of modern women were guaranteed paradoxically by the definition of bodily boundary, as in the advertisement for Nautilus Corsets shown in figure 5.6. To gain the benefits of freedom through containment, women were advised to determine their body type with measuring devices such as the "Berlei Indicator," available in stores.[106] In keeping with the standardized schema of ready-to-wear, but still preferring a descriptive rather than numerical system, Gossard advised women that they belonged to one of nine ideal types: "Average, Tall Slender, Short Slender, Curved Back, Short Waisted, Tall Heavy, Short Heavy, Large above Waist,

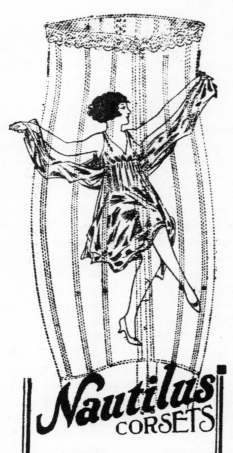

Nautilus CORSETS

The Secret of a Commanding Figure

Perfect lines are the ideal of every lover of fashion perfect freedom the ideal of every lover of comfort. The secret lies in choosing a corset designed TO FIT YOU, and in accordance with prevailing styles.

Fig. 5.6. Advertisement for Nautilus Corsets, reprinted from *Table Talk,* 20 May 1920. Courtesy of the National Library of Australia.

Large below Waist."[107] Local manufacturer Fred Burley measured thousands of Australian women and arrived at five basic figure types with thirteen variations.[108] Although these advertisements admitted that some diversity existed, they continued to type women as part of a wider visual taxonomy.

Curiously, during the years that Kellerman and others advocated the new regimes of physical health through bodily discipline, the contours of the feminine body disappeared from view in fashion plates. From 1919 to 1931 the ideal feminine shape changed from rounded with a low bust, to tubular with no curves, and then to narrow-waisted, with small high breasts and slim hips. The streamlined body of the mid-twenties was no longer in evidence. In a 1919 plate in the *Australian Home Journal*, clothes marked out the contour of breast and hips, although the rigid Edwardian line had softened considerably. In 1925, another plate in the same magazine gave no evidence of a body under the dress. Perhaps the mid-twenties "line" was a concession to ready-to-wear, which still struggled to fit the obdurately diverse feminine body. (Interestingly, by 1931, in a plate in a Foy and Gibson department store catalogue, the contour of the body began to reappear.[109]) This mid-twenties line, "as straight as a string,"[110] contradicted the traditional gendering of beauty expressed in William Hogarth's assertion that the curved line was more beautiful than the straight.[111] The "boyish silhouette" seemed at first glance to reduce the Bathing Beauty's proudly annotated contours into a strict absence of declaration, as if in modest reluctance to show the body's lines in such detail. Whether the body was made independent by its muscular control or relied on the corset for "preservation of line," it adhered to the imperative of silhouette. The body which did not adhere to "line" was scathingly criticized by the *Home*, which was committed to the lines of modernism. Rubens's and Giotto's nudes, "with their buxom curves, their heavy eyelids, those boiled-fish eyes," spilled into the abject, namely the undisciplined. To modern eyes they looked "mere meat," unformed, passive, and unworked. The traditional feminine body was targeted because of its susceptibility to "lavishness." The *Home* equated the modern with simplicity, identifying "the mode of the moment" as "the single straight line":

> This is the day of stark simplicity of line, of corners, angles, slimness, sharpness. . . . In this time of ultra-civilisation it is the mannered beauty that is admired. We conventionalise our pictures and our women. Reduction to simplicity, to the least possible number of essentials, is the mode of the moment. The single straight line is the ideal towards which

we strive, though the unfortunate mistake of nature in lumbering us with two arms and two legs has rendered this uncommonly difficult.[112]

Lois Banner's study of American beauty finds that beauty culture appropriated the feminist political aim of freeing women from cultural constraints—often through adapting the notion of a healthy body to these aims. This sense of "unlimited possibility" made all women potentially beautiful.[113] Modern beauty was about eschewing the unnecessary constraints of traditional femininity. It was about liberty, and was the logical expression of the Modern Woman's having "cultivated her mental powers, the result of hard fought battles against prejudice, [which] has enabled woman to use her powder puff with perfect peace of mind."[114] Appearing beautifully was a way for women to express their new place in modern society and the independence they had won.

What was admirable about the "flat figure," one commentator wrote, was "the dexterity with which the feminine softness was disguised beneath straight garments."[115] Much humor turned on confusion over which layer, body or clothing, defined the modern silhouette. An exasperated couturier told his bulging client, "It is ze figure of Madame that must be altered to fit ze robe!"[116] And perhaps he was not wrong, as ready-to-wear standardized sizing increasingly replaced personalized fittings. The first items of clothing to be mass-produced were army uniforms, then men's suits, and then loose-fitting women's and children's clothes.[117] With the advent of standardized clothing, the notion of alteration seemed to apply increasingly to the body and less and less to clothing. Elizabeth Wilson writes that the "strangeness of clothes" is created by the linking of the biological to the social body. Like the exasperated couturier, clothes force us to acknowledge the body as "an organism in culture, a cultural artefact even," rendering its boundaries "unclear."[118] 1920s beauty culture insisted that the boundaries that marked out the modern feminine body were markedly different from the boundaries of the premodern woman.

In 1923 Lindsay Bernard Hall, the director of the National Gallery from 1892 to 1935, stated that woman should be judged "by the standards of her time" and "standards, like fashions are ever changing."[119] What changed with modern standards was not only form, but form as a technique and a practice of bodily regulation and containment. A rather disgruntled *Truth* declared the Venus de Milo dethroned by the modern silhouette. It decried the fact that the feminine body "must be distorted to fit the costume."[120] While this was nothing new,

bodily discipline, constraint, and molding had never disguised themselves so effectively as liberation, freedom, and mobility. The ancient
body may have been invoked by physical culturists as an exemplary
product of the disciplined, self-developing citizen, but to others premodern bodies evidenced a failure of containment; it did not emit
signs of regulation or, as one woman put it, "I don't know a woman
who wouldn't agree with me that the Venus de Milo was nothing to
write home about—the great fat thing!"[121]

The modern feminine body had to negotiate dangerous boundaries which marked off the impermissible "stout" and "lank." "The laws
of proportion" decreed that if fat made up less than one-twentieth of
her weight a girl was lank, and if more than one-ninth "the unhappy
term 'obesity' looms up before us with all its clumsy bulk."[122] The
language of body normalcy intersected with notions of the feminine
body as "naturally" requiring intervention from medicine, because
women's "bodily functions are more complicated."[123] Treatments
abounded for obesity and lankness. A bath salt called Leichner 1001
claimed that when added to a warm bath it activated the cells lying
under fat layers to "break up unwanted fatty tissues."[124] Most advertisements were evasive about the method or type of treatment, calling
instead upon the expertise of "psychological science" and relying on
the new trope of the "before and after" illustration.[125] Flesh could be
"produced" or dissolved at will.[126] Straying outside the bounds of body
normalcy could even be fatal: "Heat This Summer Will Kill Hundreds
of Over-Fat People," a 1917 advertisement warned. It went on to show
a woman shrinking through three stages, because its product "reduces
fat people to normal."[127] Reduction and enhancement were part of a
system of bodily accounting in which an arithmetic of measurement
became part of women's daily regimen.

The subjection of women's bodies to such systems of bodily accounting implicated the logic of capitalist exchange in techniques of
appearing. In the advertisement shown in figure 5.7 for the film *The
American Venus*, which was aimed at theater operators, *Everyone's* directly linked the feminine body to monetary exchange. Measurement
constructed the feminine body not only as standardized, but as able
to be construed as spectacle within a system of equivalences between
profit margins and corporeal margins. As more and more of the body
came out from under clothes, it had to be "accounted for" by the
women who made spectacles of themselves. However, the restrictions
of measurement and bodily accountability did not suffice to deflect a

FIG. 5.7. Advertisement for *The American Venus*, reprinted from *Everyone's*, 14 April 1926. Courtesy of the Mitchell Library, State Library of New South Wales.

disapproving if not censoring gaze from women manifestly invested in their appearance.

Enter Stage the Modest Beauty

Women who participated in beauty culture and beauty competitions risked the charge of self-absorption, and of being overly attentive to their image. As Felski notes, unlike similar male types whose identities were also circumscribed by visual style, such as the Dandy, in modernity's representational systems women "lack the self-consciousness which their presence inspires in others. They embody artifice naively, as it were, without being able to raise it to the level of philosophical reflection."[128] The Dandy was self-reflective about the significance of his visual style, but modern women were simply caught in the logic of the modern spectacle like a moth in a flame. At worst such women were merely conceited.

As the focus of community condemnation the print competitions had to legitimate the self-scrutiny and posing that they requested from their women competitors. The *Sunraysia Daily* assured readers that "a lovely woman has the right to admire herself. But she should do it subtly, secretly, not openly and blatantly." In spite of running a beauty competition it joined in the frequent condemnation of feminine vanity:

> Unfortunately, however, there are women that appear to be watching themselves while they speak, listening to themselves, visualising themselves. Their vanity is colossal. Greedy for admiration, they cannot see a man without wanting to annex him. Such women are incapable of real love. They are too engrossed in themselves. Their main, sometimes their only interest in life is a daily pandering to their own insatiable vanity. . . . One of the most appalling sights is the woman that will not surrender to age. Her vanity will not allow her to admit that her day is over, and in some wonderful way she flatters herself that she still looks young and beautiful.[129]

Although appearing beautifully required youthfulness, it was decried as immature. The vain woman was not unlike the Screen-Struck Girl, overly identified with spectacle, specifically the image of idealized beauty, and thus self-deluded. In the case of the print competitions, the problem of the Beauty Contestant's immodesty had to be circumvented for the show to go on. Charity and regional pride, for which "a girl should not mind coming into the limelight,"[130] could cancel out the charges of immodesty and vanity. The *Sunraysia Daily* also deployed popularized psychology, arguing that it was a "generally accepted psychological fact" that for those young women who showed a passion for their own dress "suppressed desires are the most dangerous."[131] It was better for such young women to express their desires than to fixate on them because they were prohibited.

By 1922, as the newspaper competitions flourished, commentaries and opinions multiplied about how fascinated young women were by their visual appeal and how much they desired its publicity. *Argus* and *Truth*, which had missed the boat in holding the competitions, ran images such as the cartoon shown in figure 5.8, in which a despairing older woman is left out of the new obsession with beauty competitions. These newspapers became forums for scathing condemnation of the Beauty Contestants and the commercial benefits they brought to rival papers, not to mention photography studios and even jewelry stores.[132] *Truth* questioned how a modest woman could "exhibit her charms to the public gaze" to be "gaped" at. It used the theatrical

TRAGEDY OF A BEAUTY COMPETITION

How a "Great' Newspaper Circulation is Produced!

FIG. 5.8. Cartoon by Dennis Connelly, reprinted from *Truth*, 8 September 1923. Courtesy of the State Library of Victoria.

backgrounds of many of the entrants to point to the Beauty Contestant's association with the commodity spectacle, picturing her as seeking a "bundle of banknotes and a place in the spotlight."[133] It questioned the procedures of competitions, especially those in which girls appeared on theater stages in bathing "togs" and were measured by committees that included men.[134] Finally, it blamed the overwhelming effects of publicity and fame for the suicide of Dulcie Barclay, Miss Queensland of 1926. Her success caught her in "the web of feminine modernism"; it "engulfed" her and "deprived her of her reason." Like the Screen-Struck Girl, she was caught in the disorienting glare of the modern feminine spectacle. Barclay lost more than her virtue; she "floundered, lost her moorings and took her life."[135]

By 1926, feminist organizations were protesting against "the degradation of our national womanhood" through the "cheapening" public exhibition and "parading" of young women in beauty competitions.[136] They denied that the competitions were representative of Australia's beauty and named them "a good advertisement" for the newspapers, but not for the girls of Australia who were left to "suffer the indignity brought upon them by a few." The contestants exhibited "an unreasoning and unhealthy love of publicity," their plight was "pitiable and demoralising," and no amount of prize money could "compensate them for the dignity and modesty they had lost."[137] The groups were aggrieved particularly by the manner of display, with women in "semi-nude" bathing costumes, and by the "vulgar publication of photographs."[138]

Feminists objected that the contests were founded in "sex bias, otherwise why was only woman's form exploited?" Their conditions meant an entrant was "judged and measured as if she were an animal," while her "spiritual attributes" failed to rate. The women agreed that "something sacred" which "involved the finer graces of character" that inhered in beauty was being traded for a kind of beauty that "was purely physical."[139] The Woman's Christian Temperance Union argued that "true beauty is wholly spiritual, shining out in the face and making life lovely in the only true sense."[140] The sense that women's character and inner life were lost through their visual reproduction in images presaged the later feminist catchword of "sex object" in protests which also originally concentrated on beauty competitions.[141] And yet, as Judith Smart argues, women's organizations were forced to concede that the contests provided a "route to civic visibility," which made them "consistent with their own" aims.[142]

In Sydney, the Committee of the Council of Churches passed a resolution similar to that of the women's organizations: "womanly modesty is being exploited for mercenary purposes. We regard such competitions as calculated to lower the sense of public respect for the womanhood of the state, as well as to impair the sense of modesty, which should ever be the charm and protection of womanhood."[143] In 1926, their protest entered parliamentary question time and the premier of New South Wales gave notice that he would give the matter "every consideration."[144] A Member of the Legislative Assembly, Mr. Hill, was disconcerted by the tendencies toward publicity and commercialism the contests fostered in girls "who are essentially vain, eager for notoriety and greedy for prizes." The new opportunities mass culture afforded for celebrity particularly offended this political critic.

Public prominence, in his view, should be the reserve of the "great," who displayed "reticence about personal achievements." Granting celebrity to a "useless" and "unimportant" class of girl invited the public "to glorify the wrong people." And he denied that this "manner of girl" could be representative of Australian national character, since "the very nature of the means by which she won recognition negatived that modesty and dignity which, whatever the ignorant and foolish may believe, still distinguishes the Australian girl born of good stock and brought up under wholesome conditions."[145] A correspondent to the *Sun News-Pictorial* agreed that "every decent schoolboy and schoolgirl despises 'skite' [boasting]."[146]

Since Eve Gray, the *Evening Star* winner, was already a renowned stage beauty, emphasizing her modesty seems to have been even more important.[147] She was said to be "natural and unaffected"; "even without the setting of the stage, without the lights and the accompanying aids to beauty, Miss Gray looked extremely handsome." Betty Tyrrell, the *Herald* winner, had also worked on the stage, yet she was portrayed as "A Domesticated and Contented Young Bride."[148] Gray entered the competition when Ashby Studios asked her permission to enter her stage portrait. While she confessed to always having "a desire to face the footlights," she specifically averred that "I did not seek publicity" in entering the contest. In a later product endorsement, she said winning a beauty contest felt "Dreadful, most embarrassing." She wished she could "escape" from the "large, staring crowd" that seemed to follow her everywhere.[149] A reporter found "nothing of the experienced woman of the world about her . . . she was refreshingly ingenuous and girlish."[150] And of course, neither winner had thought she would succeed. Tyrrell declared, "It was the last thing I expected," and when told she was the most beautiful woman in Victoria she replied, stunned, "but, I'm not."[151] While discussion of Eve Gray and Betty Tyrrell continued in the metropolitan dailies, the film *Exit the Vamp* was succeeded in theaters by *Enter Stage the Modest Beauty*.[152]

Jill Julius Matthews documents how late-nineteenth-century physical culture had to dissociate self-cultivation from narcissism and allay anxieties that the muscular body was androgynous, in order to embrace "women's desire for modern bodies." In her work on the Women's League of Health and Beauty in the 1930s, Matthews notes that both beauty culture and physical health culture, including the growth of calisthenics, executed some of the "popular demands" of modernity—especially that of self-improvement.[153] In its activities, the Women's League implemented the standardization and mechanization of mass production that many of its members toiled under daily.[154] It particularly had to counter the association of display with narcissism. Matthews believes it did so through the ideal of self-transformation, and that "modern bodies had not only to be desired, they had to be created." Its members, she writes, might well be "on stage, showing off their bodies, but really they were having fun, enjoying themselves tremendously. . . . exhibitionism was renamed loyalty." This disassociation, crucial to the Women's League's respectability, was effected through its "ethic of desexualised fun," which, through strategic use of the uniform and of posed exercise routines, successfully achieved a "controlled exhibitionism." This "demure" display recast feminine spectacle as "the perfect physical beauty that comes from radiant health: wholesome, not pornographic, unself-conscious not narcissistic."[155] Appearing publicly was legitimated by physical culture, which added impetus to the emerging cult of the Bathing Beauty.

The burgeoning beauty industry had to similarly repudiate vanity and exhibitionism. In the 1910s and 1920s, women physical culturists countered the "disreputable" and "wicked" reputation of "women's self-conscious cultivation of physical beauty"[156] with rights discourse— it was women's right and duty to pursue beauty through the techniques of modernity. As long as the young women were out to attract not a sexualized gaze, but rather an admiring gaze, their appearing was a reputable activity. Practices of appearing, however, could be branded narcissistic when they actively sought a desiring gaze. As an alternative to the inadmissible, but evident, desire of young women to publicly expose and pose themselves as beautiful spectacles, beauty culture invoked the incontestable status of the natural: adorning oneself and attracting the gaze of men was a timeless and natural tendency in women, who were, after all, the fairer sex.

The Freshness of Right Living

The intersection of beauty culture and gendered identity posed a contradiction in modernity's understanding of the feminine. The transformation of women through consumption contradicted the naturalness with which the feminine was paradigmatically associated. To overcome this contradiction, the "natural" was discursively reaffiliated with older ideals of inner virtue understood as health. The idea of beauty as health deflected the sense that modern beauty involved trickery, imitation, and techniques of camouflage. It insured against the artificial and the perception of illusion in modern feminine spectacle. The "triumph of real charm"[157] thus belonged to the girl who "emanated the freshness of right living,"[158] defined as health, efficiency, hygiene, scientific treatment, self-development, and self-care. These "significatory effects of the body"[159] became the modern signs of inner virtue.

Yet a paradox remained in the ways the natural was invoked to treat and intervene in the body. "Superfluous" hair became a "hideous growth" like a tumor, from which one "suffered," but of course a woman could be "cured" to become a "normal woman again."[160] Similarly, "a muddy skin, over-dry or over-greasy; dull discoloured eyes; a coated tongue; haggard cheeks, are all things to be ashamed of"[161] rather than insignia of a body in varying states of health. Fashion phenomena such as the bob were recommended with the pervasive logic of science: "there is something distinctly unhealthful, now that we know so much about antisepsis and hygiene, in carrying round those superfluous masses of hair that collect dirt and germs."[162] Under Madame Alwyn's beauty regime the body could resist natural processes, and health itself was a kind of treatment; she wrote, "age is not a matter of years—it is a matter of condition."[163] She was supported by other advertisements: "Choose your age. Don't accept the verdict of the years. Be forty if you must, but never for an instant look it."[164] Women who did not appear to their best advantage were unnatural. The desire to appear beautifully may have "naturally" inhered in women; nevertheless it was expressed through their reliance on treatments and aids. In advertisements the mantra recurred—in "all women there is an instinctive perception of beauty and a longing for it."[165] Beauty was "the birthright of Every Woman" and her natural "ambition."[166] "The desire to look pretty is firmly implanted in the mental make up of every woman, and it's no use going against nature."[167] Modern beauty culture effected "the displacement of the natural from the body to its inorganic accoutrements."[168] Beauty aids themselves became natural, and the body more like a system of allocated parts requiring regular intervention, supervision, and care.

Greek dance was revived in this period in an effort to counter a perceived loss of balance in the modern body, beleaguered by "jerky, uncontrolled and neurotic" movements because of a lack of "coordination" and "intention." Training and control of the "whole muscular mechanism of the body" would "economise" energy and diminish the "expenditure of nervous force." This ancient technique intersected with the modern belief that self-control and self-development are important parts of "good citizenship," itself reflected by the love of and ambition for beauty.[169] It was in this sense that the modern appearing woman evinced the significatory effects of the modern subject through emitting the signs of self-control and self-advancement. "Scientific physical exercises will strengthen and tone the internal muscle tissue, which in turn reflects on the facial contour," advised Madame Alwyn, pictured in the women's magazine *Herself* wearing a leotard and balanced on her toes.[170]

The rationalized discursive tendencies of the period were directed to women's bodies and their sexuality. In Kerreen Reiger's analysis of the "ideology of technical rationality," she sees the growth of the state sector during this period as instrumental in modern bureaucratization and the rise of a professional-managerial class which sought to intervene in women's lives on numerous levels. One significant discourse was the domestic economy movement, which proposed a model of the efficient housewife through the scientific management or Taylorization of household tasks.[171] Reiger points to a contradiction between positing women as natural, maternal, and domestic and seeing the feminine body, the home, and child-rearing as requiring intervention through modernized techniques of efficiency and organization. The same contradiction was at work in beauty culture: as it advocated a body liberated from physical constraints, it also inculcated a regime of techniques of appearing as a means to achieve this natural body. The ambivalence around changed definitions of feminine beauty—as on the one hand inhering in women and on the other hand able to be acquired through artificial means—affected the confidence with which people looked upon the ideal beauty as representative of their city, region, nation, and race. Feminine beauty figured prominently in the mirror of national identity, but the ways in which beauties could become representative—through artificial techniques and printed photographic portraits—made them seem a poor reflection to some.

The Representative Beauty

The Beauty Contestant won public acclaim at the same time that the celebrity beauty emerged. This celebrity beauty was exemplified in the person of Annette Kellerman and propagated by many of the leaders of cosmetics and fashion houses, such as Coco Chanel and Elizabeth Arden.[172] Feminine beauty had a long tradition of renown, generally through the society networks and journals which published fashion plates and product endorsements by favored debutantes or women from "the younger set."[173] The Riley sisters of Sydney, "tall, dark, handsome with the figures of statues," were remembered decades after they promenaded "the block" (Melbourne's Collins Street).[174] Beauty renown was a mode of personalizing the conventions of anonymity that surrounded women's presence in cosmopolitan space.

The iconography of the Beauty Contestant was circumscribed by the Business Girl, Outdoor Girl, and Bathing Beauty, because all four were present in public places. Thousands of readers, many of them in rural towns, participated in the *Sun*'s Beautiful Business Girl competition of 1923, which registered 600,421 votes. The *Evening Sun*'s Queen of the Beaches competition ran in the summer of 1923–24.[175] "Do You Know These Girls?" asked a feature spread of girls on the beach.[176] The emphasis on public display seeped into techniques of appearing, with one front-page photo showing two young women being instructed by a dance teacher "in the art of looking attractive at the seaside."[177] In the 1926 Miss Australia competition, the final field of competitors—again narrowed from photographs—appeared to the judges in bathing costumes, sportswear, and walking and evening dress, all appropriate for public settings.[178]

The analogy in beauty competitions between the feminine body and public space predisposed the Contestant to becoming the representative beauty of regions and nations. If the printed photograph added the prize jewel of mass renown to the Beauty Queen's crown, it also added a new impetus, through the represent*ation* process, of represent*ativeness*. But at every turn commentary would disavow both the contrivance of image production through which these women gained renown and the fact that they had scrutinized themselves, compared themselves to contemporary ideals of feminine beauty, deployed techniques of appearing, and struck a pose. Great effort was made to reinstate the natural in these beauties, in order to confirm its significance to Australian national identity. The representative beauty then, had an important, if not conflicting, role to play. She had to embody national standards, some of which (such as whiteness) were unacknowledged but categorical.

A Distinct Racial Type

The sense that the "digger" (soldier) of World War I represented "our finest young men" helped to spur the quest for feminine national representativeness and "race-type." The *Herald*

FIG. 5.9. Advertisement for Ovaltine, reprinted from *Australian Home Journal*, 2 January 1928. Courtesy of the Mitchell Library, State Library of New South Wales.

claimed that in the photographs submitted to its competition it could trace "a distinct racial type—firmly molded chin, slightly aquiline nose, and steadfast eyes—denoting in a feminine way the same qualities which won for our young Australian manhood in its days of stress and trial the admiration of the world."[179] The Australian "type" of beauty in many ways came to be modeled on nationalistic perceptions of the digger. Feminine beauty "corresponded" to the "distinct type of manhood"[180] represented by the Australian soldier, frank and no-nonsense (not artificial) and imbued with "Australia's healthy, outdoor development," as lauded in the advertisement for Ovaltine shown in figure 5.9.[181] *Society* published Ethel Castilla's poem "An Australian Girl":

> Her frank clear eyes bespeak a mind
> Old-world traditions fail to bind
> She is not shy
> Or bold, but simply self possessed,
> Her independence adds a zest[182]

Accounts of the Beauty Contestant insisted on feminine beauty as a definitional quality of Australian womanhood. The altered emphasis on the "purely physical" meant that visually discernible racial distinction was sought. Climate, material wealth, and an intermingling of the British races were said to have produced the distinctive features of the Australian white "race." Aboriginality was expressly disavowed; it was in no way part of this national visual landscape.

The rising popularity of physical culture and the similarity of the Mediterranean and Australian climates occasioned the view that "the standard of beauty perfected in Ancient Greece" could be realized in Australia. The Australian beauty swam, played tennis, rode, played golf, and, like the Greek ideal, was unhindered by restrictive clothing.[183] As if to prove the comparison, Beryl Mills came to the first Miss Australia competition laden with sporting awards—the "best all-round sport" at Perth University, she held championships in swimming and diving, competed on the state hockey team and the varsity rowing team, and was a "fine" equestrienne and tennis and golf player.[184] But the Australian beauty had also to strike a balance with exercise, since "women should be soft, gracious creatures, not semi-men, with great knots of muscles to rob them of their natural charm."[185] The margins of bodily beauty were cut even finer in the standardized sizing of ready-to-wear.

The state winners in the earlier *Lone Hand* contest were seen as typically Australian "out-door" girls, athletic, with "Nature's ruddy glow on the cheeks," all having "simple" tastes and habits.[186] The Victorian winner, Miss Buckridge, used nothing but "cold water and a hard towel" for her complexion. She was prohibited from using powders by her father, although she did pad her hair. Her favorite drink was water. She never went to dances (going early to bed) and since she played tennis she never tight-laced. Self-effacing, she protested to the reporter, "I'm not worth writing about."[187] Mrs. Hoppe, the *Lone Hand*'s winner in New South Wales, whose "vivacity, sparkling health and exuberance" were said never to have been captured in a photograph, "however perfect," was prevented from pursuing a career in the theater by her father and was thereby "saved for what is, after all, the best career for a beautiful girl—matrimony." Though her father was evidently concerned about this public appraisal of his daughter, he did find her winning a beauty competition more respectable than "going on the stage." Mrs. Hoppe also eschewed "adventitious aids to beauty," prescribing cold water, rest, and avoidance of worry.[188] For the *Lone Hand* the competition was "a question of upholding the Aus-

tralian girl's reputation for beauty,"[189] and the paper hoped this assertion would overcome any virtuous misgivings of potential entrants. In
the 1922 competitions, the Beauty Contestant was still "fond of exercise and open air" and was disinclined to use "artificial aids."[190] Australian beauty as the contests depicted it was "natural," "unschooled
and unrestrained."[191]

Thus the "abundance of fresh air, and of clear sunshine, was said
to play a dominant part in bringing perfection of the human form,
and loveliness to the face." Outdoor freedom and leisure "operate[d]
in producing magnificent people," and beauty was key to meeting the
eugenic goal of racial distinction and purity. In doing so the Australian
beauty was "the ideal of the mother of humanity."[192] That all the British races intermingled in Australian marriages meant that the Australian girl could even claim to represent an "improved Britannia": "The
beauty of the Australian girl, therefore, reflects not only our seas and
sun and skies, but the material advantages with which Australia has
been blessed. She is living proof of how exceedingly good this Australia of ours is, and a living prophecy of how beautiful the Australia of
the future shall be."[193]

The *Herald* contest paid homage to empire, claiming that British
beauty surpassed that of all other races—but fortunately was "reproduced in Australia."[194] However, Australia (its eyes averted at all times
from its history before British invasion) had not yet had time to develop "a distinctive type of national beauty." Although Australians
were "gold colonists," their "virile and adventurous" type of beauty
was as yet inherited rather than "nationalised."[195] The director of the
National Gallery argued that beauty was based in science rather than
in mere visual gratification, since it "has a distinctive race value." It
should be adjudged as "a manifestation of the 'central form' and embodiment of our race." The beauty ideal was really a "common denominator" which "coincided with the original type of which we are
innately conscious and look for in the perpetuation of our species."[196]
At the same time, some saw race-type dissolving into "a more common, perhaps more cosmopolitan type," because commerce was
breaking down national boundaries and modernity made travel easier
and thus reduced the effect of distance.[197] The Beauty Contestant,
however, remained hoisted on the national flagpole, perhaps in reaction to modernity's racial "melting pot."

If racial intermingling, albeit of British "races," could compromise
Australian inheritance, then the environment was even more significant in "building the face" or "face architecture."[198] The benefits of the

Australian climate were thus "fairly claimed" in Eve Gray, the *Evening News* winner—even though she was, in fact, British born. That she had grown up under Australian skies "played the greatest part in developing such perfection of face and form."[199] In addition, the fact that the entrants had come "from all corners of the state" made Eve Gray an indisputably "representative" beauty.[200] The number of photographs submitted allowed the *Evening News* to declare that "the Australian girl is the equal, if not the superior, of her sister in any of the European capitals." Comparing these pictures with those entered in overseas competitions "proved this conclusively."[201] Feminine beauty both shored up local identity and reached out to a sense of global visual presence.

Representativeness was also sought from the regional beauty, who defined the local community just as much as did the district football team or fallen digger.[202] In the Mildura regional competition the contest was hailed as creating an "exhilarating new interest in the district" and doing "even more than cricket is doing to cement the Sunraysia settlements together." Moreover, the "friendly rivalry" would somehow ensure "a friendlier, happier community six months hence."[203] The print beauty contest enabled the Beauty Contestant to move from small communities in regional districts to state competitions, and finally to the national stage with the Miss Australia contest in 1926. This language of regional and national rivalry intensified during the later competitions. The *Herald* reported Sydney residents being "roused to fury" by a visiting American who said Australian women "lacked beauty" and did not compare with his countrywomen.[204] After the *Evening News* winner was announced, the *Herald* sniped that "New South Wales has no monopoly of Australian beauty. Victoria has its full share"[205] of "rival beauties" and Miss Gray "has reason to fear for her supremacy."[206] The *Illustrated Tasmanian Mail* had grander ambitions, expecting its winner to "excel both Paris and Sydney."[207]

Beauties represented not only their nation-states, but also those states' aesthetic sensibilities and racial distinction.[208] Nations vied not just to produce the finest beauty, but to prove through their judgment that they had the most refined appreciation of beauty, a mark of their civilization. By comparison "the savage," who was infantile and without aesthetic sense (and, more ominously, culturally finite), "had little sense of beauty."[209] The *Sun* captioned the image of a Turkish beauty with "she did not win a competition, because Turkey has not reached that stage of " 'civilisation' yet."[210] Art "was born among the Western peoples," who found beauty encapsulated in the female form because

FIG. 5.10. Illustration by
Stan Cross, reprinted from
Smith's Weekly, 5 April
1919. Courtesy of the State
Reference Library, State
Library of New South
Wales.

(tautologically) it excelled all other forms, "animate or inanimate," in
beauty.[211] Modern women's techniques of appearing became evidence
of national progress. Thus one commentator argued that it was "the
cult of fashion by our womanhood that diverts the race from stag-
nation," whereas the "bovine" races, uninterested in fashion, lacked
"the lever of modern progress. . . . the cult of fashion and its ever-
increasing demands, is the prime motive power for the continued
struggle and advance of the race."[212] Techniques of appearing—as long
as they manifested visual competency through the care of the self—
were markers of a civilized society.

The earlier tradition of using the feminine spectacle to symbolize
nation and geographic space recurred in images like figure 5.10. Here
the "peril to the white cradle"[213] was represented as a potential corruption of the white feminine body by "personages of involved an-
cestrage."[214] The white woman is threatened with sexual violation,
represented by the phallic weapons penetrating the domesticated

space of the nation, and she defends this space with her fragile arm, entwining her body with the symbolic machinery of national defense. This image not only used the feminine to symbolize white nationhood—rendered with the timelessness of classicism—but, not unlike the Beauty Contestant, constructed feminine spectacle itself, as long as it was modest, as a motif of white nationhood.

Developments in print media enabled reproduced photographs of individual women to represent the nation, much as line drawings had used feminine beauty to represent notions of national victory, progress, and the motherland. The Beauty Contestant became the insignia of a new national pictorial self-consciousness. Using the older associations of feminine beauty with national ideals and the formations of celebrity that were emerging in response to photographic portraiture, nations competed for racial supremacy through the fertile symbolism of robust young women. The print media made the Australian beauty, like the Anzac and the local Screen Star, a means of attaining national visibility on the international stage that was amenable to the visual taxonomies of eugenics and its quest for discernible racial distinction. Through this peculiar process of national self-placement, the publicized Beauty Contestant offered herself as reproduced image, which stabilized not only the identity of the Modern Woman, but national identity as feminine.[215] However, the beauty of nations made public visibility double-edged—it implied that women were included in—or excluded from—national and modern identity by beauty or visual dereliction. If techniques of appearing—such as self-scrutiny and comparison to a feminine ideal—were the means to locate the self within a wider community of significatory acts, women could not feel themselves included in the modern scene if they were not beautiful.

In her work on fashion, Valerie Steele argues that the emulation of idealized beauty did not reflect women's oppression as "sex objects." Seeing the basis of fashion as sexual, she says that changes in women's modes of self-representation reflected "shifting attitudes toward sexual expression" and women's consistent desire to look beautiful. As such, dress liberation of itself never greatly affected fashion and beauty; rather, it was from the acceptance of "artifice and sexual attractiveness, that modern fashion and the modern beauty industry developed."[216] The desire to appear beautifully was also systematically constructed by beauty culture, assisted by the inauguration of mass-produced ideals through the reproduction of the Beauty Contestant as spectacle. Women's responsiveness to commodity beauty culture and their participation in beauty contests suggests that they submitted docilely to prescriptive gendered symbolism, particularly its insistence that they represent the nation and the modern. Yet women could also find pleasure in the ways that beauty culture invited them to enact the modern subject by using techniques of appearing—namely, attention to and care of the self, corporeal regulation, self-transformation, and mastery, which could lead to national representativeness and democratized visual status. Ambivalences about the relationship between beauty and the Modern Woman remained—beauty had become an elaborate technique of the body which modern discourses sought to naturalize.

Feminine ideals were delimited by size, age, and race. Throughout the twentieth century, as visibility has increasingly become the precondition and expression of cultural presence and participation, beauty has narrowed the cast of women under the public eye and thus affected women's access to the cultural field. Appearing was a practice circumscribed by colonial visions and deeply invested in power relations in which race remained a structuring absence in the realization of feminine ideals. Beauty cast the Modern Woman as the privileged object in the modern picture of life. It inhabited her definitionally, to the core of her meaning: the Modern Woman was a beautifully appearing woman, and Aboriginal and elderly women, who could not appear beautifully, could not be modern. The woman who did not scrutinize herself and compare herself to the feminine ideal—as the techniques of appearing demanded—did not merit appraisal or visual presence, and she could not represent the Australian nation. This new requirement of visual comparison and competition between women legitimated a delimited model of the modern feminine ideal—one that was invested with colonial visions and that seemed destined to leave many women out of the modern scene.

Chapter 6

The "Primitive" Woman in the Late Colonial Scene

The first time Irene saw her full-length reflection in the wardrobe mirror she was very frightened and took a long time to believe it was herself—she thought that she was much more handsome.[1]

Irene was an Aboriginal girl taken "direct from a camp" at twelve years of age to be "trained" as the domestic servant of a contributor to the *Australian Woman's Mirror*. This contributor added to the journal's series of articles on the efficiency of the "Abo. Maid." The mistress "had to tolerate the company of [Irene's] mother and younger sister for a fortnight" after Irene was effectively stolen from her community. During the 1920s, Aboriginal peoples were forcibly relocated from their traditional lands to reserves, for "protection" and to allow white access to their lands, and impressed as laborers, particularly as pastoral and domestic workers.[2]

Irene's "primitivism"[3] was constructed through a number of well-established tropes, many of which still circulate in popular and institutional meanings of Aboriginality. Her grasp of English was poor, she worked at her menial domestic tasks sporadically and did not always complete them, but (unlike the Modern Woman) she approached some with childlike joy: "she is never happier than when her arms are deep in soapsuds."[4] Popular discourse also constructed Aboriginal and Islander women as primitive by their relation to their own images: they could not imagine themselves as under an appraising gaze, or stand before the mirror like the white woman, self-conscious and managing their own visual effects. If they did attempt to be modern appearing women, their techniques of appearing revealed them to be, like Irene, comically inept and unsightly.

Cartoons in many humor magazines of the 1920s, as well as serious newspapers, depicted the primitive woman as having confused, comic, and aberrant understandings of the meanings of her visibility in the modern scene. Appearing was a technique in white modern women's practice of gender, and Aboriginal women evinced their primitiveness by their failure as such technicians.[5] When Aboriginal, Islander, or even African women appeared in the modern scene they did so as abject or as racial fetishes: they failed to appear as modern women. Within the Australian colonial scene, appearing, as a practice of modern femininity, thereby accomplished a number of the discursive tasks of imperialism.

Irene's purported "first" apprehension of herself as an image to others was construed as crossing a threshold into white domestic spatiality. Her mistress represented Irene's coming face to face with herself, experiencing herself as image, as a defining, civilizing moment in her "training" in the practices of white feminine modernity. But as a servant to this modernity, at one remove as its invisible handmaid, Irene disobliged by failing to appreciate the meaning of her reflection: she could not "believe it was herself." In experiencing that space between herself and her image as delusional—"she thought that she was much more handsome"—Irene saw herself in the mirror in the space in which white women usually stood. Appearing as image to herself and others placed Irene in the colonially inscribed position of possessing her visual effects and of being required to master and appraise herself. But she did not appear beautiful to herself, suggesting this was a visual condition in which Aboriginal women were destined to fail.

The visual taxonomy imposed on Indigenous Australians—a "fixation on classification" that, as Marcia Langton writes, "reflects the extraordinary intensification of colonial administration of Aboriginal affairs from 1788 to the present"[6]—often served eugenic notions of blood purity and miscegenation. Skin color—"full-blood," "half-caste," "quadroon," "octoroon"—indicated parentage and was sometimes an index of the corruption of white decadent or modern hypercivilization. In the "constant search for appropriate characterization"[7] of colonized Aboriginality, techniques of appearing adopted the discursive tasks of racial exclusion, construction of the racial other, and recognition of white modern femininity. When Aboriginal women appeared in the modern scene, their failure to believe in themselves as images recurred throughout the tropes of exoticism, racial fetishism, and racial abjection to cast them as not appearing white, and therefore not modern.

I take the term "Aboriginality" from Marcia Langton's work on the textual processes of intersubjectivity between "the subjective experience of both Aboriginal people and non-Aboriginal people who engage in any intercultural dialogue."[8] Langton points out the pivotal importance of the fact that identity positions are textually inscribed by racial and gendered significatory processes, which are also historically contingent. She identifies three broad categories of cultural and textual constructions of "Aboriginality," both colonial and anti-colonial:

> The first is the experience of the Aboriginal person interacting with other Aboriginal people in social situations located largely within Aboriginal culture. The second is the stereotyping, iconising and mythologising of Aboriginal people by white people who have never had any substantial first-hand contact with Aboriginal people. The third is the construction generated when Aboriginal and non-Aboriginal people engage in actual dialogue, where the individuals test and adapt imagined models of each other to find satisfactory forms of mutual comprehension.[9]

It is the second category of textual inscription of Aboriginality that recurs in images of the 1920s, although colonial representations were often used in colonizing women's accounts of how they experienced colonized women, such as that of Irene's mistress. Colonizing women did not merely use available discourses of racial difference; they also invested their accounts with colonial constructions that granted their racial difference power over the Aboriginal other. The racial exclusions effected through women's techniques of appearing proved amenable to such accounts.

The term "primitive" lacks authenticity in itself and functions through ensembles of representational tropes as what Marianna Torgovnick calls "grist for the Western fantasy-mill." She sees primitivist discourse as "fundamental to the Western sense of self and Other," part of powerful symbolic systems which "have slipped from their original metaphoric status to control perceptions." Primitivist discourse fulfills the West's yearning to explore its prehistory and origin, to investigate the natural order, and to gain access to the essential, to degeneracy and nobility. The primitive is squarely placed within the exchange value of Western discursive networks. Torgovnick writes, the West's fascination with the primitive has to do with its own crisis in identity, with its own need to clearly demarcate subject and object even while flirting with other ways of experiencing the universe. Few periods of history have been more concerned than modernity with the articulation of the psychological subject and the cultivation of the individualistic self; yet the fascination with other possibilities, possibilities perhaps embodied in primitive societies, remained acute.[10]

The primitive intersected gender to reinforce modernity's disjunction of object and subject, which was increasingly ambiguous, with the subject said to be "fragmenting" like Lotus Thompson, before and within the proliferating spectacles of the modern perceptual field. Since appearing is precisely the conflation of object and subject—the syncretic moment of the subject experiencing itself as object, or the object experiencing itself as subject—the primitive woman was recruited to help reinforce this foundational divide. She could be object, but representations of her experiencing herself as image, that is as appearing, show her as unable to transcend the racially inflected space of mimicry. When she appeared, it was only in mimicry of white women, and of course she could only be "not quite white." She only succeeded in appearing to be comic, abject, or reduced to fetishized object—the meaning that imbued her image never positioned her as subject. She did not appear to be modern.

"Mine tinkit we plurry fine actors"

Irene's response to her reflection in the mirror was symptomatic of colonial constructions of primitive spectatorship before the mechanically reproduced image. The Aboriginal spectator was childlike: irrational, excitable, impressionable, unable to distinguish representation from reality, and vulnerable to transformation through mimicry. Another "Abo. maid" was expected to react to having her photograph "in the Missus' paper" with the "excitement" and "delight" of the "piccaninnies."[11] Her childlike pleasure, like Irene's fright, evinced an irrational, disproportionately emotional response. Irene's inability to experience herself and her image within a unity of identity, a subjective whole or ego-ideal, meant that the only space available to her before the mirror was mimicry of whites' self-mastery over their images.

Such mimicry by Aboriginal people was often cast as delusional, impressionable, and dangerous. Thus the 1927–28 Royal Commission into the Moving Picture Industry recommended, under the heading "The Film and Native Races," "That no moving picture film shall be screened before audiences of aborigines or natives of the Mandated Territories unless such film has been passed by the Censorship Board for such exhibition."[12] While its recommendations were never implemented in legislation, evidence had been given to the commission by a former Chief Inspector of Aborigines, J. T. Beckett, who had testified before the commission. He believed it dangerous to allow Aboriginal and Islander people access to some genres of film. Similarly, *Everyone's* wrote that whereas whites looked upon the cinema as entertainment, "with native races the same equanimity is not preserved, vivid and lasting impressions are retained by the natives, and frequently their imagination is riotously aroused. The film exerts a powerful influence over the natives and could by design instil into their minds dangerous and sinister motives."[13] In Beckett's view "the aborigine" (undifferentiated and universalized) was little interested in the "sex film"— perhaps because of his construction as a member of "a dying race," with its associations of impotency, both sexual and cultural. But he not only was interested in but tended to imitate the heroes of the American "gunman" films. And his mimicry of white subject positions as textually inscribed in cinema could corrupt him; Beckett argued that such films were "helping him to contempt for the old wholesome prohibitions," though it is not clear whether Beckett meant traditional Aboriginal customs or prohibitions imposed by whites—often whites had prohibited obedience to older laws. Beckett was drawing upon a pervasive sense of latent criminality in the primitive, who, like the cowboy, often disputed land tenure and stock possession. Aborigines were always already deviant under colonial law, and their deviancy made it easy to naturalize their incarceration and dispossession. The "island primitive," on the other hand, in spite of being as "child like as his brother of Australia," was greatly influenced by the "sex film"; he and his fellows were "all eyes and ears for a subject which they readily understand," resulting, Beckett argued, in a growing list of sexual offenses against white women in New Guinea and Papua.[14]

Although the Royal Commission recommended that Aboriginal and Islander people be banned from cinematic spectatorship, they were nevertheless used in the colonial scene to represent the primitive. In 1912, Aborigines from the Yarrabah Mission near Cairns and the Barambah Government mission reserve appeared in an American production filmed in Northern Queensland. "Infinite tact and patience were required before the camera wheel could begin to turn," perhaps as the technologies of modernity attempted to overcome the incongruity of having the premodern within their visual field. However, one young man, dubbed "Reefcomber," was adept at performing the ethnographic primitive realism required by the filmmakers. Though he was disqualified from star status as "not a very promising specimen to look at," Reefcomber's acceptance of payment in tobacco led him to "muster" other volunteers. They could enact contemporary ideas of primitive realism because they were visually coherent with the landscape: "it was wonderful how the crouching and almost nude black figures were instantly lost to sight among the black stones which strewed the natural stage—their lissom figures glided through the bush."[15] Aboriginal women were constructed as visually anomalous in the modern scene partly by this notion of Aboriginal coherence, to the point of indistinctness or camouflage, in the natural landscape, as opposed to the modern. Whereas white women were luminous and distinct when depicted in a natural environment, Aboriginal women were often positioned as part of it. This spatial assignation reflected a form of social Darwinism, constructing the modern subject through his or her visual presence in the modern scene and subsuming the visual identity of the primitive within the "wilderness."

The Aboriginal extras were also anomalous in the modern visual scene because, being premodern, they represented the past. Witnessing this display of natural origin and "savage delirium," the reporter prophesied that "the camera was recording the last pages of the history of a dying people."[16] He wrote of the camera as merely recording the demise of the primitive, but in fact, as an insignia of modern technologies, it played a more instrumental role in what Ross Gibson has dubbed "the sinister glamour of modernity."[17] The camera was co-opted into the conventions of the colonial gaze, the expansionist mapping of territories becoming an imperial aesthetics, which disqualified the primitive subject from the colonial representational matrix. At times the metaphor of the camera as an instrument of racial advancement and decline was brutally literal. On the box office success of the American film *The Vanishing Races,* local film industry personality Gayne Dexter wrote that the scalps of the American Indians who toured the country to promote it should be hung from the exhibitors' belts "as trophies of sure-shooting showmanship."[18] Similarly, *Aussie* featured a cartoon that depicted the Aborigine as the raw material of industrialized image production. Two smartly dressed young women in London discuss the imperial progress of one of their beaux: "He wrote that he's making thousands of pounds catching blackfellows and boiling them down for ink."[19] If colonialism sought a universal language through the reproduction of images, as in cinema, it was an imperial language which universally pictured Indigenous people as out of place in the modern scene and thereby as culturally finite.

The notion of "a dying race" had particular resonance in this representational process of othering within modernity, conscious of itself as the dawn of progress, development, and change. While white moderns imaged themselves at the beginning of their social narrative, they imaged primitive peoples at the end of theirs: invisibility was a symptom of their actual disappearance. The imperial significatory scene was more than a symptom of genocide; it was implicated in its tragic effects.

In 1928, after the Royal Commission had issued its recommendations, 450 Aborigines, again from the Barambah mission reserve, were given an exclusive showing of a film featuring the American Screen Star Eva Novak, *The Romance of Runnibede* (1928), in which they had appeared as extras.[20] The film exploited the mythology of native abduction of white women—it crudely disavowed, by inversion, the prevalent practice of abducting and sexually exploiting Indigenous women.[21] This colonial parable allowed for both the symbolic congruence of the feminine with the natural, while securing woman's presence, and indispensable labor, in the imperial home through her rescue from the premodern. Woman's detainment in the private realm thus became her emancipation from sexual exploitation and imprisonment by natives. The film was promoted with the teaser "A white girl captured by blacks—torn from her home, her lover, and all she held dear—carried off into the depths of the bush—perhaps to a fate more terrible than death."[22] The observer from *Everyones* lampooned the Aboriginal audience's response, assuming the voice of "Jackie," a male Aboriginal spectator: "Mine tinkit we plurry fine actors. But since look at Eva Novak blackfella missus too much proud. Want flash clobber and cooked sheep ebery day, want gibbit sixpence, gibbit jewelry, gibbit mia-mia, gibbit motor car, walk-about spend 'em cash."[23] Part of the spectacle for this "Jackie" was the effect of the cinema on his "missus" and her naive mimicry of the racially inscribed position of the white Modern Woman. The reporter's parody was at one with a comic tradition that turned on the incongruity of Aboriginal women's visibility in the modern perceptual field.

The Wages Being Very Small

In the 1928 cartoon from the *Bulletin* that is shown in figure 6.1, Mary's "missus" is peeling off the gloves which have been protecting the fairness of her hands. She stands, attired in the smart lines of the aviatrix, on the threshold of the domestic realm, from which she can depart at will because she has mastered the technologies of mobility and conquered time and distance. The information she possesses about the outside world is "first-hand"—she handles it, she is within it. She stands over Mary, whose hands are too large for gloves. Mary sits in a puddle in sartorial indefinition, her hair unruly, her features projected in a kind of simian, fleshy excess compared to the precisely rendered lines of her mistress. As a liminal figure, primitive yet domesticated, Mary scrubs her mistress's modern threshold. The cleanliness of whiteness reflects the disciplined surface of the white subject. Mary's "child of nature" naiveté seeks to have the intangible symbols of Christianity tangibly confirmed. She is excluded from the category of the Modern Woman through a complex interweaving of binary oppositions. Mary is neither mistress nor master of modern technologies; she sits on her feet, historically immobile. She is elbow-deep in menial domestic labor, unlike the Modern Woman,

FIG. 6.1. Cartoon by B. E. Minns, reprinted from *Bulletin*, 18 April 1928. Courtesy of the State Library of Victoria.

SEEKING FIRST-HAND INFORMATION.
"You bin come home in aeroplane, missus?"
"Yes, Mary."
"You bin up alonga clouds, missus?"
"Yes, Mary."
"Then you tellit this-Mary true. Did bush mish'ary pullem mine leg 'bout heaben?"

who has found avenues of escape in scientific management, labor-saving devices, and, less commonly admitted, imperial subjection. Mary's hands refer back to a mode of manual labor that is preindustrial. Her missus's hands are effectively protected from history; they handle the present and are carefully preserved against signs of age and work. Mary is unfashionable because, as primitive, she is torpid against the visual flux and transience of modernity. She evinces no mastery over her appearance; because it is black, her surface is not disciplined. Her mistress stands, almost in long shot before her like a Screen Star, holding her gaze and not bothering to return it. The mistress's understated features are cool and reserved; she appears modern. Through these binarisms Mary does not really "appear" as primitive. She does not appear in the sense in which I have been using the term—she does not emit the signs of intentionality and control over her visual effects. Nor does she seem aware of the modern perceptual field and how to achieve visual congruence within it. Mary appears as "primitive" through not appearing.

The racial difference of Aboriginal women was repeatedly cast as visual abjection. For example, a 1926 header in the *Australian Woman's Mirror* depicts the sinewed, excessively scoured face of an Indigenous servant who holds a pie and looks across at the profiled pure lines of her employer, around whom the pie's aroma delicately wafts.[24] In mirroring each other, these opposites reflected the equation of whiteness with modern beauty and Indigeneity with visual dereliction. Modern beauty (as much as liberation from domestic drudgery) was specifically founded in racial exclusion, and arguably remains so. Fleshy excess and gangly skinniness were the measures of banishment from the intersecting categories of modernity, beauty, and femininity and were textually inscribed or mapped over the features and body of the Aboriginal woman. Either she was in excess or she did not measure up to the standards of beauty that through self-regulation defined the Modern Woman.

In a 1926 cartoon in the humor magazine *Adam and Eve*, an overweight Aboriginal woman in oversized men's boots, carrying a patched sack, wrongly believes that the diversity of commodity products before her can accommodate her racial difference. She stands with her dog on this side of an elegant shop counter, pointing out a pair of black stockings, asking the dignified attendant to "Gibbit plurry flesh-color pair, boss." She improperly supposes that commodity aesthetics offer her a range of images that she may occupy, thereby enacting the subject position of the modern appearing woman.[25] And yet Aboriginal

women's relation to commodity culture was determined by their exile
from monetary exchange. The fact is they generated white income
through unpaid or poorly paid labor, particularly as domestic servants.
Thus the categories of sexual difference, race, and class were articulated through each other in representations of Aboriginal domestic
servants. Anne McClintock, in her analysis of colonial constructions
of race, gender, and sexuality, writes that "[t]hrough the rituals of
domesticity, increasingly global and more often than not violent, animals, women and colonized peoples were wrested from their puta-
tively 'natural' yet, ironically, 'unreasonable' state of 'savagery' and
inducted through the domestic progress narrative into a hierarchical
relation to white men."[26] But McClintock is acutely aware that this
hierarchical relation, particularly in the realm of imperial domesticity,
also existed between colonial and colonized women. The mistress of
another Aboriginal servant, Topsy, thus wrote unselfconsciously of her
charge as having "been in my possession" for six months, and claimed
Topsy only needed "warm garments, plain food and kind words, the
wages being very small."[27] In this self-confirming logic, Topsy had no
commodity desires, because she had no consumer means or command. Aboriginal women neither occupied the space of the commodity spectacle nor were able to performatively enact a consumerist subjectivity. Their visual dereliction recurs in another *Bulletin* cartoon.[28]
Mary is hard to make out against the foliage around the white
woman's door, with her ragged hem, simian mien, and disproportion-
ate feet. She is positioned opposite the carefully shod and groomed
luminosity of the white woman, who tells Mary that she has no bottles
to give her as her husband doesn't drink. "By Cripe," Mary replies,
"that bad fella! How you get 'em picture-show money." Mary confuses
the white woman's husband's sobriety with marital neglect. She can
access the modern spectacle only through an indigent economy based
on drunkenness—bottle returns—while white women's spectatorship
constitutes a ticket to the modern scene.

Aboriginal women were often depicted as workers on cattle sta-
tions, as portrayed in the Hugh Maclean cartoon shown in figure 6.2.
They were thus removed from the metropolis and cosmopolitan sartorial codes. Twice removed from commodity culture, both geograph-
ically and because they were outside, yet cruelly subject to, the imperial control of commodity capital, their visual effects were a pretense
that worked against them by casting doubt on their moral character,
as was done in the cartoon shown in figure 6.3. In another cartoon,
"Mary," as she was universally called, inappropriately assumes the

"Why don't you let her marry Warrigal?
I'm paying him good wages."
"She's too plurry good lookin' for Warrigal!"

FIG. 6.2. Cartoon by Hugh Maclean, reprinted from *Aussie*, 14 April 1927. Courtesy of the Mitchell Library, State Library of New South Wales.

pose of a white lady. Her friend, with a ragtag baby in her arms and a smoking pipe in her mouth, asks, "Wot, no for you smokit pipe, Mary?" Mary strikes a Greta Garbo pose, her bare feet planted beside her dingo. "No plurry fear," she replies, her nose in the air. "Man smokit pipe, lady smokit sickerette."[29] The visual codes of primitivism were projected, excessive, simian features, enormous feet, and spidery thinness or fleshy excess. "The geometry of the body maps the psyche of the race,"[30] and such a body cannot be included in the category "good lookin'," which was specified, by omission, as white (see fig. 6.2). Another contributor to the "Abo. maid" series assigned her maids a less evolved womanhood, writing, "they were both fearlessly like baboons, even down to their having hairy faces and short thick hair."[31]

Mimicry of modern types such as the "pflapper," as shown in figure 6.4, was even more misplaced, since the primitiveness of the Ab-

"My word! Lucky pfeller, that one, she bin lady's companion."
"By cripes! More like native companion, minetinkit."

FIG. 6.3. Cartoon by Hugh Maclean, reprinted from *Aussie,* 15 April 1929. Courtesy of the Mitchell Library, State Library of New South Wales.

original woman could not be disguised or layered over. The Aboriginal woman was unaware that her racial abjection could not overcome her attempts at white mimicry. She had so little mastery over her self-perception that she could not perceive herself as unsightly. In the same series of articles on the efficiency of the "Abo. maid," another "Topsy" amused her mistress with her inherent ineptness in techniques of appearing. "She has little vanities like the white girl, using face-cream, powder and even lip-salve with weird results." She was also comic when she failed to realize that her skin color rendered such interventions pointless. Thus "Country Mother" wrote in amusement that Topsy said her mother "always made her wear a hat in the Summer to prevent freckles!"[32]

The colonized woman who mimicked whiteness was recognized neither by difference nor by identity. Whereas mimicry by the Flapper could playfully destabilize the "natural" signs of femininity, showing gender to be performative, race mimicry, according to Homi Bhabha,

"Hooray! Close up get it married quickly now, mine tinkit."
"Py cripes, flash pflapper that one! Poor ol' mother never had that much clothes in 'er plurry life!"

FIG. 6.4. Cartoon by Hugh Maclean, reprinted from *Aussie*, 15 February 1928. Courtesy of the Mitchell Library, State Library of New South Wales.

was a colonial imposition on the identity of the colonized, showing them to be imperfect and flawed: "almost the same, but not white."[33] Susan Willis writes, "as replicants, black versions of white cultural models are of necessity secondary and devoid of cultural integrity."[34] And writing of colonized Africans, McClintock positions this necessity as further evidence of the "threshold" and "liminal" status of the colonized. "Inhabiting the cusp of prehistory and imperial modernity, the 'improved specimen' is seen as the living measure of how far Africans must still travel to attain modernity."[35]

In addition, the primitive subject might have no sense of the imperial narrative of racial improvement through the civilizing effects of dress, and would therefore go to no pains with it. In recurring imagery the primitive "needed guidance in order to emerge into modernity, the cultural equivalent of adulthood."[36] The primitive man, absurdly attired in a misplaced waistcoat with its cuffs around his ankles, could

Are You a MARKED MAN?

It marks the man—the suit he wears. It writes style in big, bold letters all over him, or else it writes something else. The fit of the collar, the way the shoulders are made, the length of the coat, all must be right or you are a marked man—as far as good taste is concerned.

VEREY-PHILLIPS clothes represent something more than all-wool fabrics. Our Specialist Cutters combine the talent of designing style clothes with comfort, ease, and permanency. VEREY-PHILLIPS cater specially for members of the Theatrical, Sporting, and kindred professions.

VEREY-PHILLIPS

Tailors Only.   131-133 KING ST., SYDNEY

FIG. 6.5. Advertisement for Verey-Phillips, reprinted from *Australian Variety and Show World*, 8 July 1920. Courtesy of the Mitchell Library, State Library of New South Wales.

not cut it in the significatory system of the modern subject. He looks wistfully on in figure 6.5 as the Modern Man strides off into the future, carrying the signs of his civilization as visual style: "in big bold letters all over him." If the modern subject left premodern custom behind, he did it by getting dressed. The ways that Aboriginal peoples did in fact have their own practices of appearing did not figure in this construction of the naked savage. "Tommy," in another cartoon, is told he can hardly be recognized with his beard shaved. Not unlike Irene, Tommy replies, "I close up didn't know me plurry self, boss, w'en I lookit in glass, 'sep' by me voice."[37] The primitive obligingly excuses himself from the modern scene: he cannot discern himself as image. Similarly, the *Sun News-Pictorial* pictured "Black Pug," an Aboriginal boxer, with suit, hat, and cane. The caption tells readers that his manager "could make him a boxer, but not a gentleman. Has the tailor succeeded?"[38] Aboriginal people might become spectacles because of their "natural" abilities as boxers and athletes. Yet becoming spectacles as gentlemen was less likely. Instead, "Black Pug" dressed up in white men's attire was a curiosity on the illustrations page.

Race and gender were entangled in the colonial social order as the modern subject was dressed as either male or female. Another contributor to the series on the "Abo. maid" reported that she insisted that the "gins," who "were not very keen on clothes," wear dresses. In the Northern Territory, such insistence subjected Aboriginal women to a revival of the European sumptuary laws of the early modern period. A 1911 ordinance prohibited Aboriginal women from wearing male clothing in the company of white men,[39] foreclosing sexual ambiguity or deviance. Still, the nuances of white sartorial codes were lost on "Amelia," according to her mistress—who perhaps was incapable of grasping Amelia's subversion: "Amelia, who is six feet tall, came in to wait on the table one night dressed in a cerise petticoat and light-blue striped shirt with the tail hanging out all around. A red handkerchief tied over her head and elastic-side boots two sizes too large completed the ensemble."[40]

The Revenge of the Jungle on Civilization

At the very time when the colonial scene attempted to visually expel the "primitive" from the modern by continually invoking it in imagery of the "premodern," ideas about "man's" essentially primitive nature were given a new lease on life and fresh circulation as jazz became popular and cultural forms were appropriated from "exotic" countries. Japanese motifs appeared in Art Deco designs and African motifs in modernist painting; the uncovering of the Luxor caves sparked a rash of Egyptian-derived designs in fashion; and, not least, the popular impact of jazz was immense. But exoticism posed its own problems. In particular, many feared that these cultural forms would excite primitive behaviors, especially in impressionable modern girls. The Modern Woman's love of the exotic provoked a ready association—that if she loved to dance to jazz, she would therefore desire the primitive man's gaze and more. The Modern Woman became a scapegoat for a kind of cultural miscegenation, through music, dance, and fashion, that would bring out her essentially primitive nature. As Felski notes, "the figure of woman serves as a recurring cipher of the pre-modern within modernity itself."[41] The Modern Woman's love of adornment, which was both universalized and ahistoricized, expressed her essential nature, itself not far removed from imagined tribal custom.

Industrialized nations of the 1920s shared a penchant for cultural appropriation and exoticism. Australia derived the cult of the sheik from British popular fiction, and jazz from sheet music, British and American bands touring the dance halls, phonograph records, and cinema. Both of these crazes reflected a kind of globalized primitive in two ways; they were "representative" of cultures that were cast as anachronistic in modernity and history, and they fascinated modern women by appealing to their increasingly uninhibited and thus essentially uncultured nature. The sheik had entered popular culture in 1919 in the best-selling pulp novel *The Sheik,* written by Edith Maude Hull, "the retiring wife of a Derbyshire farmer."[42] The remarkable public response to Rudolph Valentino's rendition of the role in the 1921 film, Miriam Hansen has argued, was due to his "ethnic otherness" being choreographed through a regime of looks, in exotic and fetishistic form, "as part of his erotic persona." The film used his ethnicity, both as Italian star and as Arabic screen character, to disrupt and reorder the polarized gendered positions of the cinematic gaze. By being positioned as spectacle and specifically as object of the mass feminine gaze, Valentino undermined the "gendered economy of vision," and was feminized as "a defence, as a strategy to domesticate the threat of his ethnic-racial otherness."[43]

The Sheik—in Australia, "sheik" would soon become a colloquial term for a man who preyed on young women in the street—called up an archaic sexual primitivism, not only in his persona, but also in the subjected, abducted, but adoring heroine. He celebrated "an ideal of masculinity: 'primitive' (as opposed to 'civilized'), virile and priapic." As for the emancipated Modern Woman, her helpless attraction to the brute force of her despotic lover revealed an inherent masochism, masked by her disdainful indifference to and independence from men. The Sheik proved that "to dominate the modern cold virago, brute force, not chivalry is needed."[44] Lyrics of a popular song situated the sheik as riding "wild and free" over the desert, his "captured bride" clinging for dear life: "Proudly he scorns her smile or tear / Soon he will conquer love by fear."[45] In Australia, this abducted heroine did not define the Modern Woman so much as her adoration of the Sheik (and Valentino) as part of her ensemble of cultured preferences. Primarily cinematic, the cult of the Sheik projected the risk

Reprinted at the G.P.O., Sydney, for transmission by post as a Newspaper.

6ᵈ *The* 6ᵈ
Triad

VIC COWDROY

VAUDEVILLE—AN IMPRESSION BY VIC. COWDROY.

From a Sydney Notebook—See page 2

JUNE 8th, 1927
PUBLISHED BY ART IN AUSTRALIA LTD. 24 BOND ST. SYDNEY.

FIG. 6.6. Cover illustration by Victoria Ethel Cowdroy, reprinted from *The Triad*, 8 June 1927. Courtesy of the Mitchell Library, State Library of New South Wales.

of miscegenation onto extant fears about the morally destabilizing modern spectacle. Attraction to both Valentino and the cinema bespoke a libidinal attachment to the image that, in the instance of the Sheik, served to disclose the primal, atavistic sexuality of modern women through their desire for representational coupling.

In Australia, jazz was also deeply infused with primitivist discourse. The modern youth who enjoyed it were thought to find through jazz a kind of savage, libidinal release. Jazz was perceived as "the revenge of the jungle on civilisation"[46] and "a nigger shuffle"[47] provoking "tottering ape-like convulsions which express the primitive savage."[48] Both as a dance craze and as a widespread entertainment form in revues and vaudeville minstrel shows,[49] jazz ambiguously linked the categories of race and gender. In the image of jazz portrayed in figure 6.6, primitive and modern women occupy the same social and significatory space. They are the historical bookends between which modernity placed its narrative of the present as a departure from the native's immaturity. It was a narrative haunted by the Modern Woman's uninhibited expression of primordial desires, particularly for adornment. Importantly, it was as spectacle that the primitive and Modern Woman mirrored each other. However, whereas the primitive woman mimicked the Modern Woman's status as spectacle, the Modern Woman's fascination with exoticism revealed her as essentially primitive. The English dancer Ivy Shilling said in an interview in *Society*, "The Negro element in modern dancing is, I think, a throwback. It appeals to the spark of savagery that lurks under many shirtfronts and evening dresses."[50] The interview was titled "Is Jazz a Passing Phase?" as indeed it was; the images of white moderns passing themselves off as primitive, and of these essentially primitive modern people passing themselves off as civilized. The appeal of jazz and the exotic made clear that techniques of appearing were also techniques of racial passing, in which whiteness affected the sophistication and decadence of performance.

The Charleston was said to have originated in a club called The Jungle Casino in Charleston, South Carolina, invented by a regular patron some time in 1913. It swept the United States as part of the jazz craze after it was featured in the all-black musical *Runnin' Wild*.[51] It did not gain widespread respectability until it was performed in London by the Prince of Wales, but its origins remained a point of anxiety and fascination across modern nation-states. In Australia, a series of visiting dance couples such as Andree Flo and Valentine Adami, along with an influx of American gramophone recordings, sheet music, and (beginning in 1923) an influx of American touring jazz bands, occasioned enormous interest in jazz.[52] A San Francisco violinist, "Roaming Romaine," opened jazz dance halls, such as the Crystal Palace Hall and the Salon de Luxe in 1914. He toured nationally with a jazz band in mid-1918, playing at some of the big public dance halls. A baritone, Belle Sylvia, filled Sydney's Fuller National Theatre in June 1918, and later the Bijou theater in Melbourne, with the "Big American Musical Craze."[53] *Everyone's* would later claim Joe Aronson as "the pioneer of jazz in Australia." Aronson was a saxophonist who moved to Australia in 1922 from the "Far East," bringing "syncopation" to Melbourne's Wattle Path Palais and putting together local jazz bands, which broadcasted new American songs on radio station 3LO.[54]

Desire for jazz not only evinced the atavism of emancipated, and thus uninhibited, youth, it also threatened miscegenation, because jazz's cultural contamination could crescendo into sexual and racial contamination. Jazz was denounced as "Americanisation," but its abil-

ity to intoxicate young Australian women with "Negro rhythm" racialized its danger. The *Sydney Morning Herald* wrote that jazz was the
revenge of "African exiles" for the slave trade: "The American Negro
has impregnated the whole American people, and through them the
civilised world, with the barbaric culture of the jungle through the
medium of jazz."[55] Fear that young white women would be culturally
"abducted" by jazz savagery peaked in 1928, when the Hughes cabinet
voted to deport Sonny Clay's Colored Idea, a touring band of African-
American musicians and dancers, and institute a ban on black per-
formers, which stayed in force until 1954. *Truth* and the Commonwealth Investigation Branch organized a joint raid on an East
Melbourne flat and claimed to have uncovered one of the "orgies"
allegedly conducted there regularly since the arrival of the "coons."[56]
Everyones thought Sonny Clay "much maligned" and deplored the
characterization of jazz as "rhythm loomed up [depicted] as a degen-
erate menace." Still, it remarked that Clay's troupe "played a little too
'hot' for local tastes," suggesting that young women "not fully edu-
cated to the mysteries of 'blues'" had fallen under their spell, as
though jazz were some kind of cabbalistic hex or incantation.[57] But
the Australian sheet music industry, together with dance halls, the
vaudeville circuit, and the gramophone industry, had too much to lose
from the threat of cultural miscegenation—they sought to sanitize jazz
by localizing it with songs such as "Kelly Gang Jazz" and "The Digger's
Jazz."

   Excessive love of adornment was seen as a sign of modern decadence and return to the primitive. In the 1929 cartoon from *Beckett's
Budget* shown in figure 6.7, it was also linked with ostentation,
through well-established tropes of anti-Semitism. The Modern
Woman's excessive interest in her own visual effects cast her as
crossing racial divides: primitive ornamentation was proof that "the
same decorative instinct"[58] was common to all women as part of their
essential nature. This association of the primitive with visual decadence enacted a kind of representational assimilation, which continually invoked Aboriginal women in imagery to shore up essentialist
meanings of modern femininity. It denied the cultural specificity of
Indigenous women: their techniques of appearing only became visible
in order to illustrate their own inability to be modern. The popular
press delighted in tales of colonial mimicry, of Native American prin-
cesses and "the vain children" of the Solomon Islands bobbing their
hair.[59] These stories showed that, paradoxically, it was woman's constant nature to be visually inconstant, following the cycles of fashion.

JEW—ELS.

FIG. 6.7. Cartoon reprinted from *Beckett's Budget,* 19 April 1929. Courtesy of the State Reference Library, State Library of New South Wales.

If modernity forever and indelibly altered the feminine, the essential-ized premodern woman's love of fashion and her mimicking of colo-nial women demonstrated that susceptibility to change was itself un-alterable in woman.

Primitive rituals in adornment, particularly those that violated the natural body, were a ready trope of barbarity. "We exclaim in amused disgust at the blackened teeth, ringed noses and clay-bleached hair of the South Sea Island belles, and countenance this truly savage pro-ceeding ourselves."[60] The fear that white women might undermine more than the traditional foundations of their gendered identity, and "blend" their race identity with the primitive through 1920s exoticism, was expressed in fashion commentary.[61] Animal skins and feathered hats merely revealed the Modern Woman as "primeval." "She may deny it, she may advance a thousand proofs of her culture and civilisation . . . but the moment she begins to dress, or think of dress, she becomes a primitive savage."[62] Whereas disciplining the body through dress encoded the self-development that was central to modernity's evolutionary maturity, ornamentation spoke of an instinctual and infantile devotion to visual stimuli. White men dressed: women, like primitives, adorned themselves. To look to the "savage for fresh inspirations" was to look with an "impotent"[63] gaze; "impotent" because it recognized difference and, rather than rejecting it, sought to incorporate the signs of the primitive. The taste for the exotic demonstrated a unidirectional flow of colonial appropriation and ransacking, but one which left a suspicion that the thieves were in fact the real primitives.

Around the globe, primitive societies were "rifled" for exotica "to give new flavour to jazz age dress, matching the 'primitives' of Negro music with African designs and ornament,"[64] as capital insinuated itself into nascent colonial markets and plundered their cultural artifacts. In another *Aussie* cartoon a white girl poses before her mirror in an abbreviated tunic and exaggerated headdress. She asks her friend, "Do you think that my costume is rather original, Peggy?" "Oh my dear, yes! Almost Aboriginal!" Peggy replies.[65] At times, cultural appropriation "revealed" that the Modern Woman, in her "frankness" of dress, was reverting to an antediluvian, primal sexuality. A *Beckett's Budget* cartoon has a lounging young wife reading the paper. "I see the Eastern women are now taking off their veils to more resemble white girls." Her much older husband dryly replies, "They'll need to take off a darned sight more than that."[66]

The spectacle of sun-bathing modern girls was further proof that modern emancipation was simply a throwback to barbarism. Such young women were "reverting to primitive man's belief that a bronzed skin adds considerably to beauty." This "desire for colour" was seen as "an amazing anomaly . . . in this white Australia of ours."[67] Skin pigment was associated with sexuality within the representational rubric of miscegenation, and posed a challenge to the visual taxonomy of the white Australia policy. That white women desired the exotic and incorporated it into their techniques of appearing incited fear of cultural, and sometimes actual, miscegenation.

It was, allegedly, fashionable society women, "white women of the highest European culture," who preferred "the arms of smokey skinned negroes, muscular as gorillas, and with the ape's brow and jaw." These women of "high social position," "chic, expensively dressed," sought out Negro athletes and "muddied the stream of the nation's blood." Miscegenation joined with feminine visual excess to indicate "utter decadence, a civilisation's neurotic degeneracy."[68] Techniques of appearing became a conduit of cultural contamination, only once removed from actual bodily and reproductive defilement, when colonial women sought the approving gaze of the primitive or the Oriental man. White women shimmered under raced spectatorship, their skin imbued with a luminosity that was thought to be overpowering to men of other races. Such women were aware of the visual effects of their racial specificity and were both depraved and lost to civilization.

At a reputed "Devil's Auction Sale" in Sydney's Chinatown "of white girls' bodies to evil-souled yellow men . . . men whose seventh heaven of delight is the possession of white flesh," the price of a new pair of stockings is ultimately the main gain for the prostitutes. At the appointed time, "a great deal of powder-puffing and lip-sticking takes place among the girls. Shingles are preened, stockings straightened, jazz garters placed just an enticing trifle lower on the knee." The article elaborately voyeurizes the scene, focusing on the young women, who are not only spectacles but visually deceptive: "she is pretty enough even now to make you turn your head and look back at her. But there is a coarseness, a stamp of vice about her that the thick coating of powder and the scarlet slash of lip-stick cannot hide."[69] The racially defiled prostitute could not disguise her contamination with techniques of appearing: precisely as spectacle she disclosed her fall from civilized grace. In that she could be recognized as having fallen outside the colonial heterosexual economy, her deviant sexuality represented something extraneous to civilized modernity. Her agency in miscegenation matches the formula McClintock observes: "colonized people were figured as *sexual* deviants, while gender deviants were figured as *racial* deviants."[70]

In 1926, Helen Stransky played a half-caste African woman named Tondeleyo in the stage production *White Cargo*. Both because she was an actress and because of the particular role she was playing, Stransky had to carefully guard herself against scandal; she was "much criticised" and rumored to be "nightly supported to the wings for her entrance" due to a heavy dope habit. In the interview accompanying the picture shown in figure 6.8, she justified her racial passing by

H.ALF-AND-HALF—A DRESSING-ROOM STUDY
Specially posed for Adam and Eve.

FIG. 6.8. Photograph of Helen Stransky, reprinted from *Adam and Eve*, 1 August 1926. Courtesy of the Mitchell Library, State Library of New South Wales.

saying she was "steeped in the traditions of Presbyterianism" and "an ardent supporter of the anti-liquor law." She insisted, "degeneration doesn't necessarily follow in the footsteps of a wicked part." Nor was Tondeleyo "wicked"; rather her promiscuity was, as one might have guessed, "natural as the dawn."[71]

Yet Stransky's passing did risk cultural miscegenation. Tondeleyo symbolically linked the primitive and Modern Woman as an "up-to-date pagan."[72] *Truth* described the heroine of this "sensational play" as "showing white women a thing or two." Tondeleyo's "artlessness, and conception of the marriage bond, as something whereby, in return for a number of bangles and a good deal of silk, she is to stay with one man for a long time, is not very much different from the modern flapper's ideals."[73] To complete the picture of a modern white girl passing as an uninhibited primitive woman, Tondeleyo's costume was "scanty but seductive,"[74] and *Truth* opined that if Parsifal had caught sight of her dimpled knee he would not have "put the silly question, 'What is a Woman?' to Kundry . . . he'd have known."[75] Stransky's performance was a "revelation of the thinness of the veneer which separated civilisation from savagery."[76] Modernity and civilization were only a veneer constituted by techniques of appearing.

When Tondeleyo reappeared as Luya, a half-caste Islander woman, in the Australian film *Adorable Outcast* (1928), her promiscuity was resolved through her marriage to the character Conn and her understanding of the significance of fidelity. Notably, the whiteness of the actress, Edith Roberts, was preserved by means of her clothing. Luya appears with her breasts covered among Islander women (from whom she ostensibly did not distinguish herself), whose naked breasts signified that their primitivism endured beyond their screen appearances. That is, they neither dressed up nor performed as primitive; rather they were props to create ethnographic realism. As reproduced image, white women seemed able to enter a cultural space that was not without its anxieties, but nevertheless allowed racial passing. The Islander extras for *Adorable Outcast* were apparently not "in costume," because clothes were part of how they were distinguished from the heroine, Luya, and the missionary women. Their nakedness signified that unlike white women they could not appear as other than themselves. The primitive woman could not appear to be primitive, she simply was. She could not achieve the status of the modern feminine subject through techniques of appearing.

A Menace to Our Vaunted Civilization

The primitive woman who "seduced" white men was distinct from the fallen, racially contaminated white woman in that it was her race, rather than her style, appeal, or display, that registered her moral ambiguity. However, as the source rather than the site of contamination, these women needed to be identified at a glance. This glance was colonial. It had complete faith that it could discern moral deviancy through race, and it thought of Aboriginal women's visual effects solely in terms of race. Such women represented a "spectre from our aboriginal past to menace our vaunted civilisation." Even when five men from the Victorian town of Sale pleaded guilty to sexual offenses against a "half-caste" girl, under sixteen, from the Lake Tyers Aboriginal Reserve, the defense exonerated them as "easily tempted" and the police denounced the girl as "just like an animal" and "a 'throw back' to the primitive without any idea of morals or restraint." They kept the reserve "under close surveillance," and said that "it is not the full-blooded abos, but the half and quarter castes, which give the most trouble."[77]

Race contamination through miscegenation was subject to the "surveillance" of the visual taxonomies of colonial eugenics. In the countless reports of young white women, who had evidently been raped and yet whose assailants were constructed as sexually entrapped, the visual style and appeal of the women and even children figures prominently. However, the half-caste girl was absented from this scene of appraisal. Her techniques of appearing failed to register because she was visually spoken for by her racial designation as "half-caste." From this placement her height, weight, and visual appeal or its lack became immaterial. It was her racial confusion that incited sexually confused behavior in white men, not her visual confusion, as was the case for the "flighty flapper." The "menace" of this incalculably mistreated young woman from Lake Tyers was that she was a liminal halfway figure in racial taxonomies, and could therefore open a Pandora's box of sexual confusion, both latent within her raced identity and manifest in her sexual "behavior" (read violation). In this scenario modernity's privileging of the visual was deployed by eugenic discourses; they each became complicit in the controlling effects of the other. The objectification of the primitive was central to the colonial gaze, invested as it was in stratifying the boundaries of the white subject by objectifying the other. The primitive skin was invested with a transparency which, under the colonial taxonomy, obligingly divulged the proportions of mixed blood. The sense that miscegenation was manifestly visible—that a half-caste could be known by skin color in a reliable correspondence of the visual and identity—was modern ocularcentrism's wish fulfillment. It was resonant with the Nazi "aim for visible, natural difference [which] recurs in its aim for ethnic purity."[78]

Representations of the sexuality of Aboriginal women and white women were interdependent; "the sexologists' images of the white woman drew upon images of the natural sexuality of the unrepressed 'primitive woman'. Likewise the promotion of purity for single Aboriginal women drew upon images of the nineteenth century white woman, as promoted by contemporary feminists."[79] Their interdependence, however, permitted no alterity—neither in image content nor in the respective and racialized procedures by which white and Aboriginal women became visible. These procedures, and what I have been calling the failure to appear modern, were themselves constitutive of racial difference. I want to conclude by turning to instances of race fetishism in order to make clear that I am not arguing that Aboriginal women were never looked at. On the contrary, they were perceived as unable to occupy modern imagery and escape the status of object. Insofar as Aboriginal women represented the primitive (and this representation reflected on the meaning of modern women's visual effects) and were subject to the disciplinary effects of colonial administrative surveillance, they were very much under scrutiny. As Gayatri Spivak writes, "Between patriarchy and imperialism, subject-constitution and object-formation, the figure of the woman disappears, not into a pristine nothingness, but into a violent shuttling which is the displaced figuration of the 'third-world woman' caught between tradition and modernization."[80] This shuttling, I believe, was in part effected by the racial specificity of techniques of appearing. They certified the object status of Aboriginal women by forbidding them, as object-images, to propose themselves as modern subjects within their cultural specificity. White modern women paradoxically became subjects in the visually intensified scene of modernity through their techniques of appearing as objects; Aboriginal women remained objects. But while this exclusion may have marginalized Aboriginal women's visibility, it did not diminish the significance of the primitive spectacle on the modern colonial scene. In fact the primitive was fetishized as a disavowed but structuring principle of the modern gaze. Anne McClintock's etymology of "fetishism" traces the indebtedness of ocularcentrism to primitivist discourse:

> In 1760, a French philosopher, Charles de Brosses, coined the term *fetishisme* as the term for "primitive religion." In 1867, Marx took the term commodity fetishism and the idea of primitive magic to express the central social form of the modern industrial economy. In 1905, Freud transferred the term fetish to the realm of sexuality and the domain of the erotic "perversions." The "sciences of man"—philosophy, Marxism and psychoanalysis—took shape around the invention of the primitive fetish. Religion (the ordering of time and the transcendent), money (the ordering of the economy) and sexuality (the ordering of the body) were arranged around the social idea of racial fetishism, displacing what the mod-

"Bai Jove, that — er — looks like — er — mistletoe! "

FIG. 6.9. Cartoon by Mick Paul, reprinted from *Aussie*, 14 November 1926. Courtesy of the Mitchell Library, State Library of New South Wales.

ern imagination could not incorporate onto the invented domain of the primitive. Imperialism returned to haunt the enterprise of modernity as its concealed but central logic.[81]

Racial fetishism was disavowed as a scopic regime, as McClintock's genealogy describes. The primitive woman as reproduced image was marked by certain distinguishing features, principally her naked breasts. She was subjected to an imperial sexual economy which exploited colonized women while disclaiming their status as sexual subjects. In the 1926 cartoon shown in figure 6.9, the carefully turned-

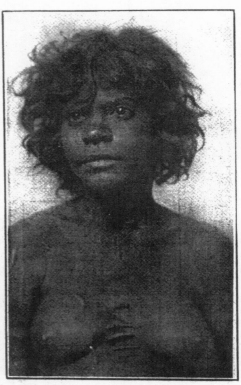

A BRUNETTE BEAUTY.—The regular oval features and beautiful eyes of this aboriginal girl might be the envy of many of

out colonial gentleman is flummoxed by the native coquette, her sexual deviancy marked by her wanton desire to cross racial divides and by her racial abjection. If she is a sexual agent, the colonial man averts his eyes. Even if described as a "brunette" beauty as in figure 6.10, the Aboriginal woman was distinguished from the modern white beauty in that she gave no sign of practicing care of the self through techniques of appearing, such as fashion. She did not discipline her surface by covering it; instead she violated it by scarring it.

Beauty Contestants were, time and time again, described as "natural" and thus representative of a frank and artless young nation. They were not, like the unnamed and thus universalized "Brunette Beauty," representative of the natural as beautiful. In representing such a universalized category, her beauty was not specified as Australian—this omission restating, at the level of representation, her dispossession. White women might have "envied" the racialized features of the Aboriginal woman, but Indigenous women could never achieve beauty in the same sense; their breasts were disinvested of the meanings of visual scandal and the privatized gaze of monogamous marriage. Needless to say, the naked breasts of the primitive woman were nevertheless subject to the voyeuristic heterosexual gaze: however, the colonial gaze was thus averted and constructed as ethnographic, innocent, and natural. It continued to pretend that it could look at Aboriginal women outside of the conventions of image possession and voyeurism by which it looked at feminine spectacle.

Modernity believed that it could unveil truth by rendering all things accessible to vision, but the "naked savage" was an ambiguous figure within this vision-centered logic. Berman finds that nakedness has been a common metaphor for "truth and stripping as self-discovery," from Shakespeare's King Lear and his "unaccommodated man" to the Marxian image of the naked exposure of capitalism's exploitation and cruelty.[82] The Western romance with the primitive was based on the unadmitted hope that the primitive would provide access to an essential, premodern man—itself a historical designation McClintock dubs "anachronistic."[83] This desire belied its own ambivalence about a perceived loss of authenticity within modernity. The primitive was assumed to be naked and also to have a childlike fondness for visual fascination which expressed itself in flamboyant codes and rituals of dress and ornament, a stereotype which would prove useful in the imperial economy of dispossession through "trinkets and beads." Primitive nudity was at times fetishized and at other times proved that "among naked savages flagrant immorality is far less common than among races accustomed to wearing clothes."[84] Nakedness without "coquetry" demonstrated the kind of "frankness in revelation" admired by those moderns who believed that dress liberation brought the benefits of "freedom of limb," hygiene, mobility, and simplicity in visual style—and who held that the visual gave access to the truth.[85] But, when gendered, the naked primitive woman merely revealed that she was sexually deviant and uncultured; when adorned or marked she was savage and infantile.

Constructing primitive feminine nudity as natural made it easier to deny that the colonial gaze was a form of sexed visual tenure, and that visual technology served as "the servant of imperial progress"[86] by enabling expansionist mapping, ethnographic classification, and the transnational language of the commodity spectacle. White moderns

Fig. 6.11. Cartoon by
W. Gill, reprinted from
Bulletin, 30 May 1928.
Courtesy of the State Li-
brary of Victoria.

EITHER WOULD DO.

Modern Papuan Missus: *"I'm bored to death. I wish there was
a club for women here."*

Her Husband: *"So do I. Or a tomahawk. I wouldn't care
which."*

looked not at the naked breasts with which primitive spectacle publicly afforded an encounter, but ostensibly at the embodiment of the
natural. In the 1928 cartoon shown in figure 6.11, the nudity of primitive women was used to suggest that they were like the Modern
Woman, seeking liberation. However, the meaning of the primitive
was anchored through nudity back to a distinct visual teleology. The
wordplay turns on an oxymoron: the Modern Woman's exposure was
about (dress) liberation, while the primitive woman was not liberated
because she was never repressed. Having no techniques of appearing
of her own, she was naturally not-dressed. The sartorial evolutionary
scale proceeded thus: modern men were dressed, modern women
were undressed, the primitive woman was never dressed. Much as the
Freudian fetish object is disavowed, primitive nudity was not directly
sexualized. Rather, the natural was fetishized for the ways that it came

to mark racial difference through visual effects, while affording un-admitted voyeuristic peeps through the keyhole of the colonial male gaze. So, in a poem called "My Abo Flapper," published in 1926, she is similar to the Modern Girl—smoking, drinking, and surfing—but not authentically modern, because not white:

> She's satin skinned and supple limbed;
> her figure's slim and straight.
> She smokes and chews and likes a booze
> (wherefore she's up-to-date);
> She takes the surf in Nature's togs, as
> ebon hued as tar—
> Whisks off her 'possum pelt and shoots
> the breakers at the bar.[87]

Her racial difference was in part marked by her not being in possession of her image, or having mastery over it; the colonial man did—which he would stridently deny if he were ever caught looking.

Thus the real scandal of the theatrical production of *White Cargo* was that it directly asked colonial spectators in its promotional posters, "Would you mammy-palaver?" (meaning flatter or wheedle the native woman).[88] The play "raised a storm of indignation because of the man-ner in which Englishmen are pictured as behaving in Negro Africa."[89] Ida Vera Simonton, author of the novel *Hell's Playground*, on which the play was based, defended Englishmen as never so "quarrelsome" or "careless of their personal appearance" as they were depicted in the play. But the play still told "of the sex hunger of the white men"[90] and of "white man's decadence."[91] The scandal of colonial men as agents of miscegenation was displaced onto the figure of Tondeleyo, "the jungle Circe, with the shamelessness of the partly civilised sav-age" and "the half-nigger vamp."[92] She was cast as "a beautiful weed drawing its life from a poisoned source [the coupling of her French father and African mother], entwining itself around all whom it came in contact [*sic*], and slowly strangling decency of thought or action in its embrace. Morality is a word without meaning to Tondeleyo. It is unknown in the vocabulary of African children."[93] Being premodern, Africans were children by definition. Their sexuality sprang from in-herent animal passion. The primitive woman was not a sexual agent: she was not "adult." Her actions instead were infantile and unwitting transgressions of modernity's mature and complex sexual edicts.

The Modern Woman's emancipated undress could also reveal, from less threatening quarters, that latent in white moderns was primitive desire. While this desire could give rise to the abomination of miscegenation, it could be expressed more safely in the uncivilized appearance of the Modern Woman. Her exposure could revert men to monkeys, drawing out the atavistic traits of a gleeful and gaping evolutionary predecessor. Thus "Uncle James" penned this verse as a "Hymn to the Modern Girl":

> And I feel as though my soul were slipping
> Back through the centuries;
> 'Tis all because a girl is tripping
> Along with splendid knees
> Hooray I am a monkey, skipping
> My way through friendly trees![94]

Colonial men delighted in being caught looking, it seems, as in figure 6.12, as long as they were not looking at black women. In fact, as spectacle, the primitive woman was subject to imperial administrative taxonomies of surveillance and visual tenure. What the colonial gaze could never admit was that when this visual tenure was cast over the bodies of Indigenous women, it could disclose that those looking, not the women looked at, were the agents of miscegenation. The imperial equation of looking with mapping was re-enacted through the possession of Indigenous women at the level of the eye. The fetishism and visual abjection of Aboriginal and Islander women emerged from the disavowal of the colonial gaze as visually and sexually possessing colonized women.

Aboriginal women were cast, like obese and aged women, as illegitimate and unassimilable objects in the modern scene. Their invisibility needs to be examined, because it represents more than an absence to modernity. Because of the way the parameters of the modern colonial subject were formulated, this absence structured who was "in" the modern scene. Appearing modern operated within a perceptual field replete with commodity racism, racial fetishism and racial abjection, exoticism of the Oriental and jazz, miscegenation, and the fiercely defended White Australia policy. These meanings intersected in a wider "primitivist discourse" inflected with gender, class, and sexuality in casting anomalies in the modern scene.

And yet representations of Aboriginal women showed them desiring, like white women, to appear. This desire indicated a desire to emit the signs of the Modern Woman and to have presence within the cultural institutions and visual apparatuses of modernity, and

"Come for a walk, Girlie?"   "Too right, Kiddo!"

FIG. 6.12. Cartoon by Hugh Maclean, reprinted from *Aussie*, 15 April 1929. Courtesy of the Mitchell Library, State Library of New South Wales.

therefore it was usually represented as comic. But the photograph shown in figure 6.13 of the Merry Singers and Dancers of Cummeragunga, taken around 1930, shows that Aboriginal women in this period did appear as Modern Women; they did indeed perform as spectacles.[95] Through their experiences within a touring troupe, their subject positions also intersected imagery. They resisted the colonial denial, the prohibition against colonized women positioning themselves within the modern perceptual field and enacting the performative subject position of the Modern Woman. I do not mean to argue that when Aboriginal women were depicted according to the conventions governing images of white women their visual presence in the modern scene allowed them to achieve a more desirable status, nor to defend the civilizing mission of training Aboriginal women in the

FIG. 6.13. Merry Singers and Dancers of Cummeragunga, Iris Atkinson (nee Nelson), Nona Tye (nee James), and Clare Mouton (nee Murray), photographer unknown, c. 1930, collection: V. Heap. Reproduced courtesy of the Museum of Victoria.

modern techniques of appearing. The dancers of the Cummeragunga performed a femininity inscribed with the visual tropes of the Modern Woman, showing that Aboriginal Women were not so easily prohibited from appearing and that their status as primitive objects was a fabrication of the colonial gaze.

Chapter 7

The Flapper in the Heterosexual Leisure Scene

If it's naughty to rouge your lips, shake your shoulders, shake your hips
let a lady confess I wanna be bad. . . .
This thing of being a good little goodie is all very well
But what can you do when you're loaded with plenty of
   health and vigor?[1]

While these lyrics no doubt posed a rhetorical question, in the 1920s they were provided with an emphatic answer: if a young woman yearned to exhibit that she was "loaded with plenty of heal-," she should appear as a Flapper. More than any other type of the Modern Woman, it was the Flapper who embodied the scandal which attached to women's new public visibility, from their increasing street presence to their mechanical reproduction as spectacles. The newly emerged subject position of the Flapper was constituted through a play of looks. Like other modern feminine types, the Flapper complicated the picture of the Modern Woman—and the status of the woman-object—by associating agency with her visibility. But she went further than the others by becoming a *sexual* subject through constituting herself as a spectacle and appearing in a heterosocial scene that was itself becoming increasingly informal by virtue of new leisure forms. In making a spectacle of herself, the Flapper seemed to court the gaze, specifically of men, and to assert her modernity as a sexual subject by paradoxically constituting herself as an object within the new conditions of feminine visibility.

The Flapper was a favored figure of mass cultural forms, and the depreciated value of "low" culture became associated with her. She was both indulged and made deviant by magazines that assumed a male readership, and she was at once the darling and the disdained of women's print media. Her enthrallment to the transient cycles of fashion and the scandal and liberation that were associated with her emancipated visual style made her an apposite representative of the instability, mutability, and perpetual innovation of the modern. The ambivalence that surrounded her visual status, as object and subject, attracted the modern gaze, preoccupied as it was with the recently invented category of the adolescent and its "demonstration of the difficulty of becoming subject."[2]

The term "Flapper" designated a young Modern Woman, whose realm of action and descriptive possibilities were tied closely, though not exclusively, to the visual realm. The Flapper had an extended adolescence as an emergent ideal of modern femininity, and she was internationally exchanged and received as a globalized type. She was notable for her mobility, her love of dance and movement, and her "sporting" sexual "frankness" with men, but I am interested here in exploring how she was constructed around perceptions of her visibility—how the meanings of her techniques of appearing were construed as part of the definitional parameters of this modern feminine type. This chapter will take the Flapper as a motif for the heterosexual leisure scene in order to explore the agency that was attached to modern women's spectacularization, and to ask why and how this spectacularization was sexualized, and thus both scandalized and sanctioned as heterosexual.

The World Bears Her No Aspect of Mystery

In the late nineteenth century, the term "flapper" meant "a very young harlot."[3] The Flapper has her etymology in the illicit commerce of a precociously deviant sexuality. She essentially remained a figure of young female heterosexuality, encompassing the spectrum of sexual trade, from the exchange of sex for "treats" in the manner of the "amateur" to the marriage market as entered by the society debutante. As adolescent she was a liminal figure: between virgin and bride, schoolgirl and Business Girl, she was losing her sweet tooth, shearing off her flapping braids, shortening her hems, experimenting with make-up, learning to drive—embodying the transformational flux of modern identity. As Catherine Driscoll argues, particular conditions shaped the emergence of feminine adolescence and the feminization of adolescence, including "[n]ew discourses on puberty and majority, new legislative definitions of girlhood including labor laws and the age of consent, new educational structures and expectations, new disciplined understandings of relations between citizenship, sex, and age, new production and consumption practices, and new modes of knowing the subject and its more or less desirable relations to culture."[4]

Driscoll's detailed genealogy of "the emergence of feminine adolescence as an explanatory category in the twentieth century"[5] relates the increased public visibility of young women to increased speculation about them in fields from psychoanalysis to anthropology and sociology. The Flapper exemplifies the increasing importance of popular visual culture in disseminating ideas about feminine adolescence in the 1920s and is an apposite heuristic for how girls consumed this imagery. The startling thing about this imagery is the extent to which it consciously comments on the significance of young women's visibility and their deliberate designs to attract the heterosexual gaze. If young modern women's growing public visibility generated commentary and theory across multiple discursive fields, the Flapper was the site where the meaning of that visibility for leisure and sexual rites was thrashed out, together with what it meant for modern feminine subjects to be speculated about, in the streets and in social analysis. As a figure of scandal the Flapper contravened a number of traditional understandings of the place of the feminine. She was not at home in the home. She sought out leisure and thrills rather than having any of the virtues of the hard-working Business Girl—although Flappers could also be Business Girls, as "An Ex-Flapper's Confession," in the *Australian Women's Mirror,* reveals:

> I was the most flapperish of flappers—and a business girl to boot. If my mother asked me to make a bed or iron in my own house I would have felt insulted. My money went in decorating myself, my evenings were spent at shows or dances or car rides with "our crowd." I smoked and was always ready for champagne, or cocktail, or wine or liqueur.[6]

Since the *Mirror* was not terribly sympathetic to the Flapper, this one goes the way of all "good" Flappers and redeems herself through matrimony. In the illustration from the sheet music distributed by Dinsdale of Melbourne ("On the level you're a devil") and shown in figure 7.1, the Flapper was the iconic hoyden, hotly pursued by men in top hats and tails astride a bottle of bubbly. Yet her desire for pleasure

[handwritten margin note: How hotly the Flapper paraded ... new rites]

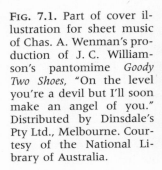

FIG. 7.1. Part of cover illustration for sheet music of Chas. A. Wenman's production of J. C. Williamson's pantomime *Goody Two Shoes*, "On the level you're a devil but I'll soon make an angel of you." Distributed by Dinsdale's Pty Ltd., Melbourne. Courtesy of the National Library of Australia.

and for the heterosexual chase was deemed excessive, as was indicated by her being "obsessed by love of dress and gaiety," which would entrap her "in the spider web of excitement." The young Modern Woman who relished showing her jazz garters in public and who flashed the "glad eye" to strange men found pleasure in breaking "the social commandments" and set out to "jazz a hectic course to perdition."[7] A single woman, she wanted more than the "coming out" of the society debutante, with her ritualized unveiling in rounds of social engagements. The Flapper diverted herself with the liberatory pleasures available to the young unmarried woman in an increasingly informal and commodified leisure scene.

Captivated by the commodity spectacle, the Flapper roused all the ambivalences felt about the female consumer, whose "perverse cravings" were seen as symptomatic of modern decadence and "an all-consuming primordial female desire."[8] Whereas men invoked the realm of production, the Flapper took her meaning from the ostensibly passive and feminized realm of consumption. She seemed to delight in the anonymity of the transitory crowd and the visual promiscuity of the metropolis, and gleefully sashayed through the streets. In doing so she rejected the national mythology that associated rurality with authenticity. She utterly rejected the lingering entanglements of mo-

THE FLAPPER'S INDISCREET FLAP

FIG. 7.2. Cartoon by Alice Solly, reprinted from *Aussie*, 15 April 1929.
Courtesy of the Mitchell Library, State Library of New South Wales.

rality surrounding the ideal of the decorous, modest, and discreet
young woman, choosing instead to pursue pleasure ostentatiously.
Cartoonists often depicted her confronting their caricatures of the
moral reform movement, "Mrs. Grundy"[9] and the wowser, as in the
family portraits shown in figure 7.2.

The genealogy of the Flapper charts the directions of transnational
commodity and cultural flows. She illustrates the place of the Modern
Girl in Western-influenced visual culture—she also appeared in To-
kyo, Beijing, Bombay, and Johannesburg—and how the Modern Girl
was received by various communities of readers and spectators, who
were poised on the cusp of the local and the global, the national and
the cosmopolitan.[10] The Flapper embodied the increasing complexity
of international power relations, as multinational corporations mobilized national types in order to localize the expanding markets of globalizing capitalism. As a shared figure, she points to the increasing cultural resonance between these countries through visual technologies
such as print and film, advertising, and the practices of commodity

exhibition. One contributor to *Aussie* "studied" the "amazing geographical array" evident in the Flapper's dress, remarking on her French gloves, American shoes and silk stockings, Italian hat, German handbag, and Swiss handkerchief.[11] Through her visual style, the Flapper spanned modernity's global commercial and representational networks, while her presence in public space simultaneously situated her before a local and scrutinizing gaze. In Australia that gaze was particularly adept at picking out American cultural imports, which it was both fascinated by and wary of.

In the United States the Flapper was identified in 1913 as "the pre-eminent model of female appearance."[12] She was associated with eye-catching, purposeless movement, especially that of the unbuttoned galoshes popular among Midwestern farming girls. The Flapper had succeeded the Gibson Girl, taking on her youth, femininity, and simultaneous high spirits and demureness.[13] In 1915 H. L. Mencken described her as "impossible to shock"; she read Havelock Ellis's works on sex, and "the world bears her no aspect of mystery."[14] Her sexual knowledge underlay the deep ambivalence felt about her; on the one hand she stood for modernity's quest for truth, but on the other hand she represented sexual agency. Commentators looked to her modes of appearing in order to discover how her modernity might affect traditional heterosexual rites.

The British Flapper was distanced from her unpalatable past as a precocious harlot between 1918, when women over thirty were enfranchised, and 1928, when younger women won "the flapper vote." According to Billie Melman, the public was obsessed with feminine sexuality during this period, and this obsession manifested itself in the definition of the Flapper: "An ambivalent notion of feminine adolescence was, it shall be recalled, central to the image of the flapper. For that historically peculiar image of the young woman as androgyne combined a blurring of the sexual identity of the modern female with mythical sexual prowess." Her ability to haunt the popular imagination in Britain also appeared in the "surplus woman" debate that occurred after the massive loss of young men's lives during World War I, fostering "fears of a perturbed, demographically imbalanced society."[15]

In Australia, these associations were adopted along with the type of the Flapper. She first appeared in the popular press as early as 1913. From his research into black-and-white drawings and popular cultural forms around 1900, Craig Judd concluded that the term derived from the sounds made by loose shoes on the pavement, similar to the unbuttoned galoshes of the American farming girls.[16] The British use of the word similarly derived from the young girl who had not yet "come out" and whose hair, whether braided or hanging, "flapped in the wind."[17] The Flapper was associated with coltish movement, often loose, uncontrolled, and erratic, that occurred outdoors or in the public eye. Bohemian columnist Dulcie Deamer wrote that the activity of the Flapper was "like the whirring movements of a clockwork toy, or even the spasmodic jerks of a just-decapitated creature."[18] This emphasis on movement would do much to associate her with the modern cinematic image both as a spectacle in movement and as a favored type in the emergent Hollywood narrative film. Her sexuality was also configured within the mobile play of looks in modernity. This mobility of looks characterized the Flapper's sexual mobility, giving rise to terms such as "flapper brackets" (motorcycle sidecars)[19] and "flapper-snatchers" (men who picked up girls for joy-rides).[20] In Virginia Scharff's history of women and motor cars, she writes that the Flapper's "appetite for self-display, for pretty clothes, and for reckless fun made her seem a perfect customer for the 'pleasure car.'"[21] She was "fast" not just in activity but in her sexual itinerancy.

In the late teens and early twenties the term "Flapper" was commonly applied to adolescent girls and sometimes children, suggesting that the androgyny of the Flapper's stylized body is only part of the story. As young women stepped into the routines of masculine street presence and workplace participation, and were even seen to challenge men in their interest in, and initiation of, sex, they were characterized as effeminate men (as distinct from the caricature of feminists as "mannish women"). But the Flapper's tubular body shape was also informed by the lanky, gangly-limbed premenarchal girl. She was the first ideal of an elongated and thus sexualized girlishness that has reappeared throughout the twentieth century in figures such as the gamine. In one child beauty competition in 1922, a special "flapper class" was set aside for girls between six and eighteen.[22] The term was used in paper patterns for girls who were not yet making their own clothes, but were nevertheless "rather scornful about what they call stodgy underwear." They were unlikely ever to wear long skirts as part of their rite of passage into womanhood, as though their highly mutable and mobile figures were nevertheless atrophied in adolescence.[23] In women's magazines the Flapper could still be figured as a child as late as 1927.[24] In a 1918 *Bulletin* cartoon a first-aid teacher asks a pointy-nosed schoolgirl still in short skirts and braids how she would treat a snakebite on his ear. "Oh, we'd put the ligature round your neck," she replies mischievously, while her classmates snicker behind their books.[25] The girlish Flapper showed none of the uncertainty of the discreet, blushing Edwardian virgin. Rather, she was all too aware of the visual effects of her emerging sexuality, which nevertheless failed to propel her into sanctioned "adult" sexual rites and nuptials, causing the adults around her consternation.

There are multiple contradictions within the meanings of the Flapper. As Driscoll notes, "the putative independence of modern women has seemed to be a problem precisely because of her immaturity, and her immaturity is defined by her dependence."[26] And there remains the unresolved question of whether she was a symbol of modernity's moral decadence, or of its newfound sexual "frankness." Nevertheless she was consistently understood as having significant consumer power, and although she was often dependent on the indulgence of fathers and "mashers,"[27] she had disposable income and therefore independence. She was willing to exploit the new technologies associated with mobility, leisure, and amusement, and she handled them adeptly. But, ever in childish pursuit of pleasure, she retained "not one, but a whole lot of sweet teeth."[28]

The Flapper remained childish even in the form of the more independent and sexualized young hoyden, often seeking pleasure and creating havoc with all the indifferent glee of Ronald Searle's later St. Trinian's schoolgirls. The copious commentary on the Flapper represented her as having deliberately and calculatingly placed herself within a heterosexual leisure scene, aware of and enjoying the impact of her visual effects. Her childishness, joy-rides, cocktails, and visits to the "flicks" made her elders worry that sexual pleasure would become her favored object and that her prolonged hedonistic immaturity would ultimately disqualify her from the traditional roles of maternity, marriage, and domesticity. One commentator remarked that such young women found "the bread and meat of marriage poor substitute for the chocolates and flowers of courtship."[29] "[M]aturity is a crucial force in structuring late modern life," in which access to the modern subject depends on entering social majority by virtue of arriving at legal age, and the Flapper is part of what Driscoll calls a terrain (which includes legislation, commentary, and social science) on which "girls are not subjects of the public sphere that identifies them by that discourse."[30] On a variety of discursive surfaces the Flapper fulfilled the status of the woman-object. Yet her imbrication of sexual agency with visual scandal produced the beginnings of a counter-version of the adult that would become enmeshed in the feminine exhibitionism and explicit display of the modern pornographic. The pornographic designation of "Adult" as the exclusively male spectator and "Girls, Girls, Girls" as the exclusively heterosexualized spectacle means that the visual sexual agency the Flapper had earlier used to access a peculiarly feminized adulthood was largely lost, until the gendered stratification of sexualized appearing and voyeurism began to be prized apart in the femme erotica of the 1980s.

In the 1920s anxiety about the purely pleasurable use of sexuality by young women mobilized a regulatory system of discourses that had already begun to surround women's sexuality. It had given rise to the 1903 New South Wales Royal Commission that inquired into the decline of the birthrate. In the 1920s, the birthrate was half that of the 1880s, a decline which was in part attributed to a "love of luxury and social pleasures" in young women.[31] In Victoria in 1916, the government introduced an act to control venereal disease which identified certain young women, such as amateurs, as its source.[32] The "new network of knowledge" about the sexuality of young single women included popular versions of Freudian psychoanalysis.[33] "Adolescence" and "Flapper" emerged together in the late nineteenth century as popular knowledge, disciplinary effect, and representational type, overtaking earlier, less scientific notions of "teenage" years as merely "stressful."[34] In 1922, the *Home Budget* wrote that Flappers between the ages of twelve and twenty were "in peril of nervous invalidism" due to their fears of adolescence.[35] While young women's healthy sexuality was "a system as vital to health as any other bodily system,"[36] it was not something to be flaunted.

But the new meanings of the sexuality of young women had contradictory effects. Under sexology "the female body became the repository of ideas not only about modernity but about sexual pleasure. Women were simultaneously objectified and rendered subjects of their own desire."[37] In the 1920s, young women were thought to use the popularized discourses of sexology to know their own desire. Also at play were psychiatric and criminological discourses that brought into view the sexuality of modern young women. Young women seemed to work this discursive and representational web into a dangerous consciousness of the sexual effects of their visual desirability. These young women—these "sex-perts," as Brodie Mack dubbed them in his 1930 cartoon shown in figure 7.3—were in fact precocious experts in the prevailing understandings of both feminine sexuality and the tech-

niques of appearing through which they were sexualized. As their sexuality became more public, their visibility became more fascinating, and their increased visibility came to signify their modernity.

Undiluted Youth

Through her visual style, the Flapper came to signify the hallmarks of modernity, such as novelty, change, youth, and innovation. Kenneth Yellis writes that what appalled people "about the Flapper, her behaviour and her dress, was precisely her modernity."[38] Dulcie Deamer considered the Flapper "today's dominant type" who "represents undiluted youth."[39] Another Sydney columnist wrote, "there are two of her in every five foot two and a bit of modernity."[40] She did not live for posterity, but "for A Good Time This Very Minute." Sensitive to her significance as a cultural type, Deamer argued she should not be relegated to the comic supplements, but rather likened to the Statue of Liberty, "towering above the variegated epoch in which we live—a sign and a portent." The Flapper was literally "looked to" for a clearer picture of modernity. In one theater review, actress Marie Prevost was described as representative of "the alluring flapper"; she "brightens the drab old world" and her self-assured visual style expressed her "natural exuberance and spirit of happy girlhood."[41] The Flapper's epochal representativeness would continue to inform ways of thinking about the modern retrospectively even into the present.

In popular histories, the Flapper would become a nostalgia figure for the "roaring twenties."[42] She has come to represent historicity itself, as a cultural marker of the 1920s as a distinct period. Women's modalities of appearing are often used as evocative historical motifs. The Flapper's bobbed hair and crêpe de Chine tube dresses have acquired historicity, becoming emblematic of the 1920s. Some charmed male historians have used her visual style as shorthand for their periodization. In *The Confident Years* Robert Murray writes that "the age of the flapper" was characterized principally by the fashion preferences of younger women, who "preferred tight non-voluptuous bosoms and the slim look."[43] George Mowry includes the Flapper among cultural items which together define "the twenties" in his *The Twenties: Fords, Flappers, and Fanatics*,[44] as does an anonymous quiz book on popular history called *Live Them Again: The Three Decades from Flappers to Flying Saucers, 1923–53.*[45] L. L. Robson has likewise characterized the twenties by innovations in young women's visual style, though he is more conscious of the historical cliché of the Flapper: "Women smoked and drank and bobbed their hair and adopted the small cloche hat which fitted tightly on the bobbed head. The vogue of rouge and lipstick spread like wildfire, and the flapper emerged—the stereotype of the period."[46] Vivian Stewart's personal account of a Sydney department store remembers Flappers as at "the height of fashion in short crêpe de Chine or silk georgette frocks with hair cropped in the new shingle style."[47] John Montgomery's earlier history of the British twenties calls up a vision of Flappers as "short-haired, boyish girls" who made free use of lipstick and make-up, which, prior to the war, had rarely been worn.[48] Similarly, for Stuart Macintyre, the Flapper's practices of appearing signified women's wider access to commercial entertainments. "Under their [screen star's] influence, Australian 'flappers' learned to bob their hair and dance the Charleston."[49]

Yet in spite of all this historical exposure, the Flapper has been characterized as a trivial historical figure precisely because her visibility is emblematic of the way modern women made spectacles of themselves. A rift that was to last the century in Western feminism emerged between those who saw feminine visibility as political participation and those who saw it as self-indulgent vanity. This polarization made it impossible to recognize the complex image of the Flapper, to see her as asserting herself as a modern subject and a sexual subject through her object status. The dichotomy was already evident at the time, as older "serious" women and the Flappers, the symbol of Modernity's youth, were distinguished through their visual styles.

While admiring the Flapper, Dulcie Deamer also criticized how she signified the modern age as "the age of youth." She satirized "the neat and nippy generation of deathless flappers," complaining they showed the modern preoccupation with "Youth, youth—nothing but youth!" She cynically wrote of the absurd imperative for women to stay forever young as symptomatic of the age's being "on the verge of immortality."[50] Flappers were said to be scornful of older women and their ideas of propriety, often because of comic ignorance of the conditions of their mothers' lives:

> When she wanted presents of any old thing, she couldn't let on she did.
> It wasn't correct to fool a man for the sake of half a quid—
> It must ha' bin a horrible world when Mother was a kid!
> To have to behave like a blinkin' nun and do what I was bid,
> And never be kissed by Jack and Ned or squeezed by a chap like Syd;
> It must ha' bin just jail for a girl when Mother was a kid![51]

Not surprisingly, older women were often perceived as antagonistic to the Flapper. Feminists such as Vida Goldstein and Rose Scott saw Flappers as misusing their hard-won independence and newfound liberty on frivolous pursuits.[52] Older women, on the other hand, were represented as overly preoccupied with hem length and resentful of being eclipsed in the modern scene by the Flapper's attention-seeking. The Flapper was advised, "you needn't care / Because the aged anywhere / Condemn the bobbing of your hair! / Their rage is envious forsooth! . . . They're rather jealous of your youth."[53] Their resentment was construed as jealousy, which in turn was taken to express an outmoded sense of visual propriety. In another cartoon, a tram conductor chats amiably about the weather, remarking, "we could do with another three or four inches." An older woman (studying the flapper's skirt) exclaims, "I should think so, indeed!"[54] *Truth* portrayed such older women as "[s]itting like owls on a dead limb on the tree of life," envious of the very thing that connoted modernity: youth, "its brave laughter and joyous unconventionality."[55]

And yet the Flapper could also modernize older women by putting to good use her transformative powers of rejuvenation and her know-how in matters romantic. In one short story she reunited poor spinster Miss Lucie with a long-lost love while boarding with her and her disapproving spinster sisters. This Flapper became "an instrument of fate," opening the closed world of the spinsters to romance. The story reiterates that the visual appeal of the Flapper is her defining quality and is even able to summon the modern, for while Miss Lucie's sisters "[d]eplored the modern girl . . . Miss Lucie often looked wistfully after the flying long legs and cropped head that seemed to her the embodiment of life and youth."[56] Her attraction to the visual effects of the Flapper's youth leads to her being "cured" of the condition of spinsterhood and her consignment to the premodern. The Flapper was ever a window of opportunity in the modern heterosexual design.

Since the Flapper was young, she was required to visually denote the difference between feminine generations.[57] Older women who mimicked her visual style unwittingly infringed on her symbolic meaning and were subject to much ridicule and censure. Considerable invective surrounded the appropriate age "to flap." Older women could only become modern by adopting the Flapper's representative visual style. Yet the mature woman "who continues flapping long after she is past the flapper age is a public nuisance,"[58] largely because she could upset the position of youth as an increasingly defining category in the taxonomy of modern women,[59] and in part because she absented herself from the role of chaperone. One commentator complained of the misconception that Flappers were girls "who had just reached that age when human beings first consent to have their faces washed without making a loud outcry." In fact, he gibed, women over forty were the "most pronounced flappers," more conspicuous because of their inappropriate "cosmetic make up and elephantine kittenishness."[60] The older Flapper could manipulate beauty techniques in order to retain a tenacious hold on youth. She defied the beauty culture doctrine that the " 'middle-aged' woman is conspicuously absent in the modern scheme of things,"[61] or rather she confirmed that middleaged women were never seen because they were disguised as young women.

The most pernicious threat posed by the older Flapper was that she might seduce young men through visually deceiving them about her age. Her techniques in visual deception—in appearing to be younger or more desirable or more chaste than she was—provoked one commentator to warn that "[t]errible revelations have occurred on sofas" through the deception of cosmetics, "the enemy of intimacy"[62]—as long as physical intimacy was the true knowledge of one's lover. Because she constituted herself as spectacle, the Flapper was deceptive, illusory, and sexually manipulative of men. Her brazen comportment was sometimes seen as a new and rebellious configuration of womanhood, yet it could also give the smart Modern Woman a bad name—particularly if, despite her maturity in age, she displayed herself as still childishly enthralled by the modern spectacle.

This desire to keep pace with the modern scene through appearing "up-to-the-minute" gave writers ways to characterize their time as excessive in its desires and unbalanced in its pursuit of pleasure. The sociologist George Simmel wrote that the rapidity of changing fashion reflected the "weakening of nervous energy" in an increasingly "nervous age."[63] The less august *Truth* was similarly disdainful, declaring war on "the menace of the flapper" who does everything "too hard, too fast and too often." Her modes of appearing, underwritten with the trope of the blasé prostitute, situated Flappers as representative of the decadent modern:

> They are jaded and bored and tired. Their crimped and marcelled hair has lost its vitality, their skins are lifeless. Unless they have a thick coating of cosmetics on their faces they look like passé women who have "gone the pace" and sounded all the depths of experience. They are bored to distraction and eternally on the look out for new excitements to stimulate interests.[64]

Because she delineated young and, by omission, aged femininity, the Flapper could also represent a kind of sexually despoiled and used-up young womanhood. Ideas of the aged, worn, and world-weary recurred in constructions of the Flapper. Deamer wrote that the "(spiritually) wrinkled flapper" had bestowed on the modern age "the indescribable feeling of a room where nearly all the oxygen has been exhausted."[65] Her desire to be scandalous grew out of the fact that "horror and astonishment are almost as essential to us as oxygen" in "a civilisation which has had its thrills 'drawn'—like its milk teeth."[66] On the one hand the aged, in the guise of the older, premodern woman, was set against the Flapper, the representative of modernity's youth; on the other hand, disquiet about the pace of the modern was expressed in the spent and slightly soiled figure of the Flapper. If the modern was youthful, the Flapper was used to warn of the consequences of "going the pace." Meanings of youth were shifting in the contradictory characteristics of the Flapper: from innocence and clumsy, innocuous animation, to a knowing and calculated use of juvenile energy and appetite with lamentable intentions.

When she wasn't making a spectacle of herself, the Flapper was an all-too-willing spectator of mass cultural forms which in their content and "appeal to baser feelings" also represented the enervated and spent modern youth. *Truth* argued that such forms of popular culture had stolen ten years "from human advancement" in their "stimulation" of "unhealthy imagination" in the jaded and thrill-seeking modern youth. They were part of the new morality founded under the compromised conditions of war, and were symptomatic of the "faster and faster" pace of the times.[67] In these accounts, modernized spectacle symbolized the loss of humanity and moral standards through the war, and the consequent excesses of youth.

You Find Her on the Movie Screen

In a series of comic narrations in *Aussie*, "Phyllis Phlapper" enthusiastically grappled with modern technologies, including the telephone, the train, and her long-suffering father's motor car. In each scenario they became playthings which exposed her to attention from unknown men. On the rare occasions when she was found at home, she created domestic anarchy, baking her father a pie that left him "fearfully ill."[68] When gadding about outdoors, her natural habitat, she was a creature of much technologically assisted action which had little dire consequence, at least to herself. After learning to drive her father's car, she felt "fearfully lucky because dad took it out the next day and he had three punctures and jammed the gears!"[69] Phyllis Phlapper was intercepted by "mashers" as she used these technologies—when crossed wires misdirected her telephone call, a man on the line posed as her boyfriend;[70] when she was on the train, an inebriated man inveigled her into playing cards.[71] Her rather optimistic belief that male strangers wished her well predisposed her to becoming "very chummy"[72] with her various companions, and yet her innocence deflected their advances through a series of missed cues. Her behavior betrayed a certain naiveté born of a too literal viewing of Hollywood films. For instance, Phyllis found it strange that her "pals" made up almost immediately after a fight, given that "it usually takes a big event to bring lovers together again, such as an illness or the child getting drowned."[73]

This flighty, dizzy young woman contradicted the knowing, self-assured Modern Girl. Yet both versions coexisted in definitions of the Flapper, because both were projections of the fear that young women were simultaneously ill-prepared for the snares and lures of public intercourse, and all too prepared. Indeed, young women, conscious of their visual appeal and schooled through popular culture in the use of their wiles, were perceived as becoming the principal lures. The contradictory implications of young women's exposure to the public eye, which we saw in the marketing of disposable sanitary napkins, recur in the doings of Phyllis Phlapper. Exposure was a danger to young women against which they must protect themselves. But in the Flapper, the danger of exposure took a new twist: the young woman who exposed herself to the public was a danger, both to herself and to others.

Part of the danger to herself derived from her exposure to, and entrapment by, the visual pleasures of modernity. She was captivated and fascinated by the modern spectacle, particularly the cinema— Rudolph Valentino was "the flapper's idol."[74] But although she was sometimes characterized as naively absorbing cinema's dramatizations as truth, like Phyllis Phlapper, the Flapper could also be unusually savvy about its limitations, while still indulging in its engrossing pleasures. Flapper columnist "Molly Masters" noted of photographs that "there's nothing like a snap to remind you of the wonderman you met a year ago—and forgot all about in a week."[75] The camera symbolically captured the volatile, mobile sexual encounters of young women. Feminine spectacle was often associated with the Flapper, and many

Hollywood films, such as *The Painted Flapper* (1924), gave her the lead role. A team of chorus dancers who appeared at Fuller's Theatre in Sydney in 1928 were called "Fuller's Eight Flappers o' Folly."[76] And the chorus girl was the "embodiment of flapperness" in one *Mustard Pot* ditty, not just because "You find her in the magazine / You find her on the movie screen," but because she appeared "With mind quite low and skirt quite high."[77] The Flapper was portrayed over and over again as spectacle and as morally "low." She endangered not only the helplessly charmed men whom she snared but also her family's reputation, because she took cues from these constructions of feminine spectacle, integrating such conventions into her own practices of appearing. Her relation to the mass spectacle made the type of the Flapper a focus of anxiety about young women's "exposure," to spectacle and as spectacle.

Her engagement in the cinema was instrumental in the construction of a female gaze, which Miriam Hansen believes unleashed a crisis through "women's massive ascendancy to a new horizon of experience." This ascendancy threatened to create an alternative public sphere that was feminized and spectacularized, and that flouted the gendered hierarchy of access to public life. If the female consumer and cinema spectator constituted a threat in their appropriation of the public gaze, the Flapper was defiant in taking pleasure in these realms and applying their principles to herself. In Australia, anxiety over the disruptive potential of the female gaze was manifest in concerns about the moral entrapment of young women in the commodity and cinema spectacles. That the Flapper should pose such threats through specular relations testified to the significance of spectacle in modernity's understanding of itself. Hansen writes,

> The challenge to the gendered hierarchy of the public sphere violated a taboo that pre-dated bourgeois sexual arrangements; the taboo on the active female gaze that pervaded traditions of representation in art, mythology and everyday life. If modern advertising and the department store had mobilized the female gaze in the service of consumption, the cinema seemed to have institutionalized women's scopophilic consumption as an end in itself, thus posing a commercially fostered threat to the male monopoly of the gaze.[78]

The youth culture of the 1920s was the first to use a feminine type to convey the specifically capitalist injunction that identity be realizable through consumer choice and immersion in visual technologies. Single young working women did not seem to fit the masculine par-

ameters of "youth" as productive and rational. By indulging in the
pleasures of mass spectacle, they defied the rational principles of the
modern masculine youth, streamlined by the new Fordist labor discipline.[79] Young working girls seemed to draw more attention by indulging in popular culture and entertainments, and choosing their
modes of appearing.

The Flapper was described as immersed in popular culture. The
enormous Palais de Dance ballroom in St Kilda, holding up to five
thousand people, was the "the Mecca for flappers."[80] A review of Anita
Loos's novel *Gentlemen Prefer Blondes* (1926) said that it should be read
by anyone "with the slightest pretensions to modernity," most especially "the longest-legged and shortest-clothed flapper on the block."[81]
Members of "the species *scribendi flapperus*" were said to be the main
participants in the "post-card craze" of the period.[82] And when cartoonist Esther Patterson promised to produce a book of portraits of
modern feminine types, it was said to be likely to be "popular among
flappers and flapperettes" because of its success in portraying "the picture girl," with whom Flappers were said to identify.[83] A number of
magazines devoted pages to Flappers, and in April 1929 *Aussie* put out
a special Flapper edition. One columnist wrote, "you see her, legions
of her about the streets, in shows, at cabarets and monopolising the
sun on the beaches."[84] Because so much attention was paid to the
leisure preferences of young women, and because they were the dominant consumers of popular culture, they became arguably more crucial to twentieth-century constructions of "youth culture" than young
men, thus feminizing it.

This feminization of youth culture probably gave young women a
greater sense of cultural inclusion and presence, itself strongly associated with what they saw and with being seen. While commentators
and older feminists were decrying the frivolous and narcissistic pursuits of young women in new mass cultural forms, young women
themselves, perhaps, saw their fascination with spectacle differently.
As they gained ascendancy, as spectators and spectacles, on the cultural stage, young women may have increasingly associated their spectacularization with social agency. As Kathy Peiss notes in her study of
the leisure practices of young working women in turn-of-the-century
New York, leisure and visual style were sites of negotiation for young
women in modern feminine identity:

> It was in leisure that women played with identity, trying on new images
> and clothes, appropriating the cultural forms around them—clothing,

music, language—to push at the boundaries of immigrant, working-class life. This public presentation of self was one way to comment upon and mediate the dynamics of urban life and labor—poverty and the magnet of upward mobility, sexual assertion and the maintenance of respectability, daughterly submission and the attractions of autonomy and romance, the grinding workday and the glittering appeal of urban nightlife.[85]

Mass culture has been derided as feminine and, as Andreas Huyssen has found, as "monolithic, engulfing, totalitarian, and on the side of regression"—abrogating the permanency, originality, and authorship of "high art" to masculinity.[86] But the daily choices that young women made in the clothes they wore, the language they used, and the leisure forms they took part in significantly reclaimed mass culture from the masculine forms of races and football in the Australian cultural imagination.[87] Arguably the Flapper filled the symbolic gap created by a leisure culture which was as yet unfigured by a feminine type. This symbolic function would play directly into a longstanding correlation of spectacle with scandal, which found all too ready confirmation as the industrialized mass spectacle. The Flapper would retain her *demi-monde* associations by looking favorably on the modern image, and by constituting herself in its likeness.

Scrupulously and Pruriently Searching for "Sin"

The association of the feminine with the mass spectacle situated it on the devalued side in a series of gendered binarisms. Traditionally, the feminine has been relegated to the side of the inauthentic, along with duplication and falsehood, while the authenticity of the original object has been attributed to the masculine. In this dichotomization, material reality has been pitted against representation, as have fascination and seduction against considered critical reception.[88] The mass-produced spectacle has been defined by its repetitiveness, its quantity rather than its quality. It is still sometimes believed to evoke an involuntary corporeal response, usually of reflex gratification, rather than appealing to the discriminating mind. As a figure of mass culture, the Flapper, characterized as frivolous and shallow, stood for the depreciation of the visible as too obvious compared to the invisible, which was "the source of value, hidden from all but the enlightened few."[89] The precedents of the scandal of the spectacle can be traced as far back as religious suspicions of "concupiscentia ocularum," Augustine's ocular desire—the ability of the image to divert the mind from spiritual concerns.[90]

The technology of printing and the increase in literacy brought about the rise of the mass image and the novel. Anxieties about the widespread availability of such material focused on its effects on the impressionable minds of women, children, the working classes, and Indigenous and migrant populations. The crowd seemed to spontaneously develop an appetite for mass cultural commodities; it was an undiscriminating, standardized response, as involuntary and essential as hunger or desire. Paula Findlen writes that pornographic culture originated in "this widened circuit of popular printed goods." "The reactions of various authorities to the appearance of erotic and obscene materials in print reflected the uneasy transition of a society from one in which access to knowledge was restricted to the social and intellectual elite to one that divulged its secrets daily and indiscriminately."[91]

The sense that knowledge and the spectacle should only be revealed in the privacy of select private libraries and institutions of learning tainted the publicized image with sexuality as anxiety about its effects on the less discerning masses crystallized around notions of exposure, indecency, and obscenity. The activity of reading had been similarly demonized, as was the mass spectacle. However, as cultural theorist Andrew Ross notes, reading was associated with masturbation until mass spectacle and industrialized pornography redeemed it in contrast as "a promise of deliverance from the orgiastic public rites."[92] That the rash and libidinous modern youth should be so hungry for mass spectacle simply evinced their carnal desires. In the 1927 *Bulletin* cartoon shown in figure 7.4, the cinema becomes an unregulated, unsupervised locale for the illicit sexuality of the simian-featured working class—a sexuality that found cover in darkened theaters and accompaniment, rather than interruption, in the moving picture. The devalued and feminized mass spectacle entered the locale of the scandalous not only because of its sexualized content, but still more because of its mode of production as reproduced spectacle. As Lynda Nead has argued with regard to pornography, "the material and cultural value of the pornographic is reduced by its reproducibility."[93] To some extent the mass spectacle, because of its mass reproduction, is tainted by the pornographic. When women, as the content of such imagery, were added to this cultural mix through the changes to visual culture in the 1920s, a kind of exposure was enacted on a number of levels. The feminine mass spectacle became sexualized and scandalized.

FIG. 7.4. Cartoon by David Henry Souter, reprinted from *Bulletin*, 28 April 1927. Courtesy of the State Library of Victoria.

The passage of explicit imagery from the private to the mass-produced set a precedent in the sexualizing of mass feminine spectacle. As Lynn Hunt shows in her analysis of pornography during the French Revolution, explicit images were used to vilify the "debauched" and feminized aristocracy, the monarchy, and the political figures of the ancien régime. However, the depiction of sexual pleasure became an end in itself, and once pornography could make a profit, "it increasingly needed no other justification." And yet, once the pornographic had "embarked on a career as a separate and distinct genre, clearly consigned to the underside of bourgeois, domestic life in the nineteenth and twentieth century," its earlier focus on the exposed feminine body began to mark a "fraternity" of the male gaze. Its mass production depoliticized and commercialized it. In Hunt's words, "the fraternal bonds of democracy were established—in pornography, at least and perhaps more broadly—through the circulation of images of women's bodies, especially through the print media and the effect of visualization through pornographic writing."[94]

The modern pornographic and feminine spectacles were entangled in the history of an increasingly fraternalized and commercialized gaze under the conditions of the reproduced image. The all-male audiences of early forms of silent cinematic pornography—the looped stag films of the 1900s, which were still shown in the 1950s—exemplified this fraternal rather than privatized gaze and the way the modern pornographic structured sexual difference into its look. But scandal was a reaction, rather than something that inhered in explicit images of women. Visual scandal was specifically the dominant cultural reaction to the publication of women's sexuality in low cultural forms.

Sexuality was brought into the realm of representation, and its erotic effects posed questions about even the most "factual" anatomy texts. In 1930, for instance, a bookseller in Sydney's Martin Place was convicted of selling obscene publications that included Aristotle's anatomy studies.[95] Censorship had initially targeted heresy rather than the sexually explicit, but by the modern era the widening of the audience for sexualized material had already prompted the founding of the vice societies of the social purity movement. In Britain, these societies assisted in pushing through Lord Chancellor Campbell's Obscene Publications Act of 1857, as well as establishing a police squad, which made such publications its exclusive concern.[96] The campaigns of the social purity movements continued to be effective. Film industries in Britain, America, and Australia voluntarily censored themselves under the movements' pressure, even before Will Hays, the president of the Motion Picture Producers and Distributors of America, established his formidable Production Code in 1930.

By the 1920s the social purity movements had gained full legitimacy, and authorities had become "very responsive to their demands."[97] But their vigilance effected a kind of exposure. The increased regulation of private sexual behavior by public institutions in the Victorian era coincided, as Foucault has argued, with a proliferation of knowledges about sexuality—itself a kind of pleasure—and its workings in the individual and society. The moral purity campaigns did not so much place sex outside the law as require that it be subject to vigilance and brought under the law's disciplinary power. As Foucault notes, sexuality became "constituted" through the law, or an effect of its operations of power.[98] Although they aimed to veil sexuality, the vice societies in fact brought it into public visibility, only to then seek its banishment. Jacqueline Rose explains the origins of these discursive shifts:

> In the second half of the nineteenth century, morality makes a spectacle of itself. Across a range of discourses this spectacle repeats itself, each time calling attention to a sexualisation which resides in the very act of looking, at the precise point where that sexuality is being most rigorously stamped out or denied.[99]

Thus "the very act" of scrutinizing women's practices of appearing only served to intensify women's exposure and eroticism. The coincidence of sexuality's entry into discourse and the increasingly feminine content of reproduced images positioned the spectacularized woman as a sexualized object. Martha Banta discerns the sexualization of feminine spectacle at work in images of American women. She writes, "everywhere Americans looked on almost every level of the nation's pictorial life, the image used with the greatest frequency to suggest the nature of desire was the image of the female."[100] Small wonder feminine spectacle became iconic in commodity culture. But the real scandal was what women themselves did with this iconicity: they adopted and negotiated it as an intrinsic part of their status as not just subjects, but specifically sexual subjects. As fashion historian Valerie Steele puts it, "whenever sex is an issue, so is looking and being seen."[101] The Flapper seemed to have this understanding built into her desire to become spectacle.

The Flapper's passion for self-adornment was characterized as an "outlet to her unconscious urgings,"[102] but also as symbolic of the modern scene's tendency for exposure. "Bookish" writes of "Short Skirted Literature":

> the tendency which makes the flapper flap in abbreviated skirts displaying calves that may be shapely, but frequently are not, and a glimpse of garter, and in low cut transparencies around the shoulders has its counterpart in the modern novel's tendency to invade bedrooms and the intimacies of life and throw off all the clothes of life with which the writers of the Victorian age were wont to cover risqué situations.[103]

As the modern type which risked the most exposure, the Flapper became a staple of comic puns and cartoons. Her vanity was written of as constituting a "fascinating" new species, *Shortskirtus Jazzgarterius:* "it is immensely vain and over burdened with sensibility. Its passionate self-adornment is well known."[104] Narcissism and exhibitionism were compatible with lingering perceptions of feminine deviancy. One columnist wrote, "our streets and public places are filled with women who are apparently trying to see how much they can leave off without being arrested." To these commentators, this fashion for exposure revealed nothing but "some perverted sort of sex-impulse."[105] Making a spectacle of oneself was condemned as "flapper manners" and reviled. "She powders her nose in public and shows her knees in trams or ferries because she thinks it is smart to do so. She combs her bobbed hair anywhere, in the theatre, in the street, in the office where she is employed. . . . [The] over-bold, over-frank, rather rude young woman of today may soon have to step aside for a younger group of girls who realize that a young woman is never more charming than when she is a little demure, and does not hide her natural modesty and sweetness under a bushel."[106] The Flapper's deliberate self-display was transgressive because she deployed public space as her own exhibition space. She was not prepared to enter the perceptual field as a mere spectator. She wanted to dominate the scene and control the anonymous play of looks within it.

"Flapperish Fashions"[107] were jokingly described as on a slippery slope to nudity in image after image of Flappers: "In our dress most of us move with the times, but flappers are not satisfied. With them it is a case of remove."[108] In another cartoon a Flapper looks at a painting of a half-nude woman and declares to the artist, "Gee! I thought it was a design for a summer evening dress!"[109] In her study of representations of the English Victorian prostitute, Lynda Nead articulates how this pleasure in display became one of "those defining features of female deviancy." She writes, "it is the issue of visibility which is ultimately at stake; women are defined as deviant in terms of their visual engagement with pleasure."[110]

Young women's apparent pleasure in exposing themselves, encapsulated by the Flapper, prompted a surveillance over women's public visibility so intense that at times it seemed ludicrous. When the newly established borough of Carrum, in Melbourne, imposed a £20 fine on anyone exposing bare arms or legs, except when immersed in the sea, *Truth* berated the council for bowing to "the dimsighted Wowser scrupulously and pruriently searching for 'sin' through his gilt rimmed specs."[111] In its portrayal of the Wowser, *Truth* toyed mischievously with the image of censors seeking out hidden sights in order to expose them to public opprobrium. It delighted in portraying such people as clerical puritans who went to extraordinary lengths, including using a magnifying glass, to uncover the indecency in modern women's practices of appearing. Effectively it played on the paradox that censorship brought obscene material to public attention in order to have it removed from view. "Even wowsers go to the seaside sometimes— just to see what they can see, you know—but they take their pleasures very sadly." Whereas the male Wowser was a surreptitious and prurient voyeur who "wants to see the worst," the female was motivated by having nothing herself to show. Her image in cartoons was sardonically ballooned with variations of "Fancy me dressing in that outrageous costume." *Truth* claimed she would sing a different tune "if she had only been plump and pleasing, like the 'creatures' she con-

FIG. 7.5. Illustration by
Mick Paul, reprinted from
Bulletin, 13 March 1929.
Courtesy of the State Library of Victoria.

QUITE LEGITIMATE.

MAIDEN AUNT: *"Goodness! What are you doing up there?"*
FLAPPER: *"Just scoring, dear."*
MAIDEN AUNT: *"But all the men are looking at your—er—limbs."*
FLAPPER: *"Yes, dear. That's where I'm scoring most."*

demns."[112] The premodern female Wowser, peering through her
glasses like a spinster aunt, seen here in figure 7.5, was visually illegitimate in the modern scene.

Once the Wowser had singled out types such as the Flapper as
morally questionable, those types were guaranteed to become favorable within the pornographic repertoire. The caption on a nude study
in the men's magazine *Mustard Pot* says that the Flapper is willing to
show "good form on our beaches."[113] In an advertisement for "undraped photographs" from French Art Studios, modern visual technologies gave the voyeuristic male gaze access to a worldwide vista of

spectacularized feminine types, from the "Saucy Bavarian Vamp" to the "Flighty Finnish Flapper," "Lovely Prague Jewess," "Artful Arab Woman," and even "Fluffy French Flapper." This range underlined both the universality of women's spectacular eroticism and the ability of such technologies to contain and order racial difference.[114] The Flapper, one of the Western and thus modern types, figured as common to Western nations in part because she was a shared woman-object amenable to the pornographic gaze. As long as pornography made the feminine body its privileged object and continued to be aimed at a fraternal gaze, a gendered binary of spectatorship and spectacle was structured into its look.

Australia in the 1920s was equipped not only to market such scandalous material, but to import it and produce it. *Truth* advertised "Rare Books and Post Cards," in which Marie Stopes's *Married Love* was thrown in with such works as *Awful Disclosures of Maria Monk on the Secrets of Convent Life Exposed* and "full length figure studies."[115] In catalogues of "spicy French Books," the moral preoccupations of the age become staples in the pornographic imagination. *Beckett's Budget* advertised "A vivid exposure of how white girls are seduced by Chinese" and asked, with a kind of sensational moral voyeurism, "Would you like to study the quivering soul of a woman and watch her as she revels in the joy of bliss realized—and later gaze upon her as she sinks into the agonising depths of despair?"[116] The misogynistic effect of the Hays Code, in which women who experienced sex were then shown to be punished and suffering, was foreshadowed in this advertisement.

Truth also reported that "Obscene films" were being smuggled from France via the Dutch Islands and screened at a number of nightclubs in the main shopping strips of Melbourne: Chapel Street, Glen-Eira Road, Dandenong Road, Orrong Road, and St Kilda. It alleged that some films were being made locally, along with photographic "nudes of a grossly revolting character," by a "certain depraved brute in the moving picture industry."[117] Were the women who appeared in these images equally depraved? A number of court cases at this time involved young women who were indecently assaulted by men who posed as photographers and "took unusual liberties in the examining" of the girls' figures. *Truth* claimed such men succeeded in their deception because of "the commercial mania of Melbourne daily newspapers for publishing pictures of female limbs."[118] These young women were both defiled and made vulnerable to trickster photographers by their exposure to pictures of "female limbs" in the popular press. Exposed to this mass feminine spectacle, they supposedly responded by

FIG. 7.6. Souvenir program from the masquerade artists' ball of 1924 held at Sydney Town Hall, August 29. Illustration by Percy Benison. Ephemera Collection of the National Library of Australia.

wishing to be reproduced as spectacles. The assumption that they did so—rather than, like the male photographers, wishing to see—can only be explained by the assignation of sexual difference through the play of looks; the pornographic image ostensibly solicited only the fraternal gaze.

"Exposed" young women were repeatedly accused of being too much encouraged by displays of the female nude. In the scandal of the 1924 Annual Artists' Ball, artists were reprehended for their "lewd" and "salacious" use of the nude.[119] When posters of the nudes which decorated the Sydney Artists' Ball of 1928 were published in *Beckett's Budget* the paper opined, "Nudity can be very beautiful and inspiring, but here it is rather disgusting."[120] While the 1924 souvenir program shown in figure 7.6 self-consciously uses feminine nudity to position artists as deliberately provoking the censure of Wowsers, *Truth* associated the annual artists' balls with the bohemian community and "society libertines," lending them the taint of "the underworld of pickpockets, thieves and dissolute hoboes." The 1924 ball was an "exhibition of lewdness and sensuality" to which women responded not by looking, but by wearing "neither a covering, a garment, nor a fancy dress—just a subtle arrangement of cloth to achieve the greatest amount of sexual suggestiveness to be paraded before the gloating eyes of drunken, leering louts."[121] The very Flapperish young woman pictured on the 1924 souvenir program, seated half-naked on an artist's palette, has the infantile and diminutive Wowser on a string, along with a more celebratory Fatty Arbuckle–like caricature. High art has sometimes shielded the female nude from censure, but these artists were not interested in being redeemed by their venerable predecessors. They wanted instead to be perceived as libertines, deliberately provoking, but nevertheless remaining out of the Wowser's reach. The devaluation of the feminine spectacle, like the pornographic, was gauged by distinguishing between the morality of mass art and high art.[122] The program cover invokes a Flapper-like figure to suggest that modern artists could admit to their own voyeuristic relation to the female nude, and that the nude herself was a visual agent, provocative, sexual, and heedless of her detractors.

Run the Gauntlet of Glad-Eye Girls

The young woman who simply "made a spectacle of herself" still provoked a scandalized gaze in the 1920s, despite young women's incursions into the public eye—or, more likely, because of them. An etiquette manual of 1919 was preoccupied with how young women publicly appeared. "Don't submit servilely to fashion"; "Don't wear too many trinkets of any kind"; "Don't supplement the charms of nature by the use of the colour-box"; "Don't overtrim your gowns or other articles of apparel"; "Don't be loud of voice in public places"; "Don't permit your voice to be high and shrill"; "Don't publicly kiss every time you come together or part"; "Don't use terms of endearment when you do not mean them"; and "Don't, young ladies, giggle or affect merriment when you feel none."[123] To "Do" all of the above, however, was to fulfill the stereotype of the Flapper. If, as the popular American commentator Elinor Glyn said, the Baby Vamp was the "It Girl,"[124] then the Flapper was deployed in the popular press as the Don't Girl, a site of moral instruction on the appearance and behavior of young women in public. The Flapper was defined by her disregard for social nicety, etiquette, and traditional mores.[125] In this respect she was emblematic of the attention-seeking unmarried girl whose modish appearance evinced her modern morality.

The *Mirror* admonished, "There is a type of girl, frivolous, crude, irresponsible and not overly burdened by morality who is always likely to come more prominently before the public gaze than others."[126] The author did not specify the nature of this gaze; it might be the disciplinary surveillance of the welfare movement, the consumerist gaze of popular culture, or the "glad eye" of street encounters. But it seems that the scandal of such young women was determined not primarily by who looked at them, but by the self-conscious intentionality of their visual effects and the fact that they actively solicited a sexualized gaze. Women's visual appeal should have remained unselfconscious and uncalculated; "the girl of good society is never 'loud' or 'flash.' She does not use her body as a lure, being sweetly unconscious of the lure of her body. . . . she is modest instinctively."[127] This expectation was seen also in more learned quarters. Sexologist Havelock Ellis, in his *Psychology of Sex*, placed modesty as "the chief secondary [sexual] characteristic of women": though not, it would transpire, of modern women like the Flapper.[128]

The Flapper's calculated visual appeal was an index of the morality of the Modern Girl. She was an opportunist in the changed conditions of feminine visibility, ever seeking eyes whose gaze would grant her the pleasures of exhibitionism. Her desire to be seen was part of her precocious hankering to take the first steps on a sexual trajectory which was scandalous, if not deviant. By soliciting sexual attention from anonymous men, she took her place alongside the "street Fairy," "privateer," and "amateur,"[129] standing in the shadow of the street prostitute. Empowered by mass culture's invitations to look, young women's gaze had acquired its own force. At the street level it sparked a network of mobile, gendered scopic encounters taking the colloquial form of the "glad eye." When young women "cast" the glad eye at the "gladsome eye" of "mashers,"[130] their mobile looks were seen to signify their sexual mobility. "Chase me clinahs" gave the "glad eye promiscuously," like the young woman with "yes, yes" in her eyes in the sheet music illustration shown in figure 7.7. They were said to be behind the persistent street harassment by mashers and "knuts," who were forced to "run the gauntlet of glad-eye girls" and yet were unfairly targeted by police as "pirates of the street."[131]

The parameters of heterosexual activity expanded during this period to include the play of looks between men and women on the street. The Flapper's desire to be seen was believed to indicate an excessive libidinous urge to be objectified by a heterosexual, anonymous, and transitory gaze. She became a cultural thought balloon, invested with the required explanation of the modern spectacle and how it

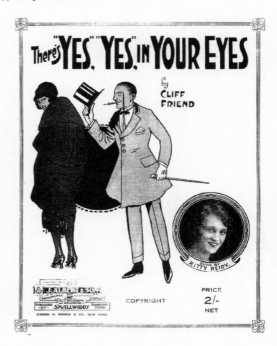

FIG. 7.7. Cover for sheet music of Cliff Friend's "There's 'Yes,' 'Yes,' in Your Eyes." Jerome H. Remick, publisher, New York and Detroit. Distributed by J. Albert and Son in Sydney (1924). Courtesy of the National Library of Australia.

reframed heterosexual relations within scopic encounters. And she illustrated that, typically, it was the feminine that carried the representational burden in the cultural redrafting of heterosexuality in the 1920s. Young desirable women were the spectacle rather than the spectator in these encounters, and their images represented the predominance of the heterosexual scene on our perceptual horizon, which has continued to this day.

The attention-seeking behavior of modern young women like the Flapper gave much cultural scope for a new legitimation of heterosexuality and an essentialized, objectifying male gaze. And yet, like the girl sipping through her straw in the cartoon shown in figure 7.8, the Flapper was unfazed by the attention; in fact she placed herself center stage and looked back expectantly, appropriating the right to her own "wild oats" or sexual agency. In men's magazines, the Flapper became a particular point of fascination and her heterosexual desirability was often enjoyed, if not eulogized. The "red hot flapper baby" "must know just how to pet," according to one ditty in *The Mustard*

THE FLAPPER'S WILD OATS

FIG. 7.8. Cartoon reprinted from *Aussie,* 14 July 1923. Courtesy of the Mitchell Library, State Library of New South Wales.

Pot,[132] and "Ycleptos," writing as an appreciative male observer in *Aussie* in 1929, devoted a poem to the Flapper:

> And many a thrill one gets
> From their twinkling feet and their figures neat
> And the way that each garment sets
> From their shining curls and their skirt that twirls
> Round their rounded knees.

But although she was a "gleeful sight," the dark side of the Flapper was never far removed. Men were warned,

> Don't be a sap, don't fall in the trap
> Be your age, my friend, be wise.
> Though chic and pert, she's an awful flirt
> And knows how to use her eyes.[133]

Flappers calculatedly objectified themselves, seeking to elicit reactions from men; they "posture in a bathing suit / Flaunting every angle" and "Deck themselves like Sheba's queen / 'Boyish' figures / Spare and lean / Ever syncopating."[134] By constituting herself as spectacle, she seemed to invite the objectifying male gaze and shore up its dominance, but her pleasure in the activity of becoming image was nevertheless threatening because of its self-referentiality, self-consciousness, and predatoriness. Thus a Bathing Beauty was photographed under a "Danger" sign in the *Sun News-Pictorial*.[135] It was as though a responsive male look only confirmed her pleasure in becoming image, and the male gaze seemed entrapped by her self-awareness as desirable image.[136] She may have known how to use her eyes, but her real threat came from her knowing how to use men's eyes. In a Percy Lindsay cartoon, two men standing in the street discuss a passing, quietly dressed young woman. "Cut in, Jim—she told a chap I know that she liked men who are game." In trepidation Jim replies, "Not me! To her sort all men are game."[137] Flappers were "not nice girls; they invited with smiles, they giggled, they ogled, they gestured."[138] Their fate was spinsterhood, since "the sensible man of today is by no means concerned with the modern flapper or the ultra-fashionable society girl as a matrimonial prospect."[139] Such a girl figured in the lyrics of a song titled "Just a Girl That Men Forget"[140] and was typecast in a play called *The Promiscuous Flapper*. She tore down all the veils of feminine mystery and thus could not stir a man to romantic love as the object of "strange ambitions and self-satisfactions he had never felt before."[141]

The Flapper incited desire, which was distinct from romantic love, and was relegated to the sexual arena of commerce and scandal. She thus became a useful figure in constructions of the culpability of deviant young women for sexual violence perpetrated by men. From 1919 to 1923 *Truth* ran numerous accounts of allegations of incest, rape, and indecent assault, presenting such experiences as the consequence of the "worthless flapper's" deviant "precocious proclivities"[142] and her calculated visual appeal. The Flapper's resistance was "very weak. She only said stop it, which, under the circumstances amounted to almost encouragement to the youth to go on."[143] In such cases, the Flapper's frankness did nothing to help her case: "in giving evidence, the girl related her story with an ease and unconcern which gave the impression that she had a first hand knowledge about worldly things much beyond her years."[144] This version of the Flapper was a "menace to young men of the community," said to repeatedly allege rape, carnal knowledge, and indecent assault. Every attempt she made to gain redress through the courts further typed her as deviant and in need of "rigorous control,"[145] generally in industrial and convent homes. Like *Truth*, *Beckett's Budget* made use of the Flapper as voyeurized spectacle while constructing her as sexually devious and damaging to men; "a flapper scorned" was liable to bring charges.[146] The high number of acquittals indicates the extent of sexual violence against women and their lack of legal redress, and the thorough undermining of the Flapper as a credible witness. Courts were advised to be "very sceptical about even the biggest certainty of any flapper when it comes to a question of identification and a man's liberty."[147]

Given the anxiety about women's heterosexual agency as expressed in their practices of appearing, it is remarkable how willing men were to surrender their sense of sexual self-possession to the calculated visual effects of the Flapper. The Flapper's attire was "a constant challenge to the baser feelings of young men,"[148] who were more or less asked to abnegate responsibility for their behavior, which was now due to the effects of feminine spectacle. The modern scene "confronted" young men with "appeals to the senses" from every direction. They were overwhelmed by the public displays of shoulders, which, on one sheet music cover, left them stuttering and gaping involuntarily.[149] The "countless exhibitions of intimate feminine attractions" were omnipresent—"leg shows" in theaters, "luscious pictures" from Hollywood, "bedroom biographies," and "half-naked bathing girls" pictured in "aphrodisiac journalism" assailed the senses, making the modern scene part of a "trying age" wherein feminine spectacle besieged men from every side.[150] The "Flapper Trapper" loved men for the pleasures they could provide but did not find pleasure in men themselves. She "fooled and fleeced" men and vampirically "cast them aside like sucked oranges," relying on abortionists[151] and divorce courts to annul her "natural" responsibility. The Flapper, "artistically hand painted,"[152] took possession of men's desire without allowing herself to be "spoken for" in marriage, thus up-ending the sexual contract. If she did marry, it was only to try "the one social novelty as yet unsampled."[153]

And yet, not unlike the Tiller Girls, the Flapper distracted men from the overly accelerated daily conditions of modernity. Glyn believed the desire men felt for the Flapper resulted from "mechanical development" and "the frightfully nervous strain" men endured in "the modern extraordinary speed of life."[154] Men, worn down by the demands of modernity, married the "fluffy" girl because they sought distraction and amusement, which the "laughing chit of idleness" effortlessly provided. She, however, was incapable of feeling genuine love "in her diminutive heart"; rather, she loved only admiration and caresses.[155] Her sexuality was visually overpronounced and yet "atrophied," because the Flapper was obsessed with capturing men "by clothing itself as little as it may. She uses the powders, the paints, and the artifices of the man-huntress."[156] A man might be drawn to her as spectacle, but she only "looked him over" in terms of his capacity to flatter with treats and presents. Overheard on the tram, one Flapper said of her weekend beau, "[H]e is soft. I pulled his leg for his week's wages again. Care for him? Huh! He gives me a good time. That's all I want from him."[157] Even worse, the Flapper was on her way to "displacing" men from their work, as cheaper clerical labor.[158] Dominate the modern scene she certainly did.

Young wives began to follow flapperish fashions as well, upsetting long-held traditions and bewildering their husbands. A short story in the *Australian Woman's Mirror* was introduced by the dilemma of husbands and wives negotiating the fashion for a shingle (short hair) and, inadvertently, the terms of the sexual contract. "Are there ANY young wives of today who haven't quarrelled with their husbands over this terrible question of shingled hair?"[159] The intention of Susie, Jim's wife, to shingle her hair went to the heart of their marriage contract as a contract of ownership over her body and visual effects. Once married, women should endeavor to make themselves visually appealing to their husbands alone. But the story of Susie's shingle highlighted the fact that, to modern women, the contract was merely symbolic, not especially relevant to the modern ideal of companionate marriage. When Jim forbids her to shingle her hair, she insists that it is her hair and she will do as she pleases with it. When he trots out her marriage vow to obey him, she replies "in a quivering voice," "Only a cad . . . would cast a thing like that in a girl's teeth—something she was just obliged to say for convention's sake. . . . That bit should have been cut out centuries ago; nobody takes it seriously."[160] If young women sought self-ownership at the level of the eye, they contravened the relational constructs of privacy, romance, and intimacy, and thus of heterosexual monogamy.

Women's new public visibility challenged the conventional possession of women's sexuality. To see a woman's hair down, for instance, had been invested with the eroticism of intimacy and sexual possession by literature and popular journalism.[161] As women bobbed their hair, discarding locks that had once been the exclusive visual domain of their husbands, many observers became uneasy. One literary critic described the domestic privilege of unbound hair as "virginal." He lamented, "Their intimacy [of husband and wife] has lost its crowning glory. They [husbands] no longer awaken near a tousled lover, but instead, a friend with dishevelled hair."[162]

Women who determined their own visual effects were taking part in the contemporary practice of equitable marriage. A 1925 cartoon in the *Bulletin* suggested that their assertions made them less vulnerable to sexual and domestic violence. "Thank Heavens I'm shingled," a cavewoman declares as she watches another be dragged off by the hair by a club-wielding caveman.[163] When the Flapper entered public space, she took with her those aspects of femininity that only husbands should be privy to. Standing by an elevator, two Flappers astound the staid gentlemen waiting nearby when one says, "Oh, they're lovely," and her friend draws attention to "them" being underwear by asking, "Have you got them on?"[164] Cartoonists had a field day with puns that transferred the theme of heterosexual exchange to the realm of the Flapper's appearing. One cartoon read, "Sydney Flappers prefer silk stockings because they like something to show for their money."[165] Once having lost the privilege of the privatized gaze, appearing modern women, not unlike the pornographic image, became commodified: as one cartoon title suggests, they were "goods in the window."[166] An "elderly husband" berates his scantily clad young wife from behind his newspaper: "I would make a woman like you pay income-tax on your figure. You wouldn't be so darned ready to reveal it then."[167] Young women were represented as prioritizing their pleasure in appearing over the romantic and increasingly sexual adventure of marriage: "I thought hubby objected to your wearing a bathing costume," a young man asks, gazing appreciatively at his acquaintance's figure. "He did," she replies. "What, changed his view?" "No, changed my husband."[168] Marital duty, configured as exclusive visual fidelity to husbands, was cast aside as young women's desire to appear to a variety of men took precedence. Engagement rings were said to "put the dampener" on some forms of amusements—perhaps because once glimpsed the look-over from men ended there.[169]

The insatiable "dress craze" of modern young women like the Flapper demonstrated the extent of "the temptation of clothes in deciding a woman's virtue."[170] "Silk stockings" had already entered the Australian lexicon by the early 1920s as code for this less detectable sexual commerce in which women exchanged sexual favors to finance the purchase of clothes, or for gifts in the form of articles of clothing.[171] And yet young women's visibility was paradoxical. These women made observers anxious partly because, despite the excesses of sexualized modes of appearing, their illicit sexual behavior was still not wholly unveiled and brought under surveillance.[172] Furthermore, they mimicked popular characterizations of the baby vamp and "gold digger," because they craved "that hectic brand of adventure introduced to them by cheap literature and pernicious moving pictures."[173] Much as sex was brought into discourse, women's techniques of appearing were brought into sex, that is, defined as sexual behavior in themselves. The agency that modern women were attaching to their techniques of appearing, the remonstrances of husbands at sharing their wives' charms with passing men, and the attempts to read women's sexuality from their visibility are all symptomatic of a dramatic shift in modern heterosexual relations: these relations were being enacted at the level of the eye. Heterosexuality was becoming an activity of looking, so that John Berger's axiom "men act, women appear" can describe not just the assignation of sexual difference through scopic relations, but the respective positions of men and women in heterosexual relations.

There was also a sense that excessive feminine exposure was a privilege of the wealthy woman, her "flaunting" a mark of her idleness. "Sassiety shemales" were accused of competing "as to who can show the greatest expanse of naked skin."[174] Excesses in exposure, particularly the bare back, were symptomatic of class decadence, the "new(de) rich,"[175] and unlike the working-class girl, society girls were hypocritically overlooked by the Wowser.[176] In Thorstein Veblen's influential *Theory of the Leisure Class*, the precondition of women's socially extended visibility was their economic dependence on men, whether they relied on sartorial upkeep within marriage or on gifts in more casual relationships.[177] His theory appears to have influenced 1920s popular discourse. For the poor, exposure meant "not having a rag to their backs,"[178] while for the wealthy, exposure was an excess of vanity and an attempt to entrap a wealthy husband. The "trapper" Flapper attracted the gaze of wealthy men as a way of "marking out her prey."[179] She was likened to the Gold Digger and the Vamp, characters in the American films being block-distributed in Australia's picture palaces during the 1920s. Glamour within the Gold Digger genre figured the fallen woman as exchanging sexual favors for fur, jewels, and luxury modernist apartments. As Lea Jacobs argues, the motifs of luxury and rise in class had a "prominent narrative function" in the fallen woman film. As a predator the Flapper type was a central character in such films, her insatiable love of finery driving the narratives of ruined men and ruinous women transgressing class divide through sexual commodification.[180] The scandal of these films was that the women did not fall but, on the contrary, rose quickly through class ranks, their luxury dress the visual manifestation of the success of their promiscuity, and thereby all the more offensive.[181] The glamour of these women barely covered the dissolute predator lurking beneath the finery. In these recurring narratives, women's visual appeal was used to disguise their true moral nature. It mesmerized men and blinded them to the women's parasitic intentions. Feminine spectacle once again was characterized as illusory and deceptive.

Paradoxically, the visual exposure of young women did not reveal their truth. Rather, girls "who flagrantly and indelicately disport them-selves on the crowded beaches . . . destroy the mystery of woman," itself a feminine "truth."[182] Flappers tricked men by pretending to be either older or younger, so that "a watchful eye should be kept on the fascinating flapper, whose appearance belies her age and leads the budding youth into the path of temptation which often puts him on the road to a police station, and more than often a felon's cell."[183] In Britain, a member of the House of Commons proposed an amendment to the criminal law requiring girls under sixteen to wear their hair long and hanging loose, for fear of the confusion they created among young men.[184] It became increasingly difficult to read young women's moral status from their visual style. In the 1920 film *The Breaking of the Drought,* two men watch the bush-heroine breaking in a horse. "My dear Gilbert, there are two sorts of women; good ones and bad ones. The bad ones are never found at home and the good ones are never found out." The pun on domestic accountability does nothing to overcome the problem that less and less could be ascertained about the sexuality of modern young women. As a reaction to this moral indeterminacy, the emerging Flapper type fulfilled what Lynda Nead calls "an appeal for absolute categories."[185] Yet the public exposure of women such as the "amateur artists" shown in figure 7.9 offered little to go by. When young women actively manipulated their visibility to effect a desirable image, their visual agency and sexual ingenuousness became a contradiction that only seemed to make them more inscru-table.

By adopting artificial, standardized, and reproduced images of women, the Flapper provoked further fears that feminine essence would be lost. A range of cosmetic products and techniques in "beauty surgery" were reinventing the feminine as reproduced not just in the printed image but in the transformations of woman's own body. Par-affin injections, hair dyes containing aphenylene diamine or lead ac-

FIG. 7.9. Cover illustration by Leonard Frank Reynolds, reprinted from *Aussie,* 15 March 1923. Courtesy of the Mitchell Library, State Library of New South Wales.

etate, acidic skin exfoliators, and their associated risk with blood poisoning illustrated the scandalous lengths women might go to in order to meet the ideals of fashion and youth. Such women were said to become "uncanny" in expression, acquiring "the face of something unnatural and inhuman."[186] "Foolish flapper fads" could have serious consequences for health. Cutting the hair too frequently, in order to maintain a bob, could result in a "pimply mange" called "the flapper's rash" on the back of the neck. The Flapper's use of cosmetics made from poisoning agents could result in "severe internal derangement and general ill-health."[187] She confirmed that "in the age of mechanical reproduction the artificial has become a determining condition for modernity"[188]—and a determining condition for her identity as modern. Her gregarious distortion of the natural self through artifice and sexualized display intensified anxieties about whether visual evidence could accurately reveal the essence, let alone the moral categories, of the feminine. For instance, the author of an article in *Truth* claims that Havelock Ellis, among other "scientists of worldwide reputation," attributes women's artifice and love of finery to "the instinctive desires of the flapper." And yet the author warns that the inherently "passive sexual role" of women means that "[h]er pretty provocative lures, her love of finery and personal adornment, her transparent little artifices in accentuating her attractions, are merely indications of the instinctive feminine desire to afford pleasure to the male animal. But to assume that the flapper is swayed by sensual longings—as sensuality is understood by man—would be absurd." While "the fascinating flapper displays an ingenuity in accentuating her sexual attractiveness that is positively uncanny . . . [it] cannot always be accepted as camouflage to conceal the carnal longings of flapperdom."[189] Again, nothing can be known from the Flapper's techniques of appearing. Whatever sexual agency she might possess was all show, and did not reach deeper than the surface effects of her self-spectacularization.

Appearing within visual technologies, the Flapper was typed as a mechanically reproduced spectacle, which was itself seen as illusory, standardized, and "untrue to life." Types were taken from film stars and the roles they tended to play—Theda Bara was a Vamp, Bebe Daniels and Louise Brooks were Baby Vamps ("the kind of woman no woman can believe is good while no man can believe is bad"[190]), and Clara Bow and Colleen Moore were Flappers.[191] In the Colleen Moore vehicle *The Perfect Flapper* (promoted by *Everyones* in the ad shown in fig. 7.10), the Flapper was in her element, surrounded by the appraising eyes of men, all vying for her (perhaps unattainable) love. Becoming spectacle located her in the center of the heterosexual field, but also cast her as having to overcome her inauthenticity in order to find real love. The Flapper was adopted from film, the very medium which had legitimated her daily quest for objectification. This did little to assuage the concern that her fluid adoption of such guises indicated a fluidity between the sexual categories of good and bad.

The type embodies a historical moment immanent within an individual, which attempts representational coherence through its common cultural perception. This is not to say that the Flapper, as a category, encompassed all sorts of modern young women, but rather that she represented young women's ability to move between multiple identities—Business Girl by day, Flapper by night, Screen Star in aspiration. As such, she began to represent the modern experience itself as a visual melting pot in which the most stringent visual taxonomies traditionally applied to women came undone.

This inscrutability figured as a loss of feminine essence and was often represented as gender mutability or the diminishment of modern young women's femininity through androgyny. It is worth noting in

FIG. 7.10. Promotional ad for *The Perfect Flapper* (1924), reprinted from *Everyones—Incorporating Australian Variety and Show World*, 3 September 1924. Courtesy of the Mitchell Library, State Library of New South Wales.

passing that androgyny and "mannish fashions" may have had their historical precedents in women's resort to cross-dressing in order to gain access to metropolitan public space. In the 1920s, androgynous appearance was another cause for scandal. Margueritte's *La Garçonne* (1922) and Radclyffe Hall's *The Well of Loneliness* (1928) were banned during this decade, suggesting that not just explicitness, but also lesbianism and gender transgression through visual ambivalence, were to be censored. The androgynous Flapper, encapsulated by the young woman shown in figure 7.11, was not averse to the gender mobility of "mannish" fashions. She was more likely to be likened to an effete young man. The boyishness of the Flapper was also seen to indicate flight from the sexual responsibilities of maternity and womanhood proper. But her androgyne was not a shying away from heterosexual activity itself; rather it was a dangerous rejection of the social institutions in which that activity should occur. As "the symbol of our era," the Flapper was said to have borrowed too much from boyish immaturity, out of a sense of feminine inferiority. She sacrificed the "dewy" youth that is peculiar to women, their "faith and wonder," to adopt the "restless self-assertion and crude, puppyish irreverence" of

THAT'S THE SORT OF GIRL ETHEL IS.
GERTIE: *"What kind of a girl is Ethel?"*
BERTIE: *"Oh, you know, old-fashioned—dam' effeminate, I think."*

FIG. 7.11. Illustration by David Henry Souter, reprinted from *Bulletin*, 19 May 1927. Courtesy of the State Library of Victoria.

young men.[192] And yet this parodying of young men only positioned her more on the side of sexual agency and self-determination. The new control these types of the Modern Woman possessed over their inconstant and versatile femininity—control which they gained through façade and artifice—associated them with the illusory feminine spectacle. But their gender mobility only intensified their sexual mobility. Paradoxically, the Flapper's androgyny seemed only to heterosexualize her, and I would argue that it did so because it was effected, like modern heterosexuality, at the level of the eye.

The self-possession of modern young women, which they gained by mastering their visibility, is manifest in Margaret Preston's 1925 painting *Flapper*, reproduced in figure 7.12. The portrait does not suggest that the flapper sat for Preston, but rather gives the impression that the artist and subject observed each other matter-of-factly and

Fig. 7.12. *Flapper* (1925). Painting by Margaret Preston (1875–1963), purchased with the assistance of the Cooma-Monaro Snowy River Fund, 1988. Courtesy of the National Gallery of Australia, Canberra.

dispassionately on a tram or ferry. By creating a type-portrait, using an anonymous model, and titling the work *Flapper*, Preston invites viewers to see her subject as symbolizing young women's public access and their self-assurance within such scopic encounters.

The "dress-liberation" with which modern young women like the Flapper were associated was another marker of the new agency that was attributed not only to women's public visibility, but to their practices of appearing. Liberated modes of dress were "the outward and visible signs of women's new Charter of Freedom and Independence."[193] Cruel, regressive customs that hid women behind veils and damaged their health with "superfluous yards of material" had been cast off, "and now the flapper has made a spring toward liberty and equality."[194] In one cartoon, a new maid is asked if she has any "encumbrances." "Not on your life! No petticoats, no corsets, no long skirts, no long hair, no gloves, no hairpins, no."[195] Similarly, the Flapper was "quite honest" about her use of beauty aids, "and prides herself like an artist on the skill of her make-up." Her "meticulous care" in "turning herself out" was, in these less condemning accounts, not a form of visual deceit or mastery over men's desires, but a forthright display of her thoroughly modern desire to improve herself. Knowing how to "make the most of the beauty youth has endowed her with" indicated that she was seeking to claim her rightful "place in the sun."[196]

Barbara Cameron writes that the "new emphasis on glamour should not be seen solely as commercial exploitation, but rather as a move towards a new type of freedom," and that the new self-image of the Flapper "answered a deep-seated need in women to assert their sexual identity." The sexual emancipation of the Flappers, in part effected through their visual style, was women's most enduring gain in this decade. Cameron provocatively concludes, "Perhaps the flappers were the most successful feminists of the twenties."[197] Insofar as feminine visibility has been associated with cultural presence and self-mastery, the traditional scandal of the spectacle was adapted to their own ends by young women like the Flapper, as they reclaimed spectacle as a site in which they could enact their modernity and their sexual agency. The Flapper responded to the spectacles of mass culture by seeing herself as a sexual subject, and she enacted this perspective in her quest for heterosexual objectification.

Within the wider modern tendency to bring sex into discourse, the Flapper vacillated in the popular imagination between representational form and a spectacularized feminine subject, each contributing to a construction of feminine sexuality that was enacted at the level of the eye. In both guises she was reproduced, either through visual technologies or through a too slavish devotion to and mimicry of the conventions of feminine spectacle. In youth culture, she displaced the male gaze and yet also dominated its field of vision. Moving across the spectrum of feminine sexual classifications, the Flapper could not be interpreted as either good or bad. She demonstrated that women who crossed cultural lines and altered or challenged their layout across the social field came in for particular surveillance, as objects of fascination and moral censure. If morality made a spectacle of itself, the Flapper seemed all too content to situate herself within dubious representational frameworks, and to play on the scandalous inferences of the spectacle. She did so purely because she took pleasure in entrapping the attention of men, her scopic prey. Ultimately, the true nature of her sexuality could never be known from her practices of appearing; instead those practices became the locale of her sexual agency. Appearing as spectacle was scandalous because, for women, such appearing became a sexual activity in itself.

When young women appeared as Flappers they toyed with the tension between cultural representation and subjective self-representation. They adopted the conventions of the mass-reproduced feminine spectacle in their self-production through appearing, demonstrating that "individuals are both the site and subjects of discursive struggle for their identity."[198] Yet the changed visual conditions in which this identity could be realized also suggested that, for modern appearing women, "visuality is the experience of Being becoming Representation."[199]

Conclusion

Feminine Identity and
Visual Culture

A funny thing happened in the time it took to finish this book. I came out from under the gaze that prompted its writing; I got older, so when I go outdoors now it's with a pram, a fractious toddler, and a distinctly lined frown. This has caused subtle and imperceptible adjustments, which have taken place minute by minute over years: changes in the seamless montage of exchanged glances in cafés, the accidental encounters with bus stop posters, the unhurried retirement of kittenish apparel to the moth-inhabited realms of the wardrobe. All of which is by the by—unless you happen to be concentrating on the ways various formations of visibility affect feminine identity.

Just as altering as the fact that I look different is that I look differently. Perhaps because I have occupied the position of the Kitten, feminine beauty had exerted a particular fascination. As I shifted out from under that gaze, the sexual posturing of Pop Kittens, Hollywood Kittens, Model Kittens, and the rest of their litter scampering across the visual horizon struck me as increasingly lackluster. It may not be chic critique to say so, but many times that posturing has struck me as ludicrous. But feminine visibility has always been more complex than first meets the eye, from its inception into mechanical reproduction and its consequent and ongoing permeation of all available perceptual surfaces, to the exclusionary effects of its racialized invocations.

Whether I'm mesmerized by the lost Australian beauty Lady Loughborough, or rolling my eyes at the amount of cleavage a shoe company requires to distract us from just how crap its shoes really are, the question remains: why do images of women elicit such passionate and polarized responses, after all this speculation? Because the imagery of women is profoundly implicated in the parameters of feminine identity. It describes the cultural sites that are available to some women and unavailable to others, and those descriptions can have prescriptive power. While these effects can exclude some women, it can enable others to occupy myriad cultural sites, and create new sites—the possibilities perpetually unfurl, fractal-like, before our eyes.

This book was intended to be not an argument for the importance of visibility, but rather a cultural history of how visibility became important. Lev Kuleshov was prescient when he stated, as I discussed in the introduction, that modern image production had enabled him to create a new woman. But this new woman was more than a composite of montaged body parts: she represented the newly emerged subject position of the modern appearing woman, who was produced, as Kuleshov's woman was, within the altered visual conditions of the modern perceptual field. We can use her appearance as a heuristic through which to explore her significance to the subjectivities of women and to the cultural spaces in which she was visible, and doing so opens a different sort of engagement between women and cultural forms.

In the 1920s modern women constituted themselves as spectacles, or "objects," assuming the status of modern subjects through the new meanings of cultural presence and social inclusion that were accruing to feminine visibility. The Western dichotomy of subject/object manifested as a cultural bias, assigning the spectator to the male position, and the spectacle to the female, in a variety of visual scenes. Yet wherever the traditional status of the woman-object was consolidated, women became able to subvert that status by occupying the images that spectacularized them, using the performative techniques of appearing. Thus did the "picture" of the Modern Woman become more complex. Because they were implicated in subject formation (rather than being simply instances of the objectification of women), the meanings and effects of these pictures also become more unstable. But the pictures opened up cultural spaces for women to occupy which were shot through with ambivalent uses and effects of power.

The articulation, assignation, and regulation of sexual difference within significatory systems produce contradictions. Modern women were able to adopt the processes of their spectacularization by managing their own images. Through techniques of appearing they were able to incorporate the principal operation of the modern spectacle—the increasing articulation of social meaning, gender, race, and power relations at the level of the eye—into the processes of their subjectivities.

But women also became subject to the representational systems they occupied. While the Flapper stole the limelight by which heterosexuality had increasingly become an activity of looking—associating not just agency, but specifically sexual agency, with her visibility—the possibilities engendered for Aboriginal women were less inviting. The modern "look" is circumscribed by colonial visions. Just when appearing modern became increasingly important to women's claims to cultural presence and participation, Aboriginal women were pictured as visual anomalies within the modern scene. Colonial visual culture formed and disseminated specific knowledges about Aboriginal femininity that were tied to the imperial venture and useful to the coercive systems of force through which dispossession and dispersal, child abduction, and labor and sexual exploitation were perpetrated. The everyday ephemera of representation effectively contributed to these dispersed yet systematic acts of colonization through a pervasive perceptual field which authorized, sanctioned, and disavowed the impact of the penetration of land-owning capitalism into traditional communities and ecologies. The repeated visual invocation and vilification of Aboriginal women was a means to consolidate their political invisibility.

In "Crossing Brooklyn Ferry," Walt Whitman records a constant play of subtle fusions of himself and the strangers who look into his face. As a man, he does not feel objectified; rather, in these encounters he can pour his meaning into those who look. Yet such looks were politically shaped and culturally contoured. The modern appearing woman was a subject position produced through scopic encounters in which social meaning and power relations were increasingly fused with industrialized image production and the regulation of the flow of looks in public space. Feminine visibility was crossed by the contradictory meanings of self-possession and possession by others, refracted through commodity exhibition and the colonial gaze.

The modern appearing woman sheds light on the dilemmas still faced by women: given the complexity of the picture of feminine visibility and its ambivalent power effects, how might women envisage the appearance of their subjectivities? How might women cast the meaning of their "look"? How might women be spectacular subjects?

Notes

INTRODUCTION

1. Jay Leyda, ed., *Voices of Film Experience: 1894 to the Present* (New York: Macmillan, 1977), pp. 249–50, quoted in Scott McQuire, *Visions of Modernity: Representation, Memory, Time, and Space in the Age of the Camera* (London: Sage, 1997), p. 80.

2. Thompson was a comedienne who began working in plays for Fuller's circuit and later joined J. C. Williamson's theater company before debuting in Australian film in 1921. She had been appearing in American films for two years when she garnered enormous publicity through the acid incident. See *Everyones: Incorporating Australian Variety and Show World*, 11 February 1925, p. 16. (*Everyones* merged several times with other journals and often changed its name.)

3. Throughout the book I will use title case when referring to types and lower case when referring to women, for example, "images of the Modern Woman influenced modern women."

4. Judith Butler, "Lacan, Riviere, and the Strategies of Masquerade," in *Gender Trouble: Feminism and the Subversion of Identity* (New York: Routledge, 1990), pp. 43–57.

5. Judith Butler, *Bodies That Matter: On the Discursive Limits of "Sex"* (New York: Routledge, 1993), p. 3.

6. Butler, *Gender Trouble*, pp. 43–48.

7. Butler writes of the Lacanian formulation, "For women to 'be' the Phallus means, then, to reflect the power of the Phallus, to signify that power to 'embody' the Phallus, to supply the site to which it penetrates, and to signify the Phallus through 'being' its Other, its absence, its lack, the dialectical confirmation of its identity." Ibid., p. 44.

8. Ibid., p. 45.

9. Joan Riviere, "Womanliness as a Masquerade," originally published in *International Journal of Psychoanalysis* 10 (1929), reprinted in *Formations of Fantasy*, ed. Victor Burgin, James Donald, and Cora Kaplan (London: Methuen, 1986), pp. 35–44.

10. Butler, *Gender Trouble*, p. 47.

11. Ibid., p. 143.

12. Ibid., pp. 143–46.

13. Ibid., p. 147.

14. I will use the term "visibility" to refer to the capacity to be seen, including self-apprehension, and "spectacularization" to refer more specifically

to the process of being exhibited and exhibiting oneself to a *public* gaze, including through mechanically reproduced imagery.

15. Tani E. Barlow et al., "The Modern Girl around the World," *Gender and History*, forthcoming. See the website for the Modern Girl around the World project at <http://depts.washington.edu/its/moderngirl.htm>, accessed 2 June 2003.

16. Andree Wright, *Brilliant Careers: Women in Australian Cinema* (Sydney: Pan, 1986), p. 20. Kellerman was the first Australian to play the lead in an American film, yet her fame accrued from diverse sources. She was a physical culture pioneer, an international swimming champion, and a vaudeville artist. When arrested by Boston police for wearing a one-piece bathing suit rather than the expected cumbersome wool dress and pantaloons, she was seen as a women's rights advocate for her belief in dress liberation. Her film stunts included diving eighteen meters into a pool containing five crocodiles, diving from the wing of an airplane, and many "scandalous" nude scenes. Interestingly, while insurers refused to insure her life, she did manage to insure her "shape" for £250,000.

17. Jacqueline Rose, *Sexuality in the Field of Vision* (London: Verso, 1986).

18. Barlow et al., "The Modern Girl around the World," op. cit.

19. These were all terms for young women who exchanged sexual favors for treats, including joy-rides, theater tickets, cocktails, and fine clothes. The Flapper often appeared in *Truth* alongside these types, who "were not professional prostitutes" and "worked in offices and shops during the day, and seek [*sic*] the bright lights at night." They were considered to be more likely to spread venereal disease, by "neglecting the precautions that the recognised 'Scarlet Woman' knows are necessary to preserve her health," and because they were difficult to identify and could not be policed, as their employers would often vouch for them. "Tarts about Town: The Lure of the Bright Lights: Flirtatious Flappers, 'Love Birds,' and 'Privateers,'" *Truth*, 29 March 1919, p. 5. (Journalists' and authors' names were not given in most newspapers of this period. Names of contributing writers and letter writers are given where published.)

20. Jonathan Crary writes, "[M]odernity is inseparable from on the one hand a remaking of the observer, and on the other hand a proliferation of circulating signs and objects whose effects coincide with their visuality." *Techniques of the Observer: On Vision and Modernity in the Nineteenth Century* (Cambridge, Mass.: MIT Press, 1994), p. 11.

21. Lawrence Grossberg, Cary Nelson, and Paula Treichler, eds., introduction to *Cultural Studies* (New York: Routledge, 1992), p. 15 n. 3.

1. THE STATUS OF THE WOMAN-OBJECT

1. Anke Gleber, "Women on the Screens and Streets of Modernity: In Search of the Female Flâneur," in *The Image in Dispute: Art and Cinema in the Age of Photography*, ed. Dudley Andrew and Sally Shafto (Austin: University of Texas Press, 1997), p. 78.

2. Ibid., pp. 74, 77, 80.

3. Quoted in ibid., p. 59.

4. Walter Benjamin, "The Flâneur" in "The Paris of the Second Empire in Baudelaire," in *Charles Baudelaire: A Lyric Poet in the Era of High Capitalism*, trans. Harry Zohn (London: Verso, 1973), p. 38.

5. Benjamin believed the genre of physiologies of urban types declined after this year, to be overtaken by physiologies of the city (such as Paris by Night), then by those of nations and animals. The types of the Modern Woman I have made the motifs of my book show that the cultural effects of this genre lingered for some time, although when applied to women they were less "innocuous" and genial and more classifying and normative. Benjamin, "The Flâneur," p. 35.

6. Ibid., p. 36.

7. Ibid., p. 55.

8. Typing was also symptomatic of the self-consciousness of the modern as a distinct historical epoch and the consequent historicization of the individual. Part of this modern self-consciousness can be attributed to people's altered experience of time. Edward Soja, in his analysis of modernity in terms of "the formative dimensions of human existence; space, time and being," defines it as "the specificity of being alive, in the world, at a particular time and place; a vital individual and collective sense of contemporaneity." Edward Soja, "History: Geography: Modernity," in *The Cultural Studies Reader*, ed. Simon During (London: Routledge, 1993), pp. 135–50.

9. Gleber, "Women on the Streets," p. 77.

10. This "image status" has paradoxically confirmed the invisible status of the female flâneur in the literature of modernity—precisely as an outcome of her excessive spectacularization as woman-on-the-street. For further analysis of the gendered dichotomy of flânerie see Susan Buck-Morss, "The Flâneur, the Sandwichman, and the Whore: The Politics of Loitering," *New German Critique* 39 (fall 1986), pp. 99–140; Janet Wolff, "The Invisible Flaneuse: Women and the Literature of Modernity," in her *Feminine Sentences: Essays on Women and Culture* (Berkeley: University of California Press, 1990), pp. 34–50; Elizabeth Wilson, *The Sphinx in the City: Urban Life, the Control of Disorder, and Women* (London: Virago, 1991); Anne Friedberg, *Window Shopping: Cinema and the Postmodern* (Berkeley: University of California Press, 1993).

11. Gleber, "Women on the Streets," p. 59.

12. "Visuality" and "vision" are distinguished by Hal Foster, cited in Martin Jay, *Downcast Eyes: The Denigration of Vision in Twentieth-Century French Thought* (Berkeley: University of California Press, 1994), p. 9.

13. John Dewey claimed that Western philosophy since Plato and Aristotle has been dominated by "a spectator theory of knowledge," in which "the theory of knowing is modeled after what was supposed to take place in the act of vision." See John Dewey, *The Quest For Certainty* (New York: Putnam, 1929), pp. 23, 214, quoted in Stephen Houlgate, "Vision, Reflection, and Openness: The 'Hegemony of Vision' from a Hegelian Point of View," in *Modernity and the Hegemony of Vision*, ed. David Levin (Los Angeles: University of California Press, 1993), p. 87. Rorty argues the West has become "obsessed with the notion of our primary relation to objects as analogous to visual perception." See Richard Rorty, *Philosophy and the Mirror of Nature* (Oxford: Basil Blackwell, 1980), pp. 162–63.

14. Jay, *Downcast Eyes*, p. 21.

15. Thomas R. Flynn, "Foucault and the Eclipse of Vision," in Levin, *Modernity and the Hegemony of Vision*, p. 274.

16. When the prisoners in the cave are "released from their bonds and cured of their delusions," accustomed to the dazzling light of the sun, they will be able to return to the cave, where, once accustomed again to the dark,

they will be able to "see a thousand times better than the remaining prisoners do and will distinguish the various shadows, and know what they are shadows of, because [they] have seen the truth about things admirable and just and good." Plato, *The Republic* (Harmondsworth: Penguin, 1975), pp. 318–24.

17. Jay, *Downcast Eyes*, pp. 26–27.

18. Plato, "The Simile of the Cave," Part VII: *The Philosophical Rules in* The Republic, 2nd ed. (Harmondsworth, U.K.: Penguin Books, 1974), pp. 320–21.

19. Luce Irigaray, *Speculum of the Other Woman*, trans. Gillian C. Gill (Ithaca, N.Y.: Cornell University Press, 1985), pp. 300–301, Irigaray's emphasis.

20. Geometric perspectivalism, a technique for picturing three-dimensional objects over the surface of a flat plane, was allegorized by Alberti as viewing the world through an open window. It arranged objects in space, "enabling artists to transcribe real appearances by figuring depth, proportion, texture and density to 'place' objects in a scene for the eye of the spectator." Scott McQuire, *Visions of Modernity: Representation, Memory, Time, and Space in the Age of the Camera* (Sage: London, 1997), p. 19.

21. Svetlana Alpers, *The Art of Describing: Dutch Art in the Seventeenth Century* (London: John Murray, 1983), p. 35.

22. Robert Romanyshyn writes that the disencarnated consumer of modern media forms derives from this Cartesian split, arguing, "The cogito project establishes a way of thinking which takes leave of its senses." Robert D. Romanyshyn, "The Despotic Eye and Its Shadow: Media Image in the Age of Literacy," in Levin, *Modernity and the Hegemony of Vision*, p. 346.

23. René Descartes, *Discourse on Method*, trans. P. J. Olscamp (Indianapolis: Bobbs-Merrill, 1965), p. 108.

24. Jonathan Crary discusses the camera obscura and its social and epistemological positioning of the human observer in *Techniques of the Observer: On Vision and Modernity in the Nineteenth Century* (Cambridge, Mass.: MIT Press, 1990), pp. 41, 25–66.

25. McQuire, *Visions of Modernity*, p. 22.

26. Levin, introduction, *Modernity and the Hegemony of Vision*, pp. 3, 2.

27. "Specular" is a term used by a range of theorists of modernity to refer to its visually magnified scene and particularly to the techniques of the observing subject within this scene. However, the term has two meanings: "pertaining to vision or sight" and "having mirroring, reflective properties." This latter meaning has particular use in Lacanian psychoanalysis. In his 1949 essay "The Mirror Stage," Lacan argued that the ego is formed through identification with an idealized image. The Lacanian subject is thus specular because the image that is identified with is specular. The term also has central significance in the work of French feminist Luce Irigaray. She uses "specular" to refer to a mirroring process in psychoanalytic theory in which the castration of the girl-child and the direction of her desire to the penis reflect "a desire for the same" back to the male subject. Indeed, because she places the feminine in "The Blind Spot of an Old Dream of Symmetry" (the title of one of her chapters), her formulation of sexual difference can evade the logic of visibility—of something to be seen which signifies that difference. Since I refer to Irigaray's work, I will avoid confusing the reader with these two meanings by using "spectacular" in describing the perceptual modern field and "specular" only in the psychoanalytic sense. See Irigaray, *Speculum of the Other Woman*.

28. This is the title of the situationist Guy Debord's treatise on the spectacle as "the perfect image of the ruling social order." Guy Debord, *The Society of the Spectacle* (New York: Zone, 1995), p. 15.

29. The development of printing had encouraged the growth of an urban reading public in Western Europe by the end of the fifteenth century. This public extended the circulation of words and images to configure "a new medium of exchange." See Paula Findlen, "Humanism, Politics, and Pornography in Renaissance Italy," in *The Invention of Pornography: Obscenity and the Origins of Modernity, 1500–1800*, ed. Lynn Hunt (New York: Zone, 1993), p. 55.

30. Jay, *Downcast Eyes*, p. 66.

31. Walter J. Ong, *The Presence of the Word: Some Prolegomena for Cultural and Religious History* (New Haven, Conn.: Yale University Press, 1967), p. 50, quoted in Jay, *Downcast Eyes*, p. 67.

32. Crary, *Techniques of the Observer*, p. 96.

33. Frederick Taylor's studies in motion and time management, *The Principles of Scientific Management*, were published in 1911 in New York. Ford's assembly line was introduced in 1913 at his factory in Highland Park, Michigan. See Stephen Kern, *The Culture of Time and Space, 1880–1918* (Cambridge, Mass.: Harvard University Press, 1983), pp. 92, 115.

34. Scopic devices, such as the camera, began to be developed in the 1820s. Their later co-option into entertainment forms coincided with the advent of the steam train and of architectural innovations in space, light, and height, all creating new perceptual and spatiotemporal fields. See Wolfgang Schivelbusch, "Excursion: The Space of Glass Architecture," in his *Railway Journey: Trains and Travel in the Nineteenth Century*, trans. Anselm Hollo (Oxford: Basil Blackwell, 1980), pp. 50–56.

35. McQuire, *Visions of Modernity*, p. 55.

36. Miriam Hansen, *Babel and Babylon: Spectatorship in American Silent Film* (Cambridge, Mass.: Harvard University Press, 1991), p. 84.

37. This phrase was coined by materialist historian Jean-Louis Comolli. Comolli wrote that the second half of the nineteenth century "lives in a sort of frenzy of the visible . . . of the social multiplication of images; ever wider distribution of illustrated papers, waves of prints, caricatures, etc . . . of a geographical extension of the field of the visible and the representable. . . . The whole world becomes visible at the same time as it becomes appropriatable." Jean-Louis Comolli, "Machines of the Visible," in *The Cinematic Apparatus*, ed. Teresa de Lauretis and Stephen Heath (New York: St. Martin's, 1980), p. 122, quoted in Linda Williams, *Hard Core: Power, Pleasure, and the "Frenzy of the Visible"* (London: Pandora, 1990), p. 36.

38. Crary, *Techniques of the Observer*, p. 285.

39. Marshall Berman, *All That Is Solid Melts into Air: The Experience of Modernity* (Harmondsworth: Penguin, 1982), p. 138.

40. Crary contends that industrialized vision's requirement of a productive observer resituated perception in the body, and through optics (the knowledge of this visionary body) was able to subject these observers to systems of power which regulated and governed them. Crary, *Techniques of the Observer*, p. 150.

41. The astronomer P. J. C. Janssen used this phrase in 1888, as quoted in McQuire, *Visions of Modernity*, p. 37.

42. Stephen Houlgate, "Vision, Reflection, and Openness," p. 96.

43. Theodor W. Adorno, *Negative Dialectics*, trans. E. B. Ashton (London: Routledge and Kegan Paul, 1973), pp. 139–40.

44. Debord, *Society of the Spectacle*, p. 17.

45. Maxim Gorky evoked "the Kingdom of Shadows" in describing his first encounter with the spectacle of cinema (rather than the film footage

itself) at Lumière's screening in Paris at the Aumont café after 1895. He wrote, "Before you life is surging, a life deprived of words and shorn of the living spectrum of colours—the grey, the soundless, the bleak and dismal life." Quoted in Gregory J. Edwards, *The International Film Poster: The Role of the Poster in Cinema, Art, Advertising, and History* (London: Columbus, 1985), pp. 17–18.

46. These "viewing positions" are not only that of the newly constituted spectator before visual technologies such as photojournalism, the camera, and the cinema, but also the vantage of the train, the electric light, and the high-rise building. See Schivelbusch, *Railway Journey*.

47. Crary, *Techniques of the Observer*.

48. Berman writes that modernity had a capacity "to generate forms of 'outward show', brilliant designs, glamorous spectacles, so dazzling that they can blind even the most incisive self to the radiance of its own darker life within." Berman, *All That Is Solid*, p. 138.

49. Irigaray, *Speculum of the Other Woman*, pp. 300–301.

50. The association of the feminine with reproduction, or producing copies rather than being originary, locates it epistemologically with semblance, image, and appearance rather than essence. Under the logic of Western knowledge traditions the modern woman sees (with deficient material eyes) and appears (as copy) imperfectly. This epistemic bias against the woman-object had cultural effects in modernity.

51. Cartoon, *Beckett's Weekly*, 10 February 1928, p. 6.

52. Mack's cartoon has its precedent in European revolutionary political satire, which made the nakedness of women's bodies representative of political truth. Explicit imagery of women represented the rejection of the Church's "veiled" hypocrisy and the European monarchies' political deception, fraud, and decadence. See the essays in Hunt, ed., *Invention of Pornography*. The transition from political uses of the obscene to commodity uses is a defining shift in the modern pornographic.

53. Mack's drawing is precisely a drawing, but I believe he, like the advertisement in figure 1.1, comments on the Modern Girl's visibility, and the conditions of that visibility are photographic and cinematic technologies.

54. See A. G. L. Shaw and H. D. Nicolson, "The Age of Electricity," in *Australia in the Twentieth Century: An Introduction to Modern Society*, ed. A. G. L. Shaw and H. D. Nicolson (Sydney: Angus and Robertson, 1967), pp. 102–10.

55. In a review of the stage comedy *The Silver Fox*, which was presented in December 1928, the character of the young girl luring the hero from an unhappy marriage is described as "The artful flapper." *Aussie*, 15 December 1928, p. 79.

56. Paul Kelly and Susan Lord, "Driven to Distraction: Going to the Movies with Walter and Siegfried," *Cineaction*, no. 34 (June 1994), p. 23.

57. Gail Finney, *Women in Modern Drama: Freud, Feminism, and European Theater at the Turn of the Century* (Ithaca, N.Y.: Cornell University Press, 1989), p. 13. The film starred Louise Brooks, who was billed in many promotional publications throughout the 1920s as a quintessential Flapper, a type of Modern Girl who was particularly immersed in her own appearance and the (hetero)sexual power and pleasures she could get from it. Interestingly, Brooks herself denied that the Flapper ever existed "except in Scott Fitzgerald's mind and the antics he planted in his mad wife Zelda's mind." See Barry Paris, *Louise Brooks* (London: Mandarin, 1990), p. 130.

58. Louise Brooks writes in her collection of autobiographical essays, "At the time Wedekind produced *Pandora's Box*, in Berlin around the turn of the century, it was detested, condemned, and banned. It was declared 'immoral and inartistic'. If in that period when the sacred pleasures of the ruling class were comparatively private, a play exposing them had called out the dogs of the law, how much more savage would be the attack upon a film faithful to Wedekind's text which was made in 1928 in Berlin, where the ruling class publicly flaunted its pleasures as a symbol of wealth and power." She adds that the play had been condensed five years earlier into the film *Loulou* by Danish actress Asta Nielson. The anti-heroine was a "man-eater" who, having devoured her victims, "dropped dead in an acute attack of indigestion." See "Pabst and Lulu" in Louise Brooks, *Lulu in Hollywood* (London: Arena, 1982), p. 94.

59. Rita Felski, *The Gender of Modernity* (Cambridge, Mass.: Harvard University Press, 1995), p. 5.

60. Ibid., p. 4.

61. Nell Evans, a former factory worker, speaking in 1919 before a joint conference of the Young Women's Christian Association and the Australian Christian Movement entitled "What Are Girls Coming To?" *Age*, 2 May 1919, p. 6. Quoted in Julie Tisdale, "Venereal Disease and the Policing of the Amateur in Melbourne during World War I," in *Lilith: A Feminist History Journal*, no. 9, autumn 1996, p. 33.

62. The first issue announced that *"Helen"* (the magazine) was "an out and out feminist. . . . Stage managed, written and—I almost said printed—by women." *Helen's Weekly*, editorial, 8 September 1927, p. 43. The hesitation at "printed" speaks of how difficult it was for women to be visible and effective in a press dominated by men.

63. Evangeline, "Is Woman Losing Her Charm: And Is Feminine Appeal a Vanishing Quantity?" *Helen's Weekly*, 10 November 1927, p. 52.

64. E. H. Maguire, "The Modern Girl," *Aussie*, 14 September 1923, p. 45.

65. "Are We Growing Decadent?" *Society*, 1 November 1925, p. 16.

66. Denise Riley, *Am I That Name? Feminism and the Category of "Women" in History* (London: Macmillan, 1988).

67. Marilyn Lake makes this point when she writes, "a tension becomes apparent between women's positioning as sexual objects and their constitution as sexual subjects." Lake, "Female Desires: The Meaning of World War II," *Australian Historical Studies* 24, no. 95 (October 1990), p. 274.

68. Teresa de Lauretis, *Alice Doesn't: Feminism, Semiotics and Cinema* (Bloomington: Indiana University Press, 1984), p. 38.

69. Simone de Beauvoir, *The Second Sex*, H. M. Parshley, trans. and ed. (Harmondsworth: Penguin, 1986), pp. 548, 557, 543, 641.

70. For Carole Pateman, the exchange of women lies at the heart of the social contract and places women in a paradoxical relation to the civil order: "women are property, but also persons." As persons they hold property in their own persons, which they can exchange, as obedience, for the protection of the civil realm; however, as women they are property and can only be exchanged. It is only by disavowing their difference (which the fetish aims at) that women can enter into the foundational contract of civil society—the exchange of their property in themselves through which, like men, they can "transform their natural freedom into the security of civil freedom." The status of the woman-object is only confirmed if her ability to attain subject status in

the social contract comes through disavowing her sexual difference. Carole Pateman, *The Sexual Contract* (Cambridge: Polity, 1988), pp. 6, 57.

71. Beauvoir, *Second Sex,* p. 189.

72. Ibid., p. 672.

73. Ibid., p. 189.

74. Ibid., p. 630.

75. Ibid., p. 361.

76. This formulation from Beauvoir was immensely important to the emphasis on women's sexual liberation later, though it became harder to understand that women could be simultaneously objects and subjects, particularly as the anti-pornography movement gained ascendancy from the late 1960s to the early 1980s.

77. Beauvoir, *Second Sex,* pp. 436, 626, 727.

78. Iris Marion Young, "Throwing Like a Girl: A Phenomenology of Feminine Body Comportment, Motility, and Spatiality," in *Throwing Like a Girl and Other Essays in Feminist Philosophy and Social Theory* (Bloomington: Indiana University Press, 1990), p. 15.

79. Ibid., p. 143. Young argues that "the three modalities of feminine motility are that feminine movement exhibits an *ambiguous transcendence,* an *inhibited intentionality,* and a *discontinuous unity* with its surroundings," p. 147, Young's emphasis.

80. Ibid., p. 155.

81. Berger, *Ways of Seeing,* p. 47.

82. Ibid., p. 46.

83. Sandra Bartky, "Foucault, Femininity, and the Modernization of Patriarchal Power," in *Feminism and Foucault: Reflections on Resistance,* ed. Irene Diamond and Lee Quinby (Boston: Northeastern University Press, 1988), p. 71.

84. Laura Mulvey, "Visual Pleasure and Narrative Cinema," *Screen* 16, no. 3 (autumn 1975), pp. 6–18.

85. The "sex wars" were confrontations between anti-pornography groups and feminists who opposed their constructions of sadistic male sexuality, female victimhood, and explicit lesbian pornography and their use of discrimination laws to restrict sexually explicit material. See Carole S. Vance, "More Danger, More Pleasure: A Decade after the Barnard Sexuality Conference" in *Pleasure and Danger: Exploring Female Sexuality,* ed. Carole S. Vance (London: Pandora, 1992), pp. xvi–xl. In Australia, the confrontation was between anti-censorship libertarians and anti-pornography feminists, some of whom, such as Sheila Jeffreys, came from Britain and elsewhere.

86. In a later essay, Mulvey reconsidered the female spectator's potential for "masculine identification," which, "in its phallic aspect, reactivates for her a fantasy of 'action' that correct femininity demands should be repressed." Laura Mulvey, "Afterthoughts on 'Visual Pleasure and Narrative Cinema' Inspired by 'Duel in the Sun' (King Vidor, 1946)," in *Framework,* nos. 15–17 (1981), p. 15. See examples of these approaches in Gaylyn Studlar, "Masochism and the Perverse Pleasure of the Cinema," *Quarterly Review of Film Studies* 9, no. 4 (1984), pp. 267–82; and Elizabeth Cowie, "Fantasia," *m/f,* no. 9 (1984), pp. 71–104.

87. Mary Wollstonecraft, in her *Vindication of the Rights of Woman,* wrote that genteel women are "slaves to their bodies" because they are "taught from their infancy that beauty is woman's spectre, the mind shapes the body, and roaming around its gilt cage, only seeks to adore its prison." Mary Wollstone-

craft, *Vindication of the Rights of Woman* (1792; Harmondsworth: Penguin, 1982), p. 131. See Catharine A. Mackinnon, *Feminism Unmodified: Discourses on Life and Law* (Cambridge, Mass.: Harvard University Press, 1987).

2. THE CITY GIRL IN THE METROPOLITAN SCENE

1. "Circular Addressed to Parents by the Education Departments throughout Australia with Regard to Sex Hygiene" (c. 1925), reproduced in *Australia's Women: A Documentary History*, ed. Kay Daniels and Mary Murnane (St. Lucia: University of Queensland Press, 1980), pp. 146–48.

2. In 1927, Johnson and Johnson enlisted the advice of Lillian Gilbreth, Professor in Industrial Psychology at Rutgers University and full partner in her husband's engineering firm, in designing and marketing sanitary napkins. Gilbreth—having first advised against the name "Flush Down"—surveyed some three thousand American women. She found that women's new mobility in the public realm as travelers, professionals, students, consumers, shop girls, and factory hands had made laundering homemade pads distasteful and inconvenient. The materials were too bulky to travel with undetected, and women felt exposed when laundering them in shared dormitories and rented accommodation. Gilbreth found that the pad's commercial viability would be largely determined by "comfort and inconspicuousness." Gilbreth argued that it would be "unnecessary that any effort be made to make them appear decorative," and that the containers should not be "too well known in shape," their color not "so deep that it shows through the wrapping paper nor distinctive in shade." Vern L. Bullough, "Merchandising the Sanitary Napkin: Lillian Gilbreth's 1927 Survey," *Signs* 10, no. 3 (spring 1985), p. 626.

3. In a Johnson and Johnson advertisement in the American *Ladies' Home Journal*, the company claimed to have solved "the old embarrassment of purchasing." It announced, "In order that Modess be obtained in a crowded store without embarrassment or discussion, Johnson and Johnson devised the Silent Purchase Coupon. . . . Is there a woman anywhere who will not be grateful for this method of silent purchase?" "The Silent Purchase Coupon," advertisement, *Ladies' Home Journal*, June 1928, p. 14. The image accompanying the coupon shows a woman adjusting her hat before a mirror, preparing to leave the house and enter into public view. But significantly she is also obscured from view by her cloche hat, and her reflection is available only to herself. The image suggests that a private view of herself and the intimacy of self-knowledge can be maintained despite public exposure. In Australia, Kimberly-Clark made a similar gesture toward discretion in purchasing. In a full-page advertisement the company told the reader that "It is easy to buy without saying 'Sanitary pads' by simply asking for 'Kotex'. . . . It comes in a blue box which has no printing except the name 'Kotex.' " Advertisement, *Green Room*, 28 February 1927, p. 25. Kleinert's Kez makes the same promise: "There is only one KEZ packed *in the grey box with the blue line*" (their emphasis). "Modern Womanhood Must Know No Embarassment [*sic*]: Kleinert's Kez," advertisement, *Australian Woman's Mirror*, 12 June 1928, p. 2.

4. Gail Reekie, *Temptations: Sex, Selling, and the Department Store* (St. Leonards, N.S.W.: Allen and Unwin, 1993), p. 89.

5. " 'My Dear! . . . Of Course You Can Go!': Kleinert's Sanitary Lingerie," advertisement, *Australian Woman's Mirror*, 14 May 1929, p. 31.

6. Bullough, "Merchandising the Sanitary Napkin," p. 626.

7. The semantics of the names of the later products are interesting. They pitted references to menstruation against its linguistic expulsion, as in "Menex." The name "Modess" affixes the feminine "-ess" to a reference to modesty (though another reading might see a reference to "modern goddess"). My thanks to Jordie Albiston for pointing this out.

8. "Menex: It's an Open Secret," advertisement, *Australian Woman's Mirror*, 4 June 1929, p. 36.

9. "Menex: It's So Perfectly Simple," advertisement, *Australian Woman's Mirror*, 18 June 1929, p. 13.

10. "Modern Womanhood Must Know No Embarassment" [*sic*]. Odor became another modality for exposing the secrets of the feminine body. An advertisement for "Odorono" tells of the fate of a woman who "had looks, charm and attracted men" but "suffered all unknowing from excessive underarm perspiration." Because she did not take "special precautions," men "failed to ask if they might call again." Advertisement, *Australian Woman's Mirror*, 16 April 1920, p. 2.

11. "Easily Disposable Menex: The Modern Hygiene," advertisement, *Home*, 1 May 1930, p. 95.

12. "Menex: Easily Disposable: It's an Open Secret," advertisement, *Australian Woman's Mirror*, 4 June 1929, p. 36.

13. "Modern Woman Must Know No Embarassment" [*sic*].

14. To differing degrees these discourses construed reproduction, in the words that sexologist Havelock Ellis is quoted as saying, as "the final end of the individual," but "more obviously woven into the structure of women." "A Student in Sex—He and She," *Lone Hand*, May 1919, p. 38. Menstruation in women was a manifestation of the axiom that "the female animal everywhere is more closely and for a longer period occupied with that process of reproduction which is Nature's main concern." Women were thereby positioned as nature's "protégé," and their interests identified with those of nature. Ibid. Yet in spite of the timelessness of the feminine body, under modernity it was recast as subject to change or modification, at least in the sense that it could apply the tools of modern science to itself. Menstruation, formerly a "distressing event," was "now but an incident." "Menex Easily Disposable: A Distressing Event . . . Now But an Incident," advertisement, *Australian Woman's Mirror*, 21 May 1929, p. 52.

15. "Show Her the Way: Kleinert's Ladies' Protective Necessities," advertisement, *Australian Woman's Mirror*, 16 October 1928, p. 19.

16. Ibid.

17. "Easily Disposable Menex: The Modern Hygiene."

18. My thanks to Marilyn Lake for this point.

19. "Easily Disposable Menex: The Modern Hygiene."

20. "Menex Easily Disposable: A Distressing Event . . . Now But an Incident."

21. "Show Her the Way: Kleinert's Ladies' Protective Necessities."

22. " 'My Dear! . . . Of Course You Can Go!': Kleinert's Sanitary Lingerie."

23. "Menex: It's an Open Secret."

24. *Living Melbourne, 1896–1910,* documentary film (ScreenSound Australia, the National Screen and Sound Archive, 1988).

25. Graham Shirley, "Australian Cinema: 1896 to the Renaissance," in *Australian Cinema,* ed. Scott Murray (St. Leonards, N.S.W.: Allen and Unwin, 1994), pp. 5–44.

26. "Melbourne Cup," 3 November 1896, sequence filmed by Maurice Sestier and Walter Barnett, in *Living Melbourne, 1896–1910.*

27. "Wellington Parade," 1898, sequence filmed by Joseph Perry for the Salvation Army, ibid.

28. "Paddle Ferry," circa 1910s, sequence in *Sydney City Life, 1899–1948,* documentary film (ScreenSound Australia, the National Screen and Sound Archive, 1995).

29. "Tram Car in George St.," circa 1900, ibid. There may be many more women on the pavement but they are difficult to see under the shop awnings.

30. "Horden Brother Store, Pitt St.," ibid.

31. "Marvellous Melbourne: Queen City of the South, 1910," sequence in *Living Melbourne, 1896–1910.*

32. "Swallows and Ariel Factory, 1905," ibid.

33. "Ramblings around Sydney," *Sydney City Life.*

34. "Cop in Parramatta Road," circa 1920s, ibid.

35. "Using Underground Railway," circa 1920s, and "Railway Square—Moving Hordes," circa 1920s, ibid.

36. "Women Hold Hats," 1934, ibid.

37. See Charles Fox and Marilyn Lake, "The Sexual Division of Labour," in their *Australians at Work: Commentaries and Sources,* ed. Charles Fox and Marilyn Lake (Ringwood, Vic.: McPhee Gribble, 1990), pp. 143–86.

38. According to census figures, in 1891 women constituted 10.6 percent of the commercial, clerical, and sales workforce, and in 1921, 22.4 percent. Whereas we see a rise in this sector from a percentage of women of 6.6 in 1891 to 17.2 of the total workforce in 1921, women's participation in paid domestic work dropped from 42.5 percent of the workforce in 1891 to 34.5 percent in 1921. Jill Julius Matthews, *Good and Mad Women: The Historical Construction of Women in Twentieth-Century Australia* (North Sydney: Allen and Unwin, 1984), pp. 53–54.

39. Australia's "woman question" in the 1880s and 1890s was the question of how to respond to the efforts of women's organizations to reform labor and other areas. "The so-called 'public' and 'private', the world of waged work and the world of the family became contested sites." Patricia Grimshaw, Marilyn Lake, Ann McGrath, and Marian Quartly, *Creating a Nation, 1788–1990* (Ringwood, Vic.: McPhee Gribble, 1994), p. 155.

40. Pamela Niehoff argues that the New Woman was represented by four categories: "the flapper, the modern leisured woman, the thinking woman and the resourceful woman." See her "The New Woman and the Politics of Identity," in *Strange Women: Essays in Art and Gender,* ed. Jeanette Hoorn (Melbourne: Melbourne University Press, 1994), p. 38.

41. See Susan Magarey's discussion of the New Woman as she was figured in Australian novels of the 1880s and 1890s, "History, Cultural Studies, and Another Look at First Wave Feminism in Australia," *Australian Historical Studies,* no. 106 (April 1996), p. 104. These same questions had been raised in Britain including in Grant Allen's 1895 novel *The Woman Who Did* (reprint, Oxford: Oxford University Press, 1995).

42. Katie Holmes, " 'Spinsters Indispensable': Feminists, Single Women, and the Critique of Marriage, 1890–1920," *Australian Historical Studies* 29, no. 110 (1998), p. 79.

43. Glenna Matthews, *The Rise of Public Woman: Woman's Power and Woman's Place in the United States, 1630–1970* (New York: Oxford University Press, 1992), pp. 147–72, 148, 171, 153–54.

44. Marilyn Lake, *Getting Equal: The History of Australian Feminism* (St. Leonards, N.S.W.: Allen and Unwin, 1999), p. 56.

45. Andrew Brown-May, *Melbourne Street Life: The Itinerary of Our Days* (Kew, Vic.: Australian Scholarly Publishing, 1998), pp. 104–107, 59.

46. Sally Murray, interview by Claire Williams, 6 March 1987, transcript of sound recording (New South Wales Bicentennial Oral History Project, TRC 2301 INT.34, Oral History & Folklore Collection, National Library of Australia).

47. Indeed, in one American account a Flapper causes the narrator to swerve on the footpath and he feels that "it would not surprise her over much if I stepped to the very edge of the gutter, and removed my hat as if apologising for trespassing on preserves that belonged to her." G. Stanley Hall, "Flapper Americana Novissima," *Atlantic Monthly* 129 (June 1922), p. 772.

48. K. F. Gerould, "The Smoking Car," *Harper's Monthly Magazine*, no. 144 (February 1922), p. 320.

49. "His Last Stand," cartoon, *Aussie*, 15 April 1929, p. 35.

50. See Marilyn Lake, *The Limits of Hope: Soldier Settlement in Victoria, 1915–1938* (Melbourne: Oxford University Press, 1987).

51. Heather Radi, "1920–29," in *A New History of Australia*, ed. F. K. Crowley (Melbourne: William Heinemann, 1974), p. 359.

52. *Farmer's Advocate*, 14 September 1917, quoted in Stuart Macintyre, *1901–1942: The Succeeding Age*, vol. 4 of *The Oxford History of Australia*, ed. Geoffrey Bolton (Melbourne: Oxford University Press, 1986), p. 41. Metaphors of engulfment point to the feminization of mass culture through the maternal. See Devon Hodges and Janice L. Doanne, "Undoing Feminism in Anne Rice's Vampire Chronicles," in *Modernity and Mass Culture*, ed. James Naremore and Patrick Brantlinger (Bloomington: Indiana University Press, 1991), p. 159.

53. See Marilyn Lake's analysis of the "Bushman" and the "Lonehand" in "The Politics of Respectability: Identifying the Masculinist Context," *Historical Studies* 22, no. 86 (April 1986), pp. 116–31. The turn to manufacturing was seen to be creating new economic alliances with the United States and weakening ties with Britain, the vanguard of the old morality. American investment in Australian businesses reached sixty million pounds in 1929. See J. Rickard, *Australia: A Cultural History* (London: Longman, 1988), p. 191. Hostility ran high to "Americanisation," and particularly to American cultural exports.

54. "The Return of the Prodigal Daughter," cartoon, *Bulletin*, 8 January 1925, p. 24.

55. Feminists responded to this lost supervision by casting themselves as "mothers of all the city." See Lake, *Getting Equal*, p. 58.

56. "Tarts about Town," *Truth*, 29 March 1919, p. 5.

57. "Flats and Flappers," *Truth*, 24 September 1921, p. 7.

58. "The Vortex: How Country Girls Are Drawn In," *Truth*, 1 July 1922, p. 5.

59. Ibid.

60. Another article tells the story of three young women who came to the city. Once there, one of them was "plucked from behind the typewriter" by prostitution because of her poverty. The next became a thief because "she longed to be as well dressed as the other girls" and the "lure of finery got too much." The last was a lonely junior teacher who was enticed to parties and ended up "dying at the hands of an incapable nurse." The three tragedies of

the City Girl—prostitution, thieving, and abortion—were the city's reply to the three young women's "call of youth." "Lonely Girls Who Go Astray: They Find Companionship, but Pay Heavily for It," *Beckett's Budget,* 9 December 1927, p. 16.

61. "Sydney's Underworld—Ruins Country Girls," *Green Room Pictorial,* 20 September 1926, p. 27.

62. "The Cost of Sin—Country Girls Pay the Price," *Green Room Pictorial,* 27 August 1926, p. 28.

63. *Satan in Sydney* (1918), poster advertising showing at the Lyric Theatre, from the Document Collection of ScreenSound Australia, the National Screen and Sound Archive.

64. Cecil Mann, "A Country Wife," *Bulletin,* 27 May 1926, p. 7.

65. "What Little Girls' Hands Are Made For," cartoon, *Bulletin,* 7 August 1924, p. 22.

66. H. H. B., "The Dancing Flapper," *Aussie,* 14 July 1923, p. 44.

67. "Girls Dare to Be Old Fashioned," reprinted in Katie Holmes and Marilyn Lake, eds., *Freedom Bound II: Documents on Women in Modern Australia* (St. Leonards, N.S.W.: Allen and Unwin, 1995), p. 51.

68. Without population growth white Australians were said to be threatened with "[n]ational extinction." "First Australian Baby Week: Today and Tomorrow Our Nation Must Look to the Babies," *Lone Hand,* 2 March 1920, p. 13. New South Wales Industrial Commissioner A. B. Piddington declared in 1926 that "Australia is a dying race," the birthrate having declined from 42.5 births per 1000 women in 1874 to 25.3 per 1000 in 1924. "The Vanishing Race," *Green Room Pictorial,* 27 August 1926, p. 35.

69. *Working Woman* reported on the conditions in one quilt factory in Sydney. Factory girls had nowhere to eat lunch, the toilets were never cleaned, there were no windows or ventilation on the ground floor, and kapok flew constantly through the air. "Conditions of a Quilt Factory," *Working Woman,* 1 August 1931, p. 3. In Victoria, Margaret Cuthbertson had been inspecting factories for thirty years by 1927. She found similar conditions common: poor ventilation, dirt and filth, and excessive working hours. "Australia's Working Girls: 'Admirable!' Says Miss Cuthbertson, after 30 Years," *Adam and Eve,* 3 May 1927, p. 26.

70. Myra Morris, "The Factory Girl," *Lone Hand,* 1 February 1921, p. 38.

71. "Slums and Sterility," *Truth,* 2 June 1923, p. 1.

72. See Linda Gordon, *Woman's Body, Woman's Right: A Social History of Birth Control in America* (New York: Grossman, 1976).

73. Lorine Pruette, *Women and Leisure: A Study of Social Waste,* American Women: Images and Realities series (1924; New York: Arno, 1972), p. 6.

74. A. R. Wadia, "The Moloch of Industries," in *The Ethics of Feminism: A Study of the Revolt of Woman* (New York: George H. Doran, 1923), pp. 76, 114.

75. "Why They Won't Marry the Modern Girl," *Delineator,* December 1921, p. 2.

76. Anthony M. Ludovici, *Lysistrata: Or Woman's Future and Future Woman* (London: Kegan Paul, Trench, Trubner, 1924), pp. 36, 42, 45, 49.

77. Judith R. Walkowitz, *City of Dreadful Delight: Narratives of Sexual Danger in Late-Victorian London* (Chicago: University of Chicago Press, 1992), p. 67.

78. Ibid., p. 10.

79. Kathy Peiss, *Cheap Amusements: Working Women and Leisure in Turn-of-the-Century New York* (Philadelphia: Temple University Press, 1986), p. 62.

80. Jessie Ackermann, "The Business Girl," in *Australia from a Woman's Point of View* (Melbourne: Cassell, 1913), p. 288.

81. Ibid.

82. For an account of the appointment of police matrons at the Sydney central lock-up, see Lake, *Getting Equal*, p. 59.

83. South Australia already had twelve policewomen, while four had been appointed in New South Wales. "Our Sydney Streets: Women Police Patrols Needed," *Herself*, 13 July 1928, p. 10.

84. Ackermann, *Australia*, p. 283. Contemporary cartoonist Alex Gurney punned on "factory hands and legs," showing young women sitting and standing at the factory entrance with skirts above their knees. Cartoon in *Beckett's Weekly*, 27 January 1928, p. 27.

85. See Julie Tisdale, " 'The Future Mothers of the Race': Venereal Disease and the Amateur in Melbourne during World War I," B.A. honors thesis, Monash University, 1994.

86. "Red Pepper Issue" (no. 2) of the *Mustard Pot* (1928), p. 17.

87. *Truth*, 21 January 1922, p. 3.

88. *Truth*, 18 February 1922, p. 4.

89. "Mashers and Maidens," *Truth*, 29 April 1922, p. 5.

90. Ibid.

91. Ellis calls the social separation of men and women in public space—chivalry—"an unhealthy ideal . . . according to which a woman was treated as a cross between an angel and an idiot." Havelock Ellis, *The Task of Social Hygiene*, 2nd ed. (London: Constable, 1927), p. 58.

92. In Australia, Marie Stopes's ideas were taken up and disseminated by sex educationist Marion Piddington. See Katie Holmes, *Spaces in Her Day: Australian Women's Diaries of the 1920s and 1930s* (St. Leonards, N.S.W.: Allen and Unwin, 1995), p. 89.

93. Bernhard A. Bauer, *Women and Love*, trans. Eden and Cedar Paul (London: William Heinemann, 1927), p. 43.

94. E. R. Wembridge, "Petting and the Campus," *Survey*, no. 54 (1 June 1925), p. 395.

95. In 1919, *Table Talk* gave women readers self-defense advice, to help them counter the risks of traveling to and from work unescorted. "Jiu-Jitsu and Its Advantages," *Table Talk*, 27 February 1919, p. 21. Women who knew Jiu-Jitsu were ready to take on the sexual danger which attended their movements in the metropolis and which was a staple feature of newspapers like *Truth*.

96. Lynne Frame, "Gretchen, Girl or Garçonne? Weimar Science and Popular Culture in Search of the Ideal New Woman," in Katharina Von Ankum, ed., *Women in the Metropolis: Gender and Modernity in Weimar Culture* (Berkeley: University of California Press, 1997), p. 13.

97. For example, "Seen around Sydney," *Stage and Society*, 16 December 1921, p. 4.

98. "A Traffic Hold Up," *Green Room Pictorial*, 27 September 1926, p. 12.

99. "Flighty Flappers: Pavement Nymphs: Behaviour Shocks Sargent Spring," *Beckett's Budget*, 7 September 1928, p. 21.

100. "Fair Interlopers: Women Who Swamp the Labour Market," *Truth*, 13 May 1922, p. 1.

101. "Bare Knees: Fashion's Latest Fad," *Truth*, 29 April 1922, p. 5.

102. "Traffic Signals: Sydney Enforcement," *Adam and Eve*, 1 July 1926, p. 60.

103. Matthew Williams, "Traffic Problems," in *Australia in the 1920s* (Sydney: Trocaders, 1984), p. 53; illustration of Detroit traffic aid, July 1929, *Royalauto*, in *Royalauto*, June 1996, p. 60. My thanks to Jodie Brooks for bringing this reference to my attention.

104. Andreas Huyssen, "The Vamp and the Machine: Fritz Lang's Metropolis," in *After the Great Divide: Modernism, Mass Culture, Postmodernism* (Bloomington: Indiana University Press, 1986), p. 70.

105. Dunlop used the improbability of women drivers to advertise the reliability and safety of their tires, and included snapshots from a transcontinental drive by Mrs. G. Sandford and Miss S. Christie in 1927, from Sydney to Perth, Darwin, Melbourne, and back to Sydney. Interestingly, in the 1920s cars seem to have been marketed as urban, comfortable, and convenient for women drivers, where earlier advertising had emphasized adventure and frontierism for male drivers. *Bulletin*, 4 August 1927, p. 25. See also Virginia Scharff, *Taking the Wheel: Women and the Coming of the Motor Age* (Albuquerque: University of New Mexico Press), 1992.

106. See an advertisement for Australian General Motors in the Melbourne *Bulletin*, in which women in a 1929 Chevrolet pass a billboard in which an audience stands before the slogan "The World's Best Choice." 12 December 1928, pp. 30–31.

107. "The 'Song of the Flapper-Ace'" appears in the Sydney City Girls' Amateur Sports Association fundraising publication *"Johnnie" You're a Bird*, 1930, Mitchell Library, State Library of New South Wales. "Johnnie" is Amy Johnson. Similarly, the American Elinor Smith, who in 1929 at seventeen years of age broke the record for a solo endurance flight, was known as "The Flying Flapper." Her photograph appeared in the *Australian Woman's Mirror*, 16 July 1929, p. 11. Sydney City Girls' Amateur Sports Association, *"Johnnie" You're a Bird*, Mitchell Library, State Library of New South Wales, p. 10.

108. "The Age of Indiscretion," *Bulletin*, 12 March 1925, p. 16.

109. "The Self-Respecting Typiste," *Bulletin*, 13 December 1919, p. 34.

110. "No Bait Provided," *Bulletin*, 10 April 1919, p. 16.

111. Home Lover, "Can the Business Girl Be Taken Seriously? Or Is She Merely a 'Pocket Money' Industrialist?" *Helen's Weekly*, 29 September 1927, p. 20.

112. "Readers Disagree With the writer in 'Helen's' Business Woman's Number who said the Business Girl is a Pocket Money Industrialist," *Helen's Weekly*, 15 December 1927, p. 44.

113. "The Typist's Employer: Eden Conditions Reversed—Adam Tempts Eve," *Adam and Eve*, 1 November 1927, p. 6.

114. "Wanted," *Working Woman*, 1 June 1931, p. 4.

115. "'Grooming' as an Asset: Keeping Spruce for Business," *Helen's Weekly*, 29 September 1927, p. 57.

116. "'Beauty Is Mean Advantage': Some Plain Talk by a Plain Girl Who Has Suffered Unfair Competition," *Beckett's Budget*, 2 August 1927, p. 9.

117. "Beauty Is a Bar to Business: In Which a Sydney Girl Tells How Her Good Looks Are a Hindrance," *Beckett's Budget*, 19 July 1927, p. 7.

118. C. G. Hartley, *Women's Wild Oats: Essays on the Refixing of Moral Standards* (London: T. Werner Laurie, 1919).

119. Department of Labour and Industry, Board of Trade, *Transcript and Proceedings of the Inquiry into the Cost of Living of Adult Female Workers, 1918* (holdings 2/5768, Mitchell Library, State Library of New South Wales). See also Gail Reekie's description of Farmer's Department Store's promotion of the "Smart Business Girls Campaign," *Temptations*, p. 32.

120. Rural Workers' Union Case 1912 Commonwealth Arbitration Reports, 72, reprinted in Holmes and Lake, *Freedom Bound II*, p. 13. Justice H. B. Higgins.

121. *The Age*, 5 June 1919, reprinted in Holmes and Lake, *Freedom Bound II*, p. 30.

122. Letter to the editor, *The Sydney Morning Herald*, 20 February 1934, reprinted in Holmes and Lake, *Freedom Bound II*, p. 74.

123. "The Story of a Woman, by a Woman," in *The Revolutionary Socialist* (Sydney: Socialist Labor Party of Australia, 1927), p. 5.

124. Similarly, in the United States, Thomas H. Russell (general secretary of the Clean Language League of America) wrote of how it was impossible for young women to live on five dollars a week when their expenses averaged eight dollars. The loss of virtue was framed by exploitation: "American womanhood is in grave peril solely and only because American manhood profits from the helplessness of womanhood to enrich itself." Russell, *The Girl's Fight for a Living: How to Protect Working Women from Dangers Due to Low Wages* (Chicago: M. A. Donohue, 1913), p. 17.

125. See Lake, *Getting Equal*, p. 56.

126. Ackermann, *Australia*, p. 289.

127. Elizabeth Wilson, *The Sphinx in the City: Urban Life, the Control of Disorder, and Women* (London: Virago, 1991), p. 120.

3. THE SCREEN-STRUCK GIRL IN THE CINEMATIC SCENE

1. "Making Movies (and Money)," *Aussie*, 15 October 1924, p. 14. Lovely's original surname was Lehmann, which she concealed because she was illegitimate. She had toured Australia with her mother and Sarah Bernhardt and later Nellie Stewart and become a stage favorite before she began making films with the Australian Life Biograph Company in 1911. Her American career began with Bluebird Productions (part of Universal Studios), which renamed her Louise Lovely. She left Universal when they refused to grant her a salary increase and prevented her from working with Pathé Studios. Although Universal blackballed her, she re-emerged a year later as a Fox and Goldwyn Studio star. See Andree Wright, *Brilliant Careers: Women in Australian Cinema* (Sydney: Pan, 1986), pp. 21–29.

2. See Ray Edmondson and Andrew Pike, *Australia's Lost Films: The Loss and Rescue of Australia's Silent Cinema* (Canberra: National Library of Australia, 1982), p. 19.

3. Wright, *Brilliant Careers*, p. 26.

4. Edmondson and Pike, *Australia's Lost Films*, p. 19.

5. See the catalogue accompanying *Focus on Reel Australia: A Collection of Early Australian Feature Films* (Hendon, S.A.: National Film and Sound Archives, 1990), p. 47.

6. "Oh! Oh! Louise Lovely," *Truth*, 25 October 1924, p. 1.

7. "Louise Lovely's Latest Lurk: Attracting the Screen Struck," *Truth*, 18 October 1924, p. 1.

8. Walter Benjamin, "The Work of Art in the Age of Mechanical Reproduction," in Benjamin, *Illuminations*, ed. Hannah Arendt, trans. Harry Zohn (Suffolk: Fontana, 1973), pp. 238, 231.

9. Benjamin, "The Work of Art," p. 231.

10. Gail Jones has written an imaginative account of an encounter between the visual apparatus of early cinema and a young provincial Russian girl who becomes terrified by the experience of spectatorship and leaves the cinema overwhelmed and distressed. See Gail Jones, "Modernity," in her *House of Breathing* (Perth: Freemantle Arts Centre Press, 1992), pp. 11–19.

11. Benjamin, "The Work of Art," p. 233.

12. Paul Kelly and Susan Lord, "Driven to Distraction: Going to the Movies with Walter and Siegfried," *Cineaction*, no. 34 (1995), p. 21.

13. Patrice Petro, *Joyless Streets: Women and Melodramatic Representation in Weimar Germany* (Princeton, N.J.: Princeton University Press, 1989), pp. 57–64.

14. Rita Felski, *The Gender of Modernity* (Cambridge, Mass.: Harvard University Press, 1995), p. 95.

15. See Jill Julius Matthews, "Which America?" in *Americanization and Australia*, ed. Philip Bell and Roger Bell (Sydney: University of New South Wales Press, 1998), pp. 29, 20, 16.

16. "What Films Should We Make?" *Bulletin*, 1 April 1926, p. 3.

17. Dianne Collins, "The Movie Octopus," in *Australian Popular Culture*, ed. Peter Spearritt and David Walker (Sydney: Allen and Unwin, 1979), p. 107.

18. Nancy F. Cott, "The Modern Woman of the 1920s, American Style," in *Toward a Cultural Identity in the Twentieth Century*, ed. Françoise Thébaud, vol. 5 of *A History of Women in the West*, ed. Georges Duby and Michelle Perrot (Cambridge, Mass.: Belknap Press of Harvard University Press, 1994), p. 77.

19. Peter Wollen, "Cinema/Americanism/The Robot," in *Modernity and Mass Culture*, ed. James Naremore and Patrick Brantlinger (Bloomington: Indiana University Press, 1991), p. 42. American filmmaker D. W. Griffith was quite explicit about cinema and Americanization, asking, "Are we not making the world safe for democracy, American Democracy, through motion pictures?" Quoted in Stephen Kern, *The Culture of Time and Space, 1800–1918* (Cambridge, Mass.: Harvard University Press, 1983), p. 209.

20. "The Moving Picture Business," *Bulletin*, 15 September 1921, p. 7.

21. Simon Brand, *Picture Palaces and Flea Pits: Eighty Years of Australians at the Pictures* (Sydney: Dreamweaver, 1983), p. 80; Collins, "Movie Octopus," p. 103.

22. Edmondson and Pike, *Australia's Lost Films*, p. 18.

23. "The Yankee Film Monopoly," *Bulletin*, 6 October 1921, p. 7. (After two trials ending in hung juries, Arbuckle was acquitted in March 1922.)

24. "What Films Should We Make?"

25. Joan Long and Martin Long, *The Pictures That Moved: A Picture History of the Australian Cinema, 1896–1929* (Richmond, Vic.: Hutchinson, 1982), p. 118.

26. Ina Bertrand, ed., *Cinema in Australia: A Documentary History* (Kensington: University of New South Wales Press, 1989), p. 73. See also Collins,

"Movie Octopus," for a history of women's organizations' demands for censorship. The Australian term "wowser" means a self-righteous prude, a puritan. An alderman of Sydney City Council, Mr. Norton, called an opponent "the white-whiskered wowser from Waverley." Premier Jack Scadden defined it as "a person who made more fuss about a girl showing an inch of petticoat than about a dozen families living in poverty." *Truth*, 26 October 1922, p. 5.

27. Hon. Hugh D. McIntosh, M.L.C., speech to the New South Wales Legislative Council, Sydney, 12 August 1925, transcribed in *Everyones*, 19 August 1925, p. 5.

28. Quoted in Collins, "Movie Octopus," pp. 105, 109.

29. "The Plague of 'Pictures,'" *Bulletin*, 28 July 1921, p. 7.

30. "Behind the Scenes: Fight for Movie Supremacy: Hollywood Interests Digging In," *Truth*, 9 July 1927, p. 7.

31. "The 'Pictures for Australia,'" *Bulletin*, 10 December 1925, p. 12.

32. "Exchange Men's Rejoinder to That 50 Per Cent Restriction," *Everyones—Incorporating Australian Variety and Show World*, 24 October 1923, p. 15.

33. National Council of Women of New South Wales, *Biennial Report* (Sydney, 1919–20), pp. 37–38.

34. "Australian Movies: A Real Start at Last," *Adam and Eve*, 1 March 1927, p. 24. The *Bulletin* used Hollywood scandal, particularly the Arbuckle case, to suggest that "the pictured glorification of crime, extravagance, vulgarity and sensuality which comes to us from America" (from "Yankee Film Monopoly") might well accurately reflect that "there is very little in modern life in America to deserve respect" (from "Respect"). America, admitted the *Bulletin*, "may have boys and girls who can enjoy life without considering that their 'flaming youth' entitles them to despise all ideas of chastity, sobriety and decency. It may have wives who respect the marriage vows enough not to leap at another man the instant he offers their 'starved souls' luxury if the husband is poor, or incessant hectic love-making if he is rich. It may have rush men who enjoy a quiet evening at home and shopwalkers who would rather spend their spare time working the garden than in ruining the newest shopgirl" (from "Respect"). But the paper suspected that American film was true to the American national character. "Respect—and the Pictures," *Bulletin*, 10 February 1927, p. 11, and "The Yankee Film Monopoly."

35. "Australian Movies: A Real Start at Last," *Adam and Eve*, 1 March 1927, p. 24.

36. "The 'Pictures' for Australia," *Bulletin*, 10 December 1925, p. 12. The *Bulletin* argued that Australia and Britain could produce "interesting scenic and industrial pictures and clean minded comedies which would be far more entertaining to a healthy minded public than American slop." "The Moving Picture Business."

37. Bertrand, *Cinema in Australia*, p. 71.

38. M. R. Megaw, "Happy Ever After: The Image of Women in Four Australian Feature Films of the Nineteen Twenties," *Journal of Australian Studies*, no. 7 (1980), pp. 67–69. There were a number of Australian films produced about urban women, such as *The Woman Suffers* (1918) and *Know Thy Child* (1921), a film about illegitimacy and social justice. However, except for the McDonagh sisters' films (which were criticized as un-Australian), urban

women tended to be embroiled in troubled narratives, unlike the idealized girl of the Bush.

39. "'Everyones' Extends a Helping Hand to the Australian Producer," *Everyones,* 9 February 1927, p. 30.

40. "Enter Madame," *Everyones,* 22 December 1926, p. 3.

41. "Australian Girls' Achievement: Three Sisters Produce a Film," *Herself,* 13 July 1928, p. 4. See also Kerryn L. Amery, *Hidden Women: Locating Information on Significant Australian Women* (Carlton, Vic.: Melbourne College of Advanced Education, 1986), pp. 90–100, and Wright, *Brilliant Careers,* pp. 34–40.

42. "At Last!—Picture Production in Australia on a Solid Basis," *Lone Hand,* 20 March 1920, p. 30.

43. Quoted in Wright, *Brilliant Careers,* p. 5.

44. "Enter Madame."

45. "An Actress in Australian Productions," *Theatre Magazine,* 1 July 1913, p. 34.

46. Bertrand, *Cinema in Australia,* pp. 115–16.

47. "Screening Beautiful Women—and Others," *Everyone's—Variety and Show World,* 12 April 1922, p. 8. Perhaps in response to the evidence before the 1927 Royal Commission regarding the American monopoly on film distribution in Australia, *Everyones* later softened its pro-combine line and offered "a helping hand to the Australian producer," asking, "Could you build up a reputation in your script for an Australian star?" "'Everyones' Extends a Helping Hand to the Australian Producer."

48. Quoted in Collins, "Movie Octopus," pp. 110–11.

49. "The Plague of Pictures."

50. Tom Gunning, "An Aesthetics of Astonishment: Early Film and the (In)Credulous Spectator," *Art and Text,* no. 34 (spring 1989), p. 37.

51. Bertrand, *Cinema in Australia,* p. 73.

52. Of course, in order for paparazzi images to effect this sense of a "live" encounter between star and audience, they must disavow that their images are also reproduced, hence the emphasis on unauthorized "snaps" and the repeated magazine stories on "stars without their make-up." The paparazzi want to claim that their cameras, unlike all others, see things as they really are. Liz Conor, "Nicole Kidman and the Commodity Star," *Metro,* no. 127–28 (June 2001), p. 98.

53. William K. Everson, "The Mid 1920s: The New Dominance of the Female Star," in his *American Silent Film* (New York: Oxford University Press, 1978), pp. 194–204.

54. "Oh! Oh! Louise Lovely."

55. "Beauty No Object," *Picture Show,* 1 September 1923, p. 36.

56. "Plays, Players, and Films," *Truth,* 12 January 1924, p. 8.

57. "Film Star's Morals," *Australian Woman's Mirror,* 10 May 1927, p. 10. This article gives a firsthand account of the nightclubs and drug taking in Hollywood. Arbuckle is featured as dancing a drunken "Salome" impersonation until collapsing on the dance floor. The article reports that studios were concentrating on the moral and sexual behavior of stars offscreen because they were losing thousands of dollars on films featuring Arbuckle.

58. "Hitting the High Spots at Hollywood with Movie Stars," *Truth,* 5 February 1927, p. 1.

59. "Morals of Movieland: Wild Parties and Orgies," *Truth*, 12 November 1921, p. 4.

60. "The Hollywood Girl: Under-developed and Over-exposed," cartoon, *Humour*, 12 September 1924, p. 28.

61. "Morals of Movieland."

62. "Australian Film Actress Disillusioned," *Everyones: Incorporating Australian Variety and Show World*, 11 February 1925, p. 16.

63. Wright, *Brilliant Careers*, p. 18.

64. "Australian Film Actress Disillusioned."

65. Examples include "Girls and the Movies," *Everyones: Incorporating Australian Variety and Show World*, 28 February 1923, p. 6; "Star Gives Sound Advice to Movie-Mad Maids," *Everyones: Incorporating Australian Variety and Show World*, 18 March 1926, p. 25. The latter focuses on Mabel Moore, a screen aspirant who pawned two diamond rings bought on credit to finance her pilgrimage to Los Angeles.

66. "Tragedies of the Moving Picture World: Billie Burke's Warning," *Everyone's*, 1 December 1920, p. 9. This was an interview with Billie Burke, a stage actress who rejected an apparently promising film career to devote time to her child and then return to theater. Interestingly, she found the camera "not human" to perform for, and that there was less talent and more reliance on beauty in the film studio.

67. "The City Mother (Police Department)," quoted in "City of Pretty Girls: All Want to Be Film Stars," *Everyone's*, 16 February 1921, p. 7.

68. "Girls and the Movies."

69. Ibid.

70. "Ladies of Poverty Row: Girls Who Fail in Hollywood, Where Ten Thousand Are Waiting for a Chance," *Home*, 1 January 1927, p. 52. A still from *Along Came Ruth* published in the *Australian Woman's Mirror*, showing Viola Dana being kissed, depicted the Hollywood adventure as romance. Its caption read, "Another reason why a film career appeals to the romantic flapper." *Australian Woman's Mirror*, 10 February 1925, p. 29.

71. "City of Pretty Girls: All Want to Be Film Stars," *Everyone's*, 16 February 1921, p. 7.

72. "Ladies of Poverty Row."

73. Ibid.

74. "City of Pretty Girls."

75. "Film Neurosis," *Truth*, 27 August 1928, p. 16.

76. "Our Moving Picture Swindlers: Picture Acting Schools and Methods Adopted by Picture Teachers: A Timely Warning to Screen Struck Girls: Government Control Wanted," *Green Room*, 1 June 1921, p. 4.

77. "Scoundrels of Moviedom," *Green Room*, 1 August 1921, p. 19.

78. "Our Moving Picture Swindlers."

79. "Re: Great Actresses," *Everyones*, 15 July 1925, p. 26.

80. Marilyn Lake, *Getting Equal: The History of Australian Feminism* (St. Leonards, N.S.W.: Allen and Unwin, 1999), p. 69; "Woman Censor Wanted," *Everyones*, 3 November 1926, p. 6.

81. See Geoff Brown, "Eleanor Glencross and Ivy Weber: In and out of Parliament," in *Double Time: Women in Victoria, 150 Years*, ed. Marilyn Lake and Farley Kelly (Ringwood, Vic.: Penguin, 1985), pp. 344–53.

82. "The New Censor Boards," *Everyones: The Motion Picture Authority*, 5

December 1928, p. 1. This article also welcomes the addition of Mrs. M. Liddell, a journalist, to the censors' board. Perhaps her profession, as distinct from the domestic sphere Mrs. Glencross represented, earned her more respect, for her journalism was cited as an indication of her "impartiality" and "breadth of vision."

83. Patrice Petro, "Perceptions of Difference: Woman as Spectator and Spectacle," in *Women in the Metropolis: Gender and Modernity in Weimar Culture*, ed. Katharina von Ankum (Berkeley: University of California Press, 1997), p. 44. See also her analysis of Metzian psychoanalytic film theory (Christian Metz, *Film Language: A Semiotics of the Cinema*, trans. Michael Taylor [New York: Oxford University Press, 1974]), in which the spectator identifies with himself as pure act of perception—with his own look—and thereby gains a sense of subjective coherence through processes of fetishism and voyeurism. The theories of Christian Metz have been highly influential in feminist film theory since Laura Mulvey's classic argument (discussed in chapter 1) that gender difference in spectatorship can be discerned through the identification of men with an active, controlling, and sadistic gaze in order to disavow the castration of the woman-object. In the classic film text, female spectators identify with the sexualized woman-object, and their passivity is associated with being the object of the look, the spectacle. In order to create the possibility of an active gaze for women spectators, Mulvey later reworked her argument to allow women to identify with the male gaze across the binary divide of gender. See Laura Mulvey, "Visual Pleasure and Narrative Cinema," *Screen* 16, no. 3 (autumn 1975), pp. 6–18, and "Afterthoughts on 'Visual Pleasure and Narrative Cinema' Inspired by 'Duel in the Sun' (King Vidor, 1946)," *Frameworks*, nos. 15–17 (1981), pp. 12–15.

84. Quoted in Petro, *Joyless Streets*, p. 47. See Christian Metz, *Psychoanalysis and Cinema: The Imaginary Signifier*, trans. Celia Britton, Anwyl Williams, Ben Brewster, and Alfred Guzzetti (London: Macmillan, 1982), and Mary Ann Doane, "Film and the Masquerade: Theorizing the Female Spectator," *Screen* 23, nos. 3–4 (1982), pp. 74–87.

85. Petro, *Joyless Streets*, p. 49.

86. "Screen Struck: Foolish Flapper: Yankee Actor," *Truth*, 15 September 1923, p. 2.

87. "Girls! Which of You Have Not Longed to Be a Movie Star?" advertisement for Ashby Studios, *Everyones: Incorporating Australian Variety and Show World*, 8 August 1923, p. 20; "In Search of a Film Star!" advertisement for Ashby Studios, *Ladies Designer*, 1 May 1923, p. 10, and 1 June 1923, p. 44.

88. Like the articles in *Everyones*, many of these ads maintained that the Screen Star was not always a beauty. "Remember, it is not beauty, the screen seeks—It is the Film Face—The Film Type." Advertisement for Ashby Studios, *Society*, 1 September 1923, p. 39.

89. "Is Fortune Waiting for You?" *Picture Show*, 1 May 1923, p. 50.

90. "Have You Booked Miss 1928?" Advertisement for Paramount Studio, *Everyones*, 4 January 1928, pp. 17–19.

91. Quoted in Matthew Williams, "Out on the Town—Amusements of the 1920s," in *Australia in the 1920s* (Sydney: Trocaders, 1984), p. 56.

92. "Australian Girls Wanted for American Movies: Universal Needs Them with Brains and Ability," *Australian Variety and Show World*, 10 June 1920, pp. 10–11.

93. "Universal Gets Potential Star in Australian Girl," *Australian Variety and Show World*, 24 June 1920, p. 8.

94. "Australian Girls Wanted for American Movies."

95. "Are You Fit for the Films?" *Picture Show*, 1 May 1923, pp. 24–25. In the American *Ladies' Home Journal*, Clara Bow and Joan Crawford endorsed Lux Toilet Soap. Camera techniques, they said, created new conditions for "velvety beauty"; "The loveliness of her skin under the fierce lights of the close-up is more important to a screen star than any other kinds of beauty." "'Smooth Skin the Greatest Loveliness,' Say Leading Motion Picture Directors," *Ladies Home Journal*, October 1928, p. 161.

96. For example, "Australian Screen Types," *Adam and Eve*, 1 January 1928, p. 11.

97. Sally Alexander, "Becoming a Woman in the 1920s and 1930s," in *Metropolis London: Histories and Representations since 1880*, ed. David Feldman and Gareth Stedman Jones (London: Routledge, 1991), pp. 256, 249, 264, 265.

98. Ibid., p. 249.

99. "Herbert Brenon, Paramount Director, Gives Sound Advice to Motion Picture Aspirants," *Stage and Society*, 13 December 1923, p. 44.

100. "Are You Fit for the Films?"

101. Benjamin, "The Work of Art," op. cit., p. 238.

4. THE MANNEQUIN IN THE COMMODITY SCENE

1. Orwell, "A Cold Beauty," *Aussie*, 15 October 1921, p. 46.

2. William Leach, "Transformations in a Culture of Consumption: Women and Department Stores, 1890–1925," *Journal of American History* 71, no. 2 (September 1984), pp. 319–42.

3. *Australian Woman's Mirror*, 1 September 1925, p. 11.

4. "Paris Exhibition of Decorative Art: Idols That Paris Applauds," *Home*, 1 October 1925, pp. 36, 48.

5. Jennifer Craik, *The Face of Fashion: Cultural Studies in Fashion* (New York: Routledge, 1994), p. 99.

6. William Leach, "Strategists of Display and the Production of Desire," in *Consuming Visions: Accumulation and Display of Goods in America 1880–1920*, ed. Simon J. Bronner (New York: W. W. Norton, 1989), p. 113.

7. Martin Pumphrey, "The Flapper, the Housewife, and the Making of Modernity," *Cultural Studies* 1, no. 1 (January 1987), pp. 179–94.

8. Walter Benjamin, "The Flaneur," in *Charles Baudelaire: A Lyric Poet in the Era of High Capitalism* (London: Verso, 1973), pp. 35–40.

9. Worth's employer, Gagelin, had used live models since the 1860s. See Craik, *Face of Fashion*, p. 76.

10. Ibid., p. 77.

11. Gail Reekie, *Temptations: Sex, Selling, and the Department Store* (St. Leonards, N.S.W.: Allen and Unwin, 1993), p. 145.

12. The highest paid mannequin in the world, Mademoiselle Suzette, sued her firm when they dismissed her for allegedly disclosing some of their designs to other fashion houses. *Australian Woman's Mirror*, 5 June 1928, p. 14.

13. Stephen Kern, *The Culture of Time and Space, 1880–1918* (Cambridge, Mass.: Harvard University Press, 1983), p. 189.

14. Craik, *Face of Fashion*, p. 77.

15. "Moulded Her to His Heart's Desire," *Sun News-Pictorial*, 5 October 1923, p. 8.

16. The *Australian Woman's Mirror* wrote that Mrs. O. Stubergh was capturing the American market in mannequins because she molded from live women and used wax casts. *Australian Woman's Mirror*, 27 January 1925, p. 15.

17. Manufacturing increased from 44.3 percent of the Australian gross national product in 1920–21 to 68.7 percent in 1928–29. Stuart Macintyre, *1901–1942: The Succeeding Age*, vol. 4 of *The Oxford History of Australia*, ed. Geoffrey Bolton (Melbourne: Oxford University Press, 1986), p. 202.

18. Leach, "Strategists of Display and the Production of Desire," pp. 110, 106.

19. The idea of "the masses" is said to derive from a fourteenth-century separation of the "literary and philosophical elite from the commercial, manufacturing and financial bourgeoisie." David Forgacs, "National-Popular: Genealogy of a Concept," in *The Cultural Studies Reader*, ed. Simon During (London: Routledge, 1993), p. 184. More historically pertinent is the development of consumer society through "a sharpening separation between the spheres of production and consumption from about 1870 forward." James Naremore and Patrick Brantlinger, "Introduction: Six Artistic Cultures," eds., *Modernity and Mass Culture* (Bloomington: Indiana University Press, 1991), p. 5.

20. Richard Ohmann, "History and Literary History: The Case of Mass Culture," in Naremore and Brantlinger, *Modernity and Mass Culture*, p. 31.

21. Leach, "Strategists of Display and the Production of Desire," p. 103.

22. Department stores were also coy about sexual difference. William Leach notes that department stores had separate entrances, elevators, and departments for men and women. "Everything was done to create distinct gender spaces for men and women, even as (or especially because) the exigencies of the capitalist market pulled them more closely together than ever before in the public domain." Leach, "Transformations in a Culture of Consumption: Women and Department Stores, 1890–1925," p. 331.

23. Reekie, *Temptations*, p. 24. However, Leach points out that, after the turn of the century, the newly stylized and increasingly realistic mannequins were principally female until the 1970s. Leach, "Strategists of Display and the Production of Desire," p. 112.

24. See Kerreen Reiger, *The Disenchantment of the Home: Modernizing the Australian Family, 1880–1940* (Melbourne: Oxford University Press, 1985).

25. Luisa Passerini, "The Ambivalent Image of Woman in Mass Culture," in *Toward a Cultural Identity in the Twentieth Century*, ed. Françoise Thébaud, vol. 5 of *A History of Women in the West*, ed. Georges Duby and Michelle Perrot (Cambridge, Mass.: Belknap Press of Harvard University Press, 1994), p. 330.

26. Leach, "Transformations in a Culture of Consumption," p. 336.

27. Craik, *Face of Fashion*, p. 71. See also Beverley Kingston, *Basket, Bag, and Trolley: A History of Shopping in Australia* (Melbourne: Oxford University Press, 1994).

28. Susan Porter Benson describes department stores as "adamless edens" in her *Counter Cultures: Saleswomen, Managers, and Customers in American Department Stores, 1890–1940* (Urbana: University of Illinois Press, 1986).

29. Reiger, *Disenchantment of the Home*, p. 206.

30. Reekie, *Temptations*, p. xiii.

31. Bertha Fortescue Harrison, "Advertising for the Woman," *The Reason Why: A Magazine for Advertisers*, 24 February 1909, p. 16.

32. It was necessary to "train girls as consumers." The American *Journal*

of Home Economics advised that when it came to clothes shopping, girls should "organize the data for each garment under selected headings and record it on library cards arranged alphabetically or according to topics. Helpful illustrations may be mounted on these cards. The data may be easily revised as the styles and prices change." S. Helen Bridge, "Training Girls as Consumers," *Journal of Home Economics* 13, no. 6 (June 1921), p. 247.

33. Reekie, *Temptations*, pp. 99, 104, 331, 92–93.

34. Advertisement, *Bulletin*, 14 November 1928, p. 45.

35. Elizabeth Wilson, *The Sphinx in the City: Urban Life, the Control of Disorder, and Women* (London: Virago, 1991), p. 16.

36. Judith Walkowitz, *City of Dreadful Delight: Narratives of Sexual Danger in Late-Victorian London* (Chicago: University of Chicago Press, 1992), pp. 46–52.

37. Wilson, *Sphinx in the City*, p. 68.

38. See the Myer Emporium window display, 1924–25, Melbourne University Archives, Myer Collection, Coles Myer Archives.

39. For a fond description of the grand dimensions and lavish interiors of Sydney department stores, see Vivian Stewart, "The Way They Were: A Sydney Department Store in the 1920s," *Heritage Australia* 9, no. 4 (summer 1990), pp. 20–24. For Stewart consumers too were on display in the department store. She writes, "It was the thing to dress up in hat or gloves and take the train, tram or bus to the city for the day and shop and lunch at one of the big emporiums," p. 21.

40. "The Mannequin Walk," *Australian Home Journal*, 1 April 1920, p. 41.

41. The article states that "otherwise genuinely attractive" young women "are spoiled by carelessness in standing." Thrusting the hip to one side, for example, "suggests an absolute collapse of the individual." "Standing as an Art," *Helen's Weekly*, 20 October 1927, p. 47.

42. Advertisement for Lux, *Australian Woman's Mirror*, 1 March 1927, p. 23.

43. Advertisement for Ven-Yusa the Oxygen Face Cream, *Aussie*, 15 February 1924, p. 45.

44. Advertisement for Shave Ladies' Tailors and Dressmakers, *Bulletin*, 16 December 1920, p. 42.

45. Advertisement for Palmolive Soap, *Bulletin*, 23 November 1922, p. 41. The same advertising campaign also pictures a young woman sitting demurely on a fence between two attentive men under the banner "Irresistible." *Bulletin*, 20 April 1922, p. 41.

46. *Bulletin*, 23 November 1922, p. 41.

47. Advertisement for Beecham Pills, *Australian Home Journal*, 1 September 1920, p. 36.

48. Advertisement for Vi-Glo hair treatment, *Australian Woman's Mirror*, 6 September 1927, p. 54.

49. "The Rise of Plain Jane to Social Success," advertisement for Lustre Dress Fabrics, *Australian Woman's Mirror*, 28 January 1930, p. 22.

50. "Lead Us Not into Temptation," *Bulletin*, 26 December 1928, p. 8.

51. Bernhard A. Bauer, *Women and Love*, trans. Eden and Cedar Paul (London: William Heinemann, 1927), pp. 292–93.

52. "Girls and Other Folk's [*sic*] Property: A Chat with Careless Lassies," *Everylady's Journal*, 6 November 1912, p. 655.

53. "The Economist," cartoon, *Bulletin*, 4 September 1919, p. 15.

54. "And So the World Goes Round," cartoon, *Bulletin*, 28 August 1919, p. 16.

55. "An Attractive Investment," cartoon, *Bulletin*, 29 February 1928, p. 12.

56. Sally Alexander adds that the introduction of the mass-produced sewing machine into homes played a crucial role in the passing of "the mantle of glamour" from "the aristocrat and courtesan to the shop, office, or factory girl via the film star." Sally Alexander, "Becoming a Woman in London in the 1920s and 1930s," in *Metropolis London: Histories and Representations since 1880*, ed. David Feldman and Gareth Stedman Jones (London: Routledge, 1991), p. 264.

57. "The Servant Problem," cartoon, *Bulletin*, 14 June 1923, p. 17.

58. See Andreas Huyssen, "Mass Culture as Woman: Modernism's Other," in *Studies in Entertainment: Critical Approaches to Mass Culture*, ed. Tania Modleski (Bloomington: Indiana University Press, 1986), pp. 188–207; Tania Modleski, "Femininity as Ma(s)squerade," in *Feminism without Women: Culture and Criticism in a "Postfeminist" Age* (New York: Routledge, 1991), pp. 23–34.

59. Metro-Goldwyn Mayer, advertisement for *Woman Triumphant*, *Everyones*, 1 February 1928, p. 15.

60. "Hitching a Costume to a Star," *Adam and Eve*, 1 September 1928, p. 20.

61. Ibid.

62. Gloria Swanson eulogized silk as a woman's "second heart" which "exerts a subtle influence on her thoughts." "Beautiful Clothes and Women," *Stage and Society*, 13 December 1923, p. 45.

63. "How the Movies Influence Fashion," *Home*, 1, February 1920, p. 18.

64. Scott McQuire, "The Migratory Eye: Representation, Memory, Time, and Space in the Age of the Camera" (Ph.D. dissertation, University of Melbourne, 1994), p. 73.

65. Miriam Hansen, *Babel and Babylon: Spectatorship in American Silent Film* (Cambridge, Mass.: Harvard University Press, 1991), p. 85.

66. Miriam Hansen, "Benjamin, Cinema, and Experience: 'The Blue Flower in the Land of Technology,'" *New German Critique*, no. 40 (winter 1987), p. 204.

67. Hansen, *Babel and Babylon*, p. 85.

68. Ibid., p. 86.

69. Arjun Appadurai uses this term to describe the luxury object as being more "incarnated signs than goods" and having "the capacity to signal fairly complex social messages." Arjun Appadurai, *The Social Life of Things: Commodities in Cultural Perspective* (Cambridge, New York: Cambridge University Press, 1986), p. 38.

70. While the Mannequin was a material object, like a photograph she was material in the service of imagery.

71. Raymond Bellour, "Ideal Hadaly," in *Close Encounters: Film, Feminism, and Science Fiction*, ed. Constance Penley, Elisabeth Lyon, Lynn Spigel, and Janet Bergstrom (Minneapolis: University of Minnesota Press, 1991), p. 127.

72. The Mannequin may at first sight seem to adhere to the simulacrum as it has been theorized by Jean Baudrillard. In his theory of simulation he writes of the postmodern, "It is no longer a question of imitation, nor of reduplication, nor even of parody. It is rather a question of substituting signs of the real for the real itself; that is an operation to deter every real process

by its operational double, a metastable, programmatic, perfect descriptive machine which provides all signs of the real and short-circuits all vicissitudes." Jean Baudrillard, "Simulacra and Simulations," in *Jean Baudrillard: Selected Writings*, ed. Mark Poster (Cambridge: Polity, 1988), p. 167. However, this "system of signs which devour representation," in which the "signifier supersedes the signified," belongs to what Baudrillard calls the "third order" of simulation in a long history which he takes back to feudal times. The Mannequin seems to belong instead to his "second order." Herein, representation still sought to imitate the real, rather than erase it. Baudrillard describes this second order as like that identified by Benjamin as "the age of mechanical reproduction," in which "signification came to function through the process of reproduction of 'original' representations (signs which referred to signs which, in turn referred to reality)." From "Summary of Jean Baudrillard, 'Simulations,'" in *A Critical and Cultural Theory Reader*, ed. Anthony Easthope and Kate McGowan (North Sydney: Allen and Unwin, 1992), p. 255. See also Stephen Watt, "Baudrillard's America (and Ours?): Image, Virus, Catastrophe," in Naremore and Brantlinger, *Modernity and Mass Culture*, p. 143.

73. Hansen, "Benjamin, Cinema and Experience," p. 204, *Babel and Babylon*, p. 116.

74. Rita Felski, *The Gender of Modernity* (Cambridge, Mass.: Harvard University Press, 1995), pp. 98, 99.

75. Luce Irigaray, *This Sex Which Is Not One*, trans. Catherine Porter with Carolyn Burke (Ithaca, N.Y.: Cornell University Press, 1985), p. 180.

76. "At a Mannequin Parade," advertisement for Berlei, *Home*, 2 September 1929, p. 83. See also Betty Roland's play *Feet of Clay* (1928), which retells the myth of Pygmalion and Galatea when a Melbourne sculptor falls in love with his idealized figure of a white marble woman which comes to life. Kerry Kilner and Sue Tweg, eds., *Playing the Past: Three Plays by Australian Women* (Sydney: Currency, 1995), pp. 31–54.

77. The sense that imitation is mechanical continues to inform analyses of women's consumerist subjectivity. Langman writes, "Commodified desires and images are the strings regulating a puppet show of self." Lauren Langman, "Neon Cages: Shopping for Subjectivity," in *Lifestyle Shopping: The Subject of Consumption*, ed. Rob Shields (London: Routledge, 1992), pp. 62–63.

78. Siegfried Kracauer, "The Mass Ornament" (1927), trans. Jack Zipes and Barbara Corell, *New German Critique*, no. 5 (spring 1975), pp. 67–76; "Girls und Krise," *Frankfurter Zeitung* 27 (1931), quoted in Patrice Petro, *Joyless Streets: Women and Melodramatic Representation in Weimar Germany* (Princeton, N.J.: Princeton University Press, 1989).

79. Kracauer, "Mass Ornament," p. 75.

80. Siegfried Kracauer, "Cult of Distraction: On Berlin's Picture Palaces" (1926), trans. Thomas Y. Levin, *New German Critique*, no. 40 (winter 1987), pp. 96, 92.

81. Kracauer, "Mass Ornament," p. 75.

82. Kracauer, quoted in Petro, *Joyless Streets*, op. cit., p. 65. Kracauer's analysis has resonance with popular constructions of beauty, militarism, and the rationalized, efficient feminine body. In a newspaper report of a typing competition, a journalist wrote, "young ladies are going to forget powder puffs and stray hair tendrils, and typewriters are going to rattle like machineguns under their manicured digits." "Keyboard Dianas: Clash of Typists," *Sun News-Pictorial*, 31 January 1923, p. 4.

83. Kracauer, "Mass Ornament," p. 74.

84. I do not dispute Kracauer's critique of capitalist modes of representation and perception, but rather want to question whether and why the feminine spectacle was the most useful illustration of his argument.

85. Patrice Petro, "Perceptions of Difference: Woman as Spectator and Spectacle," in *Women in the Metropolis: Gender and Modernity in Weimar Culture*, ed. Katharina von Ankum (Berkeley: University of California Press, 1997), p. 56.

86. The notion that the woman-object has an affinity with capitalist exchange derives from writings about women as objects of exchange. Within Lévi-Strauss's theory of incest taboo, the exchange of women constitutes civilization and social order through the establishment of the relations between men. It marks the passage of humanity from the state of nature to the state of culture. See Claude Lévi-Strauss, *The Elementary Structures of Kinship*, trans. James Harle Bell, John Richard von Sturmer, and Rodney Needham (London: Eyre and Spottiswoode, 1969). Luce Irigaray sees this exclusion of women from symbolic relations and language as indicating the reign of the "hom(m)o-sexual economy." The exemption of men from being exchanged and circulated makes it easier for them to recognize themselves as the same, as having the same desire, namely the desire for relations between themselves. It is "the constitution of women as 'objects' that emblematize [*sic*] the materialization of relations among men." Irigaray, *This Sex Which Is Not One*, p. 185.

87. In his theory of commodity fetishism Karl Marx stripped the commodity object of the illusion that its value derives from itself, determining that its value resides instead in the alienated labor relations between its producers. He wrote, "A commodity is therefore a mysterious thing, simply because in it the social character of men's labour appears to them as an objective character stamped upon the product of that labour." Karl Marx, "The Fetishism of Commodities and the Secret Thereof," in *Capital*, 4th ed., trans. Eden and Cedar Paul (London: Dutton, 1930), quoted in Mandy Merck, "Pornography," in *Looking On: Images of Femininity in the Visual Arts and Media*, ed. Rosemary Betterton (London: Pandora, 1987), p. 155. Marx argued that the value of the commodity object is transferred from its use value to its exchange value. The alienating effects of this process of commodity fetishism derive from "that process in which human relations come to take on the appearance in a market economy of relations between things." Andrew Milner, *Contemporary Cultural Theory: An Introduction* (St. Leonards, N.S.W.: Allen and Unwin, 1991), p. 42. For an exposition of Marxian theory of "commodity semiosis" see Andrew Ross, "The New Sentence and the Commodity Form: Recent American Writing," in *Marxism and the Interpretation of Culture*, ed. Cary Nelson and Lawrence Grossberg (London: Macmillan Education, 1988), pp. 361–80.

88. Following Jean Baudrillard, Andrew Ross argues that the signifier as exchange value can be equated with the signified as use value. He writes, "Baudrillard therefore extends Marx's critique of political economy to a critique of the economy of signification, which semiotics has provided as an analytic code for explaining all systems, and finds the same logic of exploitation and domination at work there. To put it crudely, signifier and signified correspond to exchange value and use value. Within the free circulation of a commodity system, however, the signifier is always exchanged as a sign, offering itself as *full* value, in the absence of a signified." Ross, "The New Sentence and the Commodity Form," p. 368, Ross's emphasis.

89. Wolfgang Fritz Haug, *The Critique of Commodity Aesthetics: Appearance, Sexuality, and Advertising in Capitalist Society*, trans. Robert Bock (Cambridge: Polity, 1986), p. 7.

90. Frederic Jameson, "Reification and Utopia in Mass Culture," *Social Text* 1, no. 1 (winter 1979), p. 131.

91. Marketers could count on a gap in this desire to belong to a modern collective, because consumption was now private and individualized instead of taking place in a community marketplace. The private home became its locus. Consumption promised that the buyer could be included in modernity by purchasing goods, but modernity was itself "composed of atomised individuals." Susan Buck-Morss describes Walter Benjamin's work on the dream state of mass culture in her reading of his unfinished arcades project. She argues that Benjamin saw mass culture as a "dreaming collective," unconscious of itself as a collective, and instead "composed of atomised individuals . . . who experienced their membership in the collectivity only in an isolated, alienating sense, as an anonymous component in the crowd." This concept of the atomised alienated consumer reconfigured ideas about mass culture at the point of reception. Susan Buck-Morss, "Dream World of Mass Culture," in *The Dialectics of Seeing: Walter Benjamin and the Arcades Project* (Cambridge, Mass.: MIT Press, 1993), pp. 260–61.

92. Langman, "Neon Cages," p. 47.

93. Felski, *Gender of Modernity*, p. 99.

94. Roland Marchand, *Advertising the American Dream: Making Way for Modernity, 1920–1940* (Berkeley: University of California Press, 1985), pp. 9–11.

95. Anne Stephen, "Agents of Consumerism: The Organisation of the Australian Advertising Industry, 1918–1938," in *Media Interventions*, ed. Judith Allen (Leichhart, N.S.W.: Intervention, 1981), p. 93.

96. Guy Debord, *The Society of the Spectacle* (New York: Zone, 1995), p. 24, Debord's emphasis. Debord believes the modern spectacle was contrary to the individual and to dialogue. It was "a negation of life that has invented a visual form for itself." Ultimately, in its reduction of dominant modes of production to signs, and class relations to appearances, the spectacle is contrary to, or "freezes," the Marxian historical dialectic itself. Debord's spectacle is thus "the locus of illusion and false consciousness." Debord, *Society of the Spectacle*, pp. 12, 14, 121.

97. Meagan Morris, "Things to Do with Shopping Centres," in *The Cultural Studies Reader*, ed. Simon During (London: Routledge, 1993), p. 306.

98. John Fiske writes about the creative, productive, and sometimes subversive potential within the constraints of the commodity fetish. "The commodity fetish is deeply conflicted; it bears the forces of both the power bloc and the people. It produces and reproduces the economic system, yet simultaneously can serve the symbolic interests of those subordinated by it." I would add that the symbolic interests of modern women were implicated in the processes of the commodity fetish as they gained access to the pleasures of modernity. John Fiske, "The Culture of Everyday Life," in *Cultural Studies*, ed. Lawrence Grossberg, Cary Nelson, and Paula Treichler (New York: Routledge, 1992), p. 157.

5. THE BEAUTY CONTESTANT IN
THE PHOTOGRAPHIC SCENE

My thanks to Professor Marilyn Lake for allowing research that I conducted on beauty contestants as part of her ARC Large Grant on "Women and Nation" to form the basis for this chapter.

1. "Can You Beat It?" *Sun News-Pictorial*, 27 September 1922, p. 16. According to the *Sun*, the ideal woman stood five feet five inches tall and weighed ten stone, or 140 pounds. "The Perfect Woman," *Sun News-Pictorial*, 14 September 1922, p. 13. A Miss Leiderman brought suit against the New York winner of a similar competition; Leiderman claimed that she was the "Venus of America." *Sun News-Pictorial*, 6 January 1923, p. 24, and 9 February 1923, p. 1. Dorothy Woolley advertised her figure-culture and weight-loss system in women's magazines with the same image of herself as appeared in the *Sun* and the claim that she was "Australia's Most Beautiful Model." "How to Reduce Your Weight," *Home Budget*, 1 January 1925, p. 34.

2. They were Metta Creighton (*Sun News-Pictorial*, 5 October 1922, p. 8), Eileen Shannon ("St Kilda Mermaid," ibid., 11 October 1922, p. 8), Myrtle Pallotta ("Can You Beat It?" ibid., 14 October 1922, p. 20), Dorothy Maxwell ("Another Venus," ibid., 20 October 1922, p. 10), and Mrs. V. P. McDonald ("Another Venus," ibid., 21 October 1922, p. 10).

3. The advertisement answers itself, saying that she is the girl who knows how to "keep that schoolgirl complexion." *Australian Home Journal*, 2 November 1925, p. 2.

4. "State's Most Beautiful Woman to Receive £100," *Evening News*, 1 April 1922, p. 1.

5. "Sydney's Beauty, Miss Eve Gray, Acclaimed. Can a Victorian Girl Be Found to Match Her?" *Herald*, 29 May 1922, p. 9. Eve Gray was the stage name of Evalene Garrett, a member of the J. C. Williamson theater company. In 1924 she left Australia for the London stage. See *Beckett's Weekly*, 6 January 1928, p. 27.

6. See Colleen Ballerino Cohen, Richard Wilk, and Beverly Stoeltje, eds., *Beauty Queens on the Global Stage: Gender, Contests, and Power* (New York: Routledge, 1997); and Sarah Banet-Weiser, *The Most Beautiful Girl in the World: Beauty Pageants and National Identity* (Berkeley: University of California Press, 1999).

7. Judith Smart, "Feminists, Flappers, and Miss Australia: Contesting the Meanings of Citizenship, Femininity, and Nation in the 1920s," *Journal of Australian Studies*, no. 71 (2001), p. 8.

8. See "The Hand of Time Deals Gently with Winners of Past Beauty Competition," *Sun News-Pictorial*, 3 October 1922, p. 22. The *Lone Hand* was antagonistic to American mass culture. When it closed in 1921, it wrote its own obituary, decrying the fact that public preference had "slaughtered [the paper] on the altar of Charlie Chaplinism." Its quest for the Australian beauty was probably spurred by national sentiment. "Obituary: The Passing of the *Lone Hand*," *Lone Hand*, 1 February 1921, p. 7.

9. The entries from "Westralia," Tasmania, and South Australia were forwarded to the "boards" of the other states, since those areas did not have enough entries to warrant the formation of their own state boards. Competitions also took place in "Maoriland," i.e., New Zealand.

10. "The World's Beauty: A Challenge," *Lone Hand,* 1 November 1907, pp. 12–15.

11. "Ladies Fair: Cult of Beauty: World of a Thousand Types," *Sun News-Pictorial,* 20 October 1922, p. 18.

12. "Best Figure Contest Opens at Hoyt's Sydney to Capacity," *Everyone's—Incorporating Australian Variety and Show World,* 1 October 1922, p. 99.

13. Eve Gray, the Sydney *Evening News*'s winner, was also adjudged to possess "a film face" by those "at the head of the cinematographic industry." She was filmed for a series to be exhibited in Australian cinemas and "registered perfectly" because she was "unaffected." "Miss Eve Gray's Future and the Film: *News* Winner on Pictures," *Evening News,* 17 June 1922, p. 1. Winners were also offered places in theater companies, although many of the entrants already had stage careers. "Stage Career: Openings for Winners," *Herald,* 8 August 1922, p. 5. The "final 30" of the Herald competition were filmed by Bert Cross. "Shooting the 'stars' of the *Herald* Quest," *Herald,* 5 August 1922, p. 1.

14. She was touted as a "great intellect," which made her short lecture "of enthralling interest from an intellectual point of view," but a commentator also noted that her presentation "should interest the feminine section of the audience, in view of the number of frocks exhibited by Miss Mills." " 'Miss Australia' for Lecture Tour," *Everyone's,* 10 November 1926, p. 24; "Miss Australia on the South Coast," *Everyone's,* 12 January 1927, p. 36.

15. "Glorifying the Australian Girl," *Everyone's,* 17 November 1926, p. 20.

16. "Ten Minute Séance," *Sun News-Pictorial,* 18 November 1922, p. 21.

17. Audrey Fieldhouse, a winner in a British newspaper competition, eventually married one of the many men who wrote to ask for her hand. "A Beauty Prize: Romantic End to Competition: Winner's Marriage Offers: To Wed Knight's Son," *Evening News,* 7 April 1922, p. 1; "Love and the Beauty Competition," *Illustrated Tasmanian Mail,* 24 August 1922, p. 60.

18. "Photograph Wins Husband: Sequel to Beauty Contest," *Herald,* 15 June 1922, p. 1.

19. Annette Kellerman, *Physical Beauty—How to Keep It: Annette Kellerman Illustrated* (New York: George H. Doras, 1918) pp. 14, 12.

20. Alice Jackson, "The First Beauty Competition," *Triad,* March 1927, p. 6.

21. "Man," letter to the editor, *Argus,* 8 December 1926, p. 26.

22. Kathryn Shevelow, *Women and Print Culture: The Construction of Femininity in the Early Periodical* (London: Routledge, 1989), pp. 43, 46, 50. Women's literacy increased in Europe and North America. In 1970 40 percent of women worldwide were illiterate: 83 percent in Africa, 57 percent in Asia, and 85 percent in Arab states. See Luisa Passerini, "The Ambivalent Image of Woman in Mass Culture," in *Toward a Cultural Identity in the Twentieth Century,* ed. Françoise Thébaud, vol. 5 of *A History of Women in the West,* ed. Georges Duby and Michelle Perrot (Cambridge, Mass.: Belknap Press of Harvard University Press, 1994), p. 331.

23. Rosetta Brookes, "Fashion Photography: The Double-Page Spread: Helmut Newton, Guy Bourdin, and Deborah Turbeville," in *Chic Thrills: A Fashion Reader,* ed. Juliet Ash and Elizabeth Wilson (London: Virago, 1991), p. 18.

24. See Mary Ellen Roach and Joanne Eicher, *The Visible Self: Perspectives on Dress* (Englewood Cliffs, N.J.: Prentice Hall, 1973), pp. 11–12.

25. *Australian Home Journal,* 1 August 1919, p. 1.

26. Ann Stephen, "Agents of Consumerism: The Organisation of the Australian Advertising Industry, 1918–1938," in *Media Interventions,* ed. Judith Allen (Leichhardt, N.S.W.: Intervention, 1981), p. 80.

27. Heather Radi, "1920–29," in *A New History of Australia,* ed. F. K. Crowley (Melbourne: William Heinemann, 1974), p. 390.

28. Smart, "Feminists, Flappers, and Miss Australia," p. 11.

29. "This Is the Life," *Sun News-Pictorial,* 23 February 1923, p. 4; "Perfection," ibid., 8 January 1923, p. 24; "Eyes of Youth," ibid., 10 January 1923, p. 11; "Italian Beauty," ibid., 20 February 1923, p. 19; "Parisian Beauties," ibid., 20 October 1922, p. 1; "Blonde with Brown Eyes," ibid., 20 September 1922, p. 20; "Lilies of France," ibid., 19 September 1922, p. 8; "Most Beautiful Woman," ibid., 20 December 1922, back page; "France's Six by Popular Vote," *Herald,* 11 August 1922, p. 1.

30. "Medium Weight Wins," *Sun News-Pictorial,* 23 December 1922, p. 22, "Eyebrows De Luxe," ibid., 26 October 1922, p. 19; "Parisian Beauties," ibid., 15 September 1922, p. 8.

31. C. M. Deegan, "How I Picked the Winners," *Illustrated Tasmanian Mail,* 2 November 1922, p. 12.

32. Ibid.

33. "Beauty on Trial. Story of Ayes and Noes. Judgement Reserved," *Herald,* 11 July 1922, p. 6.

34. A correspondent who called himself "Satisfied" was particularly pleased with Betty Tyrrell's win, because it proved that taste had not degenerated through the modern "life of frivolity and the admiration for the frivolous attractions which are temporary." "Is the Madonna Type Beauty's Highest Form?" letter to the editor, *Herald,* 14 August 1922, p. 8.

35. "As Others See Her," *Herald,* 26 July 1922, p. 9.

36. "Beauty on a Percentage Basis," letter to the editor, *Herald,* 24 July 1922, p. 8.

37. "Beauty Winners," *Evening News,* 15 May 1922, p. 4.

38. "Galaxy of Beauty," *Evening News,* 22 April 1922, p. 1.

39. "The Lily of Red Cliffs—Miss Lillias M. Whitney," *Sunraysia Daily,* 5 March 1923, p. 1.

40. "Sweet Seriousness—Miss Dora Nind," *Sunraysia Daily,* 12 March 1923, p. 1.

41. "Beauty—and the Beast," *Herald,* 11 July 1922, p. 4.

42. "Beauty's Jury: Searching for an Ideal," *Herald,* 28 June 1922, p. 8.

43. Judith Smart, "Feminists, Flappers, and Miss Australia," p. 10.

44. Susan Sontag, *On Photography* (Harmondsworth: Penguin, 1973), pp. 165, 164.

45. The process of sitting was written of as a novelty and curiosity by one Sydney reporter in 1846 who described "the blue glass case in which unfortunate sitters were enclosed while the process of decapitation was going on, and the consequent cadaverous, unearthly appearance which their features assumed after being subjected to this disagreeable operation." George Baron Goodman's 1842 studio closed the following year when he traveled to Hobart. In 1848 a daguerreotype studio was opened by J. W. Newland. Falk Studio followed in 1896 and Talma Studio in 1899, producing many of the photographs submitted to the newspaper beauty competitions. *Sydney Morning*

Herald, 4 May 1846, quoted in Alan Davies and Peter Stanbury, *The Mechanical Eye in Australia: Photography, 1841–1900* (Melbourne: Oxford University Press, 1985), pp. 8, 10, 102.

46. Sontag, *On Photography,* pp. 164, 59.

47. "Beauty on Trial. Story of Ayes and Noes. Judgement Reserved."

48. "Who is Eligible: Questions concerning the Beauty Contest," *Sunraysia Daily,* 7 February 1923, p. 2.

49. "Who is Eligible: Most Questions concerning the Contest," *Sunraysia Daily,* 2 March 1923, p. 6.

50. "Beauty and the Beast," *Herald,* 31 May 1922, p. 8.

51. "Who is Eligible: Most Questions concerning the Contest." Evelyn Lewis won the popularity vote and Ivy Baker won the beauty vote. "The Beauty Judge: 'Steele Blayde' Has No Desire to Officiate," *Sunraysia Daily,* 27 February 1923, p. 2. Some 823,832 votes were cast in the combined "categories," the winning beauty chosen by an artist who gave "points for qualities and minus points for defects."

52. "Pretty and Popular: She Needs to Be Both to Be Well in Front," *Sunraysia Daily,* 17 February 1923, p. 2.

53. "A Charming Example: Pioneer in Beauty Competition," *Herald,* 2 June 1922, p. 9.

54. "The Beauty Quest: Making the State Awards," *Lone Hand,* 1 October 1908, p. 629.

55. "The Beauty Quest: Final Decision," *Lone Hand,* 1 February 1909, p. 410.

56. "The World's Beauty Challenge," *Lone Hand,* 3 December 1907, p. 145.

57. "The Beauty Quest: Further Entrants," *Lone Hand,* 1 June 1908, p. 135.

58. "Australia in Search of a Daughter," *Home,* 2 August 1926, pp. 20, 76, 78.

59. "The Soldier's and Sailor's Father's Association Fund," *Society,* 1 October 1926, p. 26.

60. See Jill Julius Matthews's work on the line-up and simultaneity of movement in women's physical culture and its links to Hollywood iconography and later associations with Nazi mass spectacle and youth culture. "They Had Such a Lot of Fun: The Women's League of Health and Beauty between the Wars," *History Workshop Journal,* no. 30 (autumn 1990), pp. 22–54.

61. "What Constitutes Charm: Photographic Failures," *Illustrated Tasmanian Mail,* 21 September 1922, p. 57.

62. Marilyn Lake finds that during World War II, women increasingly judged themselves in the frames of advertisements, and mirrors figured prominently in such advertisements. See her "Female Desires: The Meaning of World War II," *Australian Historical Studies* 24, no. 95 (October 1990), pp. 267–83.

63. "The Elizabeth Arden Method Clears, Firms, and Softens Your Skin," *Home,* 1 November 1926, p. 39.

64. Melisande, "Our Complexions," *Herself, in Town and Country,* 5 November 1930, p. 19.

65. "Beauty's Time Table," advertisement for Ven-Yusa the Oxygen Face Cream, *Australian Woman's Mirror,* 10 November 1925, p. 57.

66. "Your Face Is Your Fortune: Therefore Look after It," *Australian Woman's Mirror,* 8 September 1925, p. 33.

67. Janine Jouet, "Managing Your Mouth," *Australian Woman's Mirror*, 15 March 1927, p. 30.

68. "Do You Have Lovely Lips?" *Helen's Weekly*, 15 September 1927, p. 38.

69. Teresa de Lauretis, *Technologies of Gender: Essays on Theory, Film, and Fiction* (Bloomington: Indiana University Press, 1987), p. 18.

70. Michel Foucault, *The Care of the Self*, vol. 3 of *The History of Sexuality*, trans. Robert Hurley (New York: Vintage, 1988), p. 41.

71. "The Beauty Doctor," *Sun News-Pictorial*, 8 June 1923, p. 6.

72. "The Happy Woman," advertisement for the Australasian Scale Company, *Bulletin*, 7 February 1924, p. 3.

73. "Correct Lines," advertisement for Gossard Corsets, *Bulletin*, 30 December 1920, p. 23.

74. Jeanette, "Before the Mirror," *Bulletin*, 21 November 1918, cover sleeve.

75. "Face to Face—As If You Were Another Girl," advertisement for Palmolive Soap, *Bulletin*, 22 November 1923, p. 4.

76. Placing oneself before the anticipated gaze of another enabled a Lacanian identification of the self from the place of the other, "as an object." Commodity beauty culture pegged into specular relations points of the gaze that both reasserted and transcended the self as the origin of the look, that is, in the terms of film theory, it hammered into "the field of vision" multiple points of identification. In doing so it opened up a whole new canopy of specular relations with implications for how women might effect their status as spectators and spectacles, or subjects and objects. It spawned multiple vantages of the gaze and in consequence effected at each point a certain removal of the self and a fragmenting of the subject. In looking, in being looked at, and in looking at themselves being looked at, modern women had multiple views of the self. The feminine look was conflated into the feminine spectacle as seen from the same subject position. See Christian Metz, "Identification, Mirror," in *Psychoanalysis and Cinema: The Imaginary Signifier*, trans. Celia Britton, Anwyl Williams, Ben Brewster, and Alfred Guzzetti (London: Macmillan, 1982), p. 45.

77. "The Triumph of Little Miss Ordinary," advertisement for Cecille Hairdressing Salon, *Home*, 1 July 1927, p. 83.

78. "A Dialogue between a Young Woman and Her Reflection," advertisement for Lassetter's Vitona, *Australian Woman's Mirror*, 8 September 1925, p. 65.

79. "Face to Face—As If You Were Another Girl."

80. Advertisement for Senora Sabina, *Table Talk*, 11 December 1919, p. 27.

81. "Correct Figure," letter to the editor, *Sun News-Pictorial*, 11 October 1923, p. 7.

82. "Beauty as a New Investment," *Home*, 1 December 1926, p. 19.

83. "Her Dream Comes True," advertisement for Palmolive Soap, *Home*, 1 March 1923, p. 1.

84. "Girl of 19 Accused of Bad Complexion," advertisement for Kruschen Salts, *Helen's Weekly*, 24 November 1927, p. 43.

85. "Modern Woman Must Be Beautiful," *Helen's Weekly*, 6 October 1927, p. 13.

86. Kathy Peiss, "Making Faces: The Cosmetic Industry and the Cultural Construction of Gender," *Genders*, no. 7 (March 1990), p. 157.

87. Arguably, the exposure of legs after centuries of long skirts shifted attention from the top half of the feminine body (emphasized in the era of the corset), to the bottom half (emphasized in the era of the girdle). Stage and screen stars of the 1920s have notably shorter legs than contemporary feminine ideals.

88. "In Spite of Exposure . . . or Because of It . . . ," advertisement for Hinds Cream, *Australian Woman's Mirror*, 27 January 1930, p. 91.

89. "Annette Kellerman," *Everyone's*, 16 February 1921, p. 13.

90. In July 1924 *Everyones* reported that Kellerman had retired to run a women's physical culture club on the U.S. Pacific Coast. *Everyones*, 16 July 1924, p. 25. However, she also starred in Beaumont Smith's 1924 film *Venus of the South Seas*. *Everyones*, 20 August 1924, p. 29.

91. Lois W. Banner, *American Beauty* (New York: Alfred A. Knopf, 1983), p. 267.

92. Kellerman, *Physical Beauty*, p. 29.

93. These measurements were discussed by sculptor Web Gilbert, selected as a judge in the *Herald* competition because of his "remarkable knowledge of anatomy." "Beauty's Sponsors: Judges Chosen for *Herald* Competition," *Herald*, 7 June 1922, p. 7.

94. Kellerman, *Physical Beauty*, pp. 48–49.

95. "This Beauty Business: Which Also Means This Health Business," *Adam and Eve*, 1 March 1929, p. 20.

96. Kellerman, *Physical Beauty*, pp. 21, 23, 25, 165, 166.

97. "A Natural Diet and Proper Exercise," *Adam and Eve*, 1 March 1929, p. 21.

98. The popular belief that the Modern Woman discarded the corset is disproved by a 1925 report that in the two previous years more corsets were imported into Australia than during any other period. In addition, Australia gained a reputation as a corset manufacturer, exporting £700,000 worth in 1924–25. "Credula," letter to the editor, *Australian Woman's Mirror*, 25 November 1924, p. 15. Corsets were even manufactured for girls and pregnant women. Foy and Gibson catalogue, no. 54 (1918), University of Melbourne Archives.

99. Advertisement for Gossard Corsets, *Bulletin*, December 2, 1920, p. 10.

100. This advertisement introduced the brassiere, which evolved from the bust bodice. It argued that "to attain the desired degree of slackness demanded by the fashion for an apparently uncorseted figure, one must be corseted and brassiered better than even before." *Home*, winter, 1 June 1920, p. 62.

101. "The Average Woman: How Beautiful She Is," advertisement for Berlei, *Home*, 1 March 1926, p. 86.

102. "Why Women in War Time Insist upon Gossard Corsets," advertisement, *Bulletin*, 25 November 1918, p. 33.

103. "The Corset of 1910 Aided the Critics of Corsets," advertisement for Nautilus Corsets, *Table Talk*, 24 April 1919, p. 31.

104. "The Corset of 29 Years Ago," advertisement for Nautilus Corsets, *Table Talk*, 13 March 1919, p. 31.

105. "That Elusive Charm We Call Style," advertisement for Gossard Corsets, *Bulletin*, 8 January 1920, p. 43.

106. Advertisement for Berlei, *Australian Woman's Mirror*, 14 May 1929, p. 39. See the account of Ivy Weber's work for Berlei during this period in

Geoff Brown, "Eleanor Glencross and Ivy Weber: In and out of Parliament," in *Double Time: Women in Victoria, 150 Years,* ed. Marilyn Lake and Farley Kelly (Ringwood, Vic.: Penguin, 1985), pp. 344–52.

107. "Corsets Specially Designed for YOU," advertisement for Gossard Corsets, *Home,* 1 September 1923, p. 69.

108. Cedric Flower, *Clothes in Australia: A Pictorial History, 1788–1980s* (Kenthurst, N.S.W.: Kangaroo, 1984), p. 157.

109. *Australian Home Journal,* 1 December 1919, p. 1; *Australian Home Journal,* 2 March 1925, p. 28; Foy and Gibson winter catalogue, no. 80 (Perth, 1931), p. 37, University of Melbourne Archives.

110. "Line," *Home,* 1 April 1925, p. 62.

111. Banner, *American Beauty,* p. 10.

112. Robert MacDonald, "The New Feminine Beauty: In Which We Examine the Meaning of the Modern Moulds of Form," *Home,* 1 May 1929, pp. 27–29.

113. Banner, *American Beauty,* p. 16.

114. Blanche Singleton, "War Paint: A Dissertation on Feminine Foibles," *Society,* 1 June 1925, p. 35.

115. Janine Jouet, "The New Silhouette," *Australian Woman's Mirror,* 11 February 1930, p. 28.

116. "It Was Madame That Was Wrong," *Bulletin,* 1 December 1927, p. 35.

117. Valerie Steele, *Fashion and Eroticism: Ideals of Feminine Beauty from the Victorian Era to the Jazz Age* (New York: Oxford University Press, 1985), p. 80. The development of mass-produced clothing was spurred by the invention of the sewing machine in 1851 and paper dressmaking patterns in the 1870s.

118. Elizabeth Wilson, *Adorned in Dreams: Fashion and Modernity* (London: Virago, 1985), p. 2.

119. "Beauty, Colour, and Form: How It Originates," *Herald,* 23 June 1923, p. 6. On Hall, see Leonard B. Cox, *The National Gallery of Victoria, 1861–1968: A Search for a Collection* (Melbourne: National Gallery of Victoria, 1970), pp. 43–61.

120. "Venus Vanquished: Dethroned by the Dressmakers," *Truth,* 31 July 1920, p. 5.

121. Mary C. Mallon, "Is Beauty Worth the Trouble?" *Aussie,* 14 May 1921, p. 46.

122. "The Thin Girl and The Fat Girl: Treatments for Both," *Australian Home Budget,* 1 February 1917, p. 42.

123. "Why Do Women Need Medicine More than Men?" advertisement for Beecham Pills, *Bulletin,* 14 January 1926, p. 49.

124. It also managed to leave the skin "lily-white." Advertisement for Leichner 1001, *Bulletin,* 31 July 1929, p. 41, and 30 January 1929, p. 41.

125. "The New Vacuum System for the Development of the Bust, Neck, Arms, Shoulders," advertisement, *Australian Home Journal,* 1 March 1917, p. 12; "The Eugene Corrective Eating Society," *Humour,* 12 December 1924, p. 64.

126. Sargol Herztrol Formula claimed to "produce flesh and strength" and referred to itself as among "flesh maker" products. "At the theatre, in the ballroom, or at any social gathering—well developed men and women are always admired. The beauty of their well-rounded, splendidly healthful figures is irresistibly attractive." Advertisement, *Truth,* 22 May 1920, p. 2.

127. An endorsement from a user declared, "it has made a new woman of me." Advertisement for Ti-Sarkin, *Australian Home Budget*, 1 January 1917, p. 12.

128. Rita Felski, *The Gender of Modernity* (Cambridge, Mass.: Harvard University Press, 1995), p. 110.

129. "Vain Women: The Self-Flatterer and Her Fate," *Sunraysia Daily*, 17 March 1923, p. 6.

130. "The Quest for Beauty: All in the Good Cause of Sweet Charity," *Sunraysia Daily*, 1 March 1923, p. 2. Thirty finalists for the *Herald* competition were exhibited to raise money for the Women's Hospital Appeal. Eight thousand visitors arrived in one lunch hour, and £200 was raised during one day. "Beauty Trial Ending," *Herald*, 11 August 1922, p. 9.

131. "A Pretty Girl's Rights: The Woman Passion for Lovely Clothes," *Sunraysia Daily*, 28 April 1923, p. 6.

132. Churches particularly objected to commercialism and "sensational journalism." "Methodist Church Protest," *Argus*, 4 November 1926, p. 12. Ashby Studios staged a "Movie Type" competition and would consider only photos that it had taken. Advertisements, *Ladies Designer*, 1 June 1923, p. 10, and 1 May 1923, p. 22; *Stage and Society*, 9 August 1923, p. 45. The Sidney Riley studio advertised that it could guarantee entrants "a portrait that will embody their charms to perfection, with that unexpected touch of distinction revealed that is given by a master hand in technique." By now, sitting for a photographic portrait had become a "pleasant" interlude. "*Evening News* Beauty Competition: Your Best Chance of Success," advertisement, *Evening News*, 8 April 1922, p. 7. By purchasing a five-shilling string of Astor pearls, women gained the right to submit their photographs to Sam Lands's "Palace of Gems" Prettiest Australian Girl Competition. Advertisement, *Beckett's Budget*, 16 August 1929, p. 7.

133. "Beauty as a Business," *Truth*, 12 August 1922, p. 4.

134. "Girls Juggled in Beauty Bungle," *Truth*, 9 July 1927, p. 1.

135. Reading between the lines, Barclay seems to have suffered a botched abortion or contracted venereal disease. "[S]he was left with a grievous handicap which had occurred in the first rosy years of it all, when she had been a girl unlearned in the ways of the world." "Her Best Pal's Story of Beauty's Fall," *Truth*, 26 April 1930, p. 7.

136. The National Council of Women called a meeting that was attended by three to four hundred representatives of the National Council of Women, the Australian Women's National League, the Mother's Union, the Australian Woman's Association, and the Woman's Christian Temperance Union.

137. "Beauty Competitions: Protest by Women," *Argus*, 7 December 1926, p. 18.

138. "Beauty Competitions: Meeting of Protest Arranged," *Argus*, 30 November 1926, p. 11. In the first modern beauty competition in America, in 1854, the indistinctness of the daguerreotypes submitted had in part overcome the scandal of women's appearing in person to be judged. This competition was conceived by Phineas T. Barnum, the circus operator. Banner, *American Beauty*, p. 248.

139. "Beauty Competitions: Protest by Women."

140. "Beauty Competitions: Described as Degrading," *Argus*, 9 December 1926, p. 12.

141. In 1971 Kate Millet wrote that "one might also recognize subsidiary

status categories among women; not only in virtue of class, but beauty and age as well." "Second-wave" feminism recognized the materiality of representation in beauty culture and its ideological effects. But it did not recognize women's participation in beauty culture as anything other than illustrative of their oppression. Kate Millett, *Sexual Politics* (New York: Virago, 1971), p. 38.

142. The protests faded after the 1927 Miss Australia competition and did not re-emerge until the 1970s. Smart, "Feminists, Flappers, and Miss Australia," pp. 12, 14.

143. "Beauty Competitions: Opposed by the Council of Churches," *Argus*, 15 December 1926, p. 36. A Melbourne clergyman, Rev. A. R. Ebbs, was outraged by a competition in a Melbourne suburb for the "most shapely" woman's leg. "Best Leg Contest," *Sun News-Pictorial*, 22 September 1922, p. 7.

144. "Questions in Parliament: 'Competitive Stunts' Criticised," *Argus*, 4 November 1926, p. 12.

145. "The Competition Mania: Unhealthy Tendencies," *Argus*, 10 November 1926, p. 4.

146. Letter to the editor, *Sun News-Pictorial*, 16 November 1922, p. 5.

147. Many commentators felt that women's appearing publicly was inherently immoral. In 1896 the *Bulletin* reported that overseas actresses were not paying their bills to the Falk studios in Sydney. It wrote, "Photographer Falk is not impressed with the commercial morality of many visiting 'stars' who have brought their patronage to the studio. A long experience of professional sitters is embittered by many collections of unpaid bills and petty meanness. The stage and concert platform are not training grounds for high principle, as far as photo orders are concerned." *Bulletin*, 6 June 1856, quoted in Davies and Stanbury, *Mechanical Eye*, p. 102.

148. Tyrrell had been married two months when she won. "The *Herald* Beauty Winner at Home," *Herald*, 11 August 1922, p. 6. She appeared in local and New Zealand pantomime productions. "Young Bride's Triumph," *Herald*, 12 August 1922, p. 4. Significantly, the burden of demonstrating propriety lay far less on the producers of imagery than it did on the women who were photographed. Similarly, Miles Franklin wrote in 1901 a conservative aunt's response to her granddaughter's desire to go on the stage: "Go on the stage! A granddaughter of mine! Lucy's eldest child! An actress—a vile, low, brazen huzzy! Use the gifts God has given her with which to do good in showing off to a crowd of vile bad men! I would rather see her struck dead at my feet this instant! I would rather see her shear off her hair and enter the convent this very hour!" M. Miles Franklin, *My Brilliant Career*, quoted in Andree Wright, *Brilliant Careers: Women in Australian Cinema* (Sydney: Pan, 1986), p. 3. The publicly visible woman had become a fixture in a shorthand syntax for morality; she signified the abandonment of domesticity, the sanctified realm of moral certitude.

149. "Miss Eve Gray: A Youthful Philosopher," advertisement for Mercolised Wax, *Ladies' Sphere*, 15 August 1922, p. 26. The Beauty Contestant drew huge crowds in her public appearances. Eve Gray, Betty Tyrrell, and Beryl Mills all undertook lecture tours in which they were almost mobbed by huge crowds. Gray had to be carried through a crowd at one theater. "Eve Gray at Haymarket Theatre," *Evening News*, 19 June 1922, p. 5. "Mrs Tyrell, This Very Night at the Auditorium," *Herald*, 19 August 1922, p. 9.

150. "Miss Garrett (Miss Eve Gray) Tells Her Story," *Evening News*, 29 May 1922, p. 4.

151. "Young Bride's Triumph," *Herald*, 12 August 1922, p. 4.

152. Advertisement for Film Screenings, *Herald*, 3 June 1922, p. 5.

153. Jill Julius Matthews, "Building the Body Beautiful: The Femininity of Modernity," *Australian Feminist Studies*, no. 5 (summer 1987), p. 22.

154. "They were women of the Machine Age, for whom the machine meant employment, consumer goods, modernity, individuality, pleasure. For these women, the League held out the promise of making them better able to enjoy it all." Matthews, "Such a Lot of Fun," p. 47.

155. Matthews, "Building the Body Beautiful," pp. 22, 31–33.

156. Ibid., p. 25.

157. "Health and Beauty: Some Delusions Shattered," *Canberra Times*, 27 January 1927, p. 14.

158. "Beauty Aids," *Canberra Times*, 1 October 1926, p. 4.

159. Elizabeth Grosz, *Volatile Bodies: Toward a Corporeal Feminism* (St. Leonards, N.S.W.: Allen and Unwin, 1994), p. 39.

160. "Who Could Tell I Once Suffered from Superfluous Hair?" Advertisement for Mrs. Frederica Hudson's "information and instructions to banish superfluous hair," *Bulletin*, 13 March 1929, p. 54.

161. "Cosmetics Cannot Clear a Skin Clouded by Poisons: Look in Your Mirror!" advertisement for Eno's Fruit Salt, *Australian Woman's Mirror*, 29 April 1930, p. 7.

162. "To Bob or Not to Bob," *Delineator*, June 1920, p. 72.

163. Madame Alwyn, "Heath and Beauty," *Herself*, 17 September 1928, p. 11.

164. Advertisement for Palmolive, *Australian Home Journal*, 1 June 1927, p. 16.

165. Advertisement for Gossard Corsets, *Bulletin*, 2 February 1922, p. 27.

166. Advertisement for the Iris-Dorothy System of Form Development, *Australian Home Journal*, 1 February 1919, p. 2.

167. "Beauty Culture and Health," *Australian Home Journal*, 1 July 1920, p. 41.

168. Leila W. Kinney, "Fashion and Figuration in Modern Life Painting," in *Architecture in Fashion*, ed. Deborah Fausch, Paulette Singley, Rodolphe El-Khoury, and Zvi Efrat (Princeton, N.J.: Princeton University Press, 1994), p. 299.

169. Gwen Slevers, "The Ideals of the Greek Dance and Their Application to Modern Life," *Helen's Weekly*, 27 October 1927, pp. 14–15; Irene Mulvany Gray, "Health Is the Truest Liberty," *Helen's Weekly*, 15 September 1927, pp. 14–15.

170. Madame Alwyn, "Heath and Beauty."

171. The "Electrocution" (electrification) of housework merged the domestic feminine with technology, *Aussie* reporting in 1921 that there were thirty-three different home appliances burying "the bugbear of heavy work." "The Electrocution of Housework," *Aussie*, 15 August 1921, p. 37. It seems mechanized aids for women's work had wider applications. The same article captions an image of a woman at her dressing table, flanked by an electric fan and radiator, with "You switch off the radiator and insert in the socket your vibrator."

172. All these businesses dealt in feminine visibility and sold products which promised to fortify and legitimate the experience of beauty. The same is true of their latter-day counterparts, such as lingerie manufacturer and supermodel Elle MacPherson and cosmetics manufacturer Poppy King.

173. A Kit Kat Powder advertisement features the portrait of a young society matron and reads, "Among Melbourne's lovely young people, Mrs Sydney Dalrymple stands out like some delicate etching in the midst of aquatints." Mrs. Dalrymple uses Kit Kat powder, "the Aristocrat of powders." *Home,* 1 March 1930, p. 14.

174. "Hand of Time Deals Gently with Winners of Past Beauty Competition."

175. See "Would South Melbourne Stand This?" *Sun News-Pictorial,* 12 April 1923, p. 11, for a rather risqué bathing beauty. See also "The O'Brien Girls Go to the Seaside," *Sun News-Pictorial,* 29 January 1923, p. 20.

176. "Do You Know These Girls? They Were Snapped on Sydney Beaches by Beckett's Camera Man," *Beckett's Budget,* 6 January 1928, p. 30.

177. "Beach Callisthenics," *Sun News-Pictorial,* 13 September 1922, p. 1.

178. "Beauty Quest: Heavy Primary Voting. Keen Contest," *Sun News-Pictorial,* 6 October 1923, p. 5. National comparisons continued. A similar London competition drew only fifty-five thousand votes. Also, the Australian Business Girl was perceived by London Business Girls as dressing better, but wearing too many colors and too much make-up and jewelry. "She Paints: She Doesn't Walk Well: Her Legs Are Poems," *Sun News-Pictorial,* 29 March 1923, p. 3.

179. "The Beauty Quest," *Herald,* 4 August 1922, p. 13.

180. "Beauty Trial Ending," *Herald,* 11 August 1922, p. 9.

181. "The Perfect Woman: Is She Extinct?" *Sun News-Pictorial,* 17 October 1922, p. 18.

182. Ethel Castilla, "An Australian Girl," *Society,* 1 March 1928, p. 3.

183. Commentator Dulcie Deamer believed that the shortening of skirts showed Australians were becoming an athletic, "Hellenic" race. "Every beach swarms with splendid young people, as healthily and un-self consciously next-door to nakedness as the youth of the land that built the Parthenon and fostered Plato." *Aussie,* 15 July 1927, p. 47.

184. "Australia in Search of a Daughter," pp. 20, 76, 78.

185. "The Perfect Woman: Is She Extinct?"

186. "The Beauty Quest: Making the State Awards," pp. 631–32.

187. "The Beauty Quest: Final Decision," p. 412.

188. "The Beauty Quest: Making the State Awards," p. 634.

189. "The World's Beauty: A Challenge," *Lone Hand,* 1 November 1907, p. 15.

190. "Beauty's Judges: Women Prefer Men as Critics," *Herald,* 3 August 1922, p. 5.

191. "The Beautiful Woman Is the Parent of Art," editorial, *Herald,* 12 August 1922, p. 6.

192. Ibid.

193. "Land of Beauty," *Evening News,* 1 April 1922, p. 4.

194. "Deals in Beauty: *Herald* Pictures Discussed," *Herald,* 21 July 1922, p. 13.

195. "Beauty's Hallmarks Not Yet Nationalised," *Herald,* 22 July 1922, p. 11.

196. L. Bernard Hall, "Beauty. Colour and Form. How It Originates," *Herald,* 23 June 1922, p. 6.

197. "Beauty's Hallmarks."

198. "Beauty. Nature's Picture Gallery. A Secular Sermon," *Herald,* 27 July 1922, p. 6.

199. "Adjudged by Artists the Most Beautiful Woman in NSW: *News Beauty Search Proves Successful: Miss Evalene Garrett wins £100 Prize," Evening News*, 29 May 1922, p. 4.

200. "Pretty Girls: The Judges Work: The Stamp of Authority," *Evening News*, 29 May 1922, p. 4.

201. "Beauty Winners," *Evening News*, 15 May 1922, p. 4.

202. "Beauties of Northern Victoria," *Sun News-Pictorial*, 25 April 1923, p. 11.

203. "The Beauty Boom: What Sunrays Will Gain by It," *Sunraysia Daily*, 3 February 1923, p. 2.

204. "Pan-American Most Beautiful Girls. An Incentive for Victoria," *Herald*, 6 June 1922, p. 8.

205. "£100 for Most Beautiful Woman. The *Herald* Offers Prize. Can Victoria Eclipse NSW?" *Herald*, 30 May 1922, p. 9.

206. "Rival Beauties. Keen Contest for £100," *Herald*, 1 June 1922, p. 7.

207. "Beauty Competition," *Illustrated Tasmanian Mail*, 6 July 1922, p. 51.

208. Modernity's colonial diaspora can be seen in the pride taken in Randwick in the winner of an Indian beauty competition, H.R.H. the Maharance of Takani, also known as Elsie Forrest from Randwick, N.S.W. "Australian Girl Triumphs," *Sun News-Pictorial*, 24 January 1923, p. 1. The *Herald* claimed that its competition had "quickened" Australians' critical sense of the beautiful. "The Beautiful Woman Is the Parent of Art."

209. "Beauty. Nature's Picture Gallery. A Secular Sermon."

210. "A Turkish Beauty," *Sun News-Pictorial*, 11 January 1923, p. 18.

211. "The Beautiful Woman Is the Parent of Art."

212. Henry Fletcher, "The Society Problem," *Society*, 1 February 1925, p. 23.

213. "The Peril to the White Cradle," *Truth*, 21 June 1924, p. 1. This article reported on the 1923 immigration figures, which indicated that white Australia had been invaded by 5,568 different races. Their low average intelligence—which happened to parallel the increasing darkness of their skin—meant that "migration is filling the States with morons."

214. "The Color Question," *Truth*, 31 January 1925, p. 1.

215. Elizabeth Grosz writes of Lacan's suggestion that the "desire for a solid, stable identity may help explain our fascination with images of the human form." See her *Volatile Bodies*, p. 43.

216. Steele, *Fashion and Eroticism*, pp. 5, 10.

6. THE "PRIMITIVE" WOMAN IN THE LATE COLONIAL SCENE

This chapter deals with images that are debasing to Aboriginal peoples. My standpoint is non-Indigenous, and I acknowledge the difference between encountering such images as a white Australian and being described and situated within them as an Indigenous Australian. The images discussed here appeared across the range of print culture in the 1920s. They contributed to white women's privilege and to the subordination of Indigenous women. I wish to acknowledge those social realities, and I hope that bringing such images into the present does not add to the suffering of any Indigenous peoples, but rather helps us to remember our colonial history as part of the process of restitution and reconciliation.

I began to draft this chapter on 8 July 1998, the day the Australian senate passed the Liberal government's Native Title Amendment Act, which abolished Indigenous Australians' native title rights over pastoral leases (which cover some 42 percent of the Australian land mass). In June 1993 the Wik people had claimed native title over an area in the Cape York Peninsula, Queensland. However, the federal court ruled that native title was extinguished by pastoral leases. The plaintiffs appealed to the High Court, which overturned the ruling on 23 December 1996, holding that native title rights coexisted with pastoral leases (though they were subordinate to the rights of pastoral lease holders where there was conflict). In response, the Liberal government amended the Native Title Act (1993) with a "ten-point plan" which permanently extinguished native title rights on pastoral leases, altered claimants' right to negotiate proceedings, and made it significantly more difficult to register applications for native title. It was thus with a deepening sense of sadness and foreboding that I engaged with the following colonial representations of Aboriginal women.

1. *Australian Woman's Mirror*, 19 October 1926, p. 37.

2. See Patricia Grimshaw, Marilyn Lake, Ann McGrath, and Marion Quartly, eds., *Creating a Nation, 1788–1990* (Ringwood, Vic.: McPhee Gribble, 1994), p. 280.

3. Throughout this chapter I use "primitivism" to describe the prevalent construction of Aboriginal and Islander women as premodern in 1920s popular culture. I do not intend it to describe their actual condition or status.

4. "Another Abo. Help," *Australian Woman's Mirror*, 5 January 1926, p. 42.

5. The Australian constitution refused to include Aboriginal people in the national census. They were thus not counted as part of the national population, and did not have many of the rights of citizenship until the 1960s.

6. Marcia Langton, *"Well, I Heard It On The Radio And I Saw It On The Television": An Essay for the Australian Film Commission on the Politics and Aesthetics of Filmmaking by and about Aboriginal People and Things* (North Sydney: Australian Film Commission, 1993), p. 29.

7. Ibid., p. 28.

8. Ibid., p. 31.

9. Ibid., p. 81.

10. Marianna Torgovnick, *Gone Primitive: Savage Intellects, Modern Lives* (Chicago: University of Chicago Press, 1990), pp. 153, 9, 157.

11. "Another Abo. Maid," *Australian Woman's Mirror*, 5 January 1926, p. 56.

12. Quoted in Ina Bertrand, *Cinema in Australia: A Documentary History* (Kensington: University of New South Wales Press, 1989), p. 119. The commission's recommendations never became law.

13. "Film Commission's Report," *Everyones*, 25 April 1928, p. 6.

14. "Black Brother and the Flicks," *Bulletin*, 3 November 1927, p. 11.

15. "Aboriginal Film Actors," *Smith's Weekly*, 6 March 1920, p. 9.

16. Ibid.

17. Ross Gibson, *Seven Versions of an Australian Badland* (St. Lucia: University of Queensland Press, 2002), p. 58.

18. *Everyones*, 3 November 1926, p. 12.

19. "In London," cartoon, *Aussie*, 15 July 1922, p. 18.

20. Film executives were said to be considering "sending a troop of aborigines abroad to circus the picture as the Red Indians did with *The Vanishing Race* here." *Everyone's*, 18 April 1928, p. 7.

21. "[W]hite middle-class women were deemed to be sexually unavailable if they were single, whereas Aboriginal women were assumed to be sexually available to all." Catriona Elder, "The Question of the Unmarried Woman: Meanings of Singleness in Australia in the 1930s," Master's thesis, La Trobe University, 1992. See also "The Limits of Protection," letter from the cook at Cherubin Station to the Chief Protector of Aborigines W.A., 4 June 1925, reprinted in *Australia's Women: A Documentary History*, ed. Kay Daniels and Mary Murnane (St. Lucia: University of Queensland Press, 1980), pp. 86–87.

22. Advertisement for *Runnibede, Beckett's Weekly*, 17 February 1928, p. 19.

23. "450 Q'land Abos Admit They Are 'Plurry Fine Actors,'" *Everyones*, 18 January 1928, p. 7.

24. "The Ways of the Abo. Servant," *Australian Woman's Mirror*, 16 November 1926, p. 11.

25. Cartoon, *Adam and Eve*, 1 November 1926, p. 6.

26. Anne McClintock, *Imperial Leather: Race, Gender, and Sexuality in the Colonial Contest* (New York: Routledge, 1995), p. 35.

27. "An Abo. Maid," *Australian Woman's Mirror*, 24 November 1925, p. 42. Another contributor wrote of Aboriginal maids who were spoiled by white influence—"the civilised lubra" (first recorded 1834, "lubra" is a rural Australian pejorative colloquial term for an Aboriginal woman)—and knew their "worth too well to be a really satisfactory servant." Wingella, "The Abo. as a Servant," *Australian Woman's Mirror*, 3 August 1926, p. 10.

28. "An Inconsiderate Husband," *Bulletin*, 20 March 1929, p. 32.

29. "Lady Smokit Pipe," cartoon, *Aussie*, 15 April 1924, p. 9.

30. McClintock, *Imperial Leather*, p. 50.

31. "Abo. Servants," *Australian Woman's Mirror*, 8 February 1927, p. 43.

32. "An Abo. Maid."

33. Quoted in McClintock, *Imperial Leather*, p. 62.

34. Susan Willis, "I Shop Therefore I Am: Is There a Place for Afro-American Culture in Commodity Culture?" in *Changing Our Own Words: Essays on Criticism, Theory, and Writing by Black Women*, ed. Cheryl A. Wall (New Brunswick, N.J.: Rutgers University Press, 1989), p. 184.

35. McClintock, *Imperial Leather*, p. 66.

36. Torgovnick, *Gone Primitive*, p. 99.

37. Cartoon, *Aussie*, 15 August 1924, p. 50.

38. "Troublesome Black 'Pug,'" *Sun News-Pictorial*, 13 December 1922, p. 11.

39. Grimshaw et al., *Creating a Nation*, p. 288.

40. Dinnah and Mary were comic in their domestic ineptitude: Mary picked up the carcass of the chicken from the serving platter and sailed out of the room with it in her hands, and Dinnah took five weeks to learn to set the table. "The Ways of the Abo. Servant," *Australian Woman's Mirror*, 16 November 1926, p. 11.

41. Rita Felski, *The Gender of Modernity* (Cambridge, Mass.: Harvard University Press, 1995), p. 56.

42. Billie Melman, *Women and the Popular Imagination in the Twenties: Flappers and Nymphs* (Hampshire: Macmillan, 1988), p. 90.

43. Miriam Hansen, *Babel and Babylon: Spectatorship in American Silent Film* (Cambridge, Mass.: Harvard University Press, 1991), pp. 293, 260.

44. Melman, *Women and the Popular Imagination*, pp. 103, 101.

45. "The Sheik of Araby," music by Ted Snyder, lyrics by Francis Wheeler and Harry B. Smith, distributed by Mills Music, 1921.

46. "Jazz Music," *Gossip*, 10 December 1924, p. 31.

47. "That Is—the Charleston Craze," *Adam and Eve*, 1 September 1928, p. 34.

48. Isadora Duncan, "My Life," *Herself*, 20 January 1931, p. 32.

49. *Truth* reported in 1926 that "nigger minstrels" were at the "height of a boom in Australian vaudeville." Australia was "one step in the large Pacific vaudeville circuit," and minstrel shows had toured there since the *Argus* advertised "Rainer's Original Ethiopian Serenaders" in January 1853. *Truth*, 16 January 1926, p. 9. See Andrew Bisset, *Black Roots, White Flowers: A History of Jazz in Australia* (Sydney: Golden, 1979), p. 4.

50. Ivy Shilling, "Is Jazz a Passing Phase?" interview, *Society*, 1 September 1919, p. 1.

51. Barrington Boardman, *Flappers, Bootleggers, "Typhoid Mary," and the Bomb: An Anecdotal History of the United States from 1923–1945* (New York: Harper and Row, 1986), p. 7. Andrew Bisset writes that jazz began to sweep America after the Original Dixieland Jazz Band played at Reisenweber's Cabaret in New York, 26 January 1917. Bisset, *Black Roots, White Flowers*, p. 9.

52. "The Jazz As It Should Be Jazzed," *Table Talk*, 28 August 1919, p. 27.

53. Bisset, *Black Roots, White Flowers*, pp. 7–9.

54. "A Pioneer of Jazz," *Everyone's*, 12 December 1928, p. 107.

55. *Sydney Morning Herald*, 19 May 1934, quoted in Bisset, *Black Roots, White Flowers*, p. 42.

56. Richard Hall, "White Australia's Darkest Days," *Age*, 15 March 1997, pp. 17–23.

57. "Jazz Is a Live Corpse, from Sonny Clay to The Ingenues," *Everyones*, 12 December 1928, p. 107.

58. "Like White Feller Missus! The Shingle in the Solomons," *Adam and Eve*, 1 January 1927, p. 45.

59. Princess Newana Gayfish of the Winnebago bobbed her hair and was expelled from her tribe. "All Because of a Haircut," *Picture Show*, 1 February 1923, p. 10; "Like White Feller Missus! The Shingle in the Solomons."

60. "The Cult of Beauty: Campaigns against Curling Tongs," *Home Budget*, 17 June 1922, p. 14.

61. "A gradual blending of the civilised with the primitive is in progress." "Tyranny of Fashion: 'Why Paris?'" *New Triad*, 1 September 1927, p. 37.

62. Fred V. Coleman, "The Savage Ways of Women," *Aussie*, 15 April 1920.

63. "Tyranny of Fashion: 'Why Paris?'"

64. Elizabeth Wilson, *Adorned in Dreams: Fashion and Modernity* (London: Virago, 1985), p. 56.

65. Cartoon, *Aussie*, 15 October 1930, p. 51.

66. Cartoon, *Beckett's Budget*, 22 February 1929, p. 24.

67. "Effect of Sun-Bathing: Beneficial in Moderation—Dangerous in Excess," *Adam and Eve*, 1 September 1929, p. 15.

68. "Colored Men Fascinate: Black Pugilists and Brown Polynesians Are Wooed by White Girls in Sydney," *Beckett's Budget*, 6 January 1928, p. 5.

69. Ibid. Women visiting a reputed opium den were all noted by *Truth* observers to be "smartly and attractively dressed." Their slavery to the Chinese

men who had addicted them to opium was the basis for *Truth's* case that "Australia must be made completely white" and that "white Australia is a country for white Australians and not for yellow scum from the fever-ridden, disease-infected orient." "Where White Girls Sell Their Souls for Yellow Gold! White Australia Internally Menaced," *Truth*, 25 July 1925, p. 12.

70. McClintock, *Imperial Leather*, p. 182.

71. Helen Stransky, "Tondeleyo, Child of Nature," interview, *Adam and Eve*, 1 August 1926, p. 1.

72. Ibid.

73. *"White Cargo* Will Cause Black Looks in Some Houses but a Full House at the King's," *Truth*, 3 July 1926, p. 11.

74. Stransky, "Tondeleyo, Child of Nature."

75. *"White Cargo* Will Cause Black Looks."

76. *"White Cargo*, a Play," *Adam and Eve*, 1 June 1926, p. 13.

77. "Half-Caste Girl Menace," *Truth*, 6 December 1924, p. 9. The girl was detained by the court and then committed to the Salvation Army Home at Riddell's Creek, Victoria.

78. Linda Mizejewski, *Divine Decadence: Fascism, Female Spectacle, and the Makings of Sally Bowles* (Princeton, N.J.: Princeton University Press, 1992), p. 18. The Nazi aim was compromised by the invisibility of Jewishness.

79. Elder, "Question of the Unmarried Woman," p. 79.

80. Gayatri Chakravorty Spivak, "Can the Subaltern Speak?" in *Marxism and the Interpretation of Culture*, ed. Cary Nelson and Lawrence Grossberg (London: Macmillan, 1988), p. 306.

81. McClintock, *Imperial Leather*, pp. 181–82.

82. Marshall Berman, *All That Is Solid Melts into Air: The Experience of Modernity* (Harmondsworth: Penguin, 1982), pp. 107–109.

83. McClintock, *Imperial Leather*, p. 40.

84. "Oh, the Fashions: Coming of the Crinoline," *Truth*, 7 February 1920, p. 5.

85. "Feminine 'Modesty,' " *Home Budget*, 28 January 1922, p. 11.

86. McClintock, *Imperial Leather*, p. 125.

87. "My Abo. Flapper," *Aussie*, 14 August 1926, p. 14.

88. *"White Cargo* Will Cause Black Looks."

89. "White Cargo," *Triad*, January 1927, pp. 8, 35. Federal Senator Foll sought to include plays in the purview of the Royal Commission into the Moving Picture Industry, because of the "disgraceful" production of *White Cargo.* "Federal Ministry Suggests Royal Commission to Enquire into Moving Picture Industry," *Everyones*, 9 March 1927, p. 10.

90. *"White Cargo* Will Cause Black Looks."

91. *"White Cargo*," *Green Room Pictorial*, 20 March 1926, p. 17.

92. Ibid.

93. "White Cargo, a Play."

94. Uncle James, "Her Skirts Are Short: A Hymn to the Modern Girl," *Beckett's Budget*, 4 November 1927, p. 21.

95. This image also appeared in an exhibition at the Museum of Victoria in 1990. I thank Mary Morris, Collection Manager for Indigenous Photographs, Ethno-Historical Collection, Museum of Victoria, for permission to reproduce this image.

7. THE FLAPPER IN THE HETEROSEXUAL LEISURE SCENE

1. "I Wanna Be Bad," song by B. G. DeSylva, L. Brown, and R. Henderson, sung by Helen Kane, published by Victor R.C.A., 1929.

2. Catherine Driscoll, *Girls: Feminine Adolescence in Popular Culture and Cultural Theory* (New York: Columbia University Press, 2002), p. 7.

3. Eric Partridge, *A Dictionary of Historical Slang* (Harmondsworth: Penguin Reference, 1972), p. 324.

4. Driscoll, *Girls*, p. 57.

5. Ibid., p. 47.

6. "An Ex-Flapper's Confession," *Australian Woman's Mirror*, 19 January 1926, p. 26.

7. " 'I Hate Your Sex': Primrose Path to Perdition," *Truth*, 18 July 1925, p. 12. A letter from "Sober Minded" to the *Sun News-Pictorial* about how disgusted he was by seeing a young woman's jazz garter on a tram from Melbourne to Camberwell sparked a number of responses about the visual scandal of young women. A typical letter argued, "the present day woman is allowed too much rope in the way of immodest dressing—diaphanous blouses, muslin skirts, and silk stockings. . . . Nakedness is more pronounced each day, and if these bare-chested hussies are allowed to promenade in this fashion, heaven help the poor kids who gaze and wonder at what species they are living amongst." "The Order of the Garter," *Sun News-Pictorial*, 6 January 1923, p. 7, and 18 January 1923, p. 19.

8. Rita Felski, *The Gender of Modernity* (Cambridge, Mass.: Harvard University Press, 1995), p. 79.

9. "Mrs. Grundy" was a character in a play by Thomas Morton, *Speed the Plough* (1798), "whose name came to indicate a rigidly conventional moral propriety." Sarah Wintle, introduction to *The Woman Who Did*, by Grant Allen (1895; Oxford: Oxford University Press, 1995), p. 2.

10. See the website for the Modern Girl around the World project at <http://depts.washington.edu/its/moderngirl.htm>, accessed 2 June 2003.

11. Sally Forth, "The Flapper in the Tram," *Aussie: The Flapper Edition*, 15 April 1929, p. 66.

12. Lois W. Banner, *American Beauty* (New York: Alfred A. Knopf, 1983), p. 176.

13. The American Gibson Girl was created by the artist Charles Dana Gibson, who drew young women of uncanny prettiness, health, stature, and elegance. They derived from the increasingly common appearance of beautiful young women in public space and were also said to realize America's independent and proud spirit. Gibson's drawings embodied a national feminine ideal throughout the late 1880s and the 1890s. See Martha Banta, *Imaging American Women: Idea and Ideals in Cultural History* (New York: Columbia University Press, 1987), pp. 211–18.

F. Scott Fitzgerald's literary creation Daisy Buchanan in *The Great Gatsby* was identified with the type of the Flapper. Her pictorial counterpart was drawn by the American cartoonist John Held, Jr., whose images of party-going Flappers who petted in cars frequented the cover of the American magazine *Life* during the 1920s. The Flapper was said to be the Gibson Girl's rebellious daughter. She was personified in the United States by Anna Held, Eva Tanguay, and the Florodora girls. Both types had been preceded and personified by Ava Willing Astor, the daughter of conservative New York society leader Caroline Astor. When she and her friends played tennis wearing bloomers, *Vogue* magazine dubbed them "the moderns." See Banner, *American Beauty,* pp. 201, 146.

14. H. L. Mencken, "The Flapper," *Smart Set* 45, no. 2 (January 1915), pp. 1–2, quoted in Janet Staiger, *Bad Women: Regulating Sexuality in Early American Cinema* (Minneapolis: University of Minnesota Press, 1995), p. 2. My thanks to Julie Tisdale for this reference.

15. Billie Melman, *Women and the Popular Imagination in the Twenties: Flappers and Nymphs* (Hampshire: Macmillan, 1988), pp. 1, 80, 16.

16. See Joan Kerr, *Heritage: The National Women's Art Book: 500 Works by 500 Australian Women Artists from Colonial Times to 1995* (N.S.W.: Craftsman, 1995), p. 425.

17. Ruth Turner Wilcox, *The Dictionary of Costume* (New York: Charles Scribner's Sons, 1969), p. 139.

18. Dulcie Deamer, "The Flapper—Our Great Illusion," *Beckett's Budget,* 21 June 1927, p. 11.

19. "The Lovers," *Humour,* 20 June 1924, p. 14.

20. "Beware the Motor Prowler," *Australian Woman's Mirror,* 20 January 1925, p. 11.

21. Virginia Scharff, *Taking the Wheel: Women and the Coming of the Motor Age* (Albuquerque: University of New Mexico Press, 1992), p. 138.

22. "Auditorium Beauty Quest," *Sun News-Pictorial,* 31 October 1922, p. 9.

23. "Fashions for the Young Folks," *Australian Home Journal,* 1 March 1923, p. 29.

24. *Helen's Weekly,* 8 December 1927, p. 12.

25. "A Timely Precaution," *Bulletin,* 26 December 1918, p. 22.

26. Driscoll, *Girls,* p. 58.

27. A "masher" was a man who flirted with or made advances to women; a "mash" was an infatuation or crush.

28. "The Flapper's Tastes," *Society,* 1 December 1925, p. 41. The article likens Flappers' tastes to those of children, although it describes them as in their teens and twenties.

29. *Adam and Eve,* 1 October 1926, p. 8.

30. Driscoll, *Girls,* pp. 48, 45.

31. Patricia Grimshaw, Marilyn Lake, Ann McGrath, and Marian Quartly, *Creating a Nation, 1788–1990* (Ringwood, Vic.: McPhee Gribble, 1994), pp. 226, 194.

32. Julie Tisdale, "Venereal Disease and the Policing of the Amateur in Melbourne during World War I," *Lilith: A Feminist History Journal,* no. 9 (autumn 1996), p. 43.

33. Catriona Elder, "The Question of the Unmarried Woman: Meanings of Singleness in Australia in the 1930s" (Master's thesis, La Trobe University, 1992), p. 20.

34. Banner, *American Beauty,* p. 102.

35. "Frightened Flappers," *Home Budget,* 4 March 1922, p. 9.

36. Elder, "Question of the Unmarried Woman," p. 24.

37. Katie Holmes, *Spaces in Her Day: Australian Women's Diaries of the 1920s and 1930s* (St. Leonards, N.S.W.: Allen and Unwin, 1995), p. 93.

38. Kenneth A. Yellis, "Prosperity's Child: Some Thoughts on the Flapper," *American Quarterly* 21 (spring 1969), p. 45.

39. Dulcie Deamer, "We Can All 'Flap,'" *Aussie: The Flapper Edition*, 15 April 1929, p. 46.

40. Nea Barry, "Two Flappers," *Aussie*, 15 April 1929, p. 44.

41. Dulcie Deamer, "The Flapper as a Profound Symbol," *Aussie*, 15 August 1929, p. 43.

42. See Alan Jenkins, "Bobs, Shingles, and Camibockers," in *The Twenties* (London: Heinemann, 1974), pp. 58–63 and 70–78; "Images of the Ideal," in Banta, *Imaging American Women*, p. 380.

43. Robert Murray, *The Confident Years: Australia in the Twenties* (Ringwood, Vic.: Penguin, 1978), p. 159.

44. George E. Mowry, "The Flapper," in *The Twenties: Fords, Flappers, and Fanatics* (Englewood Cliffs, N.J.: Prentice Hall, 1963), pp. 173–75.

45. *Live Them Again: The Three Decades from Flappers to Flying Saucers, 1923–53* (New York: Simon and Schuster, 1953), pp. 13–21. See also Jenkins, *The Twenties*.

46. L. L. Robson, *Australia in the Nineteen Twenties: Commentary and Documents* (West Melbourne: Nelson, 1980), p. 65.

47. Vivian Stewart, "The Way They Were: A Sydney Department Store in the 1920s," *Heritage Australia* 9, no. 4 (summer 1990), p. 21.

48. John Montgomery, *The Twenties: An Informal Social History* (London: Allen and Unwin, 1957), p. 61.

49. Stuart Macintyre, *1901–1942: The Succeeding Age*, vol. 4 of *The Oxford History of Australia*, ed. Geoffrey Bolton (Melbourne, Oxford University Press, 1986), p. xvii.

50. Dulcie Deamer, "When Flappers Are Immortal," *Australian Woman's Mirror*, 27 September 1927, p. 8.

51. "The Barbarous Past," *Stage and Society*, 5 April 1923, p. 32.

52. See Grimshaw et al., *Creating a Nation*, p. 239.

53. "The Flapper," *Truth*, 24 January 1925, p. 1.

54. Cartoon, *Aussie*, 15 March 1927, p. 51.

55. "Dress—and Undress: More Wailings from Wowse," *Truth*, 28 January 1922, p. 6.

56. "Flowers and a Flapper," *Australian Woman's Mirror*, 13 December 1927, pp. 8, 60.

57. The Flapper was said to place herself on the youth side of the divide between the generations by her use of fashion and slang. She called a good thing "maddest goat," "cruel," or "simply wicked" and a boring thing "awful biscuit" or "jolly newspaper." *Australian Woman's Mirror*, 26 January 1926, p. 37. The *Bulletin* reasoned that the Flapper's speech was "a series of ugly exclamations" because women in general use "a monotonously small vocabulary." "Sex and Language," *Bulletin*, 12 July 1923, p. 3.

58. "Flapping the Flappers," *Truth*, 12 August 1922, p. 1.

59. Newspaper contributors opined that the "flappers of long years ago / Are still the flappers of today." Jim Dowling, "A Flapper Seventeen," *Aussie*, 15 April 1929, p. 5. Another contributor's poem sets out to name "The seven ages of woman": (1) infant, (2) schoolgirl, (3) Flapper, (4) Flapper, (5) Flapper, (6) Flapper, and (7) Flapper. *Bulletin*, 12 January 1928, p. 32.

60. "Flappers and Floppers," *Aussie*, 14 April 1927, p. 44.

61. Advertisement for Palmolive, *Home*, 1 December 1925, p. 117.

62. Arnold Bennett, *Our Women: Chapters on the Sex-Discord* (London: Cansell, 1920), p. 82.

63. Georg Simmel, "Fashion" (1904), in *On Individuality and Social Forms: Selected Writings,* ed. Donald N. Levine (Chicago: University of Chicago Press), 1971, p. 302.

64. "War on the Flapper: Demand for Return of Old-Fashioned Girl," *Truth,* 14 June 1924, p. 9.

65. Dulcie Deamer, "The Flapper—Our Great Illusion," *Beckett's Budget,* 21 June 1927, p. 11. Alice Jackson replied the following week with "The Flapper—The World's Hope!" *Beckett's Budget,* 28 June 1927, p. 11.

66. Dulcie Deamer, "The Value of Scandal," *Australian Woman's Mirror,* 3 January 1928, p. 11.

67. "Ten Stolen Years: Inkie Pinkie Parley-Vous: 'Cinematic Exhibition' and Worse at Other Melbourne Night Dens," *Truth,* 25 September 1926, p. 9.

68. "The Trials of a Young Girl: Phyllis Phlapper Bakes a Pie," *Aussie,* 15 October 1929, p. 11.

69. "The Trials of a Young Girl: Phyllis Phlapper Learns to Drive," *Aussie,* 15 February 1930, p. 11.

70. "The Trials of a Young Girl: Phyllis Phlapper Misuses the Telephone," *Aussie,* 14 September 1929, p. 11.

71. "The Trials of a Young Girl: Phyllis Phlapper Travels by Train," *Aussie,* 15 January 1930, p. 13.

72. "Phyllis Phlapper Learns to Drive."

73. "Phyllis Phlapper Travels by Train."

74. *Everyone's,* 2 December 1925, p. 18.

75. "Molly Masters," "The Meanderings of Molly: A Page Devoted to Flappers," *Adam and Eve,* 1 October 1927, p. 44.

76. Pictured in *Everyones,* 25 July 1928, p. 54.

77. "Behold! The Chorus Girl!" *Mustard Pot,* no. 2, "Red Pepper Issue" (1928), p. 18.

78. Miriam Hansen, *Babel and Babylon: Spectatorship in American Silent Film* (Cambridge, Mass.: Harvard University Press, 1991), p. 122.

79. Antonio Gramsci viewed the 1920s as a period of sexual crisis in which sexual pleasure and liberation "came into conflict with the necessities of the new methods of work" (quoted in Peter Wollen). Monogamy is the extension of the order and precision of the machine into private life, while sexual passion is an irrational excess which, in Peter Wollen's reading, "must be expelled from the rational system of advanced industrial civilisation." See Peter Wollen, "Cinema/Americanism/The Robot," in *Modernity and Mass Culture,* ed. James Naremore and Patrick Brantlinger (Bloomington: Indiana University Press, 1991), p. 45.

80. Other dance halls in Melbourne included Carlyson's Hotel (now the Esplanade), the Wattle Park (which became the famous St. Moritz ice-skating rink), the Green Ring (standing at the site of the present concert hall), and local town halls. See Barbara Cameron, "From Charleston to Cha-Cha: The Dancing Years of Olive Rowe," in *Double Time: Women in Victoria, 150 Years,* ed. Marilyn Lake and Farley Kelly (Ringwood, Vic.: Penguin, 1985), pp. 330–34.

81. Review of *Gentlemen Prefer Blondes,* by Anita Loos, *Adam and Eve,* 1 October 1926, p. 58.

82. "Flapper's Mail," *Aussie,* 13 April 1929, p. 37.

83. "Aussie Girls," *Lone Hand,* May 1919, p. 39. The *Bulletin* reported that the book offered "cunning views of the ideal flapper." *Bulletin,* 28 November 1918, p. 38. I have been unable to locate it.

84. Barry, "Two Flappers."

85. Kathy Peiss, *Cheap Amusements: Working Women and Leisure in Turn-of-the-Century New York* (Philadelphia: Temple University Press, 1986), p. 63.

86. Andreas Huyssen, "Mass Culture as Woman: Modernism's Other," in *Studies in Entertainment: Critical Approaches to Mass Culture,* ed. Tania Modleski (Bloomington: Indiana University Press, 1986), p. 201. See Caroline Jordan's analysis of the Modernist art tradition in Australia between the wars. Male artists such as Norman and Lionel Lindsay derided Modernism as decorative and symptomatic of decadence, relegating it to the arena of women artists such as Thea Proctor and Margaret Preston. I would argue that Preston's "Flapper" portrait of 1925 in some sense personifies the resonant themes of the metropolitan young woman as spectacle (she is sitting indifferently on a tram, yet brazenly returning the gaze) and the Flapper's relation to modernism as feminized decadence through visual style and design. See Jeanette Hoorn, "Designing Women: Modernism and Its Representation in Art in Australia," in *Strange Women: Essays in Art and Gender,* ed. Jeanette Hoorn (Melbourne: Melbourne University Press, 1994), pp. 28–37.

87. The Flapper could be completely ignorant of the principles of competition in male sport. In one cartoon she stands by the fence and says, "Why not have a ball for each side and save all this squabbling?" *Humour,* 21 March 1924, p. 7. See Luisa Passerini's "The Ambivalent Image of Woman in Mass Culture" for a discussion which further complicates the feminization of mass culture and examines the intersections between its homogenizing tendencies and the agency of individual Italian young women adopting its forms. In *Toward a Cultural Identity in the Twentieth Century,* ed. Françoise Thébaud, vol. 5 of *A History of Women in the West,* ed. Georges Duby and Michelle Perrot (Cambridge, Mass.: Belknap Press of Harvard University Press, 1994), pp. 324–42.

88. James Naremore and Patrick Brantlinger offer a critique of this assumption within philosophy, and show how it lent "resistance to the serious study of visible cultural objects." "Introduction: Six Artistic Cultures," James Naremore and Patrick Brantlinger, eds., *Modernity and Mass Culture* (Bloomington: Indiana University Press, 1991), p. 3.

89. Jim Collins describes this response to mass culture. He argues, "Making fascination antithetical to 'critique' has been a stock in trade feature of avant-garde self-promotion since its inception; fascination has been made to mean uncritical acceptance, promiscuity, lack of rigour." In "Appropriating Like Krazy: From Pop Art to Meta-Pop," in Naremore and Brantlinger, *Modernity and Mass Culture,* p. 212.

90. As discussed in Martin Jay, *Downcast Eyes: The Denigration of Vision in Twentieth-Century French Thought* (Berkeley: University of California Press, 1994), p. 13.

91. Paula Findlen, "Humanism, Politics, and Pornography in Renaissance Italy," in *The Invention of Pornography: Obscenity and the Origins of Modernity, 1500–1800,* ed. Lynn Hunt (New York: Zone, 1993), pp. 58, 55.

92. Andrew Ross, "The Popularity of Pornography," in *The Cultural Studies Reader,* ed. Simon During (London: Routledge, 1993), p. 230.

93. Lynda Nead, "The Female Nude: Pornography, Art, Sexuality," in *Sex Exposed: Sexuality and the Pornography Debate,* ed. Lynne Segal and Mary McIntosh (London: Virago, 1992), p. 286. See also Jonathan Crary's discussion of the stereoscope, a popular visual device invented in 1849 that became increasingly associated with the pornographic, possibly causing its "social demise

as a mode of visual consumption." The stereoscope took on the mantle of an indecent object because of its aptitude in visualizing pornographic images. Jonathan Crary, *Techniques of the Observer: On Vision and Modernity in the Nineteenth Century* (Cambridge, Mass.: MIT Press, 1990), p. 127.

94. Lynn Hunt, "Pornography and the French Revolution," in Hunt, *Invention of Pornography*, pp. 332, 339, 329. Paradoxically, the success of the public-ization of the pornographic precipitated its private-ization through its use in the home.

95. "*Herald* Attacks Ban on Notorious Books," *Australian Budget*, 14 March 1930, p. 7.

96. This act remained in force until it was reformed in 1959, when literary merit was allowed as a defense. In 1968 censorship of the stage was abolished. Weeks notes that these changes effected a new openness, both visual and verbal, about sexuality, but that this openness was particularly realized or concentrated around "sexualization of the female body." See Jeffrey Weeks, *Sex, Politics, and Society: The Regulation of Sexuality since 1800* (London: Longman, 1989), pp. 84, 264.

97. Weeks, *Sex, Politics, and Society*, p. 217.

98. Michel Foucault, *An Introduction*, vol. 1 of *The History of Sexuality*, trans. Robert Hurley (Harmondsworth: Penguin, 1976), pp. 69, 113. He writes of "pleasure in the truth of pleasure, the pleasure of knowing that truth, of discovering and exposing it, the fascination of seeing it and telling it, of captivating and capturing others by it, of confiding it in secret, of luring it out in the open—the specific pleasure of the true discourse on pleasure" (p. 71).

99. Jacqueline Rose, *Sexuality in the Field of Vision* (London: Verso, 1986), p. 112.

100. Banta, *Imaging American Women*, p. 180.

101. Valerie Steele, *Fashion and Eroticism: Ideals of Feminine Beauty from the Victorian Era to the Jazz Age* (New York: Oxford University Press, 1985), p. 247.

102. *Stage and Society*, 1 November 1924, p. 17.

103. "The Aussie Woman," *Aussie*, 15 March 1921, p. 36.

104. "The New Zoology: The Flapper," *Stage and Society*, 15 December 1925, p. 19.

105. "Wives and Mothers," *Bulletin*, 6 April 1922, p. 7.

106. "Flapper Manners," *Australian Woman's Mirror*, 7 July 1925, p. 39.

107. "Flapperish Fashions," *Beckett's Budget*, 19 April 1929, p. 1.

108. *Aussie: The Undies Edition*, 15 February 1927, p. 33.

109. Cartoon, *Adam and Eve*, 1 August 1926, p. 21.

110. Lynda Nead, *Myths of Sexuality: Representations of Women in Victorian Britain* (Oxford: Basil Blackwell, 1988), p. 179.

111. "Bare Limbs Banned," *Truth*, 12 March 1921, p. 5. *Truth* reported that the Carrum bylaw No. 1 had been freshly posted up in the borough in 1924. "Draping Dimpled Knees," *Truth*, 19 January 1924, p. 1.

112. "Seaside Scenes," *Truth*, 3 January 1920, p. 5.

113. "The Model," *Mustard Pot*, no. 2, "Red Pepper Issue" (1928), p. 19.

114. "Be a Peeping Tom," *Beckett's Budget*, 21 September 1928, p. 29. French Art Studios, in Martin Place, Sydney, seems to have been attached to *Beckett's Budget* as a mailing and distribution center for the porn outlets along Castlereagh Street.

115. "Rare Books and Post Cards," *Truth*, 31 May 1924, p. 11.

116. "Cheap, Spicy, French Books," advertisement, *Beckett's Budget,* 10 January 1930, p. 13.

117. "Press 'Limb' Photography: Having Its Effect on Society," *Truth,* 2 February 1924, p. 4; "Photographer's Pranks: Salacious Stunts in a Studio," *Truth,* 1 February 1919, p. 5.

118. "Photographer's Pranks."

119. The modernist *Home* magazine came to the defense of the nude and its prevalence in the work of the controversial artist Norman Lindsay, in spite of Lindsay's scorn for the "decorative" work of women artists associated with *Home,* such as Thea Proctor and Margaret Preston. See Adrian Lawlor, "Numbskulls and the Nude," *Home,* 1 September 1923, p. 11. See also Mary Mackay, "Almost Dancing: Thea Proctor and the Modern Woman," in *Wallflowers and Witches: Women and Culture in Australia, 1910–1945,* ed. Maryanne Dever (St. Lucia: University of Queensland Press, 1994), pp. 26–37.

120. "Slightly Parisian: The Sydney Artists' Ball: A Rather Dull Frolic in Mittens and Carnival without Corsets," *Beckett's Budget,* 22 June 1928, p. 7.

121. "The Artists'" Ball: Sydney's Saturnalian Orgy of Revolting and Nauseating Indecency," *Truth,* 6 September 1924, p. 1. Author Dulcie Deamer, crowned "Queen of Bohemia" at a mock ceremony in 1926, had won fame by wearing a leopard skin at the 1923 Artists' Ball. See Peter Kirkpatrick, "Dulcie Deamer and the Bohemian Body," in Dever, *Wallflowers and Witches,* pp. 13–25. See also the retrospective "The Queen of Bohemia," *People,* 26 April 1950, pp. 50–53, in which Deamer is photographed doing a split and quoted as saying she was shocked by the 1924 Artists' Ball; thugs got in and "turned it into Hobohemia."

122. Nead, "Female Nude," p. 287.

123. Oliver Bell Bruce, *Don't, or Directions for Avoiding Improprieties in Conduct and Common Errors of Speech* (Melbourne: E. W. Cole Book Arcade, 1919), pp. 50–54.

124. Glyn denounced the Flapper as "a lovely, brainless, unbalanced, cigarette-smoking morsel of undisciplined sex," and "as hard as nails and cheap as dirt." Quoted in "The Flighty Flapper," *Truth,* 4 February 1922, p. 5.

125. At times the Flapper seemed to push at the boundaries only to reposition herself as "nice" within new moral fields. "A Flapper" (age sixteen) argued, "You can be naughty and still be nice / You can be good, yet taste life's spice." Reprinted in Marilyn Lake and Katie Holmes, eds., *Freedom Bound II: Documents on Women in Modern Australia* (St. Leonards, N.S.W.: Allen and Unwin, 1995), p. 52.

126. "Shirt Factory Girls: A Glimpse of Their Daily Life," *Australian Woman's Mirror,* 10 August 1926, p. 13.

127. "The Society Girl: Her Place and Her Responsibility," *Society,* 1 October 1922, p. 12.

128. Quoted in Banner, *American Beauty,* p. 65.

129. The "amateur" was a transitional figure of feminine deviancy floating somewhere between the Flapper and the prostitute. Her commerce in sexual favors exchanged for treats, including "joy rides," theatre tickets, cocktails, and presents of fine clothes, was seen as being more dangerous than the direct monetary exchange of the prostitute because of the difficulty in identifying such women. They offered men "a camouflaged respectability which

society cannot penetrate." They were held to be more responsible than the prostitute in spreading venereal disease, said to affect 10 percent of Melbourne's population. This was the figure given by Dr. James W. Barrett in "A Woman's Job," in *Bulletin*, 9 August 1923, p. 11. The Flapper often appeared in *Truth* alongside types who "were not professional prostitutes" and "worked in offices and shops during the day, and seek the bright lights at night." They were seen to be more dangerous in the spread of venereal disease by "neglecting the precautions that the recognized 'Scarlet Woman' knows are necessary to preserve her health," and because they could not be policed as their employers would vouch for them. See "Tarts about Town: The Lure of the Bright Lights: Flirtatious Flappers, 'Love Birds' and 'Privateers,'" in *Truth*, 29 March 1919, p. 5.

130. "Masher" was a term also used in the United States, apparently adopted from the Gypsy verb "to love." Fan letters were called "mash notes." See Banner, *American Beauty*, p. 238.

131. "Mashers and Misses," *Truth*, 12 February 1921, p. 5. In London in 1922, a magistrate ruled that it was not a criminal offense to exchange approving glances, and "unwanted attention" could only be legally constituted by words. "Is the Glad Eye Illegal?" *Smith's Weekly*, 18 November 1922, p. 16.

132. Another verse included "She's got to throb with passion / I want to hear her madly cry / 'Squeeze me, bite me, kiss me.'" "Cave Man Stuff," *Mustard Pot*, no. 2, "Red Pepper Issue" (1928), p. 14.

133. "Ycleptos," "The Flapper Pal," *Aussie*, 15 April 1929, p. 15.

134. "Alec," "The Eternal Flap," *Aussie*, 25 March 1929.

135. "At Last," *Sun News-Pictorial*, 3 November 1922, p. 7.

136. The imbalance in population due to the deaths of men in the war prompted popular newspapers to speculate that "surplus shes" were becoming more skilled and more overt in attracting men to marriage. *Truth* called it "playing a man-attracting game," in "Lovely Woman," *Truth*, 10 September 1921, p. 5.

137. "The Huntress," cartoon, *Bulletin*, 13 February 1929, p. 11.

138. C. G. Hartley, "The Myth of the Virtuous Sex," in *Women, Children, Love, and Marriage* (London: Heath Cranton, 1924), p. 8.

139. *Everyones*, 3 June 1925, p. 12.

140. The song's lyrics include the lines "Dear Little Girl, they call you a vamp / A Flapper with up-to-date ways / You may shine brightly just like a lamp / You'll burn out one of these days." The cover of the sheet music pictures a fashionable young woman standing forlornly alone outside a church. "Just a Girl That Men Forget," sheet music (Sydney: D. Davis, date unknown).

141. "What the Flappers Miss: Joys That Jazz Cannot Give," *Adam and Eve*, 1 February 1927, p. 37.

142. "Boy Mad: Worthless Flapper of Fifteen: Makes Awful Accusation against Her Father," *Truth*, 23 June 1923, p. 4. This Flapper was "well-developed for her age" and cast "a coquettish glance at her interrogator."

143. "Flapper Fun: Indecent Assault Charge," *Truth*, 12 December 1920, p. 5. See also "A Flapper's Frolics: Charge of Carnally Knowing," *Truth*, 23 October 1920, p. 5; "A Wayward Wench: Fifteen-Year-Old Flapper's Fall," *Truth*, 29 May 1920, p. 7.

144. "Mary's Misadventure: Country Flapper's Fall," *Truth*, 24 January 1920, p. 9.

145. "Clara's Capers: Flighty Flapper's Frolic," *Truth*, 20 September 1919, p. 5.

146. "Flapper Scorned," *Beckett's Budget*, 21 October 1927, p. 11.

147. "Flappers' Charges: Some Who Gave Evidence against Innocent Men," *Beckett's Budget*, 30 December 1927, p. 11.

148. G. A. Maxwell, a barrister, defending a client against charges of indecent conduct. Quoted in "Dress and Decency," *Truth*, 26 February 1921, p. 5.

149. "You Tell Her I S-T-U-T-T-E-R," sheet music (Sydney and Melbourne: J. Albert and Son, 1922).

150. "Sex-Stuff and Crime," *Bulletin*, 18 July 1928, p. 8.

151. *Truth* reported that the number of girls seeking such "relief from shame" was "legion," the Women's Hospital treating 150 cases of septicemia every week. "150 Babies Murdered Every Week in Melbourne," *Truth*, 10 December 1927, p. 1. See Janet McCalman, *Sex and Suffering: Women's Health and a Women's Hospital: The Royal Women's Hospital, Melbourne 1856–1996* (Carlton, Vic.: Melbourne University Press, 1998).

152. "Flapper—or Trapper of Men: New Type of Girlhood Invades Society—Hard, Cold, and Selfish," *Truth*, 26 April 1924, p. 9.

153. Dulcie Deamer, "That Married Look," *Australian Woman's Mirror*, 7 September 1926, p. 10. Deamer is again cynical about the Flapper. She continues, "Marriage meant someone to be 'wonderful' to them all the time, not just between tennis sets or in the home-going taxi—someone to shoulder the small complexities that ruffle even the existence of a half-divine twentieth century flapper."

154. Elinor Glyn, "The Present Day Flapper," *Society*, 1 April 1927, p. 36.

155. "The Fluffy Girl: Why Men Marry Her," *Everyone's: Incorporating Variety and Show World*, 15 June 1921, p. 7.

156. "Daughters of Destiny," *Truth*, 17 July 1920, p. 5.

157. "Bits for Flappers: What They Say about Each Other," *Everyone's*, 5 May 1920, p. 7.

158. "The Economic Flapper," *Smith's Weekly*, 17 April 1920, p. 1.

159. Vera G. Dwyer, "Shingle Short," *Australian Woman's Mirror*, 2 December 1924, p. 7. The sexual contract is the original social contract that constructs the male individual and masculine sexuality through mastery and ownership of women's bodies, excluding women from the fraternity of civic subjects. Carole Pateman, *The Sexual Contract* (Cambridge: Polity, 1988). *Home* reported that one Sydney hairdresser shingled seven hundred women in two and a half months in 1924. "Neaera Gets Rid of Her Tangles," *Home*, 1 September 1924, p. 15.

160. Dwyer, "Shingle Short."

161. See Victoria Cross, "Theadora: A Fragment," in *Daughters of Decadence: Women Writers of the Fin-de-Siècle*, ed. Elizabeth Showalter (New Brunswick, N.J.: Rutgers University Press, 1993), p. 26.

162. Quoted in Mary Louise Roberts, "Sampson and Delilah Revisited: The Politics of Women's Fashion in 1920s France," *American Historical Review* 98, no. 3 (June 1993), p. 673.

163. "Thank Heavens I'm Shingled," cartoon, *Bulletin*, 19 February 1925, p. 22.

164. Cartoon, *Aussie*, 15 June 1922, p. 14.

165. Brodie Mack, cartoon, *Australian Budget*, 4 July 1930, p. 1; see also Brodie Mack, cartoon, *Beckett's Budget*, 28 March 1930, p. 1.

166. Cartoon, *Bulletin*, 2 September 1926, p. 17.

167. "The Cure," cartoon, *Bulletin*, 28 January 1926, p. 19.

168. "All Right Now," cartoon, *Bulletin*, 19 May 1921, p. 36.

169. "Should Men Wear Engagement Rings?" *Adam and Eve*, 1 December 1927, p. 45. The article is more interested in whether women should.

170. "Dress and the Devil," *Truth*, 24 February 1923, p. 6.

171. A headline in an article about the seventeen-year-old girlfriend of a gangster reads in full, "Boy Madness: Melbourne's Brigade of Girl Criminals: Lure of the Easy Life: New World of Pretty Faces and Silk Stockings." *Smith's Weekly*, 8 July 1922, p. 1.

172. An article on "The Homeless Girls of Melbourne" attempted a moral taxonomy which included two classes: "(1) The girl who would prefer death to dishonour; (2) the girl who seems destined to go wrong, but would rather go right." The article called for diagnosis and treatment on the model, and with the efficiency of medical practices. "Having classified each case with the same efficiency as we now deal with cases of small pox, typhoid fever, influenza, etc., the responsible officials would place each girl in her right class and deal with her accordingly." *Adam and Eve*, 1 July 1920, p. 5.

173. "Diary of Melbourne's Youngest 'Gold Digger,' " *Truth*, 30 October 1926, p. 9.

174. "Feasting and Fasting," *Truth*, 21 June 1919, p. 5.

175. "The New(de) Rich," cartoon, *Bulletin*, 29 April 1920, p. 16.

176. "Seaside Scenes," *Truth*, 27 November 1920, p. 5. *Truth* writes, "even if the working class wench wished to ape her 'betters' the long, strong arm of the law would not sanction these capers in the licensed halls wherein are held the dances that she and her escort can afford to attend." "Fast Flappers," *Truth*, 2 October 1920, p. 5. And "As a policemen looks upon all citizens—poor citizens—as potential criminals, so do the biased critics referred to consider women and girls of the working class, if not exactly immoral in act and deed, decidedly so by inclination." "Wayward Wenches: Frolics of Fast Flappers: Not Confined to Working Class," *Truth*, 1 January 1921, p. 5. While wealth was thought to afford women more show, it could also hide their indiscretions, such as illegitimate pregnancy.

177. Thorstein Veblen, *The Theory of the Leisure Class: An Economic Study in the Evolution of Institutions* (New York: Macmillan, 1899), pp. 70–73, 82–83.

178. "One Man's Meat Is Another Man's Poison." Cartoon opposes a scene of half-dressed children with a scene of two young women in evening dress with bare backs and low décolleté. It is captioned: "There is more distress in Sydney than after the 1917 strike. Some families haven't a rag to their backs," *Bulletin*, 15 July 1920, p. 16.

179. *Truth*, 26 April 1924, p. 9.

180. Lea Jacobs, "Glamour and Gold Diggers," in *The Wages of Sin: Censorship and the Fallen Woman Film, 1928–1942* (Madison: University of Wisconsin Press, 1991), pp. 52–64.

181. The class rise of gold diggers was censored by the Motion Picture Producers and Distributors of America, and their fall was reinstituted in film. After 1934 "suffering and punishment" were meted out to the offending her-

oine, as recommended by Joseph Breen of the Production Code Administration. Ibid., p. 115.

182. "Surf Bathing and Your Complexion," *Lone Hand*, 25 October 1919, p. 31.

183. "Shocking Stories of Loose Morality at St Kilda," *Truth*, 26 February 1927, p. 9.

184. "Flapping the Flappers."

185. Lynda Nead, *Myths of Sexuality: Representations of Women in Victorian Britain* (Oxford: Basil Blackwell, 1988), p. 180.

186. Bennett, *Our Women*, p. 82.

187. "'Beauty Surgery': The Risks It Entails," *Australian Woman's Mirror*, 24 August 1926, p. 28; "Women's Craze for Beauty," *Australian Woman's Mirror*, 6 October 1925, p. 16; "Use Cosmetic Sense," *Helen's Weekly*, 15 September 1927, p. 43; "A Doctor's Warning to Flappers," *Literary Digest* 91 (30 October 1926), pp. 21–22. *Gossip* warned Flappers to "beware of bobbing toward baldness," citing "numerous doctors" who asserted that men's baldness was due to the too frequent cutting of their hair. "Are You Bobbing?" *Gossip*, 19 June 1924, p. 21. *Gossip* later reported that a Sydney medico believed young women were afflicted with a "shingle flu." "The Shingle-Flu," *Gossip*, 25 February 1925, p. 9.

188. Raymond Bellour, "Ideal Hadaly," in *Close Encounters: Film, Feminism, and Science Fiction*, ed. Constance Penley, Elizabeth Lyon, Lynn Spiegel, and Janet Bergstrom (Minneapolis: University of Minnesota Press, 1991), p. 127.

189. "The Fascinating Flapper," *Truth*, 8 November 1919, p. 5.

190. *Everyone's: The Mid Week Journal for the Home*, 4 September 1921, p. 22.

191. Clara Bow, who began her career as a beauty contestant winner, was cast as the "It Girl" in the film of that name, yet "It" came from author Elinor Glyn's category of indefinable sex appeal, rather than denoting a type. Bow was called "the fiery haired flapper of the screen" and "the reigning queen of flappers" in *Everyone's*, 12 January 1927, p. 43, and 1 December 1926, p. 44. Colleen Moore was dubbed a Flapper after she starred in *Flaming Youth* (1923), *Painted People* (1924), and *We Moderns* (1925). In 1926, publicity campaigns began to promote these stars as having grown up.

192. "The Flapper—Our Great Illusion."

193. "Bare Legs Are Not Immoral," *Beckett's Budget*, 23 November 1928, p. 4.

194. "Her Majesty the Flapper," *Society*, 1 December 1921, p. 16.

195. "Free as the Air," cartoon, *Bulletin*, 1 April 1926, p. 19.

196. "Philippa," "Flappery," *Aussie*, 15 May 1924, p. 46.

197. Barbara Cameron, "The Flappers and the Feminists: A Study of Women's Emancipation in the 1920s," in *Worth Her Salt: Women at Work in Australia*, ed. Margaret Bevege, Margaret James, and Carmel Shute (Sydney: Hale and Iremonger, 1982), pp. 257, 260, 262, 269.

198. Chris Weedon, *Feminist Practice and Poststructuralist Theory* (New York: Basil Blackwell, 1987), p. 97, Weedon's emphasis.

199. Norman Bryson, *Tradition and Desire: From David to Delacroix*, quoted in Jay, *Downcast Eyes*, p. 105.

Bibliography

PERIODICALS

Adam and Eve (Melbourne)
Age (Melbourne)
Argus (Melbourne)
Aussie (Melbourne)
Australian Home Budget (Sydney)
Australian Home Journal (Sydney)
Australian Variety and Show World (Sydney)
Australian Woman's Mirror (Sydney, published by The Bulletin Newspaper)
Beckett's Budget (Sydney)
Beckett's Weekly (Sydney)
Bulletin (Melbourne)
Canberra Times
Daily Guardian (Sydney)
Delineator (New York)
Evening News (Sydney)
Everylady's Journal (Melbourne)
Everyone's (Sydney; N.B.: *Everyone's* underwent a number of name changes 1919–1929. From 1929 until it ceased publication in 1937, it was known as *Everyones*. Throughout the book I reference the title from the date cited.)
Everyones (Sydney)
Everyone's—Variety and Show World (Sydney)
Everyones: Incorporating Australian Variety and Show World (Sydney)
Everyone's: The Mid Week Journal for the Home (Sydney)
Everyones: The Motion Picture Authority (Sydney)
Gossip (Adelaide)
Green Room (Sydney)
Green Room Pictorial (Sydney)
Helen's Weekly (Sydney)
Herald (Melbourne)
Herself (Sydney)
Herself, in Town and Country (Sydney)
Home (Sydney)
Humour (Sydney)
Illustrated Tasmanian Mail (Hobart)
Ladies' Designer (Sydney)
Ladies' Home Journal (Los Angeles)

Ladies' Sphere (Sydney)
Literary Digest (New York)
Lone Hand (Sydney)
The Mustard Pot (Sydney)
National Geographic (Washington, D.C.)
New Triad (Sydney)
New York Times
People (Sydney)
Picture Show (Sydney)
Reason Why: A Magazine for Advertisers (Sydney)
The Revolutionary Socialist (Sydney)
Royalauto (Melbourne)
Smart Set (London)
Smith's Weekly (Sydney)
Society (Sydney)
Stage and Society (Sydney)
Sun News-Pictorial (Melbourne)
Sunraysia Daily (Mildura)
Sydney Morning Herald
Table Talk (Melbourne)
Theatre Magazine (Sydney)
Triad (Sydney)
Truth (Sydney)
Truth (Melbourne)
Undergrowth (Sydney)
Vogue (New York)
Working Woman (Sydney)

BOOKS, ARTICLES, AND OTHER MATERIALS

Ackermann, Jessie. *Australia from a Woman's Point of View.* London: Cassell, 1913.

Adorno, Theodor W. *Negative Dialectics.* Translated by E. B. Ashton. London: Routledge and Kegan Paul, 1973.

Alexander, Sally. *Becoming a Woman: And Other Essays in 19th and 20th Century Feminist History.* London: Virago, 1994.

———. "Becoming a Woman in London in the 1920s and 1930s." In *Metropolis London: Histories and Representations since 1800,* edited by David Feldman and Gareth Stedman Jones, pp. 245–71. London: Routledge, 1989.

Allen, Grant. *The Woman Who Did.* With an introduction by Sarah Wintle. 1895. Oxford: Oxford University Press, 1995.

Allen, Judith. *Sex and Secrets: Crimes Involving Australian Women since 1880.* Melbourne: Oxford University Press, 1990.

Alpers, Svetlana. *The Art of Describing: Dutch Art in the Seventeenth Century.* London: John Murray, 1983.

Amery, Kerryn L. *Hidden Women: Locating Information on Significant Australian Women.* Carlton, Vic.: Melbourne College of Advanced Education, 1986.

Anderson, Perry. "Modernity and Revolution." In *Marxism and the Interpretation of Culture,* edited by Cary Nelson and Lawrence Grossberg, pp. 317–33. Basingstoke: Macmillan Education, 1988.

Andrew, Dudley, and Sally Shafto, eds. *The Image in Dispute: Art and Cinema in the Age of Photography*. Austin: University of Texas Press, 1997.

Appadurai, Arjun, ed. *The Social Life of Things: Commodities in Cultural Perspective*. Melbourne: Cambridge University Press, 1986.

Aveling, Marian, and Joy Damousi, eds. *Stepping Out of History: Documents of Women at Work in Australia*. North Sydney: Allen and Unwin, 1991.

Avineri, Shlomo. *The Social and Political Thought of Karl Marx*. London: Cambridge University Press, 1968.

Banet-Weiser, Sarah. *The Most Beautiful Girl in the World: Beauty Pageants and National Identity*. Berkeley: University of California Press, 1999.

Banner, Lois W. *American Beauty*. New York: Alfred A. Knopf, 1983.

Banta, Martha. *Imaging American Women: Idea and Ideals in Cultural History*. New York: Columbia University Press, 1987.

Barthes, Roland. "Mythologies." In *A Critical and Cultural Theory Reader*, edited by Antony Easthope and Kate McGowan, pp. 14–20. North Sydney: Allen and Unwin, 1992.

Bartky, Sandra. "Foucault, Femininity, and the Modernization of Patriarchal Power." In *Feminism and Foucault: Reflections on Resistance*, edited by Irene Diamond and Lee Quinby, pp. 61–87. Boston: Northeastern University Press, 1988.

Baudrillard, Jean. "Simulacra and Simulations." In *Jean Baudrillard: Selected Writings*, edited and introduced by Mark Poster, pp. 166–84. Cambridge: Polity, 2001.

———. "Simulations." In *A Critical and Cultural Theory Reader*, edited by Antony Easthope and Kate McGowan, pp. 203–206. Sydney: Allen and Unwin, 1992.

Bauer, Bernhard A. *Woman: A treatise on the anatomy, physiology, psychology, and sexual life of woman, with an appendix on prostitution*. Translated by E. S. Jordan and Norman Haine. London: Jonathan Cape, 1927.

Beauvoir, Simone de. *The Second Sex*. 1949. Translated by H. M. Parshley. Harmondsworth, Middlesex: Penguin, 1986.

Bell, Quentin. *On Human Finery*. 1947. London: Hogarth, 1976.

Bellour, Raymond. "Ideal Hadaly." In *Close Encounters: Film, Feminism, and Science Fiction*, edited by Constance Penley, Elisabeth Lyon, Lynn Spigel, and Janet Bergstrom, pp. 107–32. Minneapolis: University of Minnesota Press, 1991.

Benjamin, Walter. *Charles Baudelaire: A Lyric Poet in the Era of High Capitalism*. Translated by Harry Zohn. 1969. London: Verso, 1973.

———. "The Work of Art in the Age of Mechanical Reproduction." In *Illuminations*, by Walter Benjamin, translated by Harry Zohn, edited by Hannah Arendt, pp. 219–53. London: Fontana, 1973.

Bennett, Arnold. *Our Women: Chapters on the Sex-Discord*. London: Cansell, 1920.

Benson, Susan Porter. *Counter Cultures: Saleswomen, Managers, and Customers in American Department Stores, 1890–1940*. Urbana: University of Illinois Press, 1986.

Berger, John. *Ways of Seeing*. London: Penguin, 1972.

Berman, Marshall. *All That Is Solid Melts into Air: The Experience of Modernity*. New York: Viking Penguin, 1988.

Bertrand, Ina, ed. *Cinema in Australia: A Documentary History*. Kensington: New South Wales University Press, 1989.

Bisset, Andrew. *Black Roots, White Flowers: A History of Jazz in Australia.* Sydney: Golden, 1979.

Boardman, Barrington. *Flappers, Bootleggers, "Typhoid Mary," and the Bomb: An Anecdotal History of the United States from 1923–1945.* New York: Perennial Library, 1989.

Brand, Simon. *Picture Palaces and Flea-Pits: Eighty Years of Australians at the Pictures.* Sydney: Dreamweaver, 1983.

Bridenthal, Renate, Claudia Koonz, and Susan Stuard, eds. *Becoming Visible: Women in European History.* Boston: Houghton Mifflin, 1987.

Bridge, S. Helen. "Training Girls as Consumers." *Journal of Home Economics* 13, no. 6 (June 1921), pp. 246–49.

Brookes, Rosetta. "Fashion Photography: The Double-Page Spread: Helmut Newton, Guy Bourdin, and Deborah Turbeville." In *Chic Thrills: A Fashion Reader,* edited by Juliet Ash and Elizabeth Wilson, pp. 17–24. Berkeley: University of California Press, 1992.

Brooks, Louise. *Lulu in Hollywood.* New York: Knopf, 1982.

Broome, Richard. "Seeking Mulga Fred." *Aboriginal History,* no. 22 (1998), pp. 1–23.

Brown, Geoff. "Eleanor Glencross and Ivy Weber: In and out of Parliament." In *Double Time: Women in Victoria, 150 Years,* edited by Marilyn Lake and Farley Kelly, pp. 344–53. Ringwood, Vic.: Penguin, 1985.

Brown-May, Andrew. *Melbourne Street Life: The Itinerary of Our Days.* Kew, Vic.: Australian Scholarly Publishing, 1998.

Bruce, Oliver Bell. *Don't, or Directions for Avoiding Improprieties in Conduct and Common Errors of Speech.* Melbourne: E. W. Cole Book Arcade, 1919.

Buck-Morss, Susan. *The Dialectics of Seeing: Walter Benjamin and the Arcades Project.* Cambridge, Mass.: MIT Press, 1991.

———. "The Flaneur, the Sandwichman, and the Whore: The Politics of Loitering." *New German Critique* 39 (fall 1986), pp. 99–140.

Bullough, Vern L. "Merchandising the Sanitary Napkin: Lillian Gilbreth's 1927 Survey." *Signs* 10, no. 3 (spring 1985), pp. 615–27.

Butler, Judith. *Bodies That Matter: On the Discursive Limits of "Sex."* New York: Routledge, 1993.

———. *Gender Trouble: Feminism and the Subversion of Identity.* New York: Routledge, 1990.

Cameron, Barbara. "The Flappers and the Feminists: A Study of Women's Emancipation in the 1920s." In *Worth Her Salt: Women at Work in Australia,* edited by Margaret Bevege, Margaret James, and Carmel Shute, pp. 257–69. Sydney: Hale and Iremonger, 1982.

———. "From Charleston to Cha-Cha: The Dancing Years of Olive Rowe." In *Double Time: Women in Victoria, 150 Years,* edited by Marilyn Lake and Farley Kelly, pp. 330–34. Ringwood, Vic.: Penguin, 1985.

Canning, Kathleen. "Feminist History after the Linguistic Turn: Historicizing Discourse and Experience." *Signs* 19, no. 2 (winter 1994), pp. 368–404.

Certeau, Michel de. *The Practice of Everyday Life.* Translated by Steven Rendall. Berkeley: University of California Press, 1984.

Chartier, Roger. "Text, Symbols, and Frenchness." In *Cultural History: Between Practices and Representations,* edited by Roger Chartier, translated by Lydia G. Cochrane, pp. 95–111. Cambridge: Polity (in association with Blackwell), 1988.

Cohen, Colleen Ballerino, Richard Wilk, and Beverly Stoeltje, eds. *Beauty Queens on the Global Stage: Gender, Contests, and Power.* New York: Routledge, 1996.

Collins, Diane. "The Movie Octopus." In *Australian Popular Culture,* edited by Peter Spearritt and David Walker, pp. 102–20. Sydney: Allen and Unwin, 1979.

Collins, Jim. "Appropriating Like Krazy: From Pop Art to Meta-pop." In *Modernity and Mass Culture,* edited by James Naremore and Patrick Brantlinger, pp. 203–24. Bloomington: Indiana University Press, 1991.

Comolli, Jean-Louis. "Machines of the Visible." In *The Cinematic Apparatus,* edited by Teresa de Lauretis and Stephen Heath, p. 122 (New York: St. Martin's, 1980). Quoted in Linda Williams, *Hard Core: Power, Pleasure, and the "Frenzy of the Visible"* (London: Pandora, 1990), p. 36.

Corbin, Alain. "Commercial Sexuality in Nineteenth-Century France: A System of Images and Regulations." *Representations,* no. 14 (1986), pp. 209–19.

Cott, Nancy F. "The Modern Woman of the 1920s, American Style." In *Toward a Cultural Identity in the Twentieth Century,* edited by Françoise Thébaud, pp. 76–90. Vol. 5 of *A History of Women in the West,* edited by Georges Duby and Michelle Perrot. Cambridge, Mass.: Belknap Press of Harvard University Press, 1994.

Cowan, Ruth S. "The Industrial Revolution in the Home: Household Technology and Social Change in the Twentieth Century." *Technology and Culture* 17, no. 1 (January 1976), pp. 1–24.

Cowie, Elizabeth. "Fantasia." *m/f,* no. 9 (1984), pp. 71–104.

Craik, Jennifer. *The Face of Fashion: Cultural Studies in Fashion.* New York: Routledge, 1994.

Crary, Jonathan. *Techniques of the Observer: On Vision and Modernity in the Nineteenth Century.* Cambridge, Mass.: MIT Press, 1990.

Creed, Barbara. "Feminist Film Theory: Reading the Text." In *Don't Shoot Darling: Women's Independent Filmmaking in Australia,* edited by Annette Blonski, Barbara Creed, and Freda Freiberg, pp. 280–313. Melbourne: Greenhouse, 1987.

———. "Pornography and Pleasure: The Female Spectator." *Australian Journal of Screen Theory* 15, no. 16 (1982), pp. 67–88.

Curthoys, Anne. "Women's Liberation and the Writing of History." In *For and against Feminism: A Personal Journey into Feminist Theory and History,* edited by Anne Curthoys, pp. 2–8. Sydney: Allen and Unwin, 1988.

Damousi, Joy. "Beyond the Origins Debate: Theorising Sexuality and Gender Disorder in Convict Women's History." *Australian Historical Studies* 27, no. 106 (April 1996), pp. 59–71.

Daniels, Kay, and Mary Murnane, eds. *Australia's Women: A Documentary History.* St. Lucia: University of Queensland Press, 1989.

Davies, Alan, and Peter Stanbury. *The Mechanical Eye in Australia: Photography 1841–1900.* Melbourne: Oxford University Press, 1985.

de Lauretis, Teresa. *Alice Doesn't: Feminism, Semiotics, Cinema.* Bloomington: Indiana University Press, 1984.

———. *Technologies of Gender: Essays on Theory, Film, and Fiction.* Bloomington: Indiana University Press, 1987.

Debord, Guy. *The Society of the Spectacle.* New York: Zone, 1995.

Department of Labour and Industry, Board of Trade. *Transcript and Proceedings of the Inquiry into the Cost of Living of Adult Female Workers, 1918.* Holdings 2/5768, Mitchell Library, State Library of New South Wales.

Descartes, René. *Discourse on Method.* 1637. Translated by P. J. Olscamp. Indianapolis: Bobbs-Merrill, 1965.

Dewey, John. *The Quest for Certainty,* 23, 214. New York: Putnam, 1929. Quoted in Stephen Houlgate, "Vision, Reflection, and Openness: The 'Hegemony of Vision' from a Hegelian Point of View," in *Modernity and the Hegemony of Vision,* edited by David Michael Levin (Berkeley: University of California Press, 1993), p. 87.

Dixon, Robert. "The New Woman and the Coming Man: Gender and Genre in the 'Lost Race' Romance." In *Debutante Nation: Feminism Contests the 1890s,* edited by Susan Magarey, Sue Rowley, and Susan Sheridan, pp. 163–74. St. Leonards, N.S.W.: Allen and Unwin, 1993.

Doane, Mary Ann. "Film and the Masquerade: Theorizing the Female Spectator." *Screen* 23, nos. 3–4 (1982), pp. 74–87.

Driscoll, Catherine. *Girls: Feminine Adolescence in Popular Culture and Cultural Theory.* New York: Columbia University Press, 2002.

Edmondson, Ray, and Andrew Pike. *Australia's Lost Films: The Loss and Rescue of Australia's Silent Cinema.* Canberra: National Library of Australia, 1982.

Edwards, Gregory J. *The International Film Poster: The Role of the Poster in Cinema, Art, Advertising, and History.* London: Columbus, 1985.

Einstein, Albert. *Relativity: The Special and the General Theory, a Popular Exposition.* Translated by Robert W. Lawson. 15th ed. London: Methuen, 1960.

Elder, Catriona. "The Question of the Unmarried Woman: Meanings of Singleness in Australia in the 1930s." Master's thesis, La Trobe University, 1992.

Ellis, Havelock. *The Task of Social Hygiene.* 2nd ed. London: Constable, 1927.

Everson, William K. *American Silent Film.* New York: Oxford University Press, 1978.

Ewen, Stuart. *Captains of Consciousness: Advertising and the Social Roots of the Consumer Culture.* New York: McGraw-Hill, 1976.

Felski, Rita. *The Gender of Modernity.* Cambridge, Mass.: Harvard University Press, 1995.

Findlen, Paula. "Humanism, Politics, and Pornography in Renaissance Italy." In *The Invention of Pornography: Obscenity and the Origins of Modernity, 1500–1800,* edited by Lynn Hunt, pp. 49–108. New York: Zone, 1993.

Finkelstein, Joanne. *After a Fashion.* Melbourne: Melbourne University Press, 1996.

Finney, Gail. *Women in Modern Drama: Freud, Feminism, and European Theater at the Turn of the Century.* Ithaca, N.Y.: Cornell University Press, 1989.

Fishbein, Leslie. "*Dancing Mothers* (1926): Flappers, Mothers, Freud, and Freedom." *Women's Studies* 12, no. 3 (1986), pp. 241–51.

Fiske, John. "The Culture of Everyday Life." In *Cultural Studies,* edited by Lawrence Grossberg, Cary Nelson, and Paula Treichler, pp. 165–73. New York: Routledge, 1992.

Flower, Cedric. *Clothes in Australia: A Pictorial History, 1788–1980s.* Kenthurst, N.S.W.: Kangaroo, 1984.

Flynn, Thomas R. "Foucault and the Eclipse of Vision." In *Modernity and the Hegemony of Vision,* edited by David Michael Levin, pp. 273–86. Berkeley: University of California Press, 1993.

Focus on Reel Australia: A Collection of Early Australian Feature Films. Catalogue. Hendon, S.A.: National Film and Sound Archives, 1990.

Ford, Ruth. "Speculating on Scrapbooks, Sex, and Desire: Issues in Lesbian History." *Australian Historical Studies* 27, no. 106 (1996), pp. 111–26.

Forgacs, David. "National-Popular: Genealogy of a Concept." In *The Cultural Studies Reader,* edited by Simon During, pp. 177–92. London: Routledge, 1993.

Foucault, Michel. *The History of Sexuality.* 3 vols. Translated by Robert Hurley. New York: Vintage, 1976–88.

———. *The Order of Things: An Archaeology of the Human Sciences.* London: Tavistock, 1970.

Fox, Charles, and Marilyn Lake. "The Sexual Division of Labour." In *Australians at Work: Commentaries and Sources,* edited by Charles Fox and Marilyn Lake, pp. 143–86. Ringwood, Vic.: McPhee Gribble, 1990.

Foy and Gibson catalogue, no. 54, 1918. University of Melbourne Archives.

Foy and Gibson winter catalogue, no. 80, Perth, 1931. University of Melbourne Archives.

Frame, Lynne. "Gretchen, Girl or Garçonne? Weimar Science and Popular Culture in Search of the Ideal New Woman." In *Women in the Metropolis: Gender and Modernity in Weimar Culture,* edited by Katharina von Ankum, pp. 12–40. Berkeley: University of California Press, 1997.

Fraser, W. Hamish. *The Coming of the Mass Market, 1859–1914.* Hamden, Conn.: Archon, 1981.

Friedberg, Anne. *Window Shopping: Cinema and the Postmodern.* Berkeley: University of California Press, 1993.

Garber, Marjorie. *Vested Interests: Cross Dressing and Cultural Anxiety.* New York: Routledge, 1992.

Gasché, Rodolphe. *The Tain of the Mirror: Derrida and the Philosophy of Reflection.* Cambridge, Mass.: Harvard University Press, 1986.

Gaskill, Clarence. "Oh Sarah! Won't You Please Pull Down That Shade?" Sheet music. Distributed by Allans Music, 1925.

Gibson, Ross. *Seven Versions of an Australian Badland.* St. Lucia: University of Queensland Press, 2002.

Ginsburg, Josif. *The Hygiene of Youth and Beauty.* Sydney: Cornstalk, 1927.

Gleber, Anke. "Women on the Screens and Streets of Modernity: In Search of the Female Flâneur." In *The Image in Dispute: Art and Cinema in the Age of Photography,* edited by Dudley Andrew and Sally Shafto, pp. 55–116. Austin: University of Texas Press, 1997.

Gordon, Linda. *Woman's Body, Woman's Right: A Social History of Birth Control in America.* New York: Grossman, 1976.

Greenhide (1926). Promotional poster. Documentation Collection, Screen-Sound Australia, the National Screen and Sound Archive.

Grimshaw, Patricia, Marilyn Lake, Ann McGrath, and Marion Quarterly. *Creating a Nation, 1788–1990.* Ringwood, Vic.: McPhee Gribble, 1994.

Grossberg, Lawrence, Cary Nelson, and Paula Treichler, eds. *Cultural Studies.* New York: Routledge, 1992.

Grossman, Atina. "The New Woman and the Rationalization of Sexuality in Weimar Germany." In *Powers of Desire: The Politics of Sexuality,* edited by Ann Snitow, Christine Stansell, and Sharon Thompson, pp. 153–71. New York: Monthly Review Press, 1983.

Grosz, Elizabeth. *Volatile Bodies: Toward a Corporeal Feminism*. St. Leonards, N.S.W.: Allen and Unwin, 1994.

Gunning, Tom. "An Aesthetics of Astonishment: Early Film and the (In)Credulous Spectator." *Art and Text*, no. 34 (spring 1989), pp. 31–45.

Hall, G. Stanley. "Flapper Americana Novissima." *Atlantic Monthly*, no. 129 (June 1922), pp. 771–80.

Hall, Stuart. "Encoding, Decoding." In *The Cultural Studies Reader*, edited by Simon During, pp. 90–103. London: Routledge, 1993.

————. Introduction to *The Critique of Commodity Aesthetics: Appearance, Sexuality, and Advertising in Capitalist Society*, by Wolfgang Fritz Haug, translated by Robert Bock. Cambridge: Polity, 1986.

Hamilton, Marybeth. "'A Little Bit Spicy, but Not Too Raw': Mae West, Pornography, and Popular Culture." In *Sex Exposed: Sexuality and the Pornography Debate*, edited by Lynne Segal and Mary McIntosh, pp. 295–312. London: Virago, 1992.

Hansen, Miriam. *Babel and Babylon: Spectatorship in American Silent Film*. Cambridge, Mass.: Harvard University Press, 1991.

————. "Benjamin, Cinema, and Experience: 'The Blue Flower in the Land of Technology.'" *New German Critique*, no. 40 (winter 1987), pp. 179–224.

————. "Early Cinema, Late Cinema: Transformations of the Public Sphere." In *Viewing Positions: Ways of Seeing Film*, edited by Linda Williams, pp. 134–51. New Brunswick, N.J.: Rutgers University Press, 1995.

Hartley, C. Gasquoine. *Women, Children, Love, and Marriage*. London: Heath Cranton, 1924.

————. *Women's Wild Oats: Essays on the Refixing of Moral Standards*. London: T. Werner Laurie, 1919.

Hatcher, O. Latham. *Rural Girls in the City for Work: A Study Made for the Southern Woman's Educational Alliance*. Richmond, Va.: Garret and Massie, 1930.

Haug, Wolfgang Fritz. *The Critique of Commodity Aesthetics: Appearance, Sexuality, and Advertising in Capitalist Society*. Translated by Robert Bock. Cambridge: Polity, 1986.

Heidegger, Martin. "The Age of the World Picture." In *The Question Concerning Technology, and Other Essays*, translated by William Lovitt, pp. 115–54. New York: Harper and Row, 1977.

Higonnet, Anne. "Women, Images, and Representation." In *Toward a Cultural Identity in the Twentieth Century*, edited by Françoise Thébaud, pp. 343–96. Vol. 5 of *A History of Women in the West*, edited by Georges Duby and Michelle Perrot. Cambridge, Mass.: Belknap Press of Harvard University Press, 1994.

Hodges, Devon, and Janice L. Doanne. "Undoing Feminism in Anne Rice's Vampire Chronicles." In *Modernity and Mass Culture*, ed. James Naremore and Patrick Brantlinger, pp. 158–75. Bloomington: Indiana University Press, 1991.

Hollander, Anne. *Sex and Suits*. New York: Alfred A. Knopf, 1995.

Holmes, Katie. *Spaces in Her Day: Australian Women's Diaries of the 1920s and 1930s*. St. Leonards, N.S.W.: Allen and Unwin, 1995.

————. "'Spinsters Indispensable': Feminists, Single Women, and the Critique of Marriage, 1890–1920." *Australian Historical Studies* 29, no. 110 (1998), pp. 68–90.

Holmes, Katie, and Marilyn Lake, eds. *Freedom Bound II: Documents on Women in Modern Australia*. St. Leonards, N.S.W.: Allen and Unwin, 1995.

Hoorn, Jeanette. "Designing Women: Modernism and Its Representation in Art in Australia." In *Strange Women: Essays in Art and Gender*, edited by Jeanette Hoorn, pp. 28–37. Melbourne: Melbourne University Press, 1994.

———, ed. *Strange Women: Essays in Art and Gender*. Melbourne: Melbourne University Press, 1994.

Houlgate, Stephen. "Vision, Reflection, and Openness: The 'Hegemony of Vision' from a Hegelian Point of View." In *Modernity and the Hegemony of Vision*, edited by David Michael Levin, pp. 87–123. Berkeley: University of California Press, 1993.

Hunt, Lynn. "Pornography and the French Revolution." In *The Invention of Pornography: Obscenity and the Origins of Modernity, 1500–1800*, edited by Lynn Hunt, pp. 301–40. New York: Zone, 1993.

———, ed. *The Invention of Pornography: Obscenity and the Origins of Modernity, 1500–1800*. New York: Zone, 1993.

Huyssen, Andreas. "Mass Culture as Woman: Modernism's Other." In *Studies in Entertainment: Critical Approaches to Mass Culture*, edited by Tania Modleski, pp. 188–207. Bloomington: Indiana University Press, 1986.

———. "The Vamp and the Machine: Fritz Lang's *Metropolis*." In *After the Great Divide: Modernism, Mass Culture, and Postmodernism*, pp. 65–81. Bloomington: Indiana University Press, 1986.

Irigaray, Luce. *Speculum of the Other Woman*. Translated by Gillian C. Gill. Ithaca, N.Y.: Cornell University Press, 1985.

———. *This Sex Which Is Not One*. Translated by Catherine Porter with Carolyn Burke. Ithaca, N.Y.: Cornell University Press, 1985.

Jacobs, Lea. *The Wages of Sin: Censorship and the Fallen Woman Film, 1928–1942*. Madison: University of Wisconsin Press, 1991.

Jameson, Frederic. "Reification and Utopia in Mass Culture." *Social Text* 1, no. 1 (winter 1979), pp. 130–48.

Jay, Martin. *Downcast Eyes: The Denigration of Vision in Twentieth-Century French Thought*. Berkeley: University of California Press, 1993.

Jenkins, Alan. *The Twenties*. London: Heinemann, 1974.

Jonas, Hans. *The Phenomenon of Life: Toward a Philosophical Biology*. New York: Harper and Row, 1966.

Jones, David. Visual merchandising collection. Replicas of 1920s mannequins. Photographed by Jeremy Ludowyke.

Jones, Gail. *The House of Breathing*. Perth: Freemantle Arts Centre Press, 1992.

Jordan, Caroline. "Designing Women: Modernism and Its Representations in Art in Australia." In *Strange Women: Essays in Art and Gender*, edited by Jeanette Hoorn, pp. 28–52. Melbourne: Melbourne University Press, 1994.

Kellerman, Annette. *Physical Beauty—How to Keep It: Annette Kellerman Illustrated*. New York: George H. Doras, 1918.

Kelly, Paul, and Susan Lord. "Driven to Distraction: Going to the Movies with Walter and Siegfried." *Cineaction*, no. 34 (June 1994), pp. 20–25.

Kennedy, Hugh A. Studdert. "Short Skirts." *Forum*, no. 75 (June 1926), pp. 829–36.

Kern, Stephen. *The Culture of Time and Space, 1880–1918*. Cambridge, Mass.: Harvard University Press, 1983.

Kerr, Joan, ed. *Heritage: The National Women's Art Book: 500 Works by 500 Australian Women Artists from Colonial Times to 1995.* Sydney, N.S.W.: Craftsman, 1995.

Kingston, Beverley. *Basket, Bag, and Trolley: A History of Shopping in Australia.* Melbourne: Oxford University Press, 1994.

———. "The Freedom of the Factory." In *My Wife, My Daughter, and Poor Mary-Ann: Women and Work in Australia,* pp. 56–73. Melbourne: Nelson, 1975.

Kinney, Leila W. "Fashion and Figuration in Modern Life Painting." In *Architecture: In Fashion,* edited by Deborah Fausch, Paulette Singley, Rodolphe El-Khoury, and Zvi Efrat, pp. 270–313. Princeton, N.J.: Princeton University Press, 1994.

Kirkpatrick, Peter. "Dulcie Deamer and the Bohemian Body." In *Wallflowers and Witches: Women and Culture in Australia, 1910–1945,* edited by Maryanne Dever, pp. 13–25. St. Lucia: University of Queensland Press, 1994.

Know Thy Child (1921). Footage supplied by ScreenSound Australia, the National Screen and Sound Archive.

Kracauer, Siegfried. "Cult of Distraction: On Berlin's Picture Palaces." 1926. Translated by Thomas Y. Levin. *New German Critique,* no. 40 (winter 1987), pp. 91–96.

———. "Girls and Krise." *Frankfurter Zeitung,* no. 27, 1931. Quoted in Patrice Petro, *Joyless Streets: Women and Melodramatic Representation in Weimar Germany* (Princeton, N.J.: Princeton University Press, 1989), p. 65.

———. "The Mass Ornament." 1927. Translated by Jack Zipes and Barbara Cornell. *New German Critique,* no. 5 (spring 1975), pp. 67–76.

Lake, Marilyn. "Female Desires: The Meaning of World War II." *Australian Historical Studies* 24, no. 95 (October 1990), pp. 267–83.

———. *Getting Equal: The History of Australian Feminism.* St. Leonards, N.S.W.: Allen and Unwin, 1999.

———. *The Limits of Hope: Soldier Settlement in Victoria, 1915–38.* Melbourne: Oxford University Press, 1987.

———. "The Politics of Respectability: Identifying the Masculinist Context." *Historical Studies* 22, no. 86 (April 1986), pp. 116–31.

———. "Women, Gender, and History." *Australian Feminist Studies,* nos. 7–8 (summer 1988), pp. 1–9.

Langman, Lauren. "Neon Cages: Shopping for Subjectivity." In *Lifestyle Shopping: The Subject of Consumption,* edited by Rob Shields, pp. 40–82. London: Routledge, 1992.

Langton, Marcia. *"Well, I Heard It on the Radio and I Saw It on the Television":* An Essay for the Australian Film Commission on the Politics and Aesthetics of Filmmaking by and about Aboriginal People and Things.* North Sydney: Australian Film Commission, 1993.

Leach, William. "Strategists of Display and the Production of Desire." In *Consuming Visions: Accumulation and Display of Goods in America 1880–1920,* edited by Simon J. Bronner, pp. 99–132. New York: W. W. Norton, 1989.

———. "Transformations in a Culture of Consumption: Women and Department Stores, 1890–1925." *Journal of American History* 71, no. 2 (September 1984), pp. 319–42.

Lerner, Gerda. "Placing Women in Traditional History: A 1975 Perspective." In *Liberating Women's History: Theoretical and Critical Essays,* edited by Berenice A. Carroll, pp. 357–67. Urbana: University of Illinois Press, 1976.

Levin, David Michael, ed. *Modernity and the Hegemony of Vision*. Berkeley: University of California Press, 1993.

Lévi-Strauss, Claude. *The Elementary Structures of Kinship*. Translated by James Harle Bell, John Richard von Sturmer, and Rodney Needham. London: Eyre and Spottiswoode, 1969.

Lewis, Jane. "Women, Lost and Found: The Impact of Feminism on History." In *Men's Studies Modified: The Impact of Feminism on the Academic Discipline*, edited by Dale Spender, pp. 55–72. Oxford: Pergamon, 1981.

Leyda, Jay, ed. *Voices of Film Experience, 1894 to the Present*, pp. 249–50. New York: Macmillan, 1977. Quoted in Scott McQuire, *Visions of Modernity: Representation, Memory, Time, and Space in the Age of the Camera* (London: Sage, 1997), p. 80.

Living Melbourne, 1896–1910. Documentary film, dir. Chris Long. ScreenSound Australia, the National Screen and Sound Archive, 1988.

Long, Joan, and Martin Long. *The Pictures That Moved: A Picture History of the Australian Cinema, 1896–1929*. Richmond, Vic.: Hutchinson, 1982.

Ludovici, Anthony M. *Lysistrata: Or Woman's Future and Future Woman*. London: Kegan Paul, Trench, Trubner, 1924.

Lungstrum, Janet. "Metropolis and the Technosexual Woman of German Modernity." In *Women in the Metropolis: Gender and Modernity in Weimar Culture*, edited by Katharina von Ankum, pp. 128–44. Berkeley: University of California Press, 1997.

Macintyre, Stuart. *1901–1942: The Succeeding Age*. Vol. 4 of *The Oxford History of Australia*, edited by Geoffrey Bolton. Melbourne: Oxford University Press, 1986.

Mackay, Mary. "Almost Dancing: Thea Proctor and the Modern Woman." In *Wallflowers and Witches: Women and Culture in Australia, 1910–1945*, edited by Maryanne Dever, pp. 26–37. St. Lucia: University of Queensland Press, 1994.

MacKinnon, Catharine A. *Feminism Unmodified: Discourses on Life and Law*. Cambridge, Mass.: Harvard University Press, 1987.

Magarey, Susan. "History, Cultural Studies, and Another Look at First Wave Feminism in Australia." *Australian Historical Studies* 27, no. 106 (April 1996), pp. 96–109.

Marchand, Roland. *Advertising the American Dream: Making Way for Modernity, 1920–1940*. Berkeley: University of California Press, 1985.

Matthews, Glenna. *The Rise of Public Woman: Woman's Power and Woman's Place in the United States, 1630–1970*. New York: Oxford University Press, 1992.

Matthews, Jill Julius. "Building the Body Beautiful." *Australian Feminist Studies*, no. 5 (summer 1987), pp. 17–34.

———. "Dancing Modernity." In *Transitions: New Australian Feminisms*, edited by Barbara Caine and Rosemary Pringle, pp. 74–87. St. Leonards, N.S.W.: Allen and Unwin, 1995.

———. "Feminist History." *Labour History*, no. 50 (1986), pp. 147–53.

———. *Good and Mad Women: The Historical Construction of Femininity in Twentieth-Century Australia*. North Sydney: Allen and Unwin, 1984.

———. "They Had Such a Lot of Fun: The Women's League of Health and Beauty between the Wars." *History Workshop Journal*, no. 30 (autumn 1990), pp. 22–54.

———. "Which America?" In *Americanization and Australia*, edited by Philip

Bell and Roger Bell, pp. 15–31. Sydney: University of New South Wales Press, 1988.

Mazlish, Bruce. "The *Flâneur:* From Spectator to Representation." In *The Flâneur,* edited by Keith Tester, pp. 43–60. London: Routledge, 1994.

McCalman, Janet. *Sex and Suffering: Women's Health and a Women's Hospital: The Royal Women's Hospital, Melbourne, 1856–1996.* Carlton, Vic.: Melbourne University Press, 1998.

McClintock, Anne. *Imperial Leather: Race, Gender, and Sexuality in the Colonial Contest.* New York: Routledge, 1995.

McLuhen, Marshall. "Sight, Sound, and Fury." In *Mass Culture: The Popular Arts in America,* edited by Bernard Rosenberg and David Manning White, pp. 489–95. New York: Macmillan, 1957.

McQuire, Scott. "The Migratory Eye: Representation, Time, and Space in the Age of the Camera." Ph.D. diss., University of Melbourne, 1994.

———. *Visions of Modernity: Representation, Memory, Time, and Space in the Age of the Camera.* London: Sage, 1997.

Megaw, M. R. "Happy Ever After: The Image of Women in Four Australian Feature Films of the Nineteen Twenties." *Journal of Australian Studies,* no. 7 (1980), pp. 55–71.

Melman, Billie. *Women and the Popular Imagination in the Twenties: Flappers and Nymphs.* Hampshire: Macmillan, 1988.

Merck, Mandy. "Pornography." In *Looking On: Images of Femininity in the Visual Arts and Media,* edited by Rosemary Betterton, pp. 151–60. London: Pandora, 1987.

Metz, Christian. *Psychoanalysis and Cinema: The Imaginary Signifier.* Translated by Celia Britton, Anwyl Williams, Ben Brewster, and Alfred Guzzetti. London: Macmillan, 1982.

Millett, Kate. *Sexual Politics.* New York: Virago, 1971.

Milner, Andrew. *Contemporary Cultural Theory: An Introduction.* St. Leonards, N.S.W.: Allen and Unwin, 1991.

Mizejewski, Linda. *Divine Decadence: Fascism, Female Spectacle, and the Makings of Sally Bowles.* Princeton, N.J.: Princeton University Press, 1992.

Modleski, Tania. *Feminism without Women: Culture and Criticism in a "Postfeminist" Age.* New York: Routledge, 1991.

———, ed. *Studies in Entertainment: Critical Approaches to Mass Culture.* Bloomington: Indiana University Press, 1986.

Montgomery, John. *The Twenties: An Informal Social History.* London: Allen and Unwin, 1957.

Morris, Meaghan. "Things to Do with Shopping Centres." In *The Cultural Studies Reader,* edited by Simon During, pp. 295–319. London: Routledge, 1993.

Mowry, George E. *The Twenties: Fords, Flappers, and Fanatics.* Englewood Cliffs, N.J.: Prentice Hall, 1963.

Mulvagh, Jane. *Vogue History of Twentieth Century Fashion.* London: Viking, 1988.

Mulvey, Laura. "Afterthoughts on 'Visual Pleasure' and 'Duel in the Sun.'" *Framework,* nos. 15–17 (1981), pp. 12–15.

———. "Visual Pleasure and Narrative Cinema." *Screen* 16, no. 3 (autumn 1975), pp. 6–18.

Murray, Robert. *The Confident Years: Australia in the Twenties.* Ringwood, Vic.: Penguin, 1978.

Murray, Sally. Interview by Claire Williams, 6 March 1987. Transcript of sound recording. New South Wales Bicentennial Oral History Project. TRC 2301 INT.34, Oral History and Folklore Collection, National Library of Australia.

Myer Emporium window display, 1924–25. University of Melbourne Archives. Myer Collection. Coles Myer Archives.

Naremore, James, and Patrick Brantlinger. "Introduction: Six Artistic Cultures," in *Modernity and Mass Culture*, edited by Naremore and Brantlinger, pp. 1–28. Bloomington: Indiana University Press, 1991.

———, eds. *Modernity and Mass Culture*. Bloomington: Indiana University Press, 1991.

National Council of Women of New South Wales. *Biennial Report*. 1919–20. Sydney.

Nead, Lynda. "The Female Nude: Pornography, Art, Sexuality." In *Sex Exposed: Sexuality and the Pornography Debate*, edited by Lynne Segal and Mary McIntosh, pp. 280–94. London: Virago, 1992.

———. *Myths of Sexuality: Representations of Women in Victorian Britain*. Oxford: Basil Blackwell, 1988.

Nelson, Cary, and Lawrence Grossberg. *Marxism and the Interpretation of Culture*. Hampshire: Macmillan, 1988.

Niehoff, Pamela. "The New Woman and the Politics of Identity." In *Strange Women: Essays in Art and Gender*, edited by Jeanette Hoorn, pp. 38–52. Melbourne: Melbourne University Press, 1994.

Ong, Walter J. *The Presence of the Word: Some Prolegomena for Cultural and Religious History*, p. 50. New Haven, Conn.: Yale University Press, 1967. Quoted in Martin Jay, *Downcast Eyes: The Denigration of Vision in Twentieth-Century French Thought* (Berkeley: University of California Press, 1994), p. 67.

Paris, Barry. *Louise Brooks*. London: Mandarin, 1990.

Partridge, Eric. *A Dictionary of Historical Slang*. Harmondsworth: Penguin Reference, 1972.

Passerini, Luisa. "The Ambivalent Image of Woman in Mass Culture." In *Toward a Cultural Identity in the Twentieth Century*, edited by Françoise Thébaud, pp. 324–42. Vol. 5 of *A History of Women in the West*, edited by Georges Duby and Michelle Perrot. Cambridge, Mass.: Belknap Press of Harvard University Press, 1994.

Pateman, Carole. *The Sexual Contract*. Cambridge: Polity, 1988.

Peiss, Kathy. *Cheap Amusements: Working Women and Leisure in Turn-of-the-Century New York*. Philadelphia: Temple University Press, 1986.

———. "Making Faces: The Cosmetics Industry and the Cultural Construction of Gender, 1890–1930." *Genders*, no. 7 (March 1990), pp. 143–69.

Petro, Patrice. *Joyless Streets: Women and Melodramatic Representation in Weimar Germany*. Princeton, N.J.: Princeton University Press, 1989.

———. "Perceptions of Difference: Woman as Spectator and Spectacle." In *Women in the Metropolis: Gender and Modernity in Weimar Culture*, edited by Katharina von Ankum, pp. 41–66. Berkeley: University of California Press, 1997.

Plato. *The Republic*. Translated by Desmond Lee. Harmondsworth: Penguin, 1975.

———. "The Simile of the Cave." In Part VII: *The Philosophical Rules in* The Republic, 2nd ed., trans. Desmond Lee, pp. 316–25. Harmondsworth, U.K.: Penguin Books, 1974.

Probyn, Elspeth. *Sexing the Self: Gendered Positions in Cultural Studies*. New York: Routledge, 1993.

Pruette, Lorine. *Women and Leisure: A Study of Social Waste*. American Women: Images and Realities. 1924. New York: Arno, 1972.

Pumphrey, Martin. "The Flapper, the Housewife, and the Making of Modernity." *Cultural Studies* 1, no. 1 (January 1987), pp. 179–94.

Radi, Heather. "1920–29." In *A New History of Australia*, edited by F. K. Crowley, pp. 357–414. Melbourne: William Heinemann, 1974.

Ray, Robert B. "The Avant-Garde Finds Andy Hardy." In *Modernity and Mass Culture*, edited by James Naremore and Patrick Brantlinger, pp. 224–52. Bloomington: Indiana University Press, 1991.

Reekie, Gail. *Temptations: Sex, Selling, and the Department Store*. St. Leonards, N.S.W.: Allen and Unwin, 1993.

Reiger, Kerreen. *The Disenchantment of the Home: Modernizing the Australian Family, 1880–1940*. Melbourne: Oxford University Press, 1985.

Rickard, John. *Australia: A Cultural History*. London: Longman, 1988.

Riley, Denise. *Am I That Name? Feminism and the Category of "Women" in History*. London: Macmillan, 1988.

Riviere, Joan. "Womanliness as a Masquerade." In *Formations of Fantasy*, edited by Victor Burgin, James Donald, and Cora Kaplan, pp. 35–44. London: Methuen, 1986.

Roach, Mary Ellen, and Joanne Eicher. *The Visible Self: Perspectives on Dress*. Englewood Cliffs, N.J.: Prentice Hall, 1973.

Roberts, Mary Louise. "Sampson and Delilah Revisited: The Politics of Women's Fashion in 1920s France." *American Historical Review* 98, no. 3 (June 1993), pp. 657–84.

Robson, L. L. *Australia in the Nineteen Twenties: Commentary and Documents*. West Melbourne: Nelson, 1980.

Roland, Betty. *Feet of Clay*. In *Playing the Past: Three Plays by Australian Women*, edited by Kerry Kilner and Sue Tweg, pp. 31–54. Sydney: Currency, 1995.

Romanyshyn, Robert D. "The Despotic Eye and Its Shadow: Media Image in the Age of Literacy." In *Modernity and the Hegemony of Vision*, edited by David Michael Levin, pp. 339–60. Berkeley: University of California Press, 1993.

Rorty, Richard. *Philosophy and the Mirror of Nature*. Oxford: Basil Blackwell, 1980.

Rose, Jacqueline. *Sexuality in the Field of Vision*. London: Verso, 1986.

Ross, Andrew. "The New Sentence and the Commodity Form: Recent American Writing." In *Marxism and the Interpretation of Culture*, edited by Cary Nelson and Lawrence Grossberg, pp. 361–80. London: Macmillan, 1988.

———. "The Popularity of Pornography." In *The Cultural Studies Reader*, edited by Simon During, pp. 221–42. London: Routledge, 1993.

Russell, Thomas H. *The Girl's Fight for a Living: How to Protect Working Women from Dangers Due to Low Wages*. Chicago: M. A. Donohue, 1913.

Ryan, Edna, and Anne Conlon. *Gentle Invaders: Australian Women at Work, 1788–1974*. Melbourne: Thomas Nelson, 1975.

Samuel, Raphael. "Reading the Signs: II. Fact Grubbers and Mind-Readers." *History Workshop Journal*, no. 33 (spring 1992), pp. 220–51.

Satan in Sydney. 1918. Dir. Beaumont Smith. Copy at ScreenSound Australia, the National Screen and Sound Archive.

Satan in Sydney. 1918. Poster advertising performance at the Lyric Theatre.

Documentation Collection, ScreenSound Australia, the National Screen and Sound Archive.

Saunders, Kay, and Raymond Evans. "Visibility Problems: Concepts of Gender in Australian Historical Discourse." *Australian Historical Studies* 27, no. 106 (April 1996), pp. 142–53.

Scharff, Virginia. *Taking the Wheel: Women and the Coming of the Motor Age.* Albuquerque: University of New Mexico Press, 1992.

Schivelbusch, Wolfgang. *The Railway Journey: Trains and Travel in the Nineteenth Century.* Translated by Anselm Hollo. Oxford: Basil Blackwell, 1980.

Schwartz, Vanessa. "Cinematic Spectatorship before the Apparatus: The Public Taste for Reality in Fin-de-Siècle Paris." In *Viewing Positions: Ways of Seeing Film,* edited by Linda Williams, pp. 87–113. New Brunswick, N.J.: Rutgers University Press, 1995.

Scott, Joan W. "The Evidence of Experience." *Critical Inquiry* 17, no. 4 (summer 1991), pp. 773–99.

———. "Experience." In *Feminists Theorize the Political,* edited by Judith Butler and Joan Scott, pp. 22–40. New York: Routledge, 1992.

———. *Gender and the Politics of History.* New York: Columbia University Press, 1988.

Searles, Patricia, and Janet Mickish. " 'A Thoroughbred Girl': Images of Female Gender Role in Turn-of-the-Century Mass Media." *Women's Studies* 10, no. 3 (1984), pp. 261–83.

Shaw, A. G. L., and H. D. Nicolson. "The Age of Electricity." In *Australia in the Twentieth Century: An Introduction to Modern Society,* edited by A. G. L. Shaw and H. D. Nicolson, pp. 102–10. Sydney: Angus and Robertson, 1967.

Shevelow, Kathryn. *Women and Print Culture: The Construction of Femininity in the Early Periodical.* London: Routledge, 1989.

Shoesmith, Dennis. "The New Woman: The Debate on the 'New Woman' in Melbourne, 1919." *Politics* 8, no. 2 (November 1973), pp. 317–20.

Showalter, Elizabeth, ed. *Daughters of Decadence: Women Writers of the Fin-de-Siècle.* New Brunswick, N.J.: Rutgers University Press, 1993.

Simmel, Georg. *On Individuality and Social Forms: Selected Writings.* Edited by Donald N. Levine. Chicago: University of Chicago Press, 1971.

Smart, Judith. "Feminists, Flappers, and Miss Australia: Contesting the Meanings of Citizenship, Femininity, and Nation in the 1920s." *Journal of Australian Studies,* no. 71 (2001), pp. 1–15.

Smith-Rosenberg, Caroll. *Disorderly Conduct: Visions of Gender in Victorian America.* Oxford: Oxford University Press, 1986.

Soja, Edward. "History: Geography: Modernity." In *The Cultural Studies Reader,* edited by Simon During, pp. 135–50. London: Routledge, 1993.

Sontag, Susan. *On Photography.* Harmondsworth: Penguin, 1973.

Spearritt, Peter, and David Walker. *Australian Popular Culture.* Sydney: Allen and Unwin, 1979.

Spivak, Gayatri Chakravorty. "Can the Subaltern Speak?" In *Marxism and the Interpretation of Culture,* edited by Cary Nelson and Lawrence Grossberg, pp. 271–313. London: Macmillan, 1988.

Steele, Valerie. *Fashion and Eroticism: Ideals of Feminine Beauty from the Victorian Era to the Jazz Age.* New York: Oxford University Press, 1985.

Stephen, Ann. "Agents of Consumerism: The Organisation of the Australian Advertising Industry, 1918–1938." In *Media Interventions,* edited by Judith Allen et al., pp. 78–96. Leichhart, N.S.W.: Intervention, 1981.

Stewart, Vivian. "The Way They Were: A Sydney Department Store in the 1920s." *Heritage Australia* 9, no. 4 (summer 1990), pp. 20–24.

Studlar, Gaylyn. "Masochism and the Perverse Pleasure of the Cinema." *Quarterly Review of Film Studies* 9, no. 4 (fall 1984), pp. 267–82.

Sydney City Life, 1899–1948. Documentary film. ScreenSound Australia, the National Screen and Sound Archive, 1995.

Taylor, Frederick W. *The Principles of Scientific Management.* New York: Harper and Row, 1911.

Thomas, Julian. "Amy Johnson's Triumph, Australia, 1930." *Australian Historical Studies* 23, no. 90 (April 1988), pp. 72–84.

Tisdale, Julie. "Venereal Disease and the Amateur in Melbourne during World War I." *Lilith: A Feminist History Journal,* no. 9 (autumn, 1996), pp. 33–52.

Torgovnick, Marianna. *Gone Primitive: Savage Intellects, Modern Lives.* Chicago: University of Chicago Press, 1990.

Vance, Carole S. "More Danger, More Pleasure: A Decade after the Barnard Sexuality Conference." In *Pleasure and Danger: Exploring Female Sexuality,* edited by Carole S. Vance, pp. xvi–xxxix. London: Pandora, 1992.

Vattimo, Gianni. *The End of Modernity: Nihilism and Hermeneutics in a Postmodern Culture.* Cambridge: Polity, 1988.

Veblen, Thorstein. *The Theory of the Leisure Class: An Economic Study in the Evolution of Institutions.* New York: Macmillan, 1899.

Wadia, A. R. *The Ethics of Feminism: A Study of the Revolt of Woman.* New York: George H. Doran, 1923.

Walkowitz, Judith R. *City of Dreadful Delight: Narratives of Sexual Danger in Late-Victorian London.* Chicago: University of Chicago Press, 1992.

Walkowitz, Judith R., Myra Jehlen, and Bell Chevigny. "Patrolling the Borders: Feminist Historiography and the New Historicism." *Radical History Review,* no. 43 (winter 1989), pp. 23–43.

Waterhouse, Richard. *Private Pleasures, Public Leisure: A History of Australian Popular Culture since 1788.* Melbourne: Longman, 1995.

Watt, Stephen. "Baudrillard's America (and Ours?): Image, Virus, Catastrophe." In *Modernity and Mass Culture,* edited by James Naremore and Patrick Brantlinger, pp. 135–57. Bloomington: Indiana University Press, 1991.

Weedon, Chris. *Feminist Practice and Poststructuralist Theory.* New York: Basil Blackwell, 1987.

Weeks, Jeffrey. *Sex, Politics, and Society: The Regulation of Sexuality since 1800.* London: Longman, 1989.

Wilcox, Ruth Turner. *The Dictionary of Costume.* New York: Charles Scribner's Sons, 1969.

Williams, Linda. *Hard Core: Power, Pleasure, and the "Frenzy of the Visible."* London: Pandora, 1990.

——, ed. *Viewing Positions: Ways of Seeing Film.* New Brunswick, N.J.: Rutgers University Press, 1995.

Williams, Matthew. *Australia in the 1920s.* Sydney: Trocaders, 1984.

Williamson, Judith. *Consuming Passions: The Dynamics of Popular Culture.* London: Marion Boyars, 1986.

Willis, Susan. "I Shop Therefore I Am: Is There a Place for Afro-American Culture in Commodity Culture?" In *Changing Our Own Words: Essays on Criticism, Theory, and Writing by Black Women,* edited by Cheryl A. Wall, pp. 173–95. New Brunswick, N.J.: Rutgers University Press, 1989.

———. *A Primer for Everyday Life*. New York: Routledge, 1991.

Wilson, Annie. *Report of the Equal Moral Standing Committee*. Sydney: National Council of Women, 1919–20.

Wilson, Elizabeth. *Adorned in Dreams: Fashion and Modernity*. London: Virago, 1985.

———. *The Sphinx in the City: Urban Life, the Control of Disorder, and Women*. London: Virago, 1991.

Wolff, Janet. "The Invisible Flâneuse: Women and the Literature of Modernity." In *Feminine Sentences: Essays on Women and Culture*, pp. 34–50. Berkeley: University of California Press, 1990.

Wollen, Peter. "Cinema/Americanism/The Robot." In *Modernity and Mass Culture*, edited by James Naremore and Patrick Brantlinger, pp. 42–69. Bloomington: Indiana University Press, 1991.

Wollstonecraft, Mary. *Vindication of the Rights of Woman*. 1792. Harmondsworth: Penguin, 1982.

The Woman Suffers (1918). Dir. Raymond Longford. Copy at ScreenSound Australia, the National Screen and Sound Archive.

Wright, Andree. *Brilliant Careers: Women in Australian Cinema*. Sydney: Pan, 1986.

Yellis, Kenneth A. "Prosperity's Child: Some Thoughts on the Flapper." *American Quarterly* 21 (spring 1969), pp. 44–64.

Young, Iris Marion. "Throwing Like a Girl: A Phenomenology of Feminine Body Comportment, Motility, and Spatiality." In *Throwing Like a Girl and Other Essays in Feminist Philosophy and Social Theory*, pp. 141–59. Bloomington: Indiana University Press, 1990.

Zola, Emile. *The Ladies' Paradise*. 1883. Berkeley: University of California Press, 1992.

Index

Liz Conor completed her Ph.D. in women's studies at LaTrobe University. She is an Australia Research Council postdoctoral research fellow in the Department of English at the University of Melbourne.